INDUSTRIAL RESTRUCTURING IN EAST ASIA

TOWARDS THE 21ST CENTURY

Nomura Research Institute, Ltd. (NRI), established in 1966, is Japan's largest and most comprehensive private-sector research organization. It offers a wide range of services, including public policy research, investment and financial research, management consulting, contract research and regional planning. The company is also Japan's leading supplier of systems consulting, integration and operating services.

NRI has a staff of 2,700 and operates globally through offices in Tokyo, Yokohama, Osaka, New York, Washington, D.C., San Francisco, London, Frankfurt, Paris, Zurich, Sydney, Hong Kong, Singapore, Taipei and Seoul. NRI also manages the Nomura School of Advanced Management, one of Japan's foremost centres for management training, and is affiliated with the Tokyo Club Foundation for Global Studies, a non-partisan foundation supported by Japanese industry to promote better understanding in Japan of world issues.

The Institute of Southeast Asian Studies (ISEAS) was established as an autonomous organization in 1968. It is a regional research centre for scholars and other specialists concerned with modern Southeast Asia, particularly the multi-faceted problems of stability and security, economic development, and political and social change.

The Institute is governed by a twenty-two-member Board of Trustees comprising nominees from the Singapore Government, the National University of Singapore, the various Chambers of Commerce, and professional and civic organizations. A ten-man Executive Committee oversees day-to-day operations; it is chaired by the Director, the Institute's chief academic and administrative officer.

INDUSTRIAL
RESTRUCTURING
IN EAST ASIA

TOWARDS THE 21ST CENTURY

EDITED BY
SEIICHI MASUYAMA
DONNA VANDENBRINK
CHIA SIOW YUE

NRI
Nomura Research Institute, Tokyo

ISEAS
Institute of Southeast Asian Studies, Singapore

Published jointly by

Institute of Southeast Asian Studies   &   Nomura Research Institute
30 Heng Mui Keng Terrace   New Otemachi Building
Pasir Panjang   2-2-1 Otemachi Chiyoda-ku
Singapore 119614   Tokyo 100-0004, Japan

© 2001 Tokyo Club Foundation for Global Studies

ISEAS Library Cataloguing-in-Publication Data

Industrial restructuring in East Asia : towards the 21st century / edited by Seiichi Masuyama, Chia Siow Yue, Donna Vandenbrink.
   (ISEAS current economic affairs, 0218-2114)
  1.   Industries—East Asia.
  2.   Industries—Asia, Southeastern.
  3.   Industrial policy—East Asia.
  4.   Industrial policy—Asia, Southeastern.
  5.   Technological innovations—East Asia.
  6.   Structural adjustment (Economic policy)—East Asia.
  7.   Structural adjustment (Economic policy)—Asia, Southeastern.
  I.   Masuyama, Seiichi.
  II. Chia, Siow Yue.
  III. Vandenbrink, Donna.
  IV. Series.
HD3616 A83I421   2001   sls2001012851

ISBN 981-230-135-6 (soft cover)
ISBN 981-230-136-4 (hard cover)

ISEAS on the Internet <http://www.iseas.edu.sg/pub.html>

The responsibility for facts and opinions in this publication rests exclusively with the editors and contributors and their interpretations do not necessarily reflect the views or the policy of ISEAS, NRI, the Tokyo Club Foundation, or their supporters.

Typeset by Superskill Graphics Pte Ltd
Printed in Singapore by Seng Lee Press Pte Ltd

Contents

INTRODUCTION

PART I
INDUSTRIAL RESTRUCTURING IN
SOUTHEAST ASIAN ECONOMIES

List of Tables

List of Figures

Acknowledgements

The publication of this book was made possible through the generous funding of the research project by the Tokyo Club Foundation for Global Studies.

The editors express appreciation to the many people associated with Nomura Research Institute (NRI) and the Institute of Southeast Asian Studies (ISEAS) who contributed to this publication.

List of Contributors

Yoopi Abimanyu — Centre for Policy and Implementation Studies, Jakarta

Emilio T. Antonio, Jr. — University of Asia and the Pacific, Manila

Edward K.Y. Chen — Centre for Asian Pacific Studies, Lingnan College, Hong Kong

Chia Siow Yue — Institute of Southeast Asian Studies, Singapore

Vijayakumari Kanapathy — Institute of Strategic and International Studies (ISIS) Malaysia, Kuala Lumpur

Kai Ma — Chung-Hua Institution for Economic Research, Taipei

Seiichi Masuyama — Nomura Research Institute, Tokyo

Luis Molina — University of Asia and the Pacific, Manila

Raymond Ng — Centre for Asian Pacific Studies, Lingnan College, Hong Kong

Nipon Poapongsakorn — Thailand Development Research Institute, Bangkok

Hisashi Ono — Nomura Research Institute, Tokyo

Winston Conrad Padojinog — University of Asia and the Pacific, Manila

Cherrylyn Rodolfo — University of Asia and the Pacific, Manila

Somkiat Tangkitvanich — Thailand Development Research Institute, Bangkok

Donna Vandenbrink — Nomura Research Institute, Tokyo

Cheonsik Woo — Korea Development Institute, Seoul

Wu Zhengzhang — Development Research Centre of the State Council, Beijing

Foreword

On the cusp of the new century, the economies of East Asia are subjected to internal and external pressures to restructure. They need both to address the structural problems revealed by the financial and economic crisis of 1997–98 and to position themselves to maximise their gain in the fast-changing global economy. The Tokyo Club Foundation for Global Studies asked the leading think tanks in ten East Asian economies (the AT10) to examine the issue of industrial restructuring in their home economy. At a conference in late January 2000 the AT10 researchers presented their papers. The discussion highlighted the significant and critical issues facing these economies, mostly arising from the need to reorganise their industries to adapt to the changing technology paradigm and the demands of accelerating globalisation. In essence, the challenge of East Asian economies is to upgrade their industries to increase efficiency and innovation capability to benefit from international linkages and to increase local initiative. This volume contains the fruits of the discussion by the AT10 researchers. I am pleased that the Tokyo Club can disseminate this work in co-operation with ISEAS and NRI.

Shozo Hashimoto   January 2001
President
Tokyo Club Foundation for Global Studies

INTRODUCTION

1

Industrial Restructuring in East Asian Economies for the Twenty-First Century

Seiichi Masuyama and Donna Vandenbrink

This book is about the restructuring of industry in ten East Asian economies at the start of the twenty-first century. The subsequent chapters deal with the important issues in restructuring in these economies individually. In this overview we look at industrial structure in terms of the fundamental factors that affect the relative performance of industries in each economy, such as market structure, competitive environment, ownership and governance structure, industrial clusters, and international exposure. In other words, we discuss the industrial structures of East Asian economies from the perspective of Michael Porter's *Competitive Advantage of Nations*, although we have not followed his framework rigorously (Porter 1990). Moreover, we focus on the dynamic aspect of the region's industrial structures — the changes occurring with globalisation fuelled by liberalisation and by a paradigm shift from industrial technology to information technology (IT). We note that in the process of the structural changes in East Asian industries, the traditional "flying geese" concept is less relevant to explaining the economic and industrial development in the region and that the pattern has become less predictable. In the emerging environment, East Asian governments need to take a non-interventionist but more proactive role to accelerate regulatory reform, to align their industrial structures with the shift to information technology, and to make them more conducive to allocative efficiency, more internally driven, and more able to benefit from international network effects.[1]

THE STRUCTURE OF EAST ASIAN ECONOMIES AND
THE NEED FOR RESTRUCTURING

To begin, we need a picture of the current structure of the economies of East Asia. Although analysis of restructuring typically concerns only the industry sector, we must take a perspective that encompasses other sectors, particularly the service sector, in order to understand the structural changes that emanate from globalisation. The service sector dominates GDP in the more advanced East Asian economies such as Hong Kong, Japan, Singapore, and Taiwan, while the agricultural sector still contributes a small but significant share of value added in less developed economies such as China, Indonesia, Malaysia, Philippines, and Thailand (Table 1.1).[2] Nevertheless, the industry sector contributes over 30 percent of value added in all the economies of the East Asia region (except Hong Kong, which has become a service economy). At least one-quarter of GDP value added in these economies is from manufacturing, the major component of the industry sector.

More than four in ten workers in China, Indonesia, Philippines, and Thailand, are employed in the primary sector (which includes agriculture and mining), though this proportion is decreasing (Table 1.2). For the

TABLE 1.1
Composition of Output in East Asian Economies, 1998
(Value added as percent of GDP)

	Agriculture	Industry	Manufacturing	Services
China	18	49	37	33
Hong Kong	0	15	7	85
Indonesia	16	43	26	41
Japan	2	37	24	61
Korea	6	43	26	51
Malaysia	12	48	34	40
Philippines	17	32	22	52
Singapore	0	35	24	65
Taiwan	3	34	27	63
Thailand	11	40	29	49

Note: Industry includes mining, manufacturing, construction, and utilities.
Source: Table 12, World Bank *World Development Report 1999/2000* and Council for Economic Planning and Development Republic of China *Taiwan Statistical Data Book 1999*.

TABLE 1.2
Sectoral Composition of Employment in
East Asian Economies, 1985 and 1995
(Percent)

	Agriculture and Mining		Manufacturing		Other	
	1985	1995	1985	1995	1985	1995
China	62.4	48.6	16.7	16.2	20.8	35.2
Hong Kong	1.6	0.7	36.2	18.2	62.2	80.8
Indonesia	55.3	44.8	9.3	12.6	35.4	42.6
Japan	11.5	7.4	24.3	22.3	47.3	70.3
Korea	26.0	12.6	23.4	23.4	50.6	64.0
Malaysia	32.1	18.4	15.2	25.9	52.7	55.7
Philippines	49.6	44.4	9.7	10.0	40.7	45.6
Singapore	1.0	0.2	25.4	24.3	73.6	75.5
Taiwan	17.9	10.7	33.7	27.1	48.4	62.2
Thailand	68.6	52.1	8.0	13.4	23.4	34.5

Source: Asian Development Bank, *Key Indicators of Developing Asian and Pacific Countries* 1998, Vol. XXIX and <http://jin.jcic.or.jp/stat/stats/07IND12.html> for Japan.

other six economies, employment is concentrated in service-based activities. The share of employment in the "other", or service, category has been increasing in all the economies of the region, most dramatically in Hong Kong. At the same time, the share of employment in manufacturing increased significantly in Malaysia, Thailand, and Indonesia while it held steady in China and the Philippines, and declined in the NIEs.

In fact, the manufacturing sector is even more significant to these economies than the figures on value added and employment suggest. Management reform and innovation activities have been concentrated in this sector because of its exposure to international competition. The development of manufacturing has ignited related service sector activities, and the manufacturing sector generates the preponderance of export earnings. In all ten economies except Indonesia close to 90 percent or more of export earnings comes from manufactured products (Table 1.3). Machinery and equipment and basic light industrial products are major generators of export value for all economies in the region, with the importance of light industry (mainly textiles) declining and the weight of machinery increasing as economies develop. Electronics goods and equipment are the major and rapidly growing component of machinery

TABLE 1.3
Share of Manufactured Goods in Exports
of East Asian Economies, 1980–97
(Percent)

	1980	1990	1997
China	na	83.0	92.7
Hong Kong	94.7	96.5	98.2
Indonesia	14.0	47.2	66.0
Japan	99.3	99.6	99.6
Korea	94.2	97.2	98.6
Malaysia	47.3	71.3	89.0
Philippines	70.8	86.3	93.7
Singapore	87.5	96.0	98.1
Taiwan	90.8	95.5	97.9
Thailand	63.0	79.8	88.6

Source: UN, *Yearbook of International Trade Statistics*, various issues and Table 11-7, Republic of China, *Taiwan Statistical Data Book 1999*.

exports. Only Japan and Korea export significant amounts of transportation equipment. Electronics goods and equipment alone comprise about half or more of total exports by value in Malaysia, the Philippines, and Singapore (Table 1.4).

Historical Development Trends and Industrial Structure

The structure of industry in East Asian economies today reflects past technological conditions and policy approaches. According to the catching-up product cycle model, industrial structure evolves as an economy develops, from the simplest (imported) technology to more and more sophisticated functions of the production cycle. The sequential upgrading of production technology and industrial structure is called the "flying geese" model because the industrial structure evolves in a pattern resembling the V-formation of a flock of flying geese (Kwan 1998).

This same flying geese model is typically used to describe the relationship among the economies in the East Asia region. The image captures the connections between the industrial structures of the Asian economies at different stages of development and the dynamic, sequential nature of their development. Japan leads the East Asian flock, followed by Korea and

TABLE 1.4
Contribution of Light Industry and Machinery Manufacturing to East Asian Exports, 1996
(Percent of total value of commodity exports)

	China	Hong Kong	Indonesia	Japan	Korea	Malaysia	Philippines	Singapore	Thailand
Light industry	23.9	49.6	35.8	13.9	29.1	16.8	5.7	10.4	34.2
Machinery products	25.9	38.0	13.4	75.0	53.4	56.9	58.6	68.8	35.4
Electronics products	17.2	26.3	7.9	30.3	11.8	49.1	53.5	57.4	26.7
Transportation equipment	2.6	1.0	1.1	12.3	15.4	3.9	1.6	2.0	2.4
Total light industry and machinery products	49.8	87.6	49.2	88.9	82.4	73.7	64.3	79.1	69.6

Notes: Thailand data are 1995; all others are 1996. Light industry includes STIC divisions 6 and 8 except categories 87 and 88; machinery products includes SITC division 7 plus categories 87 and 88; electronics products include SITC categories 75, 76, and 77; transportation equipment includes SITC categories 78 and 79.
Source: Calculated from Table 5, Vol. I *UN Yearbook of International Trade Statistics 1997*.

Taiwan, and then the other, later-developing economies of the region. As applied to the economies of the Asia region, the flying-geese model depicts the latecomers replicating the development experience of the economies ahead of them. As each economy develops and its industrial structure matures, it transfers the old industries to less developed economies in the region. Each economy moves over time from labour-intensive manufacturing into more capital-intensive manufacturing as its factor endowments change and its comparative advantage evolves.

Against the overall pattern of continuing, sequential upgrading of industrial structure in the region as a whole, there is a clear distinction between economies at the head of the flock and those in the rear. Japan, Korea, and Taiwan tended to develop a comprehensive, "full-set" industrial structure within the domestic economy and to be relatively closed to foreign investment. The governments in these economies promoted domestic enterprises and encouraged indigenous technological capabilities. On the other hand, the later-developing economies in Southeast Asia pursued a more open strategy of integrating with the international division of labour under the auspices of multinational enterprises. At an earlier stage in their industrialisation, these economies jettisoned import-substitution policies and adopted export-oriented policies with liberal stances toward foreign investment. Particularly during the latter half of the 1980s, the economies of Southeast Asia utilised FDI to build their capacity to produce goods for export (Table 1.5). With the inflow of FDI these economies evolved into production platforms typically concentrating in labour-intensive assembly processes for foreign-owned firms. This development pattern was particularly conspicuous in the electronics sectors of Southeast Asian economies.

Characteristics of East Asian Industry

East Asian industrial structures have an appearance of extreme high-tech orientation. This appearance has some substance and reflects, to some extent, the latecomer's advantage. The real foundation of East Asian industries is much weaker, than it appears, however. Their high-tech industries, which grew on the basis of foreign direct investment and imported key components, consequently rely on external sources of innovation, and the economies have not developed local industrial clusters in sufficient depth. Admittedly, mutual dependence is the essence of economic globalisation, and East Asian economies have benefited from their external ties. However, lack of domestic innovative capacity and

TABLE 1.5
Ratio of Inward FDI to Gross Domestic Capital Formation, 1971–97
(Percent)

	1971–75	1976–80	1981–85	1985–90	1991	1992	1993	1994	1995	1996	1997
Japan	0.1	0.1	0.1	0.2	0.2	0.2		0.1			0.3
Korea	1.9	0.4	0.5	1.9	1.0	0.6	0.5	0.6	1.1	1.3	1.8
Taiwan	1.4	1.2	1.5	5.1	3.1	1.8	1.7	2.5	2.6	3.3	3.8
China	na	na	na	14.5	3.3	7.8	12.2	17.3	14.7	14.3	14.3
Hong Kong	5.9	4.2	6.9	12.2	2.3	7.7	11.5	10.6	7.7	11.5	9.9
Indonesia	4.6	2.4	1.0	7.6	3.6	3.9	4.3	3.8	6.7	8.9	7.0
Malaysia	15.2	11.9	10.8	43.7	23.8	26.0	20.3	14.9	11.1	12.1	12.2
Philippines	1.0	0.9	0.7	13.6	6.0	2.1	9.6	10.5	9.0	7.8	6.1
Singapore	15.0	16.6	17.4	59.3	33.6	12.4	23.0	36.1	25.6	23.1	27.3
Thailand	3.0	1.5	3.1	10.2	4.9	4.8	3.6	2.4	2.9	3.1	6.8

Source: UNCTAD, *World Investment Report*, various years.

industrial clusters may relegate East Asian industries to the less profitable areas in the international division of labour ceded by external innovators and it may deprive them of opportunities to move within the international division of labour to higher order activities.

Appearance of Extreme High-tech Orientation

According to one measure, in 1995 the Philippines, Singapore, and Malaysia outranked Taiwan and Korea in the high-tech orientation of their exports (Figure 1.1). Korea and Taiwan, on the other hand, had the highest share of medium-technology exports. When industries are classified based on R&D intensity, Singapore and Malaysia far surpass Japan and the United

FIGURE 1.1
Technological Composition of Manufactured Exports,1995

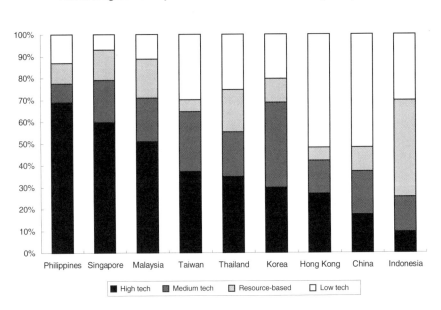

Notes: Low tech includes textiles, leather, footwear, travel goods, furniture, jewellery, toys, and plastic products. Medium tech includes, motor vehicles and parts, synthetic fibres, chemicals, fertilisers, plastics, iron, pipes, engines, motors, industrial machinery, switchgears, ships, watches. High tech includes, office, DP, telecom equipment, TVs, transistors, turbines, power generating equipment, pharmaceuticals, aerospace, optical/measuring instruments, cameras.
Source: Table 6, S. Lall et al. 1999.

States in the high-tech composition of their exports (Table 1.6). Moreover, the high-tech export share for Thailand and Korea is similar to that for Japan and the United States.

The heavy concentration of these economies in high-tech manufactured products reflects their position as latecomers able to specialise in high-growth areas. Indeed, it is largely their concentration in electronics manufacturing that makes them appear to be so high-tech oriented. It also reflects the longer time developing economies need to establish medium-technology industries, which are mostly based on mechanical engineering technology. The technology and software on which high-tech industries depend are somewhat easier to acquire than manufacturing technologies, such as machinery, which require accumulation of experience. This situation gives latecomers some advantage in the high-tech industries and accounts in part for the greater success of Southeast Asia in developing the electronics industry.

To some extent, though, this appearance of high-tech orientation is an artefact of product and industry classification methods and does not reflect the fundamental technological capabilities of these economies. Southeast

TABLE 1.6
High-tech Share of Exports, 1997

	High-tech goods' share of manufactured exports
China	21
Hong Kong	29
Indonesia	20
Japan	38
Korea	39
Malaysia	67
Philippines	12
Singapore	71
Taiwan	–
Thailand	43
U.S.	44

Note: High-tech industries defined according to direct and indirect R&D expenditure. Examples include aircraft, office machinery, pharmaceuticals, and scientific instruments.
Source: Table 19, World Bank 2000a.

Asian economies tend to be labour-intensive production nodes for corporations in Japan, the United States, Europe, and the East Asian NIEs that specialise in the more knowledge-based functions such as R&D and international marketing, and they tend to play a passive role in international production networks.

Dependence on External Sources of Innovation

Developing economies in East Asia depended and continue to depend on advanced countries as sources of innovation. According to the World Bank's analysis, two-thirds of the region's past 'miraculous' growth was due to increases in capital and labour inputs, not technology (World Bank 1993, p. 48). During the 1970s and 1980s the primary source of new production technologies in East Asia was Japan. Korea and Taiwan continue to import key components and parts, which embody technology, from Japan even as they have also became major investors in other East Asian economies (Table 1.7). China's strong household electrical appliance

TABLE 1.7
Parts and Components Trade between Japan and East Asian Economies, 1996

	Exports from Japan US$ millions	Japan's trade balance in components as a % of components exports	Trade intensity index for Japanese components
China	3,548	25.4	1.5
Hong Kong	3,500	92.4	1.0
Indonesia	2,135	82.8	2.4
Korea	4,445	71.4	2.4
Malaysia	3,959	74.0	1.5
Philippines	2,197	56.9	1.6
Singapore	3,635	78.1	1.0
Taiwan	4,514	55.1	4.3
Thailand	4,157	77.3	2.2

Note: The Trade Intensity Index measures the "tendency for two countries to trade more, or less, heavily than expected given their global importance in trade. If the intensity index is above unity, the countries are said to have a greater than expected bilateral trade based on their share in world trade."
Source: Table 5, Ng and Yeats, 1999.

industry "still relies upon continuous imports of key technology for many products, especially for top-end products" (Li 2000). Since the mid 1990s, as the basis for new products and processes shifted from production to information technology, the East Asian economies have been looking more to the United States than to Japan and the region as a source of innovation. For example, Taiwan depends more on the United States than on Japan for sourcing intermediate inputs such as data storage and telecom devices for computer and telecommunication equipment (Table 1.8).

In consequence of the tendency to rely on external sources of innovation, home-grown technological capability in the region is generally weak compared with the level of industrial development. The Southeast Asian economies and China spend far less on and have many fewer engineers engaged in R&D than Japan (Table 1.9). While the NIEs still lag well behind Japan and the United States in numbers of patents, they have largely caught up with the developed economies in their rate of R&D spending as a share of GDP.[3]

Insufficient Pool of Knowledge Workers

In part, East Asian economies had to depend on external technology by accepting FDI and importing key components to upgrade their industrial structures because many, particularly the Southeast Asian economies,

TABLE 1.8
Sources of Intermediate Inputs for
Selected Taiwan Manufacturing Industries, 1988
(Percent of total)

	Data storage	Telecom devices	Electronic components	Precision instruments	Manu-facturing
Domestic	49.8	45.05	32.3	64.3	57.8
Foreign	50.3	55.1	60.7	35.7	42.2
Japan	12.9	9.0	23.2	17.0	12.2
United States	17.6	22.4	12.9	3.8	9.2
Europe	3.0	6.6	15.1	2.5	5.3
Mainland China	1.7	3.6	2.1	1.5	2.0
Southeast Asia	8.4	13.2	5.6	2.2	4.9
Other	6.8	0.3	2.0	8.9	8.7
Total	100.0	100.0	100.0	100.0	100.0

Source: Adapted from Table 5, Schive, 1999.

TABLE 1.9
Selected R&D Indicators for East Asian Economies

	R&D scientists & engineers per million 1985–95	Number of patent applications filed by residents 1996	R&D expenditures as % of GDP
China	350	11,698	0.66
Indonesia	–	40	0.07
Malaysia	87	–	0.24
Philippines	1,299	2,414	0.22
Thailand	119	203	0.13
Hong Kong	98	41	–
Korea	2,636	68,446	2.82
Singapore	2,728	215	1.13
Taiwan	–	31,185	1.92
Japan	6,309	340,861	2.80
U.S.	3,732	111,883	2.63

Note: R&D expenditure share of GDP is 1997 or latest year available.
Source: Table 19, World Bank, *World Development Report 1999/2000*. Table III.1, *UNESCO Statistical Yearbook 1999*. Tables 6-1 and 6-3, Republic of China, *Taiwan Statistical Data Book 1999*.

lacked workers with the appropriate training and education to localise the innovation function. Elementary and secondary education systems in East Asia succeeded in meeting the rapidly growing demand for manufacturing workers, but tertiary education systems outside of Japan, Korea, and Taiwan did not turn out sufficient innovative and management talent. Only two out of each hundred people in China and Indonesia has attained a post-secondary education and the share is very small in Malaysia, Singapore, and Thailand (Table 1.10). The proportion of population with a secondary-level education also is much lower in Thailand and Indonesia compared with their neighbours. Indeed, the shortage of educated Thais has kept the wage levels of university graduates high and forced the textile industry, for example, to import management talent from India (Chapter 4). Generally speaking, enrolment in higher education rises with the level of development, but the tertiary education enrolment rate is particularly low in Indonesia and Malaysia, which is feeling the constraints of a lack of skilled labour and innovative and entrepreneurial talent. On the other hand, the Philippines enjoys a relatively high rate of tertiary enrolment and its rate of secondary

TABLE 1.10
Educational Attainment and Enrolments in East Asian Economies

	Share of population with:		Enrolments		
	Post-secondary education %	Secondary education %	Secondary enrolment ratio, 1996 %	Tertiary enrolment ratio, 1996 %	Science and engineering students as % of all tertiary students
China	2.0	34.4	70	5.6	43
Hong Kong	14.5	47.4	73	–	36
Indonesia	2.3	16.8	51	11.3	39
Japan	20.7	43.7	103	40.5	64
Korea	21.1	51.9	102	67.7	32
Malaysia	6.9	43.0	64	11.7	27
Philippines	22.0	38.5	77	29.0	14
Singapore	7.6	50.6	74	38.5	–
Thailand	5.1	13.7	56	22.1	18
Taiwan	–	–	–	–	37

Note: Secondary, post-secondary completion rates and science and engineering students are for latest year available. Enrolment ratios are gross enrolment/population in relevant age group.

Source: Table II.3, UNESCO Statistical Yearbook, 1999. Tables 6 and 8, UNESCO, *World Education Report 2000: The Right to Education*. Table 5.12, World Bank, *World Development Indicators 2000*. Table 14-6c, Republic of China, *Taiwan Statistical Data Book 1999*.

school enrolment is comparable to Hong Kong's and Singapore's. Moreover, given the need for skilled and technologically oriented graduates in these economies, the small proportion of science and engineering students at the tertiary level is inadequate, particularly in Thailand and the Philippines. Hong Kong also has a severe shortage of scientists and engineers due to the economy's heavy concentration in the service sector. While Korean engineers are somewhat less qualified than Japanese engineers, their lower wage levels make them competitive in middle technology areas (Chapter 9).

The relatively small pool of knowledge workers in East Asian economies did not pose a serious problem in the past when regional industrial development focused on the assembly function of manufacturing industries based on comparative advantage in unskilled labour. In fact, low-income economies, including China, continue to be able to depend on this advantage, but the scarcity of educated workers may inhibit growth for such economies as Malaysia and Thailand where comparative advantage in unskilled labour has weakened. Eventually, as knowledge becomes ever more necessary for their future industrialisation in the information age, insufficient numbers of knowledge workers may thwart growth in many of the region's economies.

Lacking in Supporting Industries and Domestically Owned Enterprises

In general, East Asian economies lack an adequate base of local supporting industries, including business services as well as parts and components suppliers, which generate agglomeration economies as a source of competitiveness. This did not deter investments intended to serve domestic markets, the mainstay in Southeast Asia up to the mid 1980s (and in China still), because the domestic markets tended to be protected. However, availability of competitive inputs is critical for export-oriented investments. When MNCs invest in plants in developing countries, they need to procure the best inputs in terms of quality, cost, and delivery in order to sell their output in competitive export markets. Although local sourcing may offer advantages in delivery time and cost, developing countries typically cannot supply the necessary products and services on competitive terms. Inevitably, exporting firms in developing economies must import key materials and parts from advanced and newly industrialised economies. MNCs operating in developing countries in East Asia typically use local subcontractors only for such technologically low-level activities as packaging, plating, stamping, and moulding (Thee). Japanese corporations, which had developed their own suppliers based on the *keiretsu* system at home, invited these suppliers to East Asia as a second-best solution. On the other hand, Japanese corporations might not have made sufficient efforts to develop locally owned suppliers, which could deepen industrial clusters.

Despite the overall weakness in supporting industries in the region, certain clusters did attract FDI. Locating near parts suppliers is more important for assemblers of bulky components, such as automobiles, than for assemblers of easily transportable light components, such as electronics. Thailand attracted Japanese automobile firms to invest in assembly plants in Thailand on the basis of the local machinery and metal industries that had developed under the earlier import-substitution policy. Singapore has been successful in promoting its supporting services for MNCs operating in the consumer electronics, computer, and semiconductor industries (Thee).

Malaysia and Thailand are developing similar clusters, although to a smaller extent. At the same time, underdevelopment of critical supporting industries is one reason that the electronic industry in Thailand suffers from low value added and does not contribute more toward economic growth than generating employment (Chapter 4). Thailand is one of world's largest producers of hard disk drives, but it has no indigenous firms that provide such basic services as tooling, equipment repair, clean rooms, or metal finishing (Doner and Brimble).

Closely tied to the general weakness of industrial clusters in East Asia is the weakness and lack of competitiveness of indigenous enterprises. Local suppliers of intermediate inputs and support to export-oriented producers are typically domestically owned, small and medium-sized firms (SMEs). Locally owned enterprises had been the foundation of the import-substitution strategy for many Asian economies, but these firms lost their place with the shift to FDI- and export-oriented growth strategies, which put greater competitive demands on suppliers. The region's SMEs lag even in purely domestic industries. For example, in Thailand, most value added in domestic-oriented industries comes from large enterprises; the contribution of small and medium-sized Thai enterprises is limited (Chapter 4). According to one observer, "Further development of subcontracting in Thailand is hampered by the limited technological and managerial capabilities of subcontractors, which mostly consist of SMEs" (Thee, p. 14).

Unlike most of their neighbours, Korea and Taiwan have developed strong, locally owned manufacturing enterprises. Even so, however, they get many key parts and components from Japan. Particularly in Korea the propensity to import key parts (capital goods, materials, and components) has hindered the development of local industrial linkages and domestic producers of intermediate inputs. Consequently, Korea remains a specialised production area. Moreover, although Korea's growth strategy was based on domestic firms, SMEs failed to flourish because of the emphasis on large-scale firms and protectionism and a lack of financial support (Chapter 9). In recent years, though, Korean SMEs have gained some ground.

In contrast to Korea, Taiwan developed a distinctive industrial structure based on strong independent SMEs owned by local entrepreneurs. Compared to SMEs in other Asian economies, Taiwan's SMEs have a particularly large share of export (Table 1.11). Nevertheless, Taiwan's manufacturing SMEs may not be spending enough on investment,

TABLE 1.11
Position of Small and Medium Enterprises (SMEs)
in Selected Economies
(Percent)

	SMEs Share of:			
	Firms	**Employment**	**Sales**	**Exports**
Taiwan (1994)	98.0	79.2	38.5	55.5
Hong Kong (1994)	98.4	63.3	–	–
Indonesia (1993)	97.0	–	–	–
Malaysia (1988)	92.6	40.2	19.6	–
Philippines (1998)	98.9	50.0	26.3	–
Singapore (1992)	92.0	44.0	27.0	4.7
South Korea (1994)	99.2	71.5	53.9	42.8*
Japan (1994)	99.1	78.0	–	12.6*
Australia (1994)	95.7	39.6	54.6*	–
Europe (1995)	99.8	66.5	64.9	–
United States (1995)	99.7	52.7	47.3	29.0*

Notes: Asterisk indicates data for 1993. Each country's definition of SMEs in terms of number of employees follows. Japan: below 300 in mining, manufacturing, transportation and construction; below 100 in wholesale; and below 50 in the retail and distribution industry; Hong Kong: below 50 across the board; Taiwan: below 200 in mining, manufacturing and construction and below 50 in all other industries; South Korea: below 300 in manufacturing, below 200 in construction, and below 20 in service industries; United States: below 500 across the board: EU: below 250 across the board; and Australia: below 100 in manufacturing and below 20 in the construction and service industries.
Source: Lee and Li, 1994 and Ku, 1998 as cited in Table 8.2, Jiann-Chyuan Wang, 2000.

production, and marketing of new products to create a strong enough local foundation for an information industry pyramid.[4]

At one time abundant low-wage labour in East Asian economies could offset their weak supporting industries that deprived investors of agglomeration economies. But as incomes and wage-levels rise, this comparative advantage is diminishing and the region's manufacturing industries need to find other sources of competitiveness to continue to grow. Deepening and strengthening the competence of local supporting industries will become increasingly necessary as an alternative source of competitiveness for export firms.

Weak Domestic Sector

Economic development in East Asia has been fuelled by manufacturing industries in the export sector while the domestic sector, mostly consisting of service industries is un-dynamic, inefficient, and un-competitive (except in the entrepôt economies of Hong Kong and Singapore). For example, the Philippines' service sector consists mainly of small retailers and wholesalers with low productivity (Chapter 3). Under their export-oriented growth strategy most of the region's economies maintained an open traded goods sector to ensure markets for their manufacturing industries, but they did not extend the same openness to the non-traded goods sector. Moreover, with international trade negotiations traditionally focused on traded goods, domestic markets did not feel similar pressure for liberalisation. Domestic sectors lost vigour and dynamism and this weakness is now jeopardising the overall economic health of some economies (see Masuyama 1999). The present situation in Japan shows how protected domestic sectors, particularly services, lack the dynamism to help pull the economy out of its prolonged stagnation (Chapter 11).

A particular component of the protected domestic sector, the financial sector, has become a drag on East Asian industry because of its inability to allocate capital efficiently. This misallocation is also due to inadequate corporate governance exercised by the bank-dominated financial systems of East Asia. The industrial structure in most of the region, including Japan, is seriously inefficient in utilising capital. Capital-productivity has shown a secular trend on decline since the beginning of the 1970s in Japan (Figure 1.2). In Thailand, financial liberalisation favoured capital-intensive industries and resulted in lower capital efficiency before the Asian crisis (Chapter 4).

The unbalanced treatment of the export and domestic sectors in East Asia has far-reaching economic consequences. Failure to nurture the service sector undermines the competitiveness of export industries, which depend on the efficiency of finance, transportation, distribution, and similar business services at the other end of the value chain. Admittedly, past export-oriented development strategies were structured to avoid this problem by concentrating developments in narrow geographical areas such as export processing zones where investing firms enjoyed a separate environment from the inefficient domestic economy. Neglecting the domestic service sector also limits development by under-utilising domestic demand as a source of economic growth and slows down the transition to a domestic market-led economic growth, which is necessary as East Asian economies

FIGURE 1.2
Return on Assets, Japan, 1971–98

percent

Note: ROA is operating surplus of corporations/private capital stock. Private capital stock is made nominal using the deflator for capital expenditure.
Source: Calculated by NRI from official statistics.

mature. Furthermore, the weakness in the domestic sector hampers innovation, which emanates more and more from the service sector, as demonstrated by the rapid growth of electronic commerce around the world.

Questionable Sustainability of the Current Structure

At first, the Asian economic crisis that followed the sharp decline of the Thai baht was thought to point to the inherent vulnerability of the industrial structures of the East Asian economies, which depended heavily on manufacturing for export, and particularly on electronics manufacturing. Subsequently, the inadequacy of the international financial architecture, and the financial systems and policy responses of these economies, not their weak industrial structure, have emerged as the main culprits of the crisis. Indeed, their concentration in the electronics sector proved to be beneficial for the crisis-struck economies. According to *Asian Development*

Outlook 2000, the faster-than-expected recovery in the first half of 1999 in most of the crisis-affected countries of Asia was primarily due to a pickup in global demand for electronics, which sparked an export boom in the region.

Nevertheless, there remains a crucial question whether these economies can sustain a development pattern by which they depend on the manufacturing sector linked with external innovation centres and carry an inefficient domestic sector. Dependence on external sources of innovation was in fact a convenient and appropriate strategy for economies that lacked a sufficient accumulation of technology and human resources to benefit from ongoing economic globalisation. However, the region's economies will not be able to achieve long-term growth and development in the future by continuing to rely on foreign knowledge, primarily through FDI, and without rapidly building up their indigenous innovation capabilities. Looking forward they need to make a number of specific corrections. First, they need to cope with the problem of declining comparative advantage in unskilled labour, although latecomer economies such as China and Vietnam will continue to grow on it. Second, those economies that industrialised rapidly by adapting well to the then-prevailing industrial technologies need to adapt to emerging information technologies. Third, East Asian economies need to address the low rate of return on investment, or their allocative efficiency. And finally, they need to correct their bifurcated industrial structure by improving the competitiveness of the domestic sector, particularly service industries.

All these challenges point to a need for the comprehensive restructuring of East Asian industries in order to improve the chances of sustained development. In the following sections, we analyse how the globalisation trend is accelerating industrial restructuring in East Asia and show the direction that industrial restructuring is taking in the region.

GLOBALISATION ACCELERATES INDUSTRIAL RESTRUCTURING IN EAST ASIA

Three ongoing worldwide trends are working to drive the industrial restructuring of the East Asian economies at the start of the twenty-first century:

- the paradigm shift from industrial to information technology,
- the trend toward liberalisation and deregulation, and
- the continuing globalisation of capital markets.

To some extent these forces are interrelated and their combination is spearheading economic globalisation. Advances in information technology and relaxation of national controls on foreign exchange and financial markets made possible the free flow of capital with little regard for national borders. Another force that will influence the outcome for all of the economies of the region, one that arises from within the region, is the developments in China. Our analysis in this chapter focuses on the impact of these forces on industrial structures in the region. In addition to these forces, emerging constraints of natural resources, energy, and environment, as well as the ageing populations in a large part of the region, are likely to influence the shape of the Asian economies.

Paradigm Shift from Industrial to Information Technology

In the year 2000, industrial technology such as mechanical engineering has reached maturity and information technology is advancing rapidly. The paradigm shift is driving structural changes in East Asian industries in a number of ways.

First, the paradigm shift is accelerating the transfer of mature industrial (manufacturing) technology from advanced to less-developed economies through FDI. Transfer of a new, rapidly changing technology is generally not very economical because it quickly becomes obsolete (Moritani 1998). This is particularly so if the recipient economies do not have the capacity to improve on the technology themselves. Moreover, the firm that holds the advanced technology wants to retain it in order to enjoy a competitive advantage from the dynamic technology gap. Transfer of a mature technology, on the other hand, is easier because there is no risk to the recipient of its becoming outmoded and no gain to the holder from holding on to it. Moreover, the prospect of establishing competitive advantage based on lower costs gives a firm the incentive to transfer mature production technologies, particularly through FDI. The flood of Japanese investment into Southeast Asia and China followed by the NIEs' investment in the region since the middle of the 1980s probably reflects this incentive.

Second, the shift from industrial to information technology simply increases the share of the IT industries in the economies of East Asia. Moreover, products based on digital technology such as PCs and cellular phones require a lot of assembling, which is highly labour-intensive and fits the comparative advantage of many developing economies. Output of the information technology industry, including software, is increasing, and the electronic commerce market is growing rapidly, albeit from a very low level.[5] In Korea the IT industry's share of GDP increased from 4.2 percent in 1993 to 6.3 percent in 1998. Over these five years the software and computer-related service industry grew at an annual rate of 28.8 percent, the IT equipment industry by 25.3 percent, and the communication service industry by 14.1 percent (Lee 2000).

Third, the paradigm shift to information technology increases the knowledge content of the production process as information (knowledge) substitutes for labour and capital as a production input, except perhaps in the assembly functions. This is readily seen in the increasing demand for knowledge workers and rapidly growing IT investment in the United States, which leads the transition to an IT-based economy. This may put a premium on innovation capability at the expense of knowledge-absorption capability, in which East Asia excelled in the past.

Fourth, the shift to information technology as the basis for industrial production is forcing a change in industrial organisations. Economic globalisation together with the IT revolution are undermining the competitiveness of the large, vertically integrated industrial organisations that had been the mainstays of East Asian industry in the age of industrial technology. Networked organisations that utilise out-sourcing and supply-chain management are more suited to the new IT environment than self-contained organisations such as *keiretsu* and *chaebol*. In electronics, American corporations, which have already adopted a decentralised, network-type organisation, have gained a competitive edge over Japan's integrated corporations and they are providing a model for East Asian corporations to emulate.

At the same time, the age of information technology is improving opportunities for small- and medium-sized corporations. The Internet gives smaller firms the same access to markets and information as larger firms and it eliminates the advantages of scale in some industries by giving smaller firms the opportunity to network with external firms. The adaptability, speed of management, and innovation capability that are the strengths of smaller firms are coming to the fore. Small firms can compete in non-standard production activities through the flexible manufacturing systems and individual design made possible by IT (Chen 2000). Indeed, Chinese-managed network organisations, such as Taiwan's SMEs, appear to be becoming more competitive in certain fields such as PC manufacturing.

Finally, the application of information technology changes the pattern of international production networks. During the 1980s when Japan was the world leader in industrial technology, it transferred maturing technology via FDI to other economies in East Asia. As production capacity dispersed from Japan to the region, networks formed between innovation centres and suppliers of key components and machinery in Japan and local assemblers and producers. In the 1990s, as information technology replaces industrial technology and the source of innovation moves from Japan to the United States, the production networks of East Asia are evolving. Reflecting these changes, the amount of FDI into the region from Europe and especially the United States increased relative to the amount coming from Japan. For 1993–95 the amount of FDI from the United States going into Korea, Taiwan, and China surpassed that from Japan and in the ASEAN 5 the U.S. approached the amount from Japan (Table 1.12.).

Compared to networks based on industrial technology, ones based on information technology tend to be more widely dispersed geographically because the delivery of information is much cheaper and faster than the delivery of physical goods. For example, the software industry in Bangalore, India is now closely linked to Silicon Valley. Because the United States, and Silicon Valley in particular, is the centre of innovation in information technology and Japan plays only a limited role, networks based on information technology link Asia more with the United States (and Western Europe) and less with Japan than did in traditional production networks. For example, the majority of OEM clients of Taiwan's top notebook-PCs makers are U.S., not Japanese, companies (Table 1.13).

Networks based on information technology also tend to be more open and horizontal than ones based on production technology. For example, Borrus, Ernst, and Haggard compare the production networks stemming from Cisco Systems based in California with those stemming from Japan's NEC. On one hand, Cisco's products are assembled by contracted Asian and U.S. manufacturers from components supplied by independent firms located in Asia and the United States. Cisco controls almost nothing but the specifications of the final product. In contrast, NEC controls almost every aspect from R&D to product design, engineering, manufacturing, distribution, and service through its affiliates located mostly in the country of origin; it produces the bulk of the underlying technologies, components, parts, software and subsystems internally; and it sells the finished product (Borrus, Ernst, and Haggard 2000).

Industrial networks consist of high value added core activities, mostly based in advanced countries, and peripheral activities, mostly located in developing economies. Core firms tend to control change and to retain the lion's share of profits. This tendency is particularly pronounced in networks based on information technology because of network externalities and intellectual property rights. In these networks, firms engaged in core

TABLE 1.12

Inward FDI to East Asia from Japan and Western Economies

FDI source	1990–92 Inflow		1993–95 Inflow		1996–98 Inflow	
	US$ millions	Relative to Japan	US$ millions	Relative to Japan	US$ millions	Relative to Japan
China						
Japan	3,442	1.00	14,993	1.00	11,281	1.00
United States	4,027	1.17	20,294	1.35	18,336	1.63
EU4	1,662	0.48	13,703	0.91	14,480	1.28
Korea						
Japan	617	1.00	1,133	1.00	1,024	1.00
United States	993	1.61	1,297	1.14	7,040	6.87
EU4	1,098	1.78	823	0.73	4,906	4.79
Taiwan						
Japan	1,795	1.00	1,247	1.00	1,940	1.00
United States	1,414	0.79	1,866	1.50	1,933	1.00
EU4	444	0.25	706	0.57	682	0.35
ASEAN5						
Japan	17,008	1.00	23,119	1.00	33,269	1.00
United States	10,245	0.60	18,509	0.80	12,611	0.38
EU4	13,868	0.82	27,387	1.18	31,683	0.95
Total Asia						
Japan	22,862	1.00	40,491	1.00	47,514	1.00
United States	16,679	0.73	41,966	1.04	39,920	0.84
EU4	17,072	0.75	42,619	1.05	51,751	1.09

Notes: EU4 includes France, Germany, the Netherlands and the UK combined. ASEAN5 includes Indonesia, Malaysia, Philippines, Singapore, and Thailand.
Source: Calculated from Institute for International Trade and Investment, "FDI Statistics of Major Countries of the World" (in Japanese), March 2000. Original statistics are from the United Nations, *World Investment Report*.

TABLE 1.13
External Networks of Taiwan's
Seven Top Notebook-PC Suppliers

	Major OEM Clients	Nationality
Quanta Computer	Dell	U.S.A.
	Siemens	Germany
	Gateway	U.S.A.
Acer	IBM	U.S.A.
	Hitachi	Japan
Inventech	Compaq	U.S.A.
Compal Computer Taiwan	Dell	U.S.A.
	Hewlett-Packard	U.S.A.
	DEC	U.S.A.
	Fujitsu	Japan
Twinhead International	Hewlett-Packard	U.S.A.
	Sharp	Japan
Arima Computer	Compaq	U.S.A.
CLEVO Computer	Hitachi	Japan
	Seiko Epson	Japan

Source: Adapted from Table 8.5, Wang, 2000.

activities, such as Microsoft, Intel, and Cisco, work to guard their high profitability through de facto standards and intellectual property protection while firms in peripheral activities concentrate on producing standardised commodities. The recent surge in electronics exports from East Asia seems to signal the emergence of a new international division of labour in conjunction with information technology networks: the advanced economies (particularly the United States) carry out the highly profitable innovation-oriented functions and East Asian economies produce low-margin, commoditised goods. If East Asian economies remain confined to this position, their future development prospects will be constrained, despite the rapid rise in their share of seemingly high-tech products. They must move into higher value added products to improve their long-term development prospects.

Liberalisation and Deregulation

The continuing acceptance and progress of economic liberalisation and deregulation by countries around the world has already brought change to industrial structure in East Asia. The shift by many ASEAN countries from an import-substitution industrial policy to a more liberal trade and investment policy in the middle of the 1980s attracted massive foreign direct investment that contributed to their industrialisation and to the "East Asian Miracle."[6] In fact, East Asia's mostly voluntary liberalisation centring on areas related to foreign direct investment in the export industries is serving as a model for other developing countries and furthering the process of global economic liberalisation. Moreover, a trend toward region-wide liberalisation is taking shape around AFTA in Southeast Asia and around APEC in the Asia-Pacific area, reinforcing the global trend.

Liberalisation and deregulation enhance industrial efficiency by eliminating distortions in the allocation of resources and improving efficiency (Urata 1995). For example, the cement and paper industries, in which the Philippines does not have comparative advantage, failed to flourish despite costly protection under the import-substitution policy. On the other hand, the garment industry, which developed naturally on the basis of the Philippines' comparative advantage in low-wage labour, enjoys much greater international competitiveness (Chapter 3). In Japan, de-regulation in the service sector and subsequent entry of foreign firms have introduced new products and contributed to greater efficiency (Chapter 11).

Liberalisation and deregulation have not proceeded uniformly in all sectors of East Asian economies, however. Throughout the region, the service sector remains more protected, less open, and less competitive than the manufacturing sector. Moreover, in certain economies and certain industries, state-owned enterprises maintain a deep foothold, which puts a break on industrial change. The reform of SOEs and the development of the private sector are central to China's ability to realise its transformation into a market-based economy. In Thailand, the monopoly by state-owned enterprises has constrained the development of electronic commerce (Chapter 4). The slower pace of regulatory reform in Japan and Korea compared to economies with Anglo-Saxon heritage has undermined the international competitiveness of Japanese and Korean industries by keeping them from improving innovative capacity and efficiency. In particular, reluctance to liberalise the service sector sufficiently created a competitive gap between the economies of the United States and Japan and contributed to the sluggish adoption of information technology by Japanese industry. American-led intensification of pressure for economic liberalisation during the 1990s pushed the liberalisation of the domestic sector, particularly services, to the top of the agenda in East Asia.

The Asian Financial Crisis that started in July 1997 had a strong impact on liberalisation and regulatory reform in the crisis-hit economies. In some countries, the crisis significantly accelerated these trends. Thailand, Indonesia, and Korea implemented comprehensive liberalisation and deregulation programs in conjunction with IMF assistance in the aftermath of the crisis. Korea reversed its legal and institutional framework for inward FDI from one of the most closed to one of the most open systems. Moreover, it legalised hostile corporate acquisitions (Chapter 9). On the other hand, the Asian Crisis caused backlashes against continued liberalisation in other countries as it tested fragile political and social systems to the limit. The severe crisis-induced political and social instabilities in Indonesia, an anchor of ASEAN, have increased uncertainty about the future of the regional free trade movement, AFTA. Liberalisation policy has recently slowed in the Philippines, with the imposition of limits on inward FDI to the air transport and petroleum industries (Chapter 3). The move by Singapore and Japan to establish a free trade agreement may reflect the recognition of the limits of AFTA. The different ways that East Asian economies adjusted their liberalisation policies in response to the Asian Crisis may give rise to differences in industrial efficiency and international competitiveness. There is a risk that East Asia may split along lines of economic development and political stability.

Globalisation of Capital Markets

The synthesis of IT innovation and economic liberalisation and deregulation has facilitated the globalisation of capital markets. As East Asia becomes more integrated into the global capital market, the resulting stronger corporate governance and more frequent merger and acquisition activity are accelerating industrial restructuring. Like economic liberalisation, the globalisation of capital markets has generally been a positive force on the region's economies although it showed its negative side in the Asian Financial Crisis as well.

The good performance of the U.S. economy and the growing perception of the inadequacy of their financial systems during the 1990s encouraged East Asian economies, including Japan, to shift to U.S.-style financial systems dominated by capital markets rather than the banking system. The wholesale financial liberalisation after the Asian Financial Crisis in countries such as Korea and Thailand under the influence of the IMF accelerated this change. As they have become more compatible with Anglo-Saxon systems, the East Asian systems are now more integrated into global capital markets. The trend is accelerating as American and European financial institutions increase their presence in the region, in part to take advantage of the weaker financial positions of East Asian financial institutions and of the more liberal investment environment in the wake of the Asian Crisis. China's imminent accession to the WTO will also accelerate the reform of the Chinese financial system as well as increase the presence of foreign financial institutions. Moreover, increasing competitive pressure from the globalisation of capital markets has prompted internationalisation of senior managers in some financial institutions in East Asia. For example, the Singapore government brought in foreigners to manage two state-controlled banks in its wholesale reform program of state enterprises.[7] The giant Tokyo financial market is undergoing extensive changes as a result of the Big Bang reform begun in 1998, and is expected to become much more efficient and international with an increasing presence of foreign financial institutions. This will probably have a significant impact on regional financial integration.

The acceleration of liberalisation and deregulation and the globalisation of capital markets have stimulated merger and acquisition of East Asian companies, particularly by U.S. and European firms. Indeed, the management of Korean corporations is expected to shift substantially to foreign capitals. M&A activities have increased dramatically in Japan as well. The total value of M&A deals in Japan rose from ¥1,504 billion (US$13.1 billion) in 1998 to ¥4,259 billion (US$41.7 billion) in 1999 and ¥5,059 billion (US$44.0 billion) in 2000. The value of M&As involving foreign buyers was ¥2,078 billion (US$20.4 billion) in 1999 and ¥1,097 billion (US$9.5 billion) in 2000 compared to only ¥635 billion (US$5.5 billion) in 1998.[8]

The increasing presence of capital markets in East Asia in turn has meant that capital markets have begun to play a greater role in corporate governance systems in many economies. This will bring about a better allocation of resources among industries and improve organizational structure. The realisation of governance based on capital markets, however, depends not only on legal and regulatory reforms but also on behavioural changes that require political and social maturity and consequently require the passage of time. The long transition phase will not necessarily be smooth.

China's Response to the Challenge

China stands as a potential economic giant in East Asia, and how China's development proceeds will affect industrial structure throughout the region. Since 1978 China has been aggressively restructuring to transform its economy into a market-based one and it has achieved high economic growth by implementing economic liberalisation and deregulation, primarily in the areas along the coast. The liberalisation and deregulation process should accelerate when China accedes to the WTO. China also stands to benefit from the IT revolution in the long run if it can capture the potentially great economies of scale presented by the size of the world-wide Chinese-speaking market. At the same time China continues to have a significant comparative advantage in cheap labour, and the world demands many things, including IT products and equipment, that are labour-intensive to produce. With its pool of non-skilled, low-wage labour and vast market, in the near future China may come to lead East Asia in terms of output and trade, although it is a long way from overshadowing Japan's contribution in terms of technology.

On the other hand, a number of factors handicap China's transformation into a more open economy. Its SOE system is the antithesis of a liberal, open economic system and is undermining its financial system by creating an enormous bad debt problem. The latter is a critical problem because the financial system needs to play a major role, particularly in corporate governance, in industrial restructuring. Such remnants of the planned economy and the absence of the rule of law constrain China's ability to adapt to economic globalisation. Legal infrastructure is developing gradually, but it will take time, as it needs to be supported by more mature social and political systems. Improving the efficiency of SOEs is proving to be extremely difficult and policy seems to be shifting gradually toward development of the private sector, under not insignificant political constraints. The benefits of China's accession to the WTO are expected to emerge only gradually because of the grace period and the time it will take to dissolve some of China's ingrained non-tariff barriers such as extreme regional protectionism and relationship-oriented corporate and regulatory behaviour. The actual implementation of WTO rules, like the legal structure, needs to be supported by the maturing of the political and social systems, which has yet to be realised. Moreover, the political incentives to inhibit the free sharing of information may keep China's economy from fully benefiting from the development of information technology. These constraints will create uncertainty about China's future industrial restructuring.

To the extent that China's continued development is accompanied by further liberalisation and deregulation it will mean both larger export markets and greater competition for the other East Asian economies. Although previous import-substitution policy saddled China with inefficient domestic market-oriented industries it also left the economy with moderately well developed basic technology industries such as machinery, which might play a role as supporting industries. China's potential to develop an extensive network of supporting industries poses a competitive challenge to the Southeast Asian economies, where supporting industries are inadequate. This is also true for Korea, where supporting industries are better developed than in Southeast Asia. Korea fears that unless it strengthens its innovation capability and develops its small- and medium-sized enterprises foreign investment will bypass Korea in favour of China (Chapter 9). The potential of China to ignite massive industrial restructuring in the region depends on how it resolves the constraints it now faces and whether its economy develops significantly.

DYNAMICS OF INDUSTRIAL RESTRUCTURING IN EAST ASIA

These global forces are driving an extensive restructuring of East Asian industries as they head into the twenty-first century. In the following section, we analyse the dynamics of industrial restructuring in the region in the coming years. We identify four characteristics of change in industrial structure across the region. First, the industrial structures in East Asia will come to reflect each economy's competitive advantages and each government's efforts to promote them. Second, industrial structures will be reorganised by the steps that firms take to increase efficiency and creative capacity as they try to survive the intensified competition of linking with the global economy. Third, the pattern of industrial structures will reflect the extent to which networked and self-driven organisations become the mode for industrial organisation in each economy. And finally, the industrial structures will be realigned as firms and economies seek to capture the externalities of IT and international production networks. This diversity of influences on industrial change suggests that economic and industrial development in the region will be irregular and varied. In other words, in the early twenty-first century the smooth progress of the flying geese pattern will fade and the overall pattern of development will be more unpredictable as governments and firms vary in their adaptability to the forces of change.

Global and Regional Industrial Structure Shaped by Competitive Advantage

As protective barriers fall and economies become more integrated, the location of industrial activities is based more on economic factors and less on the nationality of firms, and the pattern of industrial location reflects the *competitive* advantages of economies. The industrial structures in East Asia will reflect more and more the competitive advantages of individual economies, especially those amenable to government facilitation.

The main element of competitive advantage is relatively static comparative advantage in resources, and firms form cross-border production systems by locating separate functions in the economies that offer the best comparative advantage for each function. Knowledge-intensive industries and processes typically locate in advanced countries and labour-intensive industries and processes in developing countries. A company headquartered in Japan, such as Sony, may locate its R&D facilities in the United States, due to the availability of creative human resources, and site its assembly plants in Malaysia, due to the availability of unskilled labour. These factors in an economy's comparative advantage tend to accumulate over time as it develops.

Competitive advantage derives also from such other factors as legal and tax systems, physical infrastructure, and industrial clusters, and location decisions of multinational firms are increasingly based on these other elements. The emergence of industrial clusters, for example, can become a strong attraction to the location of industry and can significantly enhance the overall competitiveness of an economy. These days, Malaysia's attraction to MNCs, for example, is due less to its pool of unskilled labour and more to its accumulation of firms in the electronics and related industries.

Many of these other elements of competitive advantage can be shaped by government policy — by developing physical and regulatory infrastructure and by subsidising investments to enhance industrial clusters, among other things. More developed Asian economies including Korea, Taiwan, Hong Kong, Singapore, and Malaysia need to enhance these policy-dependent competitive factors in order to offset the erosion of their comparative advantage in unskilled labour due to rising wage levels. The ability of government policies to raise the skill and knowledge base of their labour resources will determine which activities these economies attract and the shape of their industrial structures in the near future. On the other hand, the industrial structure in latecomer countries in East Asia such as China, Vietnam, and Indonesia is likely to reflect their continued comparative advantage in unskilled labour more pronouncedly.

Heightened Competition Requires Efficiency and Innovation

Industrial structures will depend on how firms and economies adjust to the intensified competitive pressure of economic globalisation. For example, many of Korea's small and medium-sized enterprises are in peril as trade and investment barriers have fallen and they become exposed to competition from firms in rapidly catching up economies. The success of Singapore's government-linked corporations (GLCs) is being challenged as they are forced to compete in an ocean of sharks rather than a protected lagoon.[9] Survival in an environment of continuing liberalisation, tighter corporate governance by global capital markets, and rapid commoditisation brought about by the IT revolution demands that firms are efficient and innovative, and hence economies must offer firms an environment conducive to efficient and innovative operations.

Ongoing corporate restructuring, together with improved corporate governance brought about by economic globalisation, will raise the efficiency and innovative capability of local enterprises in East Asia. Large Japanese firms with *keiretsu* networks and Korean *chaebol* are selling off peripheral businesses, concentrating on core businesses, and delegating decision-making to lower levels in the organisation. The Asian Financial Crisis accelerated corporate restructuring in hard-hit Thailand and Korea, although less so in Thailand than in Korea, where it proceeded largely under government direction (Chapter 4).

With the spread of cross-border production networks and MNCs' application of IT to manage network activities, an individual firm's efficiency involves the efficiency of activities all along the value-chain, including transportation, distribution, and financial services, and it stretches beyond national borders. The general inefficiency of service sectors in East Asian economies is a major liability to improving the efficiency and competitiveness of firms in the region at every stage of the value-chain.

For some East Asian economies the need to differentiate themselves from the competition is shaping development strategy and structural upgrading. Typically other Asian economies see China, with its huge pool of low-cost and industrious workers and large domestic market, as the greatest competitive threat. Their success in withstanding this threat hinges on the competitiveness of their domestic inputs such as human resources, the competitive strength of their domestic and foreign corporations, and the soundness of their government policies, as well as the competitiveness of Chinese industries. Korea feels compelled to raise the technological capacity of its industries, especially its SMEs, in order to keep core industrial activities from relocating to China and to continue to attract FDI (Chapter 9). Malaysia adopted its Manufacturing-Plus-Plus (Manufacturing++) industrial development approach in recognition of competition from "newcomers with lower wages, many of which have large domestic markets and are aggressively promoting themselves as low-cost export platforms" (Chapter 5). A big question is whether Chinese industries, which are currently dominated by inefficient SOEs under heavy regional protection, will be able to raise their efficiency and innovative capability sufficiently to meet the heightened competition of the global economy, especially after China accedes to the WTO.

Transformation to Self-driven, Networked Industrial Organisations

To compete in an environment of globalisation and IT and to upgrade its industrial structure, an economy must have flexible, networked industrial organisations able to make autonomous decisions. For that matter, it needs a nexus of indigenous, self-driven industrial firms. Industrial organisations that operate as part of MNC networks rely on external organisation and management; the local core of such networks has relatively little influence on the shape and direction of business activities. To provide a local driving force to power the upgrading of industrial structure and innovation capability an economy needs a fair share of corporations with domestic capital, or, more precisely, with substantial inputs of domestic knowledge. In this region, competitive domestic firms are concentrated in Japan and the NIEs, particularly Taiwan and Korea, and they are scarce in other economies.

East Asia is coming to recognise the weakness of domestic firms and the need to strengthen the core of locally owned businesses. The Asian currency crisis revealed the consequences of Singapore's over-dependence on foreign capital and of its weak domestic corporations. Although Singaporean-owned enterprises had been encouraged by the government to develop external wings to improve cost-competitiveness and strengthen regional networks by investing in neighbouring countries, they were constrained by their overall competitive weakness (Chapter 6). Now, Singapore has started to emphasise domestic enterprise formation as the basis of economic development. Although thus far it has depended on foreign capital to the highest degree, Singapore must now create a core of enterprises based on domestic private capital if it is to be able to influence the future course of its economy. The government aspires to develop fifty indigenous world-class enterprises with core competencies to add depth and resilience to the economy (Chapter 6). Malaysia has made the development of large local enterprises geared toward regional and international markets one strategic objective of its Second Industrial Master Plan (Chapter 5). The self-organising capability of Korean firms should improve with the restructuring of the subcontracting system and the outsourcing of non-core businesses undertaken by the *chaebol* since the Asian crisis. In those industries where they have an established technological and managerial base, such as semiconductors and automobiles, Korean firms try to keep their independence by forming strategic alliances with foreign firms (Chapter 9).

Shifting Externalities of International Networks

The externalities to be gained from linking with international networks are expanding with economic globalisation and information technology, and the prospects for each economy in the region will reflect how well its industrial structure captures these benefits. As cross-border production networks proliferate, the importance of developing economies linking their industrial structures with large and powerful international networks increases. The ability to enjoy the network externalities created by the IT revolution may have even greater significance to their development prospects. Such network externalities arise from increasing returns to scale in production of IT goods.

Figure 1.3 depicts the major elements of international network externalities involving East Asia. During the 1970s and 1980s the strongest externalities emanated from Japan, the main innovation centre for maturing manufacturing technology. In addition to FDI and components, linking with Japan gave East Asian firms access to newly developed products, to procurement and distribution networks, and to some transferred technology that facilitated establishing local export-oriented manufacturing industries. Since the early 1990s, the external benefits of these links have been overtaken by the externalities emanating from the United States — the centre of IT innovation and advanced legal and accounting systems. With the ongoing changes in IT, the spread of the Internet, the continued economic liberalisation and deregulation, and the globalisation of capital markets East Asian economies have shifted from linking with Japan to linking with the United States and Europe. Japan's long economic stagnation after the bubble economy and the Asian Financial Crisis encouraged this

FIGURE 1.3
Image of Network Externalities in East Asia

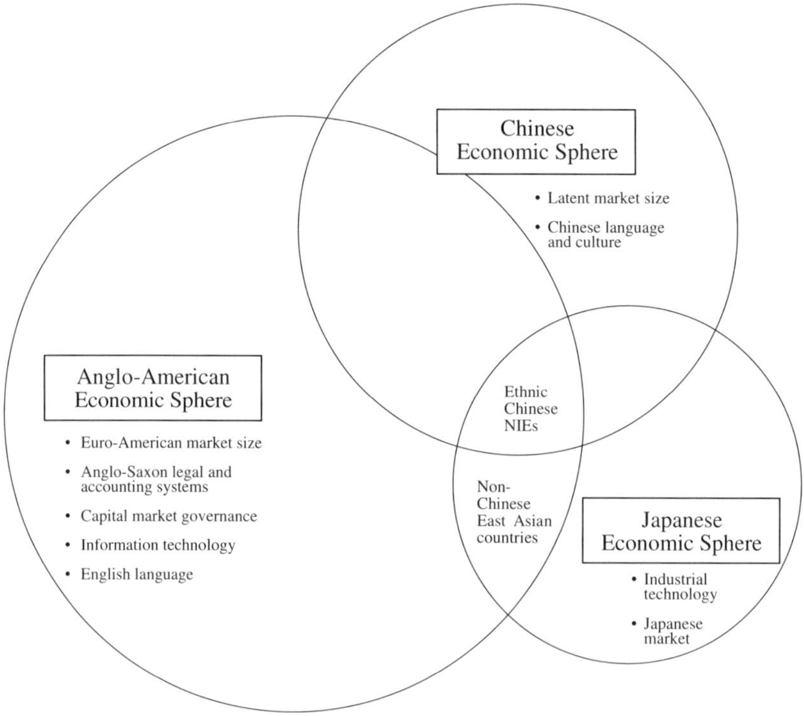

shift in network links. Europe does not offer particular attraction for international network externalities except for the size of the EU internal market. Nevertheless, European firms, particularly MNCs, have increased their presence in East Asia, perhaps as a catch-up process.

A case in point is Korea. Foreign investment into Korea has diversified recently from the traditional sources (Japan and the NIEs) to the United States and Europe, especially the latter. In 1998 over half of inward FDI to Korea came from the EU countries compared with 8 percent from Japan. Japan's share of inward FDI into Korea had stood at just under half from 1986 to 1990, but fell precipitously during the 1990s.[10] Not only did the source of FDI change, but also the sectoral destination of FDI in Korea has also changed. The share of FDI from all sources going into Korea's service sector, especially finance, telecommunications, and other business services, has risen steadily since the 1980s. European and American firms that are targeting emerging markets in China and India are using Korea as a strategic regional base. Where FDI from American and European firms had previously been directed primarily to the domestic market, it has recently focused on building export platforms in Korea (Chapter 9). During the 1990s the composition of FDI going into Asia from Europe, the United States, and Japan shifted, reflecting the changing source of network externalities.

Asian businesses are actively pursuing strategic partnerships with overseas firms, particularly American firms in the IT area. For example, Taiwanese PC manufactures have extensive OEM agreements with American firms, as mentioned previously, and Korea's Samsung Electronics is forming a strategic alliance with U.S. partners such as American Online and Amazon.com to develop e-business.

The ability to benefit from international network externalities depends in part on non-economic factors, such as language and culture. English is the predominant language of the Internet (some 80 percent of e-commerce communication at present), but the use of Chinese has increased in recent years. So far, the countries that share language, culture, and legal and accounting systems with the United States are in an advantageous position, and the Nordic countries, which have been more adaptive to the Anglo-Saxon model, made a smooth transition to the new IT environment. Taiwan and India have captured relatively more of the benefit of such externalities than their Asian neighbours as a result of having sent many students to the United States and of having a large presence of engineers in Silicon Valley. Japan's weakness in this regard is conspicuous (Table 1.14). Singapore, Malaysia, and the Philippines, where English is widely used, are also in an advantageous position.[11]

In a similar way, the sharing of Chinese language and culture may smooth access to China's vast market and production system for some East Asian economies. Their ability to link with China will influence the shape of the region over the course of the twenty-first century. In particular, to the extent that common language and culture are important in electronic commerce, particularly B-to-C e-commerce, the Chinese-speaking economies will be better positioned to serve this growing part of China's economy. Common language is also important in the growth of the software industry, as suggested by the 51 percent increase in shipments of software from Taiwan to Mainland China in 1999.[12] On the other hand, differences

TABLE 1.14
Selected Asian Countries' Links with the United States

	Average score on TOEFL July 1998–June 1999	Students studying in the US per 1,000 population 1997–1998
China	562	0.04
Hong Kong	524	1.53
India	583	0.04
Indonesia	545	0.07
Japan	501	0.37
Korea	535	0.94
Malaysia	536	0.71
Philippines	584	0.04
Singapore	–	1.26
Taiwan	510	1.44
Thailand	512	0.25

Notes: TOEFL refers to the Test of English as a Foreign Language by the Council on International Educational Exchange. Number of students studying in the U.S. per 1,000 population was calculated on the basis of population data for 1996.
Source: Complied from Research Bureau, Economic Planning Agency, 2000 and Statistics Bureau, Management and Coordination Agency 1999.

in language and culture may lengthen the time needed for Korea to develop links with China's market, despite its geographic proximity (Chapter 9).

East Asian industries will not fully realise the external benefits of IT networks if the links to international networks are based on passive acceptance of FDI. By developing their own independent innovation capacity they will have a basis on which to actively initiate participation in international networks. In this way they can increase their share of value added and continue to upgrade their industrial structures. When local East Asian firms have developed technologies to bring to market they may form strategic alliances with large multinational corporations in order to market these technologies through international networks (Chapters 7 and 9).

At the same time, East Asian governments are aware that they should not become carried away by fashion and should remain pragmatic in seeking links with network externalities. For example, the government's policy to develop Hong Kong into an innovation- and knowledge-based economy focuses on "the traditional industries where Hong Kong has already accumulated the knowledge stock and other production or marketing expertise," including tourism, media, and Chinese medicine (Chapter 7). As long as they retain comparative advantage in less skilled labour, many East Asian economies will continue to be driven by the manufacturing sector and they will continue to benefit from the transfer of mature manufacturing technology from Japan. Of course, how soon Japan transfers the old industries to East Asia depends on when it makes room by adopting information technology and strengthening its service economy.

End of the Flying-geese Pattern of Development

With the progress of globalisation and the IT revolution, the flying geese model is becoming less relevant to describe the pattern of development in East Asia. Differences in the adaptability of East Asian economies to globalisation and IT are disturbing the order of the flying geese. The flying-geese pattern of economic and industrial development in East Asia had two components: the traditional sequential development of individual "full-set" industrial structures, as seen in Japan and Korea, and the recent development of cross-border production networks through FDI. With the closer integration of economies around the globe, the full-set component is losing significance and the network component is becoming dominant.

The development pattern emerging in East Asia at the turn of the century seems to be one in which regional clusters form around each new technological breakthrough. Now we see clusters of production oriented around technology and involving economies at different stages of development. There is no longer a single economy that leads the whole flock but different leaders for each technology cluster. For example, Taiwan has overtaken Japan in the production of PCs and Korea leads Japan in the production of RAM chips.[13] Edward Chen, President of Lingnan University, Hong Kong coined the term 'aerobatics' to describe this new development pattern. Rather than a single flock of geese, he sees the clusters resembling multiple squads of stunt aeroplanes (Chen 2000).

The regional pattern of network-based development driven by FDI and the application of IT depends on the competitive advantages, including the comparative advantages, of each economy. Differences in comparative advantage tend to support a sequential flying-geese pattern of development, as industrial change accumulates through time and is orderly. On the other hand, differences in competitive advantage other than comparative advantage do not generate an obvious, predictable pattern of development. These differences arise from many factors such as market and regulatory framework, taxation, infrastructure, the development of industrial clusters, and the externalities of international networks. The competitive advantage of an economy can be influenced by the choice of policies and their implementation as well as by the networking activities of corporations. The future course of development in East Asia will depend more on the proactive involvement of corporations and governments. In general, apart from R&D spending accomplishments, the East Asian NIEs seem to have adapted better than Japan to information technology in policy development and implementation (Masuyama 2000). This may hamper the process of the less developed economies in catching up to the NIEs.

In such circumstances Japan's overwhelming position in the region will likely diminish gradually as the developing economies catch up and as the United States and Europe expand their presence. How much Japan's position recedes in the future depends on the steps that the government and corporate sector in Japan take to accommodate the forces of globalisation and information technology. Policy failures, such as the government's delayed implementation of liberalisation and deregulation, were largely to blame for Japan's recent losses in competitive advantage. Showing institutional fatigue after decades in the lead, the Japanese corporate system as well failed to adapt satisfactorily to the powerful trends of the 1990s. If they persist in such bad practices, Japan's government and corporations will hinder the upgrading of the industrial structure. This in turn will prevent Japan from transferring mature (industrial) technology to the rest of Asia and it will reduce the opportunities for networking IT and service industry innovations from Japan across Asia.

FUTURE DIRECTION OF INDUSTRIAL RESTRUCTURING POLICIES IN EAST ASIA

The East Asian economies need to adjust their industrial structures to establish a firm growth path for the twenty-first century. These economies cannot continue to grow as in the past simply by putting more inputs to work in production. The marginal gain from more and more foreign capital and more and more low-wage labour will eventually diminish, if it has not already.

To achieve sustainable long-run economic growth, East Asian governments need to focus on five areas. First, they need to facilitate the transition in structure from an industrial technology base to an information technology base. Second, they should continue to liberalise and deregulate to improve allocative efficiency as well as to create an overall environment that is conducive to innovation. Third, they need to enhance innovation capacity in order to adapt to information technology and to raise their technological self-reliance and internal drive. Fourth, they need to build up industrial clusters in order to enhance competitive advantage up and down the value chain and improve their self-driving capacity. And finally, they need to enhance the international linkages of their industries in order to maximise international network externalities. The role that East Asian governments should play in pursuing these goals is not to design interventionist industrial policy, but indirectly and proactively to create an environment to support the private sector.

Policies to Adapt to the IT Revolution

East Asian governments have placed priority on adapting the industrial structure to information technologies by encouraging local IT industries and on creating an environment for all industries to benefit from IT innovations. They have taken steps to enhance the economy's adaptability to IT by liberalising and deregulating all industries not only IT-related sectors, by raising innovation capability in the IT sector and throughout the economy, and by smoothing access to international externalities.

They have focused on developing IT-based industrial clusters and providing the IT infrastructure to attract such industries. Singapore and Hong Kong are trying to strengthen their positions as IT hubs on top of their traditional hub function as financial and transportation centres and regional headquarters for multinational corporations. Singapore seeks to become the IT hub in the Asia-Pacific region, and focuses on IT development in telecommunications, media, and electronic commerce as well as the promotion of technology development in the IT area (Chapter 6). Hong Kong has become a regional headquarters or branch office and operations site for overseas manufacturers of IT equipment and it seeks to extend this role to become an operations centre for Greater China (Chen 2000).

Malaysia's Multimedia Super Corridor project and Hong Kong's Cyberport are examples of projects to attract industrial development by putting in place the latest IT infrastructure. The Taiwan government will provide investment tax credits and low-interest loans to help companies set up electronic business networks and it is funding the National Information Infrastructure Project to accelerate the construction of IT networks.[14]

Despite efforts by all governments in the region, a regional 'digital divide' may be emerging. The NIEs are relatively well equipped to meet the challenges posed by the IT revolution, perhaps even more so than the less flexible Japan, while the other economies lag behind. International and region-wide co-operative efforts may be required to ensure that the less developed economies are able to prepare themselves adequately to access and utilise the new technologies.

Further Liberalisation and Regulatory Reform

East Asian governments need to continue to pursue liberalisation and regulatory reform in order to make the industrial structure more efficient and innovative. In fact, many of them maintained the momentum of liberalisation and regulatory reform after the Asian Crisis. This was partly because they made commitments to international organisations, but more because they realise the benefit to their economies. Moreover, they recognise that maintaining inefficient industries harms the competitiveness of efficient ones since, even in a global economy, industries benefit from the agglomeration economies of efficient nearby suppliers and business services. From now, the focus of such efforts in Asia will be the service sector, which has so far lagged behind the manufacturing sector in liberalisation and regulatory reform. Japan has begun to make progress in deregulating the service sector, although the progress has been slow and uneven in the face of strong resistance by vested interests (Endo 1999 and Chapter 11). Shocked by the Asian Crisis to see how the static domestic sector is dragging down the whole Singapore economy, the government shifted to a more open policy framework and launched a Big Bang policy in the telecommunications and finance industries (Chapter 6).

The pressure for liberalisation poses a dilemma for East Asian governments. On the one hand, liberalisation presses for more autonomous, self-driven economies where enterprises strive to differentiate products, where there is internal momentum for industrial upgrading, and where local industrial nexuses connect with international networks. This pressure calls for governments to facilitate the development of local firms. On the other hand, however, the pressure of the global and regional free trade regime constrains East Asian governments from using the traditional policy measures for nurturing infant industries — import protection and local content requirements. The rules of the WTO restrict the adoption of local content regulations, and when AFTA is fully in place it will rule out protection for infant industries within ASEAN. Already, Indonesia's national car project collapsed in the wake of the Asian Crisis and the future of Malaysia's Proton car is in question.

To build up local industries and strengthen economic autonomy, policymakers will need to look beyond traditional industrial development measures based on protection. In the future they need to design policies that promote the realisation of comparative advantage and improve overall competitive advantage. Such policies focus on strengthening industrial clusters, encouraging business formation, developing SMEs, and enhancing human resources. The global and regional trade regimes would permit governments take a direct equity stake in desirable investment projects in the private sector. Recent measures adopted by the region's governments reflect this new approach to industrial development policy. For example, the Singapore government invested in a semiconductor wafer fabricator, SemiTech, together with Texas Instruments and Hewlett Packard of the United States and Canon of Japan.

East Asian economies will use capital more efficiently as competitive mechanisms diffuse with continued liberalisation and regulatory reform, but increased efficiency also depends on improving corporate governance. Raising the standard of corporate governance in turn requires reform of the financial sector. Already, there is a strong movement to adopt a capital market-based corporate governance structure in East Asia, but more ingenuity and local input may be needed in this policy area for two reasons. First, while an American-type financial system is clearly appropriate for advanced economies such as Japan and probably the NIEs, it may not be the right answer for less-developed economies that lack sufficient information infrastructure. Second, given the inadequacy of the global financial architecture demonstrated in the wake of the Asian Crisis, the less developed economies in the region need to be able to protect themselves from being preyed on by international investors and financial institutions (Leong 2000).

Policies to Raise Innovation Capacity of Industry

With globalisation and the IT revolution pressing for more self-reliant, internally driven industrial structures, East Asian governments are turning to policies to encourage the build-up of indigenous innovation capacity.[15] Taiwan's success in developing IT enterprises through technology transfer from the Industrial Technology Research Institute (ITRI) and in providing high-technology infrastructure through the Hsin Chu Science Park provides a role model for the rest of the region. Singapore's industrial restructuring policy has shifted emphasis from cost-competition to capacity-competition, and its technology policy emphasises IT areas including telecommunications, media, and electronic commerce and biotechnology (Chapter 6). In Hong Kong, the government switched to a more active industrial and technology policy committed to developing Hong Kong as an innovation- and knowledge-based economy. It aims to strengthen competitiveness in knowledge and technology-intensive industries by enhancing the economy's technological base and resources and to raise the technology- and knowledge-content of financial service industries, such as banking, insurance and securities, in which Hong Kong is competitive (Chapter 7). Moreover, the Applied Science and Technology Research Institute is set to open in 2001 in the Tai Po Science Park in Hong Kong's New Territories. The Korean government has focused on biotechnology and new materials as frontier technology areas. China also seeks to develop software, biotechnology, fibre-optics, new energy sources, and new materials (Chapter 2).

The shift to a knowledge-intensive industrial structure needs to be undertaken in parallel with the availability of resources in each economy. The Singapore government realistically recognises that in developing domestic scientific and technological capacity it needs to focus on existing strengths and promote technology transfer and spin-offs in those areas (Chapter 6). Korea seeks to enlarge its capacity as an East Asian production platform for high value-added products and a regional innovation platform in the frontier technology area. It aspires to be a centre of excellence in applied research, systems engineering, and other leading science and technology area (Chapter 9).

Since human resources are the key to innovation capacity, there is a strong need for human resource development policy. There is an increasing recognition of the need to overhaul the educational systems in East Asia to foster creativity. The emphasis on primary and secondary education and memorisation and conformity complemented the development of manufacturing industries, but these characteristics do not serve the needs of fast-changing, IT-driven economies. For example, India and the Philippines, where the educational system is biased toward higher education, have produced competitive software industries despite their relatively low overall levels of industrial development. The Singapore government has increased fiscal spending on education, introduced programs to encourage and support life-long learning, and changed the goal of university education from increasing students' quantity of knowledge to teaching them to "learn to learn" — emphasising analytical, creative, entrepreneurial, problem-solving, and interpersonal skills (Chapter 6). Singapore has also increased competition in higher education, invited more foreign professors, and given schools greater autonomy (Chapter 6). Likewise, Hong Kong recognises that its education system needs to shed the elitism of the colonial period. In order to produce a sufficient number of knowledge workers for the information age it needs to increase its capacity for undergraduate, postgraduate, and continuing education. Moreover, the neglect of science and technology education at the undergraduate level has become a serious problem and an important issue on the reform agenda. Hong Kong established the Open Learning Institute in 1990 and the HK University of Science and Technology in 1991 and upgraded its polytechnic schools and other colleges to university status to increase the capacity of the tertiary education system (Chapter 7). While NIEs are augmenting their human resources by expanding higher education and accumulating industrial experience, the less-developed economies in East Asia are lagging in such efforts and are compelled to focus on more fundamental reform. Thailand's 1999 National Education Act started a long-term process of upgrading the education system with a key initiative to provide everyone with free basic education through the secondary level.

Developing domestic human resources through education and training is a long-term process to increase the innovative capacity of an economy. Some economies in the region are meeting their immediate need for skilled labour and knowledge workers through immigration. Recognising the limited quantity as well as quality of the domestic labour force, the Singapore government redefined human resources to include available foreign talents. It has decided to strengthen its talent scouting along the American model and it has hired foreign CEOs for state-owned firms. Malaysia also has adopted a policy to attract foreign knowledge workers. It exempts firms located in the Multimedia Super Corridor from limitations on employing foreigners. Similarly, Hong Kong government has eased immigration restrictions in order to gain access to the high quality human resources of Mainland China. There is an argument to be made that an economy's continuing openness to workers from abroad makes for a kind of Schumpeterian creative destruction that keeps it at the forefront of innovation. Indeed the attraction of brainpower from all over the world is cited as one reason for the United States' edge in IT (Jacquet 2000).

Policies to Enhance Industrial Clusters

East Asian governments acutely recognise the need to support the development of industrial clusters. Not only will the economies and efficiencies generated by clustering related industrial activities attract foreign and domestic investments, but also the intensive communication and interaction among firms in these clusters will foster the emergence of self-driven activities that East Asian economies seriously lack. Singapore's approach to industrial clusters offers a model for industrial policy in East Asia. Following the logic of Porter's *Competitive Advantage of Nations* the Singapore government seeks to form industrial clusters in electronics, petroleum refining, and marine transportation and it has invested directly in the formation of industrial clusters by establishing the Joint Investment Fund and Cluster Development Fund (Chapter 6). Malaysia moved from an industry-based approach to a cluster based-approach in 1996 with its Second Industrial Master Plan, which focuses on strengthening the service sector, the formation of an IT/Multimedia cluster, and the development of agriculture-based industries (Chapter 5). The Philippines' Export Development Plan is based on the idea that fostering industrial growth through industrial clusters is essential to longer-term success of export development and promotion efforts (Chapter 3).

Policymakers need to define industrial clusters more broadly than they have traditionally done. As we have argued, with cross-border and information technology networks, competition involves not just specific activities, but the whole value chain. The demarcation between the service and manufacturing sectors has become blurred and the competitiveness of all economic activities depends on the linkages between them. A vigorous manufacturing sector is widely recognised as a necessary condition for an economy to develop its service sector, since demand for (manufacturing support) services grows along with the manufacturing sector. For this reason, Singapore's plan for a knowledge-based economy driven by high value-added manufacturing and service exports calls for the manufacturing sector to retain a 25-percent share of the economy (Chapter 6). Similarly, Malaysia aims to maintain a 30 percent share for manufacturing as the economy diversifies into high value-added services (Chapter 5).

SMEs naturally constitute a major part of supporting industries and they play a major role in strengthening innovation capacity. Thus, promotion of SMEs is a major policy issue in industrial restructuring for East Asian governments. In Korea, which has developed centring on large firms, the development of SMEs is an urgent task. It is recognised that the key to the competitiveness of SMEs is networking (Chatper 9).

An economy's start-up environment is a major factor to developing a core of domestic enterprises centring on SMEs. East Asian economies are tending toward a venture capital model, particularly for the formation of high-tech firms. The Singapore government has shifted its SME development policy from a Japanese-style protective policy to a Silicon Valley-type venture business model. The development of venture capital and capital markets has become a major policy goal in such economies as Hong Kong, Singapore, Korea, Thailand, and Malaysia. Moreover, the development of human resources that possess not only skills but also an entrepreneurial spirit is a key to the development of venture businesses. For that purpose, it is necessary to reduce the intervention of government in business decisions through liberalisation and deregulation and to promote business education. North American and European business schools are vying for the growth markets of East Asian students through tie-ups with local universities and by setting up their own campuses in the region (Chapter 6). At the same time, Taiwan's success in spinning off high-tech ventures run by engineers from ITRI shows that government does play an important role in developing a core of technological accumulation to seed technology ventures.

Enhance International Linkage

In a world of globalising economies and a revolution in information technologies an economy's competitiveness depends crucially on maximising the benefits from the externalities of international networks. Although international linkages should basically be reinforced by fostering private-sector activities under policies that promote deregulation and liberalisation, these efforts should be supplemented to some extent by government involvement. And as discussed before, the networking environment for East Asia is changing. The attractions of linking with Japan are decreasing, relatively speaking, and the merits of linking with the United States — the innovation centre of information technology and finance and the front runner in the race for efficiency — are on the rise. The merits of linking with China are likely to grow in the long run.

East Asian governments are responding to this changed environment. Their basic policy thrust is to facilitate the human network of knowledge workers as well as the corporate network. As mentioned previously, they have adopted policies to attract foreign talents as one solution to the shortage of local talents. Many governments are encouraging domestic universities and research institutes to link with foreign universities and institutions (Economic Planning Agency 2000). Moreover, they are encouraging linkages between local knowledge workers and foreign innovation centres, particularly in the United States. For example, the Singapore government is encouraging young engineers to go to stay in Silicon Valley.

With regard to corporate networks, Singapore focuses on the role of venture capitals to bridge Singapore (and its region) and America for the sake of developing IT start-ups by Singaporeans both at home and the U.S. Through the Technopreneurship Investment Fund, the Singapore government has committed US$100 million to the US$1 billion ePlanet Fund to link Asia and the United States. The purpose of this move is to deepen the interest of U.S. venture capital firms in the investment opportunities in Asia. Singapore has also established Connect@sig in California's Bay Area as a one-stop centre to provide business services to Singaporean start-ups in the United States and to create entry points for Singaporean firms looking for contacts in Silicon Valley and for U.S. firms interested in Asia (Chia 2000).

With links to China expected to become an important competitive factor in the future, East Asian governments need to support private enterprises' attempts to build connections with the Mainland. The Singapore government has expanded both the teaching of the Chinese language and its student exchange program with China. Singapore's Infocomm Development Authority (IDA) is focusing on emerging regional IT markets in China and India, not only because of their market potential but also because of their potential as major sources of Asian content (Chia 2000). Singapore intends to utilise its multilingual and multicultural background to translate, digitise, and package the content for worldwide markets. Hong Kong hopes to serve as the operations and control centre for firms located in Greater China, while Taiwan aims to become the hub of headquarters and operations for the Asia-Pacific region (Chapter 8).

In addition to enhancing their links with the United States and China, East Asian economies need to strengthen links with neighbouring economies. Regional networks will complement and, in some sense, strengthen the position of individual economies as self-driving cores within wider international networks. The formation of AFTA by ASEAN member countries has been the main step in this direction. While the 1997–98 Asian Crisis revealed its limitations participants continue to push for the deepening of AFTA in order to maintain momentum and to respond to growing competition from China. Economic linkages involving non-AFTA economies have recently gained impetus in, for example, the moves to establish a Singapore–Japan Free Trade Agreement and a Korea–Japan

Free Trade Agreement. Japan should revise its foreign economic policies including official development assistance to focus more on supporting private sector linkages with other East Asian economies and local networks within the region. With the waning of the flying geese development mechanism, Japan is no longer always ahead of its Asian neighbours. It should formulate regional economic policies by learning from the good examples of neighbouring governments, particularly the NIEs, and it should implement policies in co-operation with them. Japan should also become much more serious in encouraging its workforce to undertake foreign language education and training — focusing on English in the short run and Chinese in the long run — in order to maintain its place in international networks.

Change in the Role of Government

The changes and challenges of globalisation and the IT revolution call for East Asian governments to take an indirect but active role in shaping the industrial development of their economies. On one hand, to promote the transition toward more efficient, self-driven, and knowledge-intensive industrial structures they need to stop directly intervening in industrial activities and concentrate on indirect measures such as deregulation and infrastructure development to strengthen locational advantage by creating a favourable environment for doing business. Government intervention in industrial activities needs to be kept at the minimum because entre-preneurship is key to innovation and self-driven industrial activities. Even the Singapore government, which is known for its successful involvement in industrial activities through government-linked corporations and other measures, is moving to emphasise private-sector initiative. On the other hand, to promote innovation and international linkages, governments need be active in pointing the direction by developing educational systems, infrastructure, and regulation and R&D policies suited to the new environment in the age of IT. Even Hong Kong, which achieved great success under its laissez-faire economic policy, has recognised the limitation of this approach for upgrading industrial structure, and it is now seriously pondering a change in the policy framework. Singapore and Taiwan, where governments were more directly involved in shaping technology changes, have been more successful in industrial upgrading than Hong Kong. East Asian governments are finding it a challenge to step into new, unfamiliar roles.

Notes

[1]   The views expressed in this chapter are solely those of the authors and do not necessarily represent the views of the authors of the other chapters. References to individual chapters appear in parentheses where appropriate.

[2]   The contribution from Indonesia (Chapter 2) concentrates on the role of the agriculture and agribusiness industries in supporting the Indonesian economy through the current crisis. Issues affecting the agricultural sector are also discussed in Chapter 10 on China.

[3]   Despite its status as an NIE Hong Kong's R&D capability is extremely poor. It has fewer scientists and engineers per capita than Thailand and only a few more than Malaysia, and its record on patent applications is similar to Indonesia's. This is partly because when Hong Kong's manufacturing facilities moved to lower wage China after the late 1970s their place was taken by service industries, which do not require significant R&D capability (Chapter 7).

[4]   "Hardware leads in infotech industry." Taipei *Journal*, 23 June 2000.

[5]   Taiwan's software sector grew thirty percent in 1999 over 1998, and Internet-related production was up 13.6 percent over 1998. "Taiwan aims for 90 percent of world supply," Taipei *Journal*, 24 March 2000.

[6]   See Masuyama (1997) for an overview of industrial policies in the East Asian economies.

[7]   "As part of Lee's reform program, the government, for instance, took the opportunity presented by the crisis to bring top foreign managers into the businesses it controls or onto their boards. By early this year two of the four biggest banks had foreign CEOs (the largest, DBS Bank is run by John Olds, an American ex-J.P. Morgan man); NOL, a big shipping line, is now run by Flemming Jacobs, a Dane formerly with Maersk; and Singapore Airlines has put the first foreigner ever (an Australian banker) on its board." Rohwer 2000, p. 105.

[8]   "Trends in Japan-related M&As in 2000" (2000nen no Nihon kigyo ni kanrensuru M&A no doko). Document circulated by Management Survey Section, Financial Research Centre, Nomura Securities, Ltd. 18 January 2001.

[9]   "The old GLC model was okay when we were in a lagoon, but when you get linked to the ocean you have to deal with sharks." Wong Kwok Seng, CEO of Singapore's Semb Corp commenting on the threat from global giants entering Asia and the demise of the old Asian conglomerate model based on relationships rather than efficiency and transparency. Rohwer 2000, p. 106.

[10] Japanese FDI to Korea increased sharply in 1999 in response to the post-crisis liberalisation there.

[11] Already, English-speaking Filipinos at Clark Special Economic Zone handle 80 percent of technical and billing inquiries for America Online, and other major Western firms including Andersen Consulting and Caltex are locating back office and customer service functions in the Philippines. See Goad 1999, pp. 8–12.

[12] "Hardware leads in infotech industry." Taipei *Journal*, 23 June 2000.

[13] In 1998 Taiwan became the world's largest supplier of notebook PCs by volume and it accounted for almost 80 percent of global output of motherboards. "Hardware Leads in Infotech Industry." Taipei *Journal*, 23 June 2000.

[14] "Taiwan coming up to speed in e-business. " Taipei *Journal*, 4 August 2000.

[15] According to a World Bank study, simultaneously raising investments in education and telecommunications and opening up to trade can increase a country's GDP growth rate as much as 4 percentage points. World Bank, 1998, "Knowledge for Development". *World Development Report 1998/99* cited in Matti Pohjola, p. 3.

References

Asian Development Bank. 2000. *Asian Development Outlook 2000*. <http://www.adb.org/documents/news/2000/nr2000039.asp.>

Borrus, Michael, Dieter Ernst, and Stephan Haggard. 2000. "Introduction: Cross-border Production Networks and the Industrial Integration of the Asia-Pacific Region." In *International Production Networks in Asia* ed M. Borrus, D. Ernst, and S. Haggard. London: Routledge.

Chen, Edward, K.Y. 2000. "The Development of the IT Industry in Hong Kong." Presentation to the Tokyo Club Foundation for International Studies' Asia Forum. Kyoto, 12 May. <http://www.tcf.or.jp/Activities/ACTtop.html>.

Chia Siow Yue. 2000. "Singapore and the IT Revolution." Presentation to the Tokyo Club Foundation for International Studies' Asia Forum. Kyoto, 12 May. <http://www.tcf.or.jp/Activities/ACTtop.html>.

Council for Economic Planning and Development. 2000. *Taiwan Statistical Data Book, 2000*. Taipei: Republic of China.

Doner, Richard F. and Peter Brimble. 1998. "Thailand's Hard Disk Drive Industry." Working paper for the Information Storage Industry Center (ISIC), University of California, San Diego. Sept. 7. <www-irps.ucsd.edu/~sloan/papers/thailandhdd.htm>.

Economic Planning Agency Research Bureau. 2000. *Annual Report on the Asian Economies* Government of Japan. June 21. <http://www5.cao.go.jp/2000/f/0621f-asia/0621f-asia-e.html>.

Endo, Yukihiko. 1999. "Can the 'Big Bang' Cure the Ills of Japan's Financial System?" In *East Asia's Financial Systems: Evolution and Crisis* eds S. Masuyama, D. Vandenbrink, and S. Y. Chia. Singapore: Institute of Southeast Asian Studies and Nomura Research Institute.

Goad, G. Pierre. 1999. "At Your Service." *Far Eastern Economic Review.* (2 September): 8–12.

Jacquet, Pierre. 2000. "Globalization and the New Economy." Presentation at the Keizai Koho Center. Tokyo. October 12.

Kwan, C. H. 1998. "The Yen, the Yuan, and the Asian Currency Crisis: Changing Fortune between Japan and China." Asia/Pacific Research Center. Occasional Papers. Institute for International Studies. Stanford University. December.

Lall, S., M. Albaladejo, and E. Aldaz, "East Asian Exports: Competitiveness, technological structure and strategies," August 1999. Preliminary draft for World Bank, *East Asia: Out of the Crisis and into the New Millennium* forthcoming.

Lee Jin Soo. 2000. "The IT Revolution in Korea." Presentation to the Tokyo Club Foundation for International Studies' Asia Forum. Kyoto, 12 May. <http://www.tcf.or.jp/Activities/ACTtop.html>.

Leong, Stephen. 2000. "East Asia under Economic Globalisation: A Malaysian Perspective." Presentation to the Tokyo Club Foundation for International Studies' Asia Forum. Kyoto, 12 May. <http://www.tcf.or.jp/Activities/ACTtop.html>.

Li Peiyu. 2000. "Importance of Foreign Direct Investment to Developing Countries." Presentation to the Tokyo Club Foundation for International Studies' Asia Forum. Kyoto, 12 May. <http://www.tcf.or.jp/Activities/ACTtop.html>.

Masuyama, S. 1997. "The Evolving Nature of Industrial Policy in East Asia: Liberalisation, Upgrading, and Integration." In *Industrial Policy in East Asia* eds S. Masuyama, D. Vandenbrink, and S. Y. Chia. Singapore: Institute of Southeast Asian Studies and Nomura Research Institute.

————. 1999. "Introduction: The Evolution of Financial Systems in East Asia and Their Responses to Financial and Economic Crisis." In *East Asia's Financial Systems: Evolution and Crisis* eds. S. Masuyama, D. Vandenbrink, and S. Y. Chia. Singapore: Institute of Southeast Asian Studies and Nomura Research Institute.

————. 2000. "Hastening to Embrace the Internet Revolution in Asia." NRI Papers 21 (1 December). <http://www.nri.co.jp/english/report/papers/index.html>.

Moritani, Masanori. 1998. *Bunmei no Gijutsushikan* (Perspective of Civilisation to the History of Technology). Tokyo: Chuokoronsha.

Ng, Francis and Alexander Yeats. 1999. "Production Sharing in East Asia: Who Does What for Whom and Why?" World Bank Research *Working Paper* 2197. Washington, D.C.: World Bank.

Pohjola, Matti. 2000. "Information Technology and Economic Growth: A Cross-Country Analysis." United Nations University Working Paper 173. January.

Porter, Michael E. 1999. *On Competition*. Cambridge: Harvard Business School Press.

————. 1990. *The Competitive Advantage of Nations*. New York: Free Press.

Rohwer, Jim. 2000. "Asia's Economy: A Precarious Balancing Act." *Fortune*. 26 June.

Schive. Chi. 1999. "A Study on Taiwan: High-tech Industries in the Spotlight." Presented at Geneva-Hong Kong Conference on Global Production: Specialization and Trade, 25–27 October, Hong Kong. <http://cepd.spring.org.tw/Speak/lingnan1.html.>

Statistics Bureau of the Management and Coordination Agency. 1999. *World Statistics* (Sekai no Toukei). Tokyo: Government of Japan.

Thee Kian Wie. n.d. Export-oriented Industrialisation and Foreign Direct Investment in the ASEAN Countries. UNU-AERC Conference on Asia and Africa in the Global Economy. <http://www.unu.edu/hq/academic/Pg_area4/Thee.html>.

UNESCO. 2000a. *Statistical Yearbook 1999*. Tokyo: Hara Shobo/UNESCO Publishing.

UNESCO. 2000b. *World Education Report 2000: The Right to Education*. UNESCO Publishing. PDL file. <http://www.unesco.org/education/information/wer/index.htm>.

United Nations. Various years. *Yearbook of International Trade Statistics*. New York: United Nations.

United Nations Conference on Trade and Development (UNCTAD). Various years. *World Investment Report*. Geneva and New York: United Nations.

Urata, Shujiro. 1995. "Trade Policy and Economic Development: A Survey of Theoretical and Empirical Studies" (in Japanese). In *Boeki Jiyuka to Keizai Hatten — Tojoukoku ni okeru Sisansei Bunseki* (Trade

Liberalisation and Productivity Growth in Asia and Latin America) ed. S. Urata. Tokyo: Institute of Developing Economies.

Wang Jiann-Chuyann. 2000. "Past and Future Role of Small and Medium-Sized Enterprises in Taiwan's Economic Development." In *Restoring East Asia's Dynamism* eds S. Masuyama, D. Vandenbrink, and S. Y. Chia. Singapore: Institute for Southeast Asian Studies and Nomura Research Institute.

World Bank. 1993. *The East Asian Miracle: Economic Growth and Public Policy.* New York: Oxford University Press.

World Bank. 1998. "Knowledge for Development." *World Development Report 1998/99* cited in Matti Pohjola UNU Working paper 173, Jan 2000 Information Technology and Economic Growth: A Cross-Country Analysis.

World Bank. 2000a. *Entering the 21st Century: World Development Report 1999/2000.* Oxford: Oxford University Press.

World Bank. 2000b. *World Development Indicators.* Washington, D.C.: World Bank.

PART I
Industrial Restructuring in Southeast Asian Economies

2

Sectoral Contribution to Indonesia's Economic Recovery
The Potential of Agriculture and Agribusiness[1]

Yoopi Abimanyu

INTRODUCTION

In mid 1997, Indonesia was hit by a currency crisis. The domestic currency depreciated by about 67 percent against the U.S. dollar between July and December 1997 and it depreciated an additional 118 percent between December 1997 and January 1998 (Figure 2.1). Even though the currency recovered about 27 percent of its value from January to April 1998, it depreciated about 83 percent from April until June 1998. After that, the exchange rate began to recover somewhat. In the year between June 1998 and June 1999, the exchange rate appreciated about 41 percent. Within that period, the exchange rate appreciation averaged about 6 percent per month.

This currency crisis caused deterioration throughout the economy. The financial and exchange rate turbulence negatively influenced economic activity, resulting in a decline in real GDP growth to 4.5 percent in 1997 from 9.3 percent in 1996 (Figure 2.2). This condition was further exacerbated by social unrest occurring in May 1998 that disrupted the production and distribution systems and triggered inflationary pressure in the real sector. Against the backdrop of these worsening developments, fuelled by the sharp deterioration of the rupiah, real output contracted even more in 1998. By the fourth quarter of 1998 the economy had contracted by 13.2 percent relative to a year earlier, with almost all sectors experiencing negative growth except for certain agricultural sectors. The economy stabilised somewhat in 1999, but through the third quarter the economy still contracted by 1.7 percent compared to one year earlier.

FIGURE 2.1
Movement of the Rupiah versus the U.S. Dollar, January 1997 to July 1999

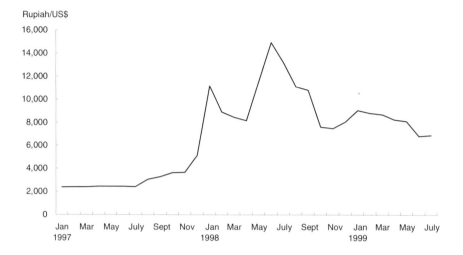

Source: Central Bank of Indonesia.

FIGURE 2.2
Indonesia's Gross Domestic Product, Q1 1994 to Q3 1999

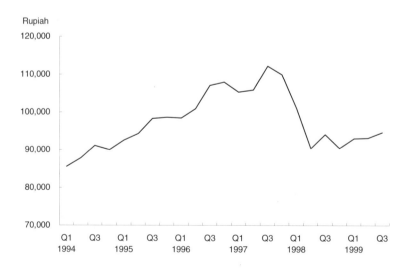

Source: Central Statistical Agency.

It has been hypothesised that agriculture was less affected by the economic contraction than other sectors because the depreciation of the exchange rate would increase demand for Indonesia's agricultural exports. This sector might help to drive the country's economic recovery. This chapter investigates how Indonesia's agricultural sector and agribusiness responded to the sharp deterioration of the rupiah. In particular, it examines whether there is a positive correlation between the depreciation of the rupiah and agricultural and agribusiness exports.

INDONESIA'S AGRICULTURAL SECTOR

The agricultural sector, including forestry and fishing, is one of the most important sectors of the Indonesian economy in terms of employment. According to the 1997 population census the share of agriculture in total employment was 44 percent, the same as in the 1995 census. This sector is also one of the largest sources of national income. In the early 1970s agriculture contributed between 40 and 50 percent of real GDP. By the early 1980s its share had declined to approximately 23 percent and in 1997 it was around 15 percent.

The drive to increase rice production from the mid-1960s showed impressive results, enabling Indonesia to achieve the goal of rice self-sufficiency in 1985. The agricultural sector's performance was less impressive in the 1990s, however. Poor weather, pest infestation, and the transfer of rice acreage to non-agricultural use caused production to contract in many areas. This led to growing concerns regarding the sustainability of rice self-sufficiency.

The focus of government agricultural policy is to maintain food security and promote efficient production, processing, and marketing of agricultural products. A key aim of the rice policy framework is to ensure food security by promoting competition in this sector. Accordingly, trade in all qualities of rice has been opened to general importers and exporters. As the rupiah strengthened and world prices fell, the domestic price of rice was declining. This prompted the government in the 1990s to provide transitional protection to rice farmers with an import tariff, while balancing the impact on consumers. The existence of the tariff will be assessed from time to time.

ROLE OF AGRICULTURE IN THE ECONOMY

Saragih (1999) suggests three reasons why agriculture is one of the only sectors that might help to rebuild the economy. First, agriculture is one of the main sectors that showed positive growth in the past several years. Even though rice production declined somewhat in 1997 as a result of severe drought, production soon increased again. The agricultural sector's share of real GDP was relatively stable at around 15 to 17 percent between the first quarter 1994 and the third quarter of 1999 (Table 2.1). It was the second largest industry in that period, followed by trade. In 1997, the industrial sector grew 5.25 percent compared to only 1.14 percent growth in the agricultural sector (Table 2.2). In 1998 however, industrial output contracted by more than 11 percent whereas agricultural output grew by 1 percent. For the first three quarters of 1999 while the industrial sector contracted by 0.5 percent (buoyed by the positive growth of oil and non-oil sub-sectors), the agricultural sector expanded by almost 2 percent. The expansion in the agricultural sector was mostly due to increased output of food, estate crops, and fisheries. These sectors grew by 1.9 percent, 2.8 percent, and 4.1 percent respectively in 1998, while they expanded by 4.0, 3.2, and 1.7 percent respectively in the first three quarters of 1999.

Second, according to Saragih, agribusiness comprises a significant share of non-oil and gas manufacturing value added, exports, and employment, while it comprises only a small share of non-oil/gas imports. This suggests that the industry imposes only a small burden on foreign exchange reserves. Third, agribusiness, which consists mostly of small and medium scale enterprises, is generally environmentally friendly and provides income and employment to low-income/low-skilled workers.

THE ROLE OF AGRICULTURE IN THE EXPORT SECTOR

In theory, the sharp depreciation of the rupiah exchange rate in 1997 and 1998 represented a window of opportunity for Indonesia's agricultural exports and it should have boosted the agricultural sector. In fact, however, the depreciation of the rupiah exchange rate was not directly followed by an increase in Indonesia's agricultural exports (Figure 2.3). Exporters may delay reacting to a change in the value of the currency, creating a gap between the timing of the changes in the exchange rate and the volume of agricultural exports. Changes in exports still do not closely follow changes in the exchange rate, however, when agricultural exports are lagged one period (Figure 2.4).

The weak response of Indonesia's agricultural exports during the recent currency crisis was surprising. Since the huge depreciation of the rupiah made Indonesian goods measured in dollars more competitive on world markets, it was expected that agricultural exports would increase. Three

TABLE 2.1
Composition of Gross Domestic Product, Q1 1994 to Q3 1999
(Percent share of constant dollar GDP)

		Agriculture	Mining	Industry	Utilities	Construction	Trade	Transportation	Financial Services	Other Services
1994	Q1	17.87	9.36	22.40	0.99	6.81	16.34	6.91	9.37	9.94
	Q2	17.30	9.21	22.68	1.04	7.57	16.63	6.93	8.97	9.67
	Q3	17.62	9.21	23.50	1.05	7.00	16.86	7.12	8.26	9.38
	Q4	14.14	9.73	24.58	1.10	7.77	17.25	7.42	8.30	9.70
1995	Q1	17.36	9.20	22.69	1.06	7.69	16.55	7.29	8.74	9.41
	Q2	17.93	9.11	22.32	1.12	7.39	16.66	7.06	9.07	9.33
	Q3	15.91	9.21	24.46	1.14	7.69	16.70	6.95	8.90	9.03
	Q4	13.46	9.46	25.90	1.14	7.66	17.02	7.18	9.04	9.14
1996	Q1	16.82	9.21	22.98	1.14	7.59	16.70	7.47	8.98	9.12
	Q2	17.23	9.06	23.07	1.19	7.50	16.60	7.15	9.22	8.99
	Q3	15.05	9.00	25.16	1.17	8.75	16.44	6.93	8.91	8.59
	Q4	12.67	9.00	27.23	1.18	7.90	17.21	7.15	9.00	8.67
1997	Q1	16.47	8.91	23.88	1.20	8.42	16.35	7.48	8.36	8.93
	Q2	15.32	9.03	24.50	1.29	8.24	16.72	7.35	8.69	8.87
	Q3	15.78	8.71	25.17	1.26	8.14	17.18	7.05	8.20	8.51
	Q4	12.02	8.95	25.76	1.31	7.85	17.59	7.46	10.32	8.73
1998	Q1	17.01	9.08	25.02	1.33	5.71	17.06	7.74	8.11	8.93
	Q2	17.62	9.94	24.18	1.53	5.27	16.25	7.38	7.65	10.18
	Q3	17.97	9.91	26.02	1.50	5.51	15.49	6.57	7.26	9.78
	Q4	16.53	10.90	25.66	1.59	5.87	15.19	6.96	7.00	10.29
1999	Q1	19.22	9.87	25.05	1.50	5.55	15.15	6.91	6.80	9.95
	Q2	18.16	9.66	25.31	1.61	5.62	15.70	6.93	6.85	10.17
	Q3	17.06	9.92	25.77	1.63	5.67	16.00	7.09	6.82	10.05

Source: Central Statistical Agency.

TABLE 2.2
Quarterly and Annual Growth of Real GDP and Selected Components
(Percent change)

		GDP	Agriculture						Industry	Trade
			Total	Food	Estate Crops	Livestock	Forestry	Fisheries		
1997	Q1	-2.49	26.71	94.88	-47.49	-10.37	0.57	-10.71	-14.50	-7.35
	Q2	0.56	-6.46	-22.79	73.75	6.67	-0.34	12.51	3.16	2.84
	Q3	6.00	9.20	-5.01	47.64	3.98	30.66	6.74	8.92	8.95
	Q4	-2.06	-25.39	-37.38	-32.20	5.56	-15.82	-0.65	0.24	0.28
	Annual	4.54	1.14	-2.85	1.61	4.92	12.62	5.79	5.25	5.98
1998	Q1	-8.03	30.14	95.46	-29.69	-11.81	16.77	-8.26	-10.67	-10.82
	Q2	-10.57	-7.34	-12.52	31.71	-3.22	-30.49	5.95	-13.58	-14.78
	Q3	4.12	6.17	-11.65	56.15	-1.02	37.81	6.48	12.04	-0.79
	Q4	-3.93	-11.60	-7.08	-24.94	2.93	-25.17	-1.68	-5.23	-5.78
	Annual	-13.20	0.81	1.90	2.76	-7.08	-1.85	4.08	-11.88	-18.05
1999	Q1	2.88	19.58	49.45	-23.90	0.98	19.15	-12.32	0.41	2.63
	Q2	0.18	-5.34	-14.63	30.60	-2.96	-11.26	12.61	1.22	3.78
	Q3	1.54	-4.60	-16.59	17.52	-1.78	9.07	7.17	3.40	3.49
	Annual	-1.66	1.82	4.01	3.17	-0.51	-8.07	1.69	-0.50	-5.69

Source: Central Statistical Agency.

FIGURE 2.3
Monthly Changes in Agricultural Exports and the Rupiah Exchange Rate,
January 1997 to September 1999

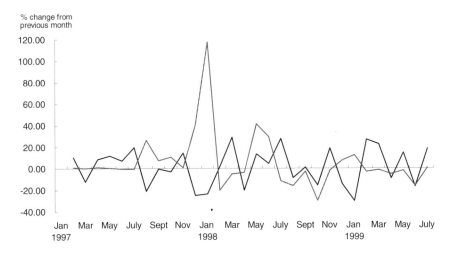

Source: Central Bank of Indonesia and Ministry of Industry and Trade.

FIGURE 2.4
Changes in Agricultural Exports Lagged
One Month and the Rupiah Exchange Rate,
February 1997 to September 1999

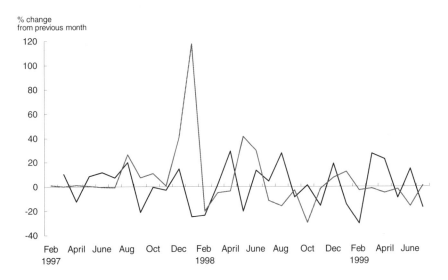

Source: Central Bank of Indonesia and Ministry of Industry and Trade.

typical explanations for why agricultural exports did not respond as expected are: the lack of trade finance caused by the collapse of the domestic banking system, the excessive dependence on imported inputs, which had become more expensive in rupiah terms, and the rising social and political instability, which caused international purchasers of manufactured goods to source from other countries.

A fourth reason is that agricultural exports suffered from a decline in the terms of trade during the economic crisis. World market prices for Indonesia's main agricultural export commodities, such as fish and shrimp, fell sharply between the first half of 1997 and the first half of 1999, and agriculture export prices generally tended downward between January 1997 and September 1999 (Figure 2.5). This decline in the prices of export goods meant that revenues from agricultural exports measured in U.S. dollars declined, even though the volume of exports continued to grow. Thus, the performance of Indonesia's agricultural exports during the economic crisis must be assessed in terms of quantity or volume as well as in terms of revenues.

To accurately distinguish the impact on agricultural exports due to changes in the exchange rate from the impact due to changes in the terms-of-trade, export value should be measured in real terms.[2] We calculated a real-value index, a time-series of agricultural export value at a constant average 1997–99 price (Table 2.3). We first divided the value of exports in current prices by the volume of exports to arrive at a base price for each month from January 1997 to September 1999. We then multiplied monthly export volume by the average of the monthly base prices to determine the value of exports, holding price constant. The implicit price deflator is the ratio of export value measured at current prices to export value measured at constant price.[3] According to this deflator, the average price of Indonesia's agricultural exports in September 1999 was 36.8 percent lower than in January 1997. Because of the decline in prices, export revenues (represented by export value at current prices) in September 1999 were only 17.90 percent higher than in January 1997, even though export volume (represented by export value at constant prices) was 86.58 percent higher.

Figure 2.6 compares January 1997-based indices agricultural exports valued at current prices and at the constant average price with the implicit price deflator. While the price deflator followed a general downward trend from January 1997 to September 1999, both nominal and real exports were more erratic. Both measures of export value fell sharply several times, particularly in 1998 and at the beginning of 1999. The value of exports generally recovered after February 1999. The coincidence of the sharp

FIGURE 2.5
Agricultural Export Prices, January 1997 to September 1999

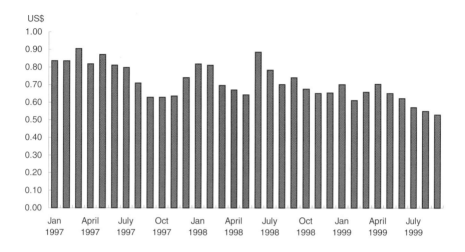

Source: Ministry of Industry and Trade.

FIGURE 2.6
Nominal and Real Value of Agricultural Exports and Implicit Price Deflator,
January 1997 to September 1999

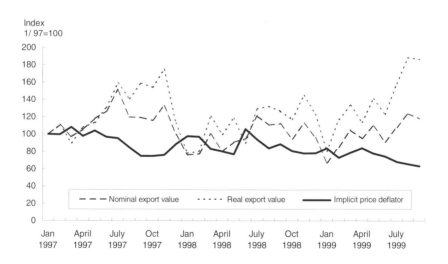

Note: Real export value is value of exports at constant average price for January 1997 to
September 1999.
Source: Ministry of Industry and Trade.

TABLE 2.3
Nominal and Real Value of Agricultural Exports and Implicit Price Deflator, January 1997 to September 1999

		Value of Agricultural Exports at:				
		Current Price		Constant Price		Implicit Price Deflator
		US$ millions	Monthly % change	US$ Millions	Monthly % change	Index 1/97 = 100	Monthly % change
1997	Jan.	531.6		443.4		1.20	100	
	Feb.	587.1	10.44	490.8	10.69	1.20	100	0.00
	March	515.4	−12.21	398.0	−18.91	1.29	108	8.26
	April	559.6	8.58	478.0	20.08	1.17	98	−9.58
	May	625.3	11.74	501.9	5.00	1.25	104	6.42
	June	670.8	7.27	578.1	15.18	1.16	97	−6.87
	July	804.0	19.86	704.7	21.91	1.14	95	−1.68
	Aug.	635.5	−20.95	625.2	−11.29	1.02	85	−10.89
	Sept.	632.6	−0.45	703.9	12.60	0.90	75	−11.59
	Oct.	614.7	−2.83	683.8	−2.86	0.90	75	0.03
	Nov.	704.3	14.57	774.4	13.26	0.91	76	1.16
	Dec.	529.3	−24.85	499.4	−35.51	1.06	88	16.53
1998	Jan.	405.2	−23.43	346.4	−30.65	1.17	98	10.40
	Feb.	411.7	1.60	354.7	2.41	1.16	97	−0.79
	March	532.1	29.22	533.5	50.39	1.00	83	−14.07
	April	424.9	−20.13	442.2	−17.11	0.96	80	−3.65
	May	482.1	13.47	524.5	18.62	0.92	77	−4.34
	June	504.1	4.57	397.4	−24.24	1.27	106	38.01
	July	643.6	27.65	573.4	44.30	1.12	94	−11.54
	Aug.	587.8	−8.67	585.0	2.02	1.00	84	−10.48
	Sept.	594.7	1.17	560.8	−4.13	1.06	88	5.54
	Oct.	502.1	−15.57	519.1	−7.44	0.97	81	−8.78
	Nov.	597.6	19.03	640.2	23.34	0.93	78	−3.49
	Dec.	511.5	−14.41	545.7	−14.77	0.94	78	0.42
1999	Jan.	357.0	−30.20	355.6	−34.84	1.00	84	7.12
	Feb.	453.8	27.11	519.0	45.95	0.87	73	−12.91
	March	556.8	22.69	590,.2	13.72	0.94	79	7.89
	April	506.6	−9.02	503,.6	−14.67	1.01	84	6.63
	May	581.8	14.84	624.1	23.92	0.93	78	−7.33
	June	484.4	−16.74	544.6	−12.74	0.89	74	−4.58
	July	574.8	18.65	702.6	29.03	0.82	68	−8.04
	Aug.	657.5	14.39	835.2	18.87	0.79	66	−3.77
	Sept.	626.8	−4.67	827.5	−0.93	0.76	63	−3.78

Source: Ministry of Industry and Trade.

downturn in the real value of agricultural exports in May 1998 with the riots in Jakarta suggests that concern about Indonesia's social and political stability may have led international buyers to divert orders to other countries.

Correlation Analysis

To formally analyse the impact of the rupiah depreciation on the agricultural sector, we calculated the correlation coefficient between average monthly exchange rate and two sets of data related to agricultural exports. One set of data, provided by the Indonesian Statistical Central Agency, covered total agricultural exports and 12 categories of agricultural commodities for the period January 1997 to September 1999. The other data set, provided by the Indonesian Ministry of Trade and Industry, covered exports for 66 agribusiness products categorised at the 9-digit level under the harmonised system (HS).

Before doing the correlation analysis, we examined the time-series properties of all the variables using the Phillips-Perron unit root test to determine the order of integration.[4] For the rupiah exchange rate data, that analysis showed that the level series is integrated on order one, while the first-difference series (month-to-month change in the exchange rate) is stationary, or integrated on order zero (Table 2.4). Thus, to avoid stationarity issues and to be able to run the correlation analysis, we used the first-difference series for all related variables.

We found no significant correlation between the first-difference of the rupiah exchange rate and the first-difference of real (constant average

TABLE 2.4
Phillips-Perron Unit Root Test on the Rupiah Exchange Rate,
January 1997 to September 1999
(t-statistics)

	Constant	Constant and trend	No constant or trend
Exchange rate level	−1.601	−1.386	−0.272
First-difference of exchange rate	−4.782	−4.840	−4.481

Note: Monthly data.

price) agricultural exports nor did we find any significant correlations between the first-differences of the exchange rate and real exports of specific categories of agricultural commodities.[5] Thus, changes in the exchange rate do not appear to be correlated with changes in real agricultural exports. However, we did find a positive correlation between the exchange rate and the real export value of fish, fats and oils, coffee, processed fish, and other processed food, when the export series were lagged six to eight months. This suggests that it takes a half a year or more for exports of some products to respond to changes in the exchange rate. Similarly, in the analysis of the 66 categories of agribusiness exports (HS 9-digit level categories) we found significant positive correlations between changes in the exchange rate and changes in real exports for nine categories of domestic agribusiness, when the export series were lagged six months. These nine categories were milk (37 percent), dried fruits and vegetables (46 percent), other prepared fruit (39 percent), prepared and preserved fish (39 percent), smoked fish (46 percent), frozen and chilled fish (41 percent) palm oil (33 percent), fried shrimp (26 percent), and other prepared food (31 percent).[6] This positive correlation for these categories of prepared food products indicates that exports of some agribusiness products did increase in response to the exchange rate depreciation when the effect of the decline in the terms of trade is taken into account.

CONCLUSION

In general, we can conclude that the drastic depreciation of the exchange rate from 1997 to 1999 did benefit Indonesia's agricultural sector and agribusiness in the short-run. The analysis of 9-digit level agribusiness exports found a significant positive correlation between changes in the exchange rate and changes in real exports for nine categories of domestic agribusiness. Nevertheless, the measured impact of the rupiah depreciation on real agricultural exports was somewhat less than we had expected.

It should be remembered that Indonesia suffered from a decline in the terms of trade at the same time as the currency crisis. The decline in agricultural commodity and agribusiness exports during the economic crisis, despite growing export competitiveness caused by the depreciation of the rupiah, was due to this terms-of-trade shock. World market prices for most of Indonesia's agricultural export commodities, such as fish and shrimp, fell sharply during the period under observation. Moreover, social and political factors, such as the sporadic rioting around Indonesia and uncertainty over political conditions in the period under observation, might have a negative impact on all types of exports, including agricultural products.

While recent economic developments in Indonesia have clearly been motivated by social and political uncertainty rather than by sound economic judgement, this situation is likely to change for the better. The installation of a newly elected government in October 1999 improved market confidence and substantially reduced political uncertainty. Economic issues and how the government handles them are likely to be the main determinants of macroeconomic indicators in the future. In particular, the market will now judge the government by what it actually does, rather than by hopes for the new government. If the government fails to live up to expectations, market sentiment could shift and the economy could fall back to the low level that prevailed for much of the past two years. With greater social and political stability the agricultural sector and agribusiness will be able to contribute to the recovery of the economy in general and to the export sector in particular.

Notes

[1] The author gratefully acknowledges the contributions of Dr. Djunaedi Hadisumarto, M. Jasin MSc, Dr. Imron Husin, Dr. Hamonangan Hutabarat, and Heny SP of the Center for Policy and Implementation Studies; Dr. L. Peter Rosner (Harvard Institute for International Development); Dr. Sahala Lumban Gaol (Ministry of Finance); Noor Fuad MSc, Widjanarko MA, and Dr. Mangara Tambunan of the Indonesian Economist Association; Dr. Budi Darmadi and Ir. Murdianto of the Ministry of Industry and Trade; Seiichi Masuyama and Donna Vandenbrink of Nomura Research Institute; Prof. Chia Siow Yue from the Institute of Southeast Asian Studies; and participants in the AT10 Researchers Meeting.

[2] The author thanks Dr. L. Peter Rosner (HIID) for help with this part of the study.

[3] The concept is similar to the concept of the GDP deflator.

[4] The null hypothesis that a unit root exists (the variable is integrated on order one) is tested by comparing the value of the t-statistic from the Phillips-Perron test for each variable to the MacKinnon 1-percent, 5-percent, and 10-percent critical values.

⁵ The commodity categories included: fish, shrimp, rubber, fats and oils, coffee, cocoa, processed fish, processed food and vegetables, other processed food, fruits and vegetables, animal feed, tea, and other agriculture goods.
⁶ The interested reader can find a fuller discussion of the results in Abimanyu 2000.

References

Abimanyu, Yoopi. 2000. "Pemilihan Sektor Yang Mampu Memberikan Kontribusi Positif Terhadap Pemulihan Ekonomi." Proceedings of the 14th Congress of the Indonesian Economist Association, Makassar, 21–23 April.

Christiano, Lawrence J. 1992. "Searching for a Break in GNP." *Journal of Business and Economic Statistics*, 10 (July): 237–50.

Chu, Chia-Sang James and Halbert White. 1992. "A Direct Test for Changing Trend." *Journal of Business and Economic Statistics*, 10 (July): 289–99.

Economist Intelligence Unit (EIU). 1999. *Country Profile: Indonesia*. London: EIU.

Enders, Walter. 1995. *Applied Econometric Time Series*. New York: John Wiley & Sons, Inc.

Estanislao, Jesus P. 1999. *East Asian Economic Crisis: The Journey to Recovery*. The 1999 Panglaykim Memorial Lecture, Jakarta, 7 April.

Food and Agriculture Organization (FAO). 1995. *Food and Agro Industries Curriculum Development in Asia*. Bangkok: FAO Regional Office for Asia and the Pacific.

Ministry of Trade and Industry, Republic of Indonesia. 1999. *Information on Exports*. Jakarta: Directorate General of Chemical, Agro and Forestry Industry.

Monthly Macroeconomic Report. Harvard Institute for International Development. Jakarta Office. Various issues.

Mudge, James. 1999. "Indonesian Non-Oil/Gas Export Performance in 1998." Paper prepared for Conference on Economic Issues Facing the New Government. Center for Development Studies, Institute for Research, Bogor University of Agriculture, Jakarta, August.

Perron, Pierre. 1989. "The Great Crash, the Oil Price Shock, and the Unit Root Hypothesis." *Econometrica*. 57 (November): 1361–1401.

———. 1990. "Testing for a Unit Root in a Time Series with a Changing Mean." *Journal of Business and Economic Statistics*. 8 (April): 153–62.

———— and Timothy J. Vogelsang. 1992a. "Short Communications: Testing for a Unit Root in a Time Series with a Changing Mean." *Journal of Business and Economic Statistics.* 10 (October): 467–70.

———— 1992b. "Nonstationary and Level Shifts with an Application to Purchasing Power Parity." *Journal of Business and Economic Statistics.* 10 (July): 301–20.

Saragih, Bungaran. 1999. "Agriculture Sector: A Promise for the New Government." Paper prepared for Conference on Economic Issues Facing the New Government. Center for Development Studies, Institute for Research, Bogor University of Agriculture, Jakarta, August.

World Bank. 1998. *East Asia: The Road to Recovery.* Washington, D.C.: The World Bank.

3

Directions for Industrial Restructuring in the Twenty-First Century
The Philippine Case

Emilio T. Antonio Jr., Winston Conrad B.
Padojinog, Cherrylyn S. Rodolfo,
and Luis Molina

Since the 1950s, the Philippines has adopted strategies ranging from import-substitution to export-orientation to bring about fundamental changes in the economic structure. In spite of five decades of effort, the Philippines lags behind its Asian neighbours, which had looked up to it at the start of the industrial development process in the 1950s.

The Asian financial crisis has provided the opportunity for the Philippine government to rethink its strategies for the twenty-first century and to consider the increasing role of the service industries in economic development. Domestic production contracted by only 0.5 percent in 1998, despite the 6.6 percent decline in agricultural value added and the 1.7 percent contraction in industrial output. It was the services sector, accounting for around 45 percent of domestic production, that prevented the economy from plunging into deep recession by posting modest growth of 3.5 percent. The service sector in the Philippines showed the most impressive growth among all service sectors in Southeast Asia during that year (Table 3.1).

As the Philippines moves into the twenty-first century, its economic structure is shifting towards a bigger services sector. The government has realised that the past bias for vertical integration and heavy manufacturing industries only misallocated resources and made downstream producers suffer the high costs of inefficiencies of the upstream players. Under the

TABLE 3.1
Growth of the Service Sector Value Added in ASEAN Economies
(Percent change)

	1993	1994	1995	1996	1997	1998
Indonesia	7.4	7.1	7.6	6.8	5.7	−16.6
Malaysia	9.7	9.5	9.2	9.5	7.7	1.2
Philippines	2.5	4.2	5.0	6.4	5.5	3.5
Thailand	9.3	8.9	9.0	4.6	−1.1	−6.8

Source: Asian Development Outlook, 1999

new administration, restructuring programs now focus on providing infrastructure, technical, and manpower development support to those downstream industries in which the Philippines has demonstrated a competitive advantage in resources, manpower skills, and linkages. Service industries have also been identified as a source of competitive advantage. However, data on the performance of the service sector are insufficient and the government lacks a comprehensive policy framework for the development of the service sector (such as Singapore and Hong Kong have adopted).

The objective of this paper is to define and examine the challenges for industrial restructuring in the Philippines in the twenty-first century in the light of the policies, market conditions, and global structural changes. First, we examine the current industrial structure of the Philippine economy and review the historical industrial restructuring experience. Then, we present case studies of four industries to highlight the reasons for success and failure of industrial restructuring efforts. Finally, we identify the key factors shaping the Philippine's industrial structure towards the twenty-first century and the government's agenda for transforming the Philippines into a service-led and knowledge-based economy.

INDUSTRIAL RESTRUCTURING EXPERIENCE OF
THE PHILIPPINES: AN OVERVIEW

Industrial restructuring involves the re-allocation of resources between and within industries, usually in response to changes in the pattern of demand, trade, or technological development. Successful restructuring programs increase the efficiency of present operations, improve production methods, and change the organisation of industry. They could be effective only as complements to sound macroeconomic policies that promote efficient, competitive supply responses by industrial enterprises. Success also depends on effective competition policies, regulatory changes, and liberalisation of factor input and final output prices, institutional services, and infrastructure.

Philippine Industrial Structure

The most significant structural change in Philippine industry occurred during the 1950s (Table 3.2). From 1946 to 1960 agriculture's share of GDP fell ten percentage points from 40 to 30 percent, while industry's share increased from 20.9 percent to 31.4 percent of GDP. Moreover, the share of the manufacturing sector more than tripled from 7.1 percent to 24.9 percent. These structural changes are indicators of industrialisation: the agricultural share declines and manufacturing outpaces other parts of the industrial sector such as mining, construction, and utilities as it provides a base for processing raw materials and for absorbing excess agricultural labour. The growth of manufacturing also makes the agricultural sector more efficient by providing it with capital goods.

Industrialisation slowed significantly since the 1970s, however, and the economic structure remained almost stagnant. The decline in the share of agriculture slowed and the shares of industry and manufacturing have decreased since 1980. On the other hand, the share of the services sector increased since 1980 and particularly during the 1990s.

TABLE 3.2
Composition of Philippine GDP by Industrial Origin, 1946–98
(Percent share of output in 1985 prices)

	1946	1950	1960	1970	1980	1990	1998
Agriculture	40.4	34.5	30.0	28.2	23.5	22.3	19.4
Industry	20.9	28.7	31.4	33.7	40.5	35.5	35.5
Manufacturing	7.1	18.1	24.9	27.1	27.6	25.5	24.9
Services	38.7	36.8	38.6	38.1	36.0	42.2	45.1

Source: National Statistical Coordination Board (NSCB).

Government Policies and Industrial Restructuring

The lack of competitiveness of Philippine manufacturing industries today is a result of the biases of past macroeconomic, trade, and tariff policies that the government implemented to directly or indirectly influence the allocation of resources within and among industries. The evolution of industrial policy can be divided into three periods according to the major policy biases.

Initial Industrialisation and Import-Substitution Phase: 1950s to mid-1960s

From the 1950s until the mid-1960s the Philippines can be characterised as having unsound macroeconomic policies on trade and foreign exchange and as a closed economy trying to achieve self-sufficiency in the production of a number of government-identified strategic products. Growth was fuelled by strong government intervention rather than by private initiative and open economic measures. The imposition of exchange and import controls ushered in a period of import-substitution from 1954 to 1961 and completely reversed the outward orientation of Philippine industries.[1]

The two major interrelated objectives of the import-substitution policy were to lay the base for a viable modern manufacturing sector and reduce the role of agriculture and to give Filipinos a larger share of economic activity. A third objective was to enhance Philippine economic independence especially vis-à-vis the United States, which was the main export market for primary products and the chief source of capital and consumer goods. Along with the bias against foreign influence and the acceptance of heavy government intervention, the overvalued currency and the liberal use of tariff walls supported the import-substitution industrialisation (ISI) strategy. The allocation of scarce foreign exchange was essentially determined by the goals of the ISI strategy. Capital and intermediate goods that favoured the finishing and assembling of imported semi-manufactures for the domestic market were considered essential imports. This practice led to the blossoming of so-called "beauty parlour" industries that simply added finishing touches to imported semi-processed inputs.

On the positive side, the ISI strategy was a practical entry point for industrialisation. It helped change the economic structure by providing the base for the growth of manufacturing value added. Gross value added in manufacturing increased by 12.9 percent per year on average for the period 1952–56. During this import-substitution phase, the government was on top of the resource allocation process and private sector initiatives were hardly recognised. In the Five-Year Economic and Social Development Program of 1957–61, for instance, the two types of industries to be given priority for national development were import-substituting industries and basic industries that lacked private capital but were needed to complement privately owned and operated industries. These industries included soft drink bottling, vehicle assembly, flour milling, spinning, textile weaving or knitting, and milk canning. Only these "preferred industries" were perceived to contribute to national development and indeed they registered high growth rates during the initial years of the plan.

During the 1950s other Asian countries looked at the Philippines as a model and followed a similar import-substitution strategy. But the Philippines was slow to take advantage of the momentum imparted by its early start in industrialisation through import substitution. Taiwan, on the other hand, was quick to exploit the skills in manufacturing that it built up and moved on to export promotion or production for domestic as well as export markets.

Philippine industrial policies in the early 1960s emphasised vertical integration. The government guided investments into the areas of highest priority in its five-year integrated socio-economic program from 1961–1965. In order of investment priority these industries were: basic metals and metal products; basic and other chemicals; pulp and paper, food processing, textiles (integration of cotton textile manufacture and expansion of ramie and synthetic fibre textile manufacture); non-metallic (cement); wood processing; and cottage industries. Such integration did not lead to significant growth in the industrial sector, however. The 5.8 percent annual rate of industrial expansion from 1962 to 1968 was way below the 10 percent annual rate from 1955 to 1961.

In sum, the initial spurt of restructuring in the Philippines was influenced largely by the government, which determined the flow of resources in the economy. Government policies led to a product mix and cost structure that was not competitive and to industrial growth that could not be sustained in open markets. The import-substituting industries became complacent under government protection and failed to adjust to the demands of changing markets at home and abroad. As the domestic market became saturated, Philippine industries remained inward looking and failed to take advantage of the post-World War II boom in export markets. But even if entrepreneurs had responded to the changing market conditions, macroeconomic policies, and the overvalued exchange rate in particular, did not support the development of the export sector. The overvalued currency and interest rate ceiling encouraged cheap capital imports and led to a bias against labour-intensive industries in the manufacturing sector. As a result, agriculture continued to employ more than 50-percent of the national labour force during the ISI phase.

Mid-1960s to 1970s

By the middle of the 1960s, the dismal results of the ISI strategy became evident. As protected local industries struggled with the effects of the foreign exchange decontrols in 1962, the government continued to intervene heavily in the industrial sector. The late 1960s also brought pressure to correct policy biases (such as reliance solely on the domestic market) which were perceived to be major stumbling blocks to economic growth. Although by the middle of the 1970s the government had recognised the important role of small and medium-industry development, it continued to emphasise vertically integrated industrial activities, and the shifting of resources from small- to large-scale industries continued.

Toward the end of the 1960s, the government recognised food insufficiency as a national problem. The remedy was to expand and restructure the industrial sector in order to help the agricultural sector to achieve self-sufficiency. The government adopted policies to encourage basic industries, such as iron and steel, and chemicals that had significant applications in agriculture and the backward integration of manufacturing and the forward integration of mining.

Before the imposition of martial law in 1972, the government put in place a number of policies to encourage exports and foreign investment. The Investment Incentives Act of 1967, the Foreign Business Regulation Act of 1968, and the Export Incentives Act of 1970 aimed at streamlining and rationalising foreign investment policies. The Board of Investments (BOI) was set up in 1970 with the mandate to draw up investment priority plans (IPPs) for industries that would receive incentives. These plans favoured heavy and integrated industries. The first IPP, for instance, identified the integrated copper plant as a priority project. Next in priority were transportation equipment manufacturing and shipbuilding. Anti-foreign sentiment was also still evident in the tasks assigned to BOI. The IPPs regulated foreign participation by classifying industries into pioneer and non-pioneer status. Only industries that had pioneer status were subject to more liberal rules of ownership.[2]

Under martial law the government took over the utilities, intervened heavily in sugar and coconut production, and designated strategic industries where it would be the driving force. These policies demonstrated the government's belief in its capability to direct industrialisation. These strategies produced some good results. One was the emergence of "non-traditional export" industries. These included manufactured goods such as garments and electronics and agricultural products such as bananas. Nevertheless, the Philippines remained predominantly inward looking. The share of non-traditional manufacturing in the volume of Philippine exports was very small compared to the newly industrialising economies. This sector comprised only 4.3 percent of total manufactured exports during the 1970s.

The macroeconomic bias against exchange rate adjustments likewise remained. While import quotas, tariffs, and foreign exchange allocation schemes were the primary instruments in the 1960s, the government relied on foreign loans to keep the exchange rate fixed. Such foreign loans more than offset the loans extended by creditors. The Philippines was missing an important requisite for effective restructuring — a reliance on market mechanisms.

Economic Crisis and Policy Reform: 1980s to the Present

For the Philippines, the decade of the 1980s was a period of economic crisis and political turbulence but also a time of significant policy reform marked by a shift from inward-looking strategy to export orientation, a more liberal stance toward foreign investment, and a gradual reduction in import tariffs. Up to 1981 tariffs on finished goods were high, while they remained low on capital and intermediate goods. Persistent balance of payments problems in the early 1980s again triggered a government program of industrial restructuring. The government was no longer the only influence on resource allocation, however. External pressure from international institutions such as the International Monetary Fund (IMF) and the World Bank became strong forces in transforming the Philippines from an inward-looking economy to an export-oriented one and for financing rehabilitation of such industries as textiles.

The World Bank Structural Adjustment Program (SAP) in 1980 served as a vehicle for adopting a more outward-looking strategy. The program included financial reforms such as interest rate deregulation and uni-banking reforms in the banking sector and fiscal reforms such as tax and non-tax measures to better mobilise domestic resources.

Reduction in tariffs and relaxation of quantitative restrictions were conditions for the strategic adjustment loans. The Tariff Reform and Import Liberalisation Programs (reduction in the list of items that required import-licensing approval from the central bank) that began in 1981 signalled a new era of industrial policy and restructuring. The liberalisation program was temporarily suspended in 1983 due to the economic crisis, but it resumed under the Aquino Administration (1987–91). Between 1981 and 1988 imports subject to restrictions fell from 47 percent of items to 10 percent and from 33 percent of import value to 14.5 percent. Executive Order 470 issued in July 1991 was another important tariff reform program. It reduced the number of commodities with high tariffs and increased the number with low tariffs over a five-year period. The average tariff would decline from 28 to 20 percent.[3]

Investment incentives were also reformed, beginning with the Omnibus Investments Code of 1981. Amendments enacted in 1983 reduced the number of incentives and eliminated some capital-cheapening measures such as accelerated depreciation and reinvestment expansion allowances. They also gave strong preference to export industries and substituted performance-based benefits for capital investments.

The poor performance of the heavy industries during the severe recession of the 1980s called into question the nine IPP projects that the government had initiated in the early 1970s to spur import substitution of intermediate goods. In contrast to these heavy industries, whose contribution to gross value added declined in the 1980s, the relatively labour-intensive industries with a solid export base, such as garments, electronics, basic metal products, and electrical machinery, enjoyed strong growth in value added.

Labour market policies were geared to the deployment of new and more efficient machinery and the use of labour-saving devices. Promotion of job and service sub-contracting aided such export industries as garments, footwear, furniture, and other light industries. The government retreated from the direct intervention it followed in the 1950s and 1960s and found a better role in such areas as education. The Aquino Administration focused on improving the means of education to meet the needs of the industrial sector.

The overall targets of the Aquino Administration were employment generation, poverty alleviation, and equitable distribution of the benefits of development. The specific objectives of industrial development were to revitalise existing industries that are economically viable and to develop internationally competitive industries that complement growth in

TABLE 3.3
Industries with Highest and Lowest Growth in
Gross Value Added, 1990–99

High Growth Industries	1990–99 Growth Rate	Low Growth Industries	1990–99 Growth Rate
Electrical machinery	13.7	Transport equipment	1.2
Machinery except electrical	7.0	Basic metals	0.3
Leather and leather products	5.6	Metal Products	–0.4
Non-metallic minerals	5.3	Textile Manufactures	–3.2
Miscellaneous manufactures	5.1	Wood and Cork products	–4.4
		Rubber Products	–4.9

Source: NSCB.

agricultural output and rural income. The plan priorities and objectives translated into the following policy thrusts:

- Improving trade and industry linkages with the agricultural and natural resources sector
- Promoting rural-based and labour-intensive micro-, cottage, and small and medium enterprises
- Co-ordinating regional and sectoral planning
- Facilitating the flow of goods and services between production and market centres and between producers and consumers
- Developing and promoting internationally competitive products that utilise indigenous materials and skilled manpower
- Reducing government participation and intervention in business in favour of a promotional and information dissemination role

In 1988 the Department of Trade and Industry formulated Ten-year Industry Sector Plans for agriculture- and forest-based industries, chemical industries, wearing apparel (textile, garments, leather goods, accessories), construction materials, mining/extracting/processing, metals and engineering, electronics, telecommunications, service industries, and gifts, toys, and housewares.

Regional industrial centres were established to put the Countryside Agro-industrial Development Strategy (CAIDS) in operation in 1991. The rationale was to develop the industrial potential of regions lying outside the national capital through investments in infrastructure and utilities.

Expansionary fiscal policy, import liberalisation, and privatisation were implemented to raise the internal efficiency and international competitiveness of the manufacturing sector.

The emphasis of the policy reforms directed towards sustaining industrial recovery shifted

- from inward-looking to more export-oriented industrialisation
- from large-scale projects to small and medium-scale industries
- from government financing to private-sector financing
- from urban-biased industrialisation to regionally balanced industrial development

Political turbulence and natural calamities interfered to reduce the effectiveness of the privatisation, liberalisation of trade and foreign investment rules, and opening up of industries to competition that were initiated in the 1980s. Reliance on market mechanisms to restructure the economy became more pronounced in the 1990s, particularly under the Ramos Administration (1992–98). Key and strategic sectors were opened to greater competition. The commitment to free trade was at the core of the administration's agenda. Attaining global competitiveness became a central theme in economic restructuring. Liberalisation and trade reforms of the 1990s changed the structure of output markets. More suppliers — local and foreign — were encouraged to enter industry. The major reforms undertaken since 1991 include:

- Liberalisation of key sectors such as telecommunications, power, airlines, insurance, shipping, and the capital market.
- Lifting restrictions on foreign exchange transactions and allowing the peso to move within a wider range consistent with a market-determined exchange rate.
- Redressing the anti-foreign bias of existing investment laws by allowing up to 100-percent foreign equity participation in all areas not specified under the Foreign Investment Negative List (Foreign Investments Act, passed in June 1991).
- Transferring minimum wage setting from the national to the regional level, which introduced some competitive forces into wage determination by allowing differences in regional priorities and exerting discipline on wage setting interventions.

The key elements of the changing industrial strategy in the Philippines are the twin objectives of privatisation and foreign investment. The government endeavours to sustain industrial recovery through the progressive expansion of the private sector and the effective implementation of a host of incentives to attract investors.

The thrust of the Vision 2000 — the Ramos Administration's blueprint for growth and development — for the Philippines is global competitiveness, expanded production of goods and services for domestic and export markets, and stronger links between agriculture and industry. To attain these major goals Vision 2000 posed the following specific objectives:

- modernisation of the production sectors through technology upgrading
- enhancement and adaptation of information technology systems in all sectors
- rural agri-industrialisation including dispersal of industries
- economic empowerment of workers and employers as partners in the development process
- greater contribution of tourism to economic growth and development

In sum, the 1990s brought the creation of a more competitive environment for Philippine industries. Export-oriented industries led the pace of industrial development in the 1990s while the integrated industries suffering from inefficiency, heavy protection, dwindling supply of raw materials, and inability to integrate forward saw large declines in their share of value added (Table 3.3).

CASE STUDIES OF INDUSTRIAL RESTRUCTURING PROGRAMS

Over the last half-century the Philippines has adopted industrial restructuring programs in order to raise competitiveness and to achieve certain political or social goals and broad economic objectives. Import-substitution strategies promote Philippine export industries and protect domestic industries from foreign competition to raise the economy's competitiveness. When the times demand industry programs to provide job security and employment, preserve national pride, or promote economic independence and self-sufficiency, these national interests take priority over international concerns such as trade agreements and investment liberalisation.

Industrial restructuring is the process bringing industry structure and performance in line with requirements of competition or national objectives. Industrial restructuring programs may involve direct or indirect interventions by the government in factor inputs (wages, energy, imported raw materials), processes (technology, skills, knowledge), and outputs (subsidies, export promotion). Such intervention comes in the form of subsidies, tariffs, deregulation, liberalisation, or fiscal incentives. Not all restructuring occurs through active government intervention. Market or competitive forces may compel industry participants to make structural adjustments independent of government support or instigation.

Four key industries, cement, pulp and paper, textiles and garments, illustrate the response of Philippine industries to various policy- and market-directed restructuring efforts.

The Cement Industry

Industry Development

The cement industry is one of the oldest manufacturing sectors in the Philippines. The first cement plant put up in 1924 in Binangonan, Rizal by the Ynchausti firm had an annual capacity of 0.6 million bags. As owner of Cebu Portland Cement Company (CEPOC) the government was a major investor in the cement industry even before World War II. By the early 1950s, three cement plants were operating in the Philippines — two of which were owned by government (Table 3.4). Later, CEPOC acquired several plants using Japanese war reparation funds.

Consumption increases until the late 1960s encouraged the entry of new players and the expansion of capacity by existing players. In 1972 the Philippines had 18 cement plants capable of producing 160 million bags annually. The industry experienced a glut following the energy crisis and the slowdown in economic activity. Production capacity increased in the late 1970s and early 1980s with the strong recovery in construction activity. Another glut occurred in 1988 when 32 cement plants operated with a combined capacity of 384 million bags.

TABLE 3.4
Cement Industry Production Capacity, 1952–99

	1952	1972	1988	1999
Number of plants	3	18	32	42
Annual capacity (million bags)	8.7	160	384	1,024

Source: Philcemcorp.

TABLE 3.5
Clinker Capacity and Composition
by Type of Process, 1988 and 1998
(Percent share)

	1988	1998
Dry	51	72
Wet	15	23
Semi-dry	34	5
Total capacity (metric tons)	7,408	21,368

Source: Philcemcorp.

In the late 1980s it became clear that most Philippine cement plants were out-dated and utilised inefficient technology. In 1988 nearly 50 percent of the plants in operation used the wet or semi-dry processes, which consumed a lot of energy, compared to the situation in Japan and Indonesia, where over 96 percent of cement plants already used the dry production process (Table 3.5). The Philippine industry's high energy-intensity made it inefficient and un-competitive. Philippine cement firms began shifting to the new technology by modernising old plants and erecting new ones. By 1998, of the 42 cement plants in operation, at least 70 percent used the dry line production process. Excess supply in the late 1990s also forced the closure of most of the wet lines.

Since the early 1950s the cement industry has relied heavily on debt, financing expansion with borrowing, particularly from government financial institutions. Calls were made for private investors, including private financial institutions as well as foreign investors, to take an active role in financing the rehabilitation of the industry during 1980s. In the late 1980s the government began to reduce its financial exposure to the industry and the private sector gradually took over through investments and loans, but debt remained the industry's main financing strategy. With the Asian Crisis of 1997–98 the peso depreciated against the U.S. dollar and lending rates increased, while construction activity slacked and cement consumption plunged. Caught with large debts, most cement firms were close to the brink. The government was not interested in bailing out the industry. Existing investors were forced to sell out to foreign equity partners, including such global players as Cemex, La Farge, Blue Circle, and Holderbank, which now account for over 85 percent of the industry's total capacity (Table 3.6).

Policy Interventions

The government has long treated the cement industry as a critical economic sector. Cement was needed to build the government infrastructure projects adopted to accelerate economic absorption and growth. The industry has benefited from government regulations and incentives, many of which served to protect the huge stake that the government accumulated over time.

The government jump-started the industry in the early 1950s as part of its import-substitution strategy. Cement imports stopped abruptly in 1949 with the imposition of import and exchange controls.[4] As domestic demand started to recover in the mid-1950s, the government provided incentives and direct financial assistance through guarantees, direct loans, and equity

TABLE 3.6
Ownership Structure of the Cement Industry, 1989 and 1998
(Metric tons)

1989		1998	
	Clinker capacity		Clinker capacity
Phinma Group		Holderbank	
Bacnotan	231	Alsons-Iligan	2,247
Hi-Cement	409	Hi-Cement	2,460
Davao Union	455	Davao	1,742
		Bacnotan	1,254
Alcantara		Cemex	
Alson Cement	429	JG-Apo	1,800
Iligan Cement	399	Solid Rizal	2,235
Madrigal-		Blue Circle	
Gokongwei		Fortune	1,260
Rizal Cement	404	Mindanao	450
Solid Cement	537	Republic	1,575
Apo Cement			
Seacem / Lim		La Farge	
FR Cement	515	FR-Lloyd's	2,121
Lloyd's	–	Continental	1,470
Sy			
Mindanao	128		
Fortune Cement	309		
Others	2,119	Others	2,754
Total	6,125	Total	21,368

Source: Philcemcorp.

investments to encourage the entry of new cement plants. Government institutions such as the Development Bank of the Philippines and the National Industrial Development Corporation extended guarantees as well as foreign loans. The Government Service Insurance System (GSIS) contributed equity funds in the form of preferred share placements. The government accommodated the industry's expansion in the 1950s and 1960s by extending loans and erecting high tariff barriers. In 1970, aware of an impending glut, the government judged the industry to be overcrowded and discouraged new applications for financing.

In order to ease the impact of the excess supply in the cement industry in the 1970s, the government extended incentives through BOI to encourage exporting. This was the beginning of the government's outward-oriented industrial strategy. In fact, the government envisioned building a cement terminal in Manila North Harbor to reduce the cost of handling cement exports. The government also instituted regulatory measures and incentives to protect its huge investments in the industry. During the 1970s, the Price Control Council (PCC) regulated cement prices predominantly to protect consumer interests.

Also around this time the Cement Industry Authority (CIA) was formed by Presidential Decree 94 to address the issues confronting the industry. The Cement Association of the Philippines was later transformed from an association of cement companies into a legal entity, the Philippine Cement Corporation (now known as Philippine Cement Manufacturers Corporation), to assist the CIA carry out its mandate.

In the 1980s, the government took steps to address the inefficiency and lack of competitiveness in the cement industry. It actively initiated rehabilitation programs and sponsored energy conversion programs, granting fiscal incentives through the BOI and preferential loan assistance from the Development Bank of the Philippines (DBP). Many of the DBP loans went bad when cement consumption contracted in the economic crisis of the mid-1980s and drastic capacity cuts were implemented. When demand began to recover in the late 1980s and early 1990s, cement imports continued to be regulated though the industry again experienced a supply shortage. Meanwhile, the BOI was still offering incentives to stimulate the rehabilitation and modernisation of the industry.

Drastic changes in government policy in the middle 1990s enabled the cement industry to finally attract private sector financial support. The deregulation of foreign exchange and capital controls and the rehabilitation of the central bank (Bangko Sentral ng Pilipinas) integrated the Philippines with the global financial system and enhanced the government's monetary policy tools. Strong foreign exchange flows and macroeconomic stability led to a decline in the cost of borrowing in both local and foreign currency.

Two policy changes that took place in the 1990s will have a significant impact on the future of the industry. First, in 1999, the BOI removed cement firms from eligibility for fiscal incentives, except for projects located in Mindanao. Second, trade agreements under the AFTA and the World Trade Organisation are gradually liberalising the industry. Tariff barriers began to fall in 1997 with the implementation of the CEPT among ASEAN members. By 2002, the domestic cement market will be largely open to foreign trade. Trade liberalisation does not appear to be an immediate threat to the domestic industry because high transport costs create a natural barrier against imports and because the price of imported cement is higher than the prevailing domestic price since the peso depreciated in 1997.

Current Structural Issues

Issues currently facing the cement industry are:

- Price controls. There are renewed calls for price controls based on the perception that the industry follows non-competitive pricing practices. After falling for two years in the aftermath of the Asian crisis, cement prices began to recover in 1999, jumping over 50 percent (from P65 per bag to over P100 per bag) in October 1999. The industry's current average break-even point, including financing charges, is around P85 per bag.
- Incentives. Most cement companies incurred losses in the aftermath of the Asian crisis. Those firms that had received BOI fiscal incentives before they were terminated in 1999 have proposed reinstating them.
- Consolidation. The cement industry is becoming more concentrated as domestic players consolidate their operations or merge with foreign cement companies in order to attain economies of scale.

Pulp and Paper Industry

Structural Changes: 1950s to the 1990s

The pulp and paper industry includes non-integrated and integrated producers of pulp and paper. Non-integrated mills produce either pulp or paper, while integrated mills manufacture both.[5] Under the present classification the industry also includes paper converters, which manufacture paper products such as envelopes or notebooks.

Pulp and paper production in the Philippines started in 1948 when the Compania de Cellulosa de Filipinas established an integrated pulp and paper mill in Bais, Negros Occidental. This mill is still in operation. Paper Industries Corporation of the Philippines (PICOP), the largest integrated pulp and paper company in ASEAN, was established in 1971 and utilises hardwood from its own timber concessions in the eastern coast of Mindanao.

Capacity utilisation in the pulp and paper industry averaged under 70 percent throughout the 1980s. At its lowest in 1985, capacity utilisation was below 30 percent. Only two integrated mills operating at full capacity could have supplied the industry's total output. Most local demand was actually met by imports, which entered the market under declarations and through outright smuggling.

The domestic industry has been stymied by a persistent shortage of raw materials. The Philippines' inflexible agrarian reform program and the huge capital outlays discouraged the development of industrial plantations to supply domestic wood for the paper mills. The number of pulping facilities increased in the 1960s and 1970s, but many did not survive because of the shortage of raw materials and the high cost of imported wood. To get around the shortage of domestic raw materials, many mills utilised cheaper imported pulp and most of the non-integrated paper mills put up during the 1970s and 1980s relied on imported or recycled waste paper.

By the late 1970s and early 1980s, it was becoming clear that the Philippines had too many mills and that fewer and larger producers were needed to exploit economies of scale. Most mills expanded using second-hand equipment. Now most of this equipment is obsolete and these old machines have not been utilized because of the difficulty of obtaining replacement parts and the lack of consulting engineers.

Private investors shunned the under-utilised, import-dependent pulp and paper industry and the technology became out-dated. The industry fails miserably in meeting environmental protection standards. Effluents and pollutants from the mills are unchecked and contaminate the water supply of areas where they operate. The currency devaluations in the 1980s further eroded the already sorry plight of most firms due to the higher cost of imported inputs.

Policy Initiatives

The Philippine pulp and paper industry existed under a prolonged import-substitution type industrial policy. Government incentives and direct investments led to a rapid increase in the number of new paper mills during the 1950s and 1960s. Concern over the Philippines' lack of a modern integrated pulp and paper mill led the government to encourage the establishment of PICOP. Despite the low rate of capacity utilisation the government continued to support the industry with incentives and high tariff protection until the early 1990s. Indeed, the pulp and paper industry is still eligible for four- to six-year fiscal incentives under the BOI's Investment Priority Plan.

Tax and customs duty exemptions as well as tax credits introduced during the 1950s became counter-productive in the 1980s. Tariffs on imported finished paper and paper products in the 1950s were intended to protect Philippine papermakers from lower cost, higher quality international competition. The high tariffs on finished products, which varied from 30 to 50 percent, kept the industry above water.[6] Effective rates of protection ranged from 8 percent to as high as 102 percent. On the other hand, the high tariff rates for finished and branded products and the low tariff rates on raw materials actually discouraged the setting up of domestic pulping facilities.

Tariffs designed to protect the wood and processed wood industry from imports in the 1950s made the cost of the paper industry's most basic raw material, industrial wood, onerously high. The tariff structure also led to under-declaration of import values and smuggling. In the 1960s and 1970s the government instituted measures to address the inadequate supply of domestic wood by encouraging paper mills to use alternative indigenous raw materials, such as bamboo (used by Bataan Pulp and Paper Mill to produce printing and writing paper), tropical hardwoods (used by Rustan Pulp and Paper Mills to produce container board), and bagasse (used by United Pulp and Paper Co. to produce sack kraft).

Government incentives to encourage equipment imports were not limited to new equipment and thus they encouraged paper mills to purchase less-expensive second-hand machines.

The government failed to attract foreign investors and financiers in the middle 1980s. Initially the Philippine pulp and paper industry survived liberalisation in 1987. High international paper prices and the tight supply of paper and board from exporting countries gave the Philippine industry some breathing space to adjust to the new environment. The industry was laden with debt, however, and the Aquino Administration eventually had to take over PICOP, the largest paper manufacturer. The government plans to convert its debt to equity, turn around the bottom line, and dispose of it through the Asset Privatisation Trust.

Measures proposed and adopted by the government in the early 1990s partly address the factors that discourage investments in the industry:

- Amend certain policies on foreign ownership of property and marketing of foreign products;
- Tap long-term credit facilities from international financial institutions;
- Provide fiscal incentives to encourage long-term export-oriented industries;
- Foster co-ordination with ASEAN member countries to regionalise the pulp and paper industry;
- Privatise and de-control government-owned mills;
- Undertake an extensive industrial tree plantation program to ensure ample supply of fibre;
- Encourage the consolidation of pulp and paper companies; and,
- Encourage the development of export markets

Current Status and Prospects

- The industry depends largely on imported inputs such as long fibres, chemicals, and waste papers. The devaluation of the peso in 1997 further increased the cost of these imported raw materials, which already comprised more than 40 percent of the industry's costs.
- Many paper and pulp mills will suffer with the tearing down of tariff barriers. With its present cost structure the Philippine industry is not likely to be able to compete with its ASEAN counterparts such as Thailand and Indonesia as liberalisation in AFTA speeds up after the year 2000. Over 10,000 Philippine employees will likely lose their jobs.
- Consumer and industrial demand for paper has already shifted to imports as a result of trade liberalisation such as the regional agreements under AFTA.

Garment Industry

Industry Profile and Structure

The garment industry has thrived with little government protection. From a group of small, cottage-based enterprises in the late 1950s the industry has evolved into a technology-based industry that has generated significant foreign exchange earnings for the Philippines and competes with semiconductors as the country's top dollar earner. Over 65 percent of domestic garment production is exported.

The garment industry's lack of linkages with the domestic textile industry proved to be a blessing. Despite many periods of peso devaluation, the industry continued to exploit the lower-priced, higher-quality textiles produced abroad. The government's role was limited to allowing the industry to import textiles duty-free. At present the garment industry imports more than 90 percent of its textile requirements.

The garment industry includes not only the manufacture of clothing and wearing apparel, such as hats, gloves, handkerchiefs, but also support services such as embroidery, printing, dyeing, knitting, laundering, finishing, and pattern and design-making. The present industry structure, technology, and performance have evolved substantially from the small, cottage-based industry that earlier replaced traditional home sewing, dressmaking and tailoring. During the 1980s direct foreign competition led to an increase in the number of firms in the industry and a decrease in industry concentration. Many of the new entrants were small but highly competitive firms. The industry cost structure improved significantly because of high labour- and capital-productivity. The industry upgraded from traditional low value added tailoring to high value embroidery and ready-made garment manufacturing.

The export earning potential of the industry attracted new garment manufacturers. The change in international demand to ready-made and high-end garments caused a shift in the type of garment firms and their export-composition. In the latter part of the 1970s the industry was primarily engaged in custom tailoring. In the 1980s, manufacture of women's, girls' and babies' garments gradually rose to dominate the industry. There was also a rise in the ready-made, embroidery, hat, and handkerchief segments in the industry. In the 1990s economies of scale and rising capital intensity led to a rapid increase in the number of medium-scale (100–199 workers) and large-scale (over 200 workers) firms.

Since the 1950s the industry has been labour-dependent, relying on the skills of Filipino workers in garment manufacturing. With the competitive cost of skilled labour in the 1950s up to the late 1980s, many U.S.-based companies invested in the Philippine garment industry. The garment industry's share of manufacturing employment declined with the shift to technology-based operations in the early 1990s (Table 3.7).

The importance of garments as an export product reflects the Philippines growing dependence on non-traditional products for foreign exchange. The growth of export receipts slowed in the 1980s and early 1990s due to competition from lower cost garment-producing countries and more attractive duty benefits (in Mexico and Caribbean Basin countries) and shorter turn-around time. The largest share of garment exports, close to 80 percent on average, goes to quota countries, including the United States, the major export destination, the EU (particularly Great Britain), and Canada. The remaining 20 percent of garment exports goes to non-quota countries including Japan, the UAE, Singapore, and Hong Kong.

Industrial Policy

The garment industry went through three stages of industrial policy evolution, import-substitution (1950s–70s), trade reform (1980s) and trade liberalisation and industrial deregulation (1990s). The industry started to grow rapidly following the 1961 passage of the Embroidery Act (RA 3137), which permitted garment manufacturers to import textiles duty free. Garment manufacturers also benefited from tax exemptions, credit, and deductions as a critical industry under the Basic Industries Act (RA 3127) and the Investment Incentives Act (RA 5186).

In the 1970s the government began to encourage exports because of the foreign exchange crisis in the late 1960s, weak domestic consumption, and the general industry glut. The strategy was made explicit with the passage of the Export Incentives Act (RA 6135) and the Export Processing Act (PD 1966). The former granted exporters more fiscal incentives in addition to those specified in RA 5186.

The Garments and Textile Export Board (GTEB) was created in 1979. GTEB plays a major role in industry regulation, undertaking multi-faceted functions to support the objectives of the industry and to optimise foreign

TABLE 3.7
Garment Industry Share of
Manufacturing Employment, 1970–98
(Percent)

	Share
1970–1974	5.8
1975–1979	10.5
1980–1984	11.8
1985–1990	15.2
1990–1994	16.0
1994–1998	16.5

Source: Bureau of Labor and Employment Statistics.

exchange earnings. The GTEB provides procedural guidelines to prospective exporters and importers of raw materials. The Centre for International Exhibitions and Missions (CITEM) handles marketing of garment industry exports and the Board of Investments (BOI) administers incentive schemes for exporters. Garment exporters who locate in designated export processing zones enjoy special incentives such as income tax holidays.

From the 1950s to the 1970s, tariff rates on machinery and raw material inputs for the textile industry were lower than rates on finished textiles. This form of industry incentive was part of the government's plan to develop an integrated textile industry to support the input requirements of garment producers. However, garment exporters preferred imported textiles because the quality of locally produced textile goods paled compared with the imported products. Thus, the government's protection of the local textile industry forced the domestic garment industry to pay higher input costs.

The Tariff Reform Program and the Import Liberalisation Program that began in the early 1980s signalled the beginning of the trade reform period. The implicit tariff rate on garment industry output went down from 10 percent in 1983 to 0 percent in 1988 while tariffs on garment industry inputs declined from 52 to 38 percent. In 1982 import restrictions on undergarments, clothing accessories, apparel, and textile fabric were removed. With the liberalisation of imports, domestic garment manu-facturers began to suffer because of their high-cost structure, and the government implemented a tax credit scheme in 1985. Under the scheme, the BOI issued tax credit certificates to local textile millers who supplied tax-and duty-free textiles to garment exporters with bonded manufacturing warehouses.

During the globalisation period of the 1990s the garment industry became ready for more international competition. The additional incentives provided in the Export Development Act (RA 7844) greatly benefited garment exporters. Government incentives supported the adoption of electronic data interchange (EDI) technology and garment manufacturers in the Philippines became the first in Asia to adopt this technology to speed processing of export documents.

Industrial Structure Issues

Under the World Trade Organisation the quota system of the garment and textile industries will gradually be phased out. The Multi-fibre Arrangement

(MFA) will be replaced with the Agreement on Textiles and Clothing (ATC) which will provide guidelines for administering existing quotas and establishing constraints while phasing out the quotas over ten years. This new world order will subject Philippine garment makers to more intense global competition.

Some areas of structural weakness in the Philippine garment industry in light of global trade liberalisation include

- Increasing wages vis-à-vis productivity levels
- Government bureaucracy
- Dependence on quota markets and weak foreign market demand
- Inefficiency of manufacturers and lack of service support
- Continuing entry of new competitors
- Rapidly changing retail trends
- Lack of coherent industry strategy

The GTEB drafted a long-term export development plan to address these issues by improving productivity; raising value-added through investments in dyeing, finishing, printing and the development of tropical fabric; enhancing design capability; expanding markets by adding high value items and brand image; and developing and opening the domestic market to garment exporters.

Textile Industry

Industry Structure

Begun in the 1950s, the textile industry immediately rose to national prominence because of its potential to reduce dependence on imports to meet domestic demand.

The textile industry includes the production of fibre and yarn, fabric, and manufacture of made-up textile articles such as ropes, carpets, and rugs. Primary processing includes spinning, weaving, knitting, and finishing and secondary processing includes manufacture of made-up textile articles. Processing that involves three or more stages is classified as integrated, while non-integrated textile processing involves only one or two stages.

The textile industry developed before the garment industry. The number of textile firms increased dramatically during the 1950s because of government protection and incentives, but the growth was not sustained into the 1960s when over-expansion and entry of new textile firms led to an industry glut. With a large share of production going to the domestic market, the textile industry was susceptible to the ups and downs of the Philippine economy. In the 1970s, the industry lost the incentive to produce innovative designs and create new textiles because of the profitability of producing for the domestic market, which was protected from foreign competitors.

From the 1980s growth in the number of textile industry establishments began to decelerate. The industry remained small throughout the 1980s with almost 70 percent of textile firms in 1988 classified as small-scale. Over sixty percent of the textile firms operating in the late 1980s were primary processors.

Philippine textile producers were practically confined to the domestic market because their costs were high relative to international textile prices. Textile exports occurred indirectly when Philippine garment exports began to pick-up in the middle 1980s. High tariffs on imported textiles from the 1950s to the 1980s kept the industry afloat. Many textile makers shut down as domestic consumers, including garment makers, turned to cheaper imported textiles when the marked was liberalised in the 1980s.

Industrial Policy

Textiles never became a major export commodity for the Philippines because of excessive government protection. The textile industry was one of the first industries given pioneer status under the import substitution regime in the 1950s. The government protected the textile industry by import and foreign exchange controls, provided liberal access to dollar allocations for the importation of machinery and raw materials, and readily granted loans and tax concessions.

In the 1960s, the government removed the quotas on textile imports, but retained high tariffs to protect domestic producers. It also maintained low tariff rates on imports of machinery and raw materials, increasing the effective rate of protection for the textile industry. Meanwhile, the Basic Industries Act and the Investment Incentives Act of the 1960s provided fiscal incentives such as tax credits and tax exemptions for the textile industry. Smuggling was rampant because of the differential between international and domestic textile prices.

Export incentives introduced by the government in the 1970s were not effective because of the distorted tariff structure and import restrictions. For instance, most of the raw material inputs of the textile industry were on the list of regulated commodities and could not be imported without government clearance.

By the end of the 1970s the government recognised that the textile industry was not internationally competitive. Studies had revealed severe operating and structural problems because of obsolete machines and equipment, lack of specialisation, poor technical processes, and high cost of production. World Bank funds were made available to the industry through the Textile Rehabilitation Program in 1982–85. With only 11 textile mills availing themselves of the loans in the depressed local and foreign markets of 1982 and 1983, the program did not succeed and the funds were returned to the World Bank.

Lessons from the Case Studies

Today the Philippine cement and garment industries are internationally competitive, with the former attracting foreign investment and the latter contributing significantly to export earnings. On the other hand, the pulp and paper and textile industries are unable to compete in the global competitive environment of the twenty-first century. These different outcomes along with the different experiences outlined in these four case studies suggest that successful restructuring of target industries includes not merely rehabilitation, modernisation, integration, and product promotion. Certain conditions must be met before restructuring programs are formulated and implemented. Industrial programs should complement general policies that promote competitiveness and efficiency. This means that successful restructuring depends on education, politics, infrastructure, and other national systems and institutions.

An effective industrial restructuring program requires

- Macroeconomic stability supported by sound macroeconomic policies (especially with respect to exchange rates).
- Removal of serious distortions in support sectors such as capital and financial markets. Government should ensure the existence of and promote solvent and sound savings, banking, and non-bank financial institutions.
- Exposure to competition through free entry and exit and tearing down barriers to trade. Competition policies should be pursued under a program of trade liberalisation and export promotion.
- Exit of government from direct investment and policy-induced industrial projects. Open markets should be complemented by the elimination of government subsidies, guarantees, and tax concessions. Private financial institutions should become channels for financing restructuring programs.

- Market determination of prices. Price controls breed inefficiency and promote rent-seeking and monopolistic behaviour. They send the wrong market signals leading to the misallocation of resources.
- Continual upgrading and new construction of physical infrastructure such as roads, power generation plants, transportation facilities, and ports.
- Access to and institutional support of information services (industry and economic statistics, trade information and data), human resource services (education, training, management), and consultancy services (legal, financial, accounting, and tax).
- Strong corporate incentives through appropriate regulation of disclosure, accounting standards and practices, bankruptcy, licensing, intellectual property rights, and fiduciary and prudential investment standards.

STRATEGIES FOR INDUSTRIAL RESTRUCTURING IN THE TWENTY-FIRST CENTURY

Developing a High Value Added Service Economy

The rapid growth of the service sector in economies around the world is attributed to the liberalisation and deregulation of service industries, technological advances, outsourcing, and the unbundling of services by the manufacturing sector. The Philippine government aims to sustain and accelerate the growth of the service sector by improving productivity and implementing reforms that effectively and efficiently meet the needs of the modern agriculture and industry sectors.

Data on the economic performance of the service sector are inadequate and it is difficult to measure the sector's contribution, particularly with the increasing tradability of services and technological advancements. National income accounts do not capture the contributions of knowledge-based industries and data on trade in services omit services delivered via IT networks or subsidiaries and affiliates in foreign markets.[7]

While the service sector has been growing rapidly as a share of total output, it has generally lagged behind the goods sector in aggregate productivity growth (Table 3.8). This situation is observed widely in both developed and developing countries. One explanation for the lag in the growth of productivity in the service sector is the measurement problem mentioned above. It is likely that productivity growth in the finance, insurance, and real estate industry as well as in private services has been under-estimated. Also, there may be less competition in service industries compared with goods-producing industries, but it is hard to quantify this impact.

Pursuing the goal of a high value added service economy requires a policy framework that recognises the role of services, particularly service exports, in Philippine economic growth. The Ramos Administration undertook regulatory reforms such as deregulation and privatisation that contributed to the rapid growth in the value added of such service industries as telecommunications and financial institutions. The liberalisation of domestic and international air transport helped improve access both within the archipelago and between the Philippines and the rest of the world. Almost 70 percent of the country's total exports, by value, was shipped by air in 1998, a marked increase over the 20 percent in 1992. The government has also provided incentives for the development of service-based industries, in the 1994 Export Development Act (RA 7844).

In 1999, the Department of Trade and Industry identified certain service industries as "in-need services," priority industries in which the Philippines enjoys a competitive advantage. These include aircraft maintenance and ground services, health services, tourism services (particularly the development of retirement villages), information technology niching, and construction services. For in-need services that are capital-intensive policy should focus on reducing the cost of capital equipment. On the other hand,

TABLE 3.8
Annual Growth in Labour Productivity by Industry, 1993–96
(Percent)

	1993	1994	1995	1996
Agriculture	−1.66	1.26	2.11	−1.34
Mining	9.61	13.13	2.95	−6.72
Manufacturing	3.45	1.62	3.59	2.49
Utilities	−8.18	3.69	11.02	3.83
Construction	1.17	1.88	−2.9	−4.0
Wholesale and retail	−0.96	0.08	−1.36	−0.95
Transportation and communications	−4.35	−3.32	−0.28	−2.67
Finance, insurance, business services	−9.91	8.01	−2.16	−2.30
Community and personal services	2.06	1.31	−0.86	0.23

Source: NSCB.

those that are labour-intensive may require incentives to reduce labour costs and training expenses. The easy entry of foreign firms to provide technology is also needed.

Export Development through Industrial Clustering

The Department of Trade and Industry's past action plans for the export sector took two tracks: creating a favourable environment for exports and investment and assisting the marketing, production, and financing of exports. As part of the second track, the DTI encouraged diversification of exports by identifying products that are selling well overseas but whose market potential has not yet been fully exploited. It has identified 14 such so-called 'product winners' for the Philippines, including consumer and industrial products, agricultural and resource-based items, as well as international services. The Philippines has specific advantages in the production of these winners due to its labour skills, unique raw materials, and design capabilities. Service industries that present future opportunities in terms of skilled employment, essential business support for export, and use of the improving infrastructure for telecommunications include: professional services, construction services, film animation, data conversion, software development, and multi-media content development.

The Philippine Export Development Plan (PEDP) of 1999–2001 identifies industry clustering as a key medium-term strategy for export promotion, recognising that successful export development depends on both fostering the growth of export industries and promoting and marketing export products. The PEDP focuses on development of industry clusters in each of the Philippines' fourteen geographical regions. A cluster chart was prepared for the Philippines based on data from the United Nations International Trade Centre (Figure 3.1). The initial clusters were chosen based on the performance of Philippine products in the world market in the past five years, industry priorities for each region, and such national objectives as regional dispersal, increased value added, product diversification, and productivity improvement. To develop strategies, the clusters were grouped in four categories based on common characteristics: factor-driven, investment-driven, innovation-driven, and trend-driven industries (Figure 3.2).

The success of these export programs depends on a number of factors in addition to the commitment of government institutions. It requires strengthening existing firms through technology transfer (including expert

FIGURE 3.1
Philippine Industry Clusters

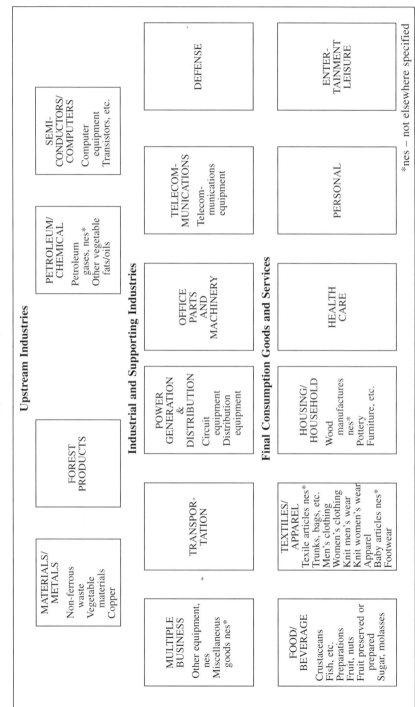

Source: Philippine Export Development Plan (PEDP) 1999–2001.

advice and regular industrial extension services), attracting foreign and domestic investors to upgrade local suppliers and subcontractors and link to sophisticated buyers, and providing support programs such as common training facilities and productivity improvement measures.

Manpower Development

An abundant supply of skilled workers has helped the Philippines attract foreign direct investment in the production of high value commodities such as electronics and software development. The Philippines now ranks just behind India as a centre for information technology in Asia. The government has recognised the need to continuously upgrade the quality of education in order to preserve this competitive edge in service exports. It must raise the quality of education in rural areas in particular if it is to attract FDI to generate employment and income opportunities there.

FIGURE 3.2
Categorisation of Industry Clusters for Export Promotion

Factor-Driven Industries		Innovation-Driven Industries	
Traditional resource base, High labour intensity Semi-skilled to highly skilled workers Existing technology base Stable or growing markets	• Furniture • Processed foods • Processed wood • Basketry and holiday décor • Jewellery • Tropical fruit	Utilise knowledge-intensive technologies High capital intensity Highly skilled labour Growing to new/ emerging markets	• Professional services • Information technology services
Investment-Driven Industries		**Trend/Opportunity-Driven Industries**	
Utilise second-wave technologies Medium to high labour intensity Semi-skilled workers Stable or growing markets	• Electronics • Automotive parts and components • Footwear • Oleo-chemicals • Mining and mineral products • Metals and engineering	Emerge following a trend Tremendous world demand Event-driven opportunities	• Hardware/software solutions for computer systems • Costume jewellery

Source: PEDP, 1999–2001.

The Commission on Higher Education and the United Nations report that the present curriculum in the Philippines is not geared to graduate a substantial number of workers suited for dynamic industrial sectors. Enrolment in the sciences and technical subjects is too low and there are minimal linkages between educational institutions and the industries that help develop student capabilities with industry requirements (Table 3.9).

The unsatisfactory quality of basic education in the Philippines was revealed by the results of the Third International Mathematics and Science Test (IMST3) administered in 1995 to 13-year old children in different countries. On the math portion of the test, Filipino students averaged only 31 percent correct. On the science, the scores of Filipino children were 77 percent below the international median for lower secondary school students and 80 percent below the international median for upper secondary school students.

Research and Development

If technology is to be the foundation of the export structure, then the Philippines must have a technology-oriented system and culture, but the

TABLE 3.9
Tertiary Technical Education Enrolments in East Asia, Number and Share of Population

	Natural Sciences		Mathematics and Computing		Engineering		Total	
	Number	%	Number	%	Number	%	Number	%
Philippines	27,200	0.040	121,000	0.178	225,700	0.333	373,900	0.551
China	167,700	0.014	99,400	0.008	971,000	0.080	1,238,100	0.102
Hong Kong	13,400	0.219	–	0.000	16,600	0.271	30,000	0.490
Indonesia	25,100	0.013	128,000	0.065	293,900	0.149	447,000	0.227
Korea	163,700	0.365	–	0.000	577,400	1.286	741,100	1.651
Malaysia	8,800	0.044	4,600	0.023	12,700	0.063	26,100	0.130
Singapore	1,300	0.039	1,400	0.042	13,000	0.391	15,700	0.472
Taiwan	16,800	0.078	32,800	0.153	179,100	0.834	228,700	1.065
Thailand	22,500	0.039	27,100	0.047	58,700	0.101	08,300	0.187

Source: UNESCO, 1997.

country currently lags behind its Asian neighbours not only in technical education but also in emphasis on R&D. It compares poorly with Taiwan, Korea, Singapore, and even China in terms of scientists and engineers engaged in R&D or in R&D expenditures as a share of GDP (Table 3.10). The Science and Technology Agenda for National Development is a comprehensive plan adopted in 1998 but it is meaningless because of a lack of genuine commitment and funding. The government is promoting ISO 9000, but the program has not been effective in getting companies to adopt the standards because it lacks incentives (Table 3.11).

The failure of Philippine institutions to focus on technology development and enhancement will impair the country's overall competitiveness. Productivity will fall if wages continue to climb and human resources cannot adapt to the high-technology, high-value activities of the future. Technological support and know-how will enhance value by preparing the manufacturing sector to upgrade from assembly and parts manufacturing to product design and testing.

TABLE 3.10
R&D Employment and Expenditures in East Asia

	Scientists & Engineers in R&D		R&D Expenditures % of GNP
	Number per million pop	Total	
Philippines (1992)	157	9,960	0.20
China (1995)	350	422,700	0.50
Hong Kong (1995)	98	574	0.30
Indonesia (1995)	0	0	0.10
Korea (1994)	2,636	117,486	2.80
Malaysia (1992)	87	1,633	0.40
Singapore (1995)	2,728	7,695	1.10
Taiwan (1995)	3,022	63,457	1.80
Thailand (1995)	119	6,899	0.10

Source: UNESCO 1997.

TABLE 3.11
ISO 9000 Certificates in Selected
Asian Countries
(Number of Companies)

	1993	1998
Thailand	9	1,236
Malaysia	224	1,707
Hong Kong	161	1,940
Philippines	4	668
Singapore	523	3,000
Indonesia	8	1,442
Taiwan	96	3,173

Source: ISO 1998.

Regulatory Reforms

The government has launched a plan to support the development of globally competitive industries. It will continue liberalisation of the trade and investment environment, provide infrastructure, develop science- and technology-based human resources, and put priority regional growth networks/centres, special economic zones, and provincial agro-industrial enterprises on a fast-track. The plan aims to make the country internationally competitive as a service provider and to develop a high-quality and high value-added service economy that effectively and efficiently meets the needs of modern agriculture and industry. Market opening measures such as the liberalisation of the domestic and international airline and telecommunications markets and the deregulation of inter-island shipping and the banking industry have already been adopted.

The government also plans to revise the Productivity Incentives Act and to pass new measures to promote electronic data interchange (EDI) and electronic commerce in trade transactions by utilising electronics, fibre-optics, and similar media and by fostering the convergence of various sectors, such as telecommunications and media and entertainment, to provide business and residential consumers with a broad array of new information services and to provide more efficient and innovative services.

Notes

The authors would like to acknowledge the research assistance provided by Ms. Annaliza G. Peña.

[1]   These policies combined with other forms of government intervention, including a usury law that capped interest rates and made capital cheap, a legislated minimum wage, credit allocation schemes that directed financial resources to areas the government identified as crucial to economic development, and rules on foreign participation in economic activities that kept them out of government-designated areas.

[2]   In their study on the impact of industrial policy reforms for the period 1983 to 1988, Medalla et al. (1995) found that the effective rates of protection for activities within the IPP were higher than the average for the manufacturing industry as a whole.

[3]   E.S. Tan, "Trade Reform in the 1990s: Effects of E.O. 470 and the Import Liberalization Programme," in Medalla et al., 1995.

[4]   The government allowed occasional imports in order to curb price increases and cover shortages as cement consumption continued to rise during the 1950s and 1960s while foreign exchange controls remained in place.

[5]   Pulp is a fibrous material derived from wood species and used in papermaking.

[6]   In the 1950s duty was 10-percent on imported kraft pulp, 30-percent on newsprint, 50-percent on kraft liners, 40-percent on fluting, and 30-percent on wood fibre/ tree printing paper.

[7]   Accounting and monitoring the services rendered by overseas contract workers have become a priority as a result of the relatively good performance of the service sector during the Asian crisis and the growth of small and medium enterprises engaged in subcontracting activities such as software and solutions development.

References

Alburo, F.A. 1985. "Philippine Trade in Manufactures Structural Change". Discussion Paper No. 8509. University of the Philippines School of Economics. August.

Ashley, E.G. and L. Shires. 1986. *A Review of the Textile Sectors with Proposed Plans & Strategies, 1986–1995.* Manila: Board of Investments. October.

Austria, M. 1994. "The Textile and Garment Industry: Impact of Trade

Policy Reform on Performance, Competitiveness, Structure." Research Paper Series No. 94-16. Manila: Philippine Institute for Development Studies.

Bautista, R.M. 1983. "Industrial Policy and Development in the ASEAN Countries." Manila: Philippine Institute for Development Studies.

Bautista, R.M. and J.H. Power & Associates. 1979. *Industrial Promotion Policies in the Philippines.* Manila: NEDA-APO Production Unit.

Belassa, B. 1981. "Industrial Prospects and Policies in The Developed Countries." Staff Working Paper No. 45. Washington, D.C.: World Bank.

Clavella, W. 1991. *Philippines by Year 2000.* Manila: Quality Bookbinding & Printing.

De Vries, B.A. 1980. "Transition toward More Rapid and Labor-Intensive Industrial Development: The Case of the Philippines." Staff Working Paper No. 424. Washington, D.C.: World Bank.

Department of Trade and Industry (DTI). 1997. "Export-led Balanced Agri-Industrialization." *Department of Trade and Industry Framework Plan.* DTI Library.

Estanislao, J.P., and F.E. Agdamag. 1981. *Sources of Philippine Industrial Growth, 1956–1978.* Manila: Philippine Institute for Development Studies.

"Industry, Services, Push Growth Rate: First Quarter Economic Report" 1996. *Philippine Development*, 22(3): 2–4.

Inoue, R. et al. 1997. *East Asian Industrial Policy Model: History of Industrial Policy.* Tokyo: Nomura Research Institute.

Jayarajah, et al., 1992. "Structural and Sectoral Adjustment: World Bank Experience, 1980–92."

Lall, S. 1993. "The East Asian Miracle Study: Does the Bell Toll for Industrial Strategy?" Development Studies Working Papers No. 67, International Development Center. London: Oxford University.

Laquindanum, L.C., ed., 1980a. "Industry Performance 1980 and Prospects for 1981." *PDCP Industry Digest.* 4(6):1–8.

―――. 1980b "Industrial Performance and Prospects for The Rest of 1980." *PDCP Industry Digest.* 4(2): 1–4.

―――. 1996a. "Pulp & Paper Industry: Investing For Growth". *PDCP Bank Industry Digest* 20(2): 1–6.

―――. 1996b "Pulp & Paper Industry: Investing For Growth". *PDCP Bank Industry Digest* 20(3).

"Leapfrogging Towards the 21st Century: A Strategy for Progress." *Philippine Development* 12 (May–June, 1995): 11–12.

Managbanag, S.G. 1995. "The Premier Agri-Industrial Hub and Trade Center of the South: Northern Mindanao (Region X)." *Philippine Development*. 12 (May– June).

Medalla, E.M. 1990. "An Assessment of Trade and Industrial Policy, 1986–1988." PIDS Working Paper Series No. 90-07. Philippine Institute for Development Studies. January.

Medalla, E.M., et al. 1995. *Catching Up With Asia's Tigers*. Vol. I. Manila: Philippine Institute for Development Studies.

Medalla, E.M., et al. 1996. *Catching Up With Asia's Tigers*. Vol. II. Manila: Philippine Institute for Development Studies.

National Economic Development Authority (NEDA). 1998. *Agri-Industrial Development Plan*. Manila: NEDA.

———. 1999. *Medium Term Development Plan for 1999–2004*. Manila: NEDA

———. 1957. *Five-Year Economic and Social Development Program for Fiscal-Year 1957–1961*. Manila: NEDA.

———. 1962. *Five-Year Integrated Socioeconomic Program for the Philippines, 1961–1964*. Manila: NEDA.

———. 1967. *Four-Year Economic Program for the Philippines: Fiscal Year 1967–1970* Manila: NEDA.

———. 1969. *Five-Year Development Program for the Philippines, 1970–1974*. Manila: NEDA.

———. Various years. *Philippine Development Report*. Manila: NEDA.

———. 1998. *The Philippine National Development Plan: Directions for the 21st Century*. Manila: NEDA.

Ofreneo, R.E. 1990. *Industrial Adjustment, Employment and Industrial Relations*. Manila:ILO-ARTEP.

———. 1980. "Ongpin Faces the Nation on TV." *Industrial Development Digest* 3(2).

Onoda Engineering & Consulting Co. Ltd. 1991. "Industrial Restructuring Studies: Cement." Makati: Development Bank of the Philippines.

Oy, L.P. 1992. "Industrial Restructuring Studies: Pulp and Paper Industry." Makati: Development Bank of the Philippines.

Pante, Filologo, Jr and E.M. Medalla. 1990. "The Philippine Industrial Sector: Policies, Programs, Performance." PIDS Working Papers Series no. 90-18 (July). Philippine Institute for Development Studies.

Philippine Chamber of Industries. 1963. "The Dynamics of Industrial Growth." Proceedings of the 10th National Convention of Manufacturing and Producers. Manila , 21–23 March.

Philippine National Bank (PNB). 1991. "Industry Update: Pulp and

Paper." *PNB Industry Studies*. Manila: PNB Department of Economic Research.

Power, J.H. 1969. "Structure of Protection in the Philippines." University of the Philippines, School of Economics.

Private Development Corp. of the Philippines (PDCP). 1973. "Portland Cement." *Studies on Philippine Industries* No. 6. Makati: PDCP.

"Prospects of Exports, Industrial Programs, Optimistic Signs for 1980s." *Industrial Development Digest* 3(1), January 1980.

"Restructuring of Manufacturing Industries: The Experience of the Textile Industries in Pakistan, Philippines, Portugal." World Bank Staff Working Papers No. 558. Washington D.C: World Bank. 1995.

Riddle, D.I. 1986. *Service-Led Growth: The Role of the Service Sector in World Development*. New York: Praeger.

Sicat, G.P. and J.H. Power. 1970. *Industrialization in the Philippines and Development*. Manila Economic Cooperation.

United Nations Industrial Development Organisation (UNIDO). 1988. "Industrial Restructuring Policies in Developing Asian Countries with Particular Attention to Textile and Garment Industry". UNIDO Industry Development Review Series, PPD. 104. Dec. 29.

UNIDO, Industrial Development Board. 1992. *Industry and Development Global Report 1992/1993*. Vienna: UNIDO.

————. 1979. *Industry 2000: New Perspective*. Vienna: UNIDO.

UNIDO Regional and Country Studies Branch. 1988. *Philippines: Sustaining Industrial Restructuring through Privatization and Foreign Investment*. Industrial Development Review Series. Vienna: UNIDO.

4

Industrial Restructuring in Thailand
A Critical Assessment

Nipon Poapongsakorn
and Somkiat Tangkitvanich[1]

Two and a half years since the Asia Crisis began there are signs of economic recovery in the East Asian countries. The crisis has had a significant impact on the structure of the Asian economies and on the structure of the manufacturing sector in particular. Due to the crisis, industrial restructuring is taking place everywhere in Asia. Japan is reforming its *keiretsu*, abandoning the traditional lifetime employment and seniority systems, and trying to nurture entrepreneurship. The Korean government made a bold attempt to split up the *chaebol* system and aggressively reform industry to promote participation of small and medium-sized enterprises. Hong Kong attempted to strengthen the manufacturing sector, realising that it had relied too heavily on the service sector.

It can be argued that even in the absence the crisis, the industrial structure of the Asian economies had already changed significantly from a few decades earlier. In the case of Thailand, the adoption of an export-led growth strategy in the early 1980s brought marked changes in the composition of national income. The share of agriculture declined from 23.2 percent in 1980 to 11.3 percent in 1997 while the share of manufacturing increased from 21.2 to 28.2 percent.

This chapter describes the shift in industry structure in Thailand during the past decade, with a focus on the manufacturing sector. At the same time, it identifies problems that need to be addressed to keep the Thai economy on a growth path, assesses the government's post-crisis restructuring initiatives, and recommends further policy steps.

Throughout the analysis, we refer to four categories of manufactured products based on input characteristics.[2] These categories are:

- Resource-based products such as processed food, mining products, rubber products, and furniture.
- Labour-based products such as garments, footwear, toys, jewellery, artificial flowers, sporting goods, and leather products.
- Capital-based products such as steel, chemicals, petroleum products, and plastics.
- Technology-based products such as electronics, medical instruments, photographic and optical equipment, and pharmaceutical products.

The reader should recognise certain limitations in this system of categorisation. It may group together products that involve very different production processes. Moreover, there may be large differences in the labour and capital requirements among individual products within each category. Technology-based products are the most difficult to define because certain products that appear to be technology-based, such as electronics and computer parts, may actually involve relatively simple, labour-based assembly operations.

THAILAND'S DEVELOPING INDUSTRY STRUCTURE

Production Structure

Agriculture was the leading sector in the Thai economy during the two decades of growth in the 1960s and 1970s. When the first National Development Plan was launched in 1961, Thailand was a typical agricultural economy. Agriculture contributed approximately 40 percent of GDP, and over 80 percent of the population were engaged in agricultural activities. Rice was the major crop and primary products for export included rubber, maize, kenaf, and tin.

Agriculture's contribution to GDP started to decline even from the beginning of the first plan period, and in 1986 the industrial sector surpassed agriculture, both in share of GDP and in rate of growth. As the economy industrialised, the service sector such as banking, finance and insurance, and transportation, which provided basic support, grew in step with it.

The declining economic importance of agriculture and rapid growth of the industrial sector are signs of the success of the export promotion strategy implemented in conjunction with the Fifth Plan (1982–86) and continuing with the Sixth Plan (1987–91). Through this strategy Thailand's manufactured products became competitive in foreign as well as domestic markets.

Export Structure

For a highly open economy such as Thailand changes in the composition of exports readily reveal the changes in industrial structure. During the mid-1970s, exports of agricultural products, mainly resource-based products made a large contribution to GDP. Along with resource-based products, capital-based products also comprised a large part of total export value. Both resource- and capital-based products played a dominant role in the economy during this period (Figure 4.1).

The situation changed when the economy was readjusted towards export promotion in the early 1980s. The manufacturing sector, especially technology- and labour-based products started to replace the agricultural sector as the driving force for exports. Exports of manufactured products surpassed agricultural exports in 1985, and the value of manufactured exports has risen dramatically since then. Exports of technology-based products increased significantly during the 1990s, and the share of technology-based products overtook the share of labour-based products (Figures 4.1 and 4.2). Technology-based products' share of total exports increased from 27 percent in 1992 to 37 percent in 1998. During the same period, resource-based products declined from 11.3 to 9.2 percent of total exports and labour-based products fell from 21.6 to 11.7 percent of total exports.

Investment Patterns

Thailand has been among the top fifteen FDI recipient countries for the past three decades (UNCTAD 1999).[3] Drawn by low labour cost, local market potential, political stability, and tax incentives, FDI has been one of the most important forces behind the shift in Thailand's industrial structure.

Since the 1980s the overwhelming number of FDI-financed projects benefiting from investment promotion measures has been in technology-based products. During the same period, the share of locally funded promoted projects in technology-based products was very small (Figure 4.3). Net flows of foreign investment show a similar pattern. Since 1980 the largest volume of net FDI flows has gone to technology-based products,

FIGURE 4.1
Composition of Exports by Input Category, 1975–97

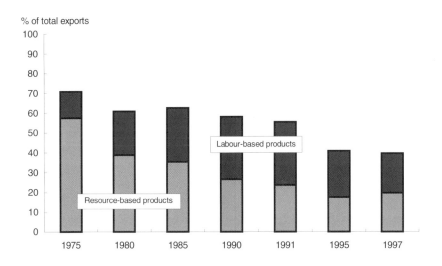

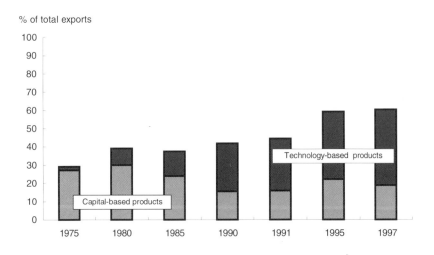

Source: Bank of Thailand.

FIGURE 4.2
Export Value of Manufactured Products by Input Classification

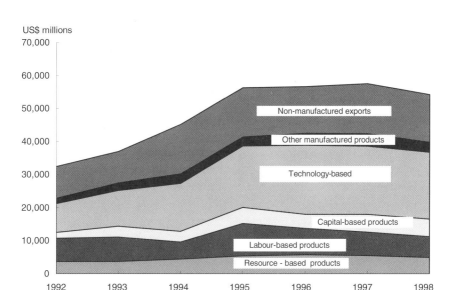

Source: Computed by TDRI from Bank of Thailand data.

considerably exceeding the net flows to resource- and capital-based products (Figure 4.4).

Thailand's major sources of foreign investment are Japan, the European Union, the United States, and the newly industrialised economies (NIEs) in Asia. Although Japan remains the largest investor, its share of FDI into Thailand declined from over 50 percent in 1988 to only approximately 30 percent in 1998. In contrast, the shares of the United States and the EU increased considerably from approximately 10 percent to nearly 20 percent. Investment from the Asian NIEs started to gain prominence in the early 1990s and the combined investment share of these economies stood at approximately 24 percent in 1998 (Figure 4.5).

Although investment promotion measures did attract FDI to Thailand, the success came at a high cost. According to a recent analysis, the redundancy rate — the proportion of promoted investment that would have occurred without incentives — was 81 percent (FIAS 1999). The same study estimated that Thailand lost 28,500 million baht in annual tax

FIGURE 4.3
Number of Promoted Investment Projects by
Input Category and Financing Source

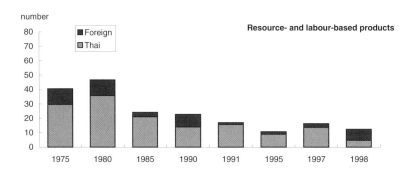

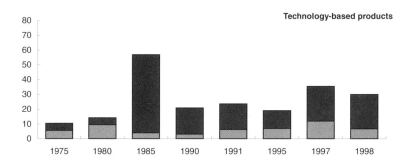

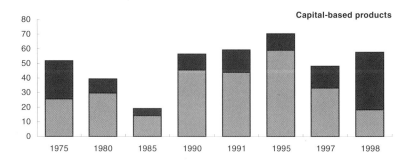

Source: Computed by TDRI from *BOI Annual Report*.

FIGURE 4.4
Net Flow of Foreign Direct Investment by Input Category of Product

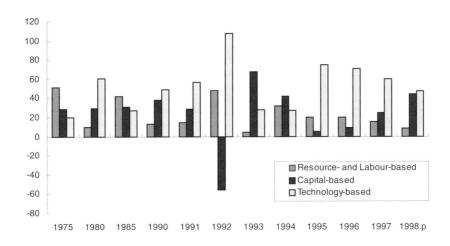

Source: Computed by TDRI from Bank of Thailand data.

FIGURE 4.5
Net Flow of Foreign Direct Investment by Source

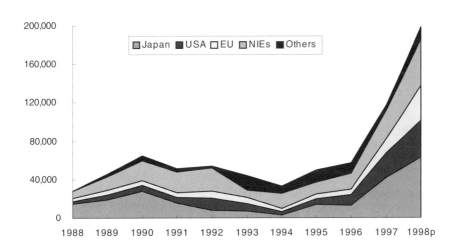

Source: Board of Investment.

revenue, about 0.61 percent of GDP, from the investment promotion measures, and the cost of 1.38 million baht per job created by the investment promotion far exceeded the opportunity cost of labour.

The pattern of investment is also characterised by the geographical concentration of industry, particularly in and around Bangkok. In 1981 Bangkok and its vicinity accounted for 75 percent of the total value of manufacturing. The figure was still 75.75 percent in 1990. After 1990, pollution, congestion, and labour shortages in the Bangkok region increasingly pressured investors to recognise the need to move industrial establishments to outlying regions — the Central region, Eastern region, or Southern region. Despite government fiscal incentives to encourage business relocation, most large-scale industries are still located in the Greater Bangkok vicinity in order to benefit from its large consumer market and the availability of better infrastructure facilities and social services.

MACRO-ECONOMIC ENVIRONMENT OF THE 1980S AND 1990S — BUILDING TOWARD CRISIS

Macro-economic Policy Adjustment

The Thai economy faced strong external pressures during the years 1980 to 1985. The second major oil price increase in 1979 had a serious impact because of Thailand's extreme dependence on oil imports. Real GDP growth was low, the inflation rate was high, and the debt service ratio was increasing due to heavy foreign borrowing at high interest rates. Faced with growing fiscal and external imbalances the government took a number of fiscal and monetary policy measures aimed at adjusting the economy to the new external parameters. These measures included two devaluations of the baht against the U.S. dollar (in 1981 and 1984), curtailment of public expenditures, vigorous revenue collection efforts, and a tight ceiling on external borrowing by the public sector.

Sound macro-economic management brought the economy back to a high growth track in the second half of the 1980s. Thailand's remarkable economic performance after 1986 is also attributed to external factors ranging from booming export demand to declining interest rates and decreasing oil prices. The combined result of these factors was two-digit GDP growth in the late 1980s.

Impacts of Financial Market Liberalisation

In the late 1980s, the Thai authorities lifted most capital controls. They liberalised repatriation of profits and dividends and removed the remaining controls to give Thai companies, including banks and finance companies, access to offshore markets for funding. By 1991, virtually all capital account transactions were unregulated. In 1993, the Bangkok International Banking Facility (BIBF) was established. The purpose of the BIBF was to facilitate the international expansion of the banking sector and reduce the cost of borrowing for Thai entrepreneurs. BIBF banks were allowed to mobilise funds abroad to lend to local companies in foreign currency. BIBF banks were subjected to the same capital adequacy and liquidity requirements as non-BIBF banks but they enjoyed tax advantages. At the same time that the capital account was liberalised, the authorities started to liberalise domestic interest rates and interest rate controls were largely abolished in 1992.

Cheap foreign loans available at a presumably risk-free fixed exchange rate fuelled speculation in the property sector as well as over-investment in the manufacturing and service sectors. Even before the crisis, over-capacity was common in capital-intensive industries, e.g., telecommunications, power generation, petrochemicals, steel, and refineries. Once the crisis struck Thailand in July 1997, the country's real sectors were left with tremendous unserviceable debts and half-idle facilities.

THE NEED FOR INDUSTRIAL RESTRUCTURING

To restart their full operation, debt-ridden companies need to undergo financial restructuring. The government facilitated the process soon after the crisis by setting up the Corporate Debt Restructuring Advisory Committee (CDRAC) under the Bank of Thailand. The CDRAC program targets large corporations, with total outstanding credits exceeding half of the non-performing loans in Thailand. Though necessary, debt restructuring by itself is not enough to make these companies more competitive. Even before the crisis, Thai firms were losing competitiveness in international markets and economic growth was slowing. Signs of low productivity and relatively weak position in export markets pointed to the need for changes in the structure of the manufacturing sector.

Low Productivity

Historically, the main source of output expansion in Thailand has been increases in inputs rather than improvements in productivity. In the early 1960s and 1970s, agricultural output increased primarily due to extension of the area under cultivation; yields remained low. In the 1980s, manufacturing output increased mainly because of pervasive inflows of investment. From the late 1980s to the early 1990s, high rates of investment in Thailand increased the growth rate of output. But during the 1990s, many East Asian economies achieved rates of output growth similar to Thailand's with lower rates of investment. This meant that investment in Thailand was relatively less productive than in neighbouring economies. As a result, Thailand required a higher rate of investment to compensate for the declining growth rate (Colaco 1998).

Competitive Market Position

Just as the competitive position of an individual company is described in terms of its products' market share and the growth rates of those markets, the competitive position of a country can be judged from the market shares of its exports and growth rates of international markets. A country is 'competitive' in the production of a particular product when its share in the global market for that product is expanding. It is considered 'dynamic' in the production of a product if its share of world trade is growing above the average rate of all other traded products (Lall 1998).

Using these definitions, a country's exported products can be classified as 'rising stars', 'falling stars', 'lost opportunities', or 'retreats' (Figure 4.6).[4] A country whose exports are mainly classified as rising stars — signifying the country is gaining market share in dynamic products, products whose markets are expanding rapidly — is in the best position. The worst situation for a country is a high proportion of 'lost opportunities', which signifies the country is losing market share in products that are supposed to be dynamic. Exports classified as 'falling stars' are preferable to 'lost opportunities', since at least the country is gaining share, albeit in a shrinking or slowly expanding market. Exports classified as 'retreats' signify that the country is moving out of stagnant products and indicate that the country is undergoing a form of restructuring.

Figure 4.7 uses these categories to compare the competitive position of Thailand and other Asian countries in international markets based on export data for 1990–95. Since the data precede the Asian crisis, they may

FIGURE 4.6
Positioning of a Country's Export Products in World Markets

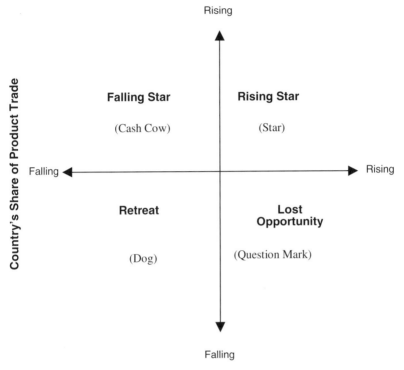

Rising

Falling

Rising

Falling

Falling Star

(Cash Cow)

Rising Star

(Star)

Retreat

(Dog)

Lost
Opportunity

(Question Mark)

Country's Share of Product Trade

Product's Share of World Trade

Source: TDRI based on Boston Consulting Group and Lall 1998.

not accurately reflect the current situation. However, they do reveal historical differences in the competitive position of these economies. With more than half (54 percent) of its manufactured exports classified as rising stars, Thailand was seemingly well positioned in international markets. Even so, Thailand was not in as strong a position as some nearby economies including Malaysia, which had 73 percent of its exports classified as rising stars, and Singapore with 69 percent rising stars. On the other hand, overall, Thailand was on a par with the Philippines and it was positioned well ahead of Indonesia and Korea and somewhat ahead of China and Taiwan. Furthermore, Thailand had a smaller proportion of exports classified as lost opportunities than all except China and Malaysia.

FIGURE 4.7
Competitive Position of East Asian Economies in Export Markets

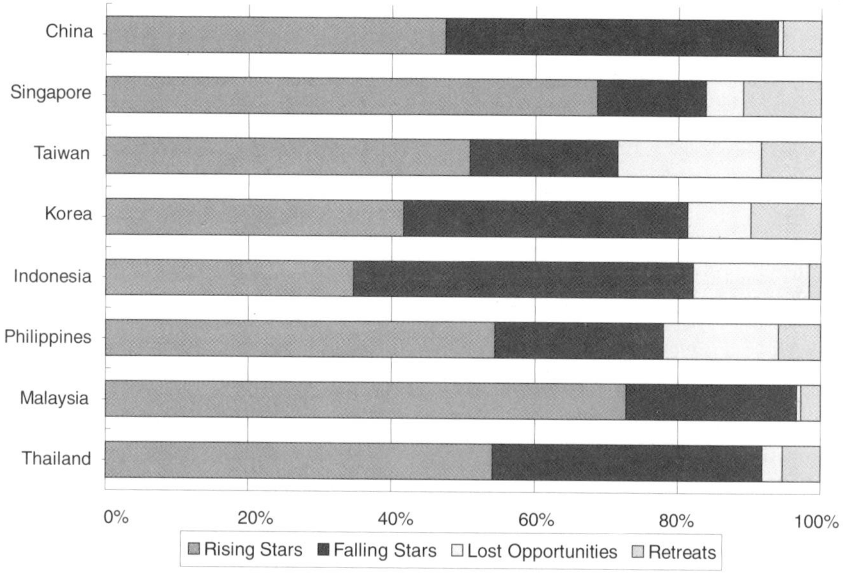

Source: Lall 1998.

A survey of manufacturing companies by the Ministry of Industry in early 1999 adds another dimension to our understanding the competitive position of the Thai manufacturing sector. Sixty-five percent of the Thai manufacturing companies surveyed identified their major competitors as domestic producers, joint-venture companies, and multinational corporations in Thailand. This indicates that most Thai companies compete locally instead of globally. Moreover, nearly half (48 percent) of the remaining manufacturing firms identify producers in low-cost countries (China and Vietnam) as their main competitors (Figure 4.8). This suggests that Thai manufacturers compete mainly at the low end of international markets where there is little product differentiation and added value is low.

Thus, although Thai manufacturers are relatively well positioned to compete in the world market, making products for market segments that are growing, they do not create high added value and remain confined to the low end of these growing markets.

FIGURE 4.8
Main Competitors Identified by Thai Manufacturing Firms

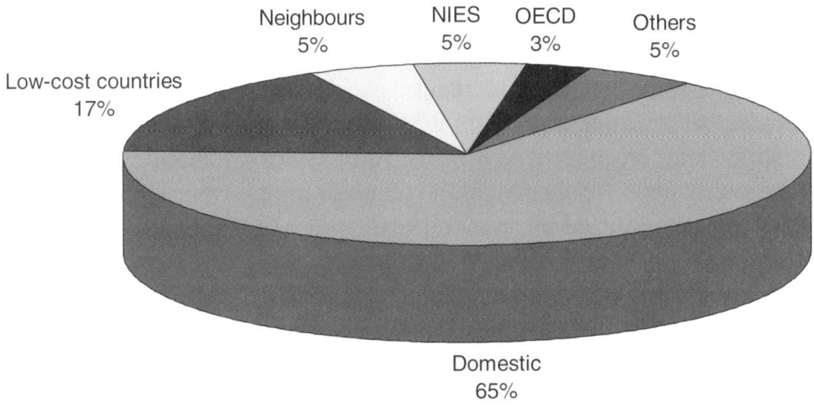

Source: Ministry of Industry

Reasons for Decline in Competitiveness

The first strain in Thailand's impressive macroeconomic performance appeared in 1996, when export growth slowed down markedly. While Thai exports grew on average 23 percent a year during the 10 years prior to 1996, growth fell to 0 percent in 1996 (Mallikamas and Pootrakool 1998). A number of short-term factors such as a cyclical slowdown in the demand for Thai exports seem to have been at play, in particular in explaining the abruptness of the decline in export growth in 1996. However, long-term factors seem to have also been at work for a period of time before 1996, as shown by the slowdown in the growth of labour-intensive exports. The erosion in competitiveness in labour-intensive goods seems to be the result of both international and domestic factors.

International Factors

International factors include the coming on-stream of new production facilities in economies with much lower income per capita and wages than Thailand: India, China, Vietnam, and the Philippines. The 1994 devaluation of the Chinese currency by about 30 percent may have been an additional factor.

Domestic Factors

Domestic factors include labour market dynamics and exchange rate policy. During 1991–1995, nominal wages in the manufacturing sector of Thailand increased by 11 percent on average, which translated into an average increase in real wages of 5 percent a year. This sustained wage growth took place despite the large disparity between rural and urban incomes and the large share of employment in the rural sector — about 50 percent of total employment. Furthermore, the increase in real wages since the mid-1980s was not matched by an increase in labour productivity (Mallikamas and Pootrakool 1998).

The exchange rate policy that linked the baht to the US dollar, until July 1997, led to an appreciation of the real effective exchange rate of the baht of about 15 percent between mid-1995 and mid-1997. As a result, labour-intensive industries such as garments and footwear were relocated from Thailand to China or Vietnam. This translated into a drop in Thailand's share of labour-intensive goods on world export markets. This loss was not, however, compensated by an increase in market share in more advanced exports.

Factors Inhibiting Competitiveness in Advanced Exports

A number of factors explain why Thailand is not gaining competitiveness and market share in more advanced products.

Quality Management

Poor management of product quality may help explain why Thai manufacturers are not positioned to compete in high-end markets. Quality management consists of actions that a company takes to ensure that its products conform to external standards and to customers' requirements. Central to the concept of quality management is the ISO9000 standard. ISO9000 is becoming increasingly prominent as more and more importers demand products manufactured according to this standard. Thus, the number of its companies that are ISO9000-certified can be viewed as a basic indicator of a country's competitiveness.

Thailand has fewer companies with ISO9000 certification than the other Asian countries except the Philippines (Figure 4.9). Thai companies did not adopt the standard widely until 1996, two years after most countries in East Asia. Moreover, almost 40 percent of the certified companies in

FIGURE 4.9
Number of Companies with ISO9000 Certification in Asian Countries

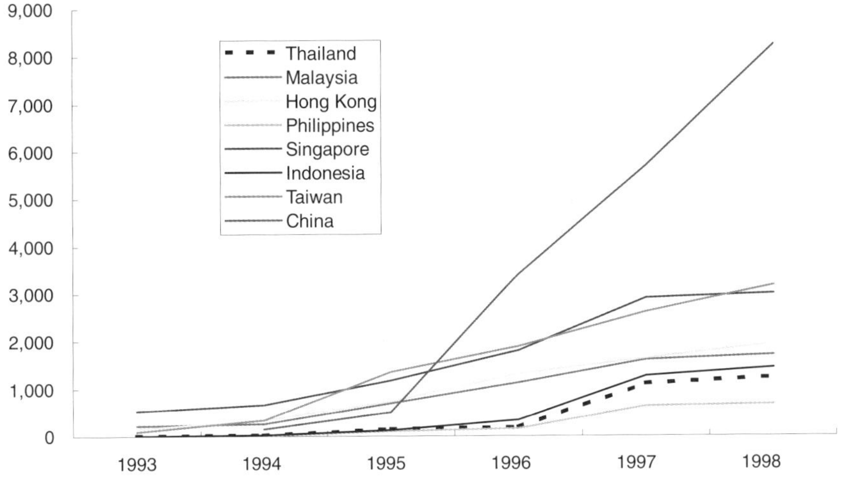

Source: ISO.

Thailand make products classified as capital-based (Figure 4.10). Surprisingly, only 20 percent of certified companies are in technology-based sectors. This share is disappointingly low since manufacturers of technology-based products are oriented to production for export. This suggests that Thai export producers have failed to keep up to the quality standards demanded in the global market.

Labour Quality

Thailand missed the opportunity to upgrade both its physical and human capital during the economic boom. Compared to bottlenecks in physical infrastructure and related services, deficiencies in human capital are the more serious drawback to improving competitiveness in advanced exports.

Education and skill levels of the Thai population lag behind those of neighbouring countries because of the neglect of secondary and higher education during the 1980s (Table 4.1). With low enrolment in secondary and technical education, Thailand has a smaller stock of skilled labour and educated workers than its competitors. The lack of skilled and trained

FIGURE 4.10
Thai Firms with ISO9000 Certification by Input Category, 1992–99

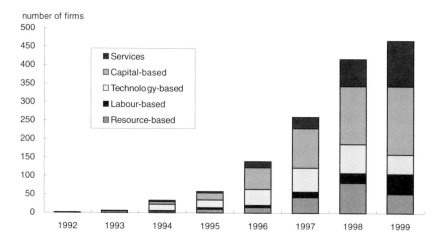

Source: Thailand Industrial Standard Institute (TISI).

TABLE 4.1
Enrolment in Secondary and Tertiary Education
in East Asian Economies

	Secondary School Enrolment Ratio	Tertiary Enrolment in Technical Fields	
	% of age group	Engineering number	Total number
Philippines	80	201,701	510,525
Malaysia	61	12,693	32,222
Thailand	49	51,949	816,256
Indonesia	45	205,086	315,325
Korea	99	437,537	730,346

Source: Middleton 1998.

labour has been a persistent obstacle to industry restructuring in Thailand. Since firms are more likely to provide productivity-enhancing training to more highly educated workers, Thailand's lack of better-educated workers acted as a brake on productivity growth.

Of particular concern is the small stock of Thais with science and engineering skills. For example, in 1995 Thailand had 119 scientists and engineers per million population, while Korea and Singapore each had more than 2,500 (Colaco 1998). As much as low growth of production capability, a lack of workers with training in science and engineering has limited Thailand's capability in design, research, and technology development, functions that are increasingly important in the industrial development process (Table 4.2).

There are also serious quality problems with Thailand's educational system. Curricula are out-dated, personnel are under-qualified, and quality and access are unevenly distributed. The present education system is not conducive to developing the skills needed for higher productivity manufacturing and information technology- and knowledge-based services (Middleton 1998).

Other Factors

While the human capital bottlenecks and failure of quality management are important, many other factors inhibit Thai firms in competing in advanced products.

• High tariffs distort the finished product and tariffs on such certain finished products are lower than on parts, components, and raw materials. Producers of advanced export products are therefore penalised by negative effective rates of protection (ERP).

TABLE 4.2
Technological Capacity of East Asian Economies

		Number of Scientists and Engineers in R&D per million population	Total R&D Expenditures as % of GDP
Thailand	1991	173	0.2
Indonesia	1988	181	0.2
Malaysia	1992	87	0.4
Philippines	1984	90	0.1
Korea	1994	2,636	2.8
Singapore	1994	2,512	1.1

Source: Colaco 1998.

- Supporting industries are weak, particularly local SMEs with the potential to subcontract with advanced industries to provide such critical inputs as plastics and rubber processing.
- The quality of infrastructure services and related facilities such as telecommunications, networks, and transportation is poor and investors must bear high operating costs to meet user demand.
- Financial institutions do not function well to provide loans to makers of advanced products. The difficulty of financial institutions in assessing the risk of such investments limits their access to credit. Moreover, financial institutions are reluctant to provide loans to this kind of activity because firms lack physical infrastructure and tangible assets as collateral.
- Government sectoral policies and administration are fragmented, leading to ineffective and misguided investment decisions and easily encouraging rent-seeking behaviour.

SECTOR-SPECIFIC RESTRUCTURING

This section discusses the restructuring needed in three industrial sectors that represent three competitive positions. The Thai electronics and computer parts industry is a rising star; the textile industry may be a falling star; and e-commerce represents a lost opportunity.

Electronics Industry

The electronics industry is composed of five sub-sectors: consumer electronics, computer parts and assembly, semiconductors, telecommunication equipment, and other electronics and related industries. Multinational companies dominate most of these sub-sectors. Most active are Japanese- and American-owned companies and more recently Taiwanese ones. A key characteristic of the electronics industry is the short life span of electronics products, especially computer-related products. For example, laptop computers usually become out-dated in three months, desktop computers in five months, hard disks in six months and monitors in a year. With the fast pace of technological innovation, manufacturers must be able to shift to new product lines quickly in order to survive. Thai electronics makers have shown considerable ability to adapt to changes in the world market (Poapongsakorn and Tangkitvanich 1999). Electronics products have become the largest export category, contributing 35 percent of total exports in certain years. Employing more than 330,000 workers, the industry has been a major source of job creation.

The electronics industry contributes little to the Thai economy except employment, however, because value added and use of local content are low. The case of a multi-million dollar hard-disk assembly factory is a good example. Although it employs over 3,500 workers, the factory adds only 5 percent to the value of the products it produces, and it procures less than 10 percent of its parts and raw materials locally (Poapongsakorn and Tangkitvanich 1999).

There are many reasons for the industry's low value added and limited use of local sources. First, distortions in the tariff structure such that tariffs on certain finished products are higher than on the component parts and raw materials penalise producers by negative effective rates of protection (ERP). For example, home electronic appliances and insulated cable wires were estimated to have an ERP in 1996 of –11.9 and –11.5 percent, respectively (Bussayawit and Saehae 1996). Second, Thailand lacks local industries in critical areas supporting the electronics sector, such as presswork and plastic and rubber processing, both because of the limited capacity of locally sourcing parts and because current tax policies inhibit the subcontracting system. Finally, the lack of qualified electronic engineers and technicians in certain areas, for example, electromagnetic interference, is a major bottleneck for upgrading the industry.

The competitiveness of Thailand's electronics manufacturers will be fully tested when the WTO Information Technology Agreement goes into effect in January 2000. Tariffs are cut to 0–5 percent for a large number of items. To maintain competitiveness, the electronics industry needs to invest more in training human resources, especially engineers and technicians. It must also acquire the ability to add more value by improving product quality, designing new products, conducting research and development, and seeking new markets.

Textile Industry

While the textile industry includes textile equipment, related petrochemical ventures, related pulp, fibre, yarn spinning, fabric weaving and knitting, fabric forming, fabric processing, and garment manufacturers, the main players in the Thai textile industry are involved in fibre, yarns, fabric, fabric processing, and garment making. The industry is widely viewed as set to become a falling star because of Thailand's rising labour costs. In

1995 annual manufacturing wages in Thailand were higher than in Malaysia and well above the level in other developing economies (Table 4.3).

Some textile industry insiders (Kittikulsingh 1999) disagree that this conclusion applies across the board. They argue that different sectors have different labour and capital input requirements so that rising wages may affect competitiveness to varying degrees. An increase in labour cost will have a significant impact on competitiveness in downstream segments, such as weaving and knitting, dyeing, printing and finishing, and garment manufacturing, which are labour-intensive.[5] Up-stream fibre manufacturing, however, is capital-based and not greatly affected by rising labour costs. The competitiveness of garment manufacturing, which can be viewed as a service-oriented industry, depends on efficient marketing as much as on labour cost. Spinning, a midstream industry, can be either labour-or capital-intensive depending on the production technology. Since spinning plants in Thailand are reasonably well equipped and not excessively labour-intensive the competitiveness of this segment should not be unduly affected by Thailand's rising wage costs.

TABLE 4.3
Annual Manufacturing Wages in
Selected Developing Economies, 1985–95
(US dollars)

	1985	1990	1994	1995	Percent Change 1985–90	Percent Change 1990–95
Singapore	7,290	10,839	17,794	26,577	48.7	145.2
Korea	3,476	9,353	14,295	17,000	69.1	81.8
Taiwan	3,832	9,826	14,469	16,200	156.4	64.9
Hong Kong	4,808	9,161	15,160	16,061	90.5	75.3
Thailand	2,392	3,522	4,917	5,450	47.2	54.7
Malaysia	3,375	3,240	4,555	5,413	–4.0	67.1
Philippines	1,257	1,802	2,857	3,650	43.4	102.6
Pakistan	1,323	1,754	2,139	2,942	32.6	67.7
Egypt	2,058	1,756	1,751	2,048	–14.7	16.6
India	1,298	1,592	1,269	1,181	22.7	– 25.8
Indonesia	921	674	1,001	1,026	–26.8	52.2
Sri Lanka	529	606	837	928	14.6	53.1
Bangladesh	557	859	1,016	736	54.2	–14.3
China	286	317	340	484	10.8	52.7

Source: UNIDO 1997.

Nevertheless, the textile industries in Thailand need modernisation. Old machinery should be replaced, staff should be trained, and marketing techniques should be re-oriented towards serving customers and securing repeat orders. Investment should focus on research and development for quality improvement. To deal with the lack of qualified staff in marketing, quality control and auditing, and textile engineering, the government should set up an industry institute to establish a standard productivity benchmark for each sub-sector, operate a high quality training program, and assist SMEs in export preparation (Kittikulsingh 1999).

E-commerce

Narrowly defined, e-commerce is the conduct of business on-line, that is, selling and buying goods and services through the Internet. The products traded may be physical products such as books, CDs, and used cars, or services such as travel and information services. This form of e-commerce is usually referred to as Business-to-Consumer (B-to-C) e-commerce. Business-to-Business (B-to-B) e-commerce focuses on supply-chain management and customer relationship management among companies. Both forms of e-commerce are growing very fast due to the proliferation of the Internet.

In developed economies e-commerce has increased the efficiency of conducting business and lowered transaction costs, both of which enhance overall competitiveness. Companies in these economies are adopting e-commerce very quickly. For example, General Electric (GE) expects to conduct almost all procurement through its electronic procurement system within five years. Other large companies are moving in the same direction.

Further adoption of e-commerce in developed economies will inevitably increase the pressure on Asian companies that trade extensively with them. Companies in the leading e-commerce sectors, e.g., wholesale and retail trade, pharmaceutical, automobile, and electronics industries are under the most pressure to adjust in order to maintain their status as suppliers to global companies. Asian companies will have no choice but to upgrade their technological and marketing capabilities and modify their business models to adapt to the fast-approaching information era. Unless they join the electronic supply chain, they will lose comparative advantage as suppliers of cheap and high quality parts and raw materials to large multinational corporations. To them e-commerce will become a 'lost opportunity'.

For this reason, it is worrying that Thailand lags behind other East Asian countries in adapting to e-commerce (Tangkitvanich 1999). Thailand ranks near the bottom of the East Asian economies in the number of SSL servers and Internet hosts per capita (Figure 4.11).[6] Tangkitvanich and Nikomborirak (1997) argued that the lower penetration of the Internet in Thailand is due in part to the existence of the state monopoly on the international communication market. Moreover, while most East Asian economies have a scarcity of IT-literate human resources, the problem seems especially acute in Thailand. The country also lags in computerisation

FIGURE 4.11
SSL Servers and Internet Hosts in East Asian Economies

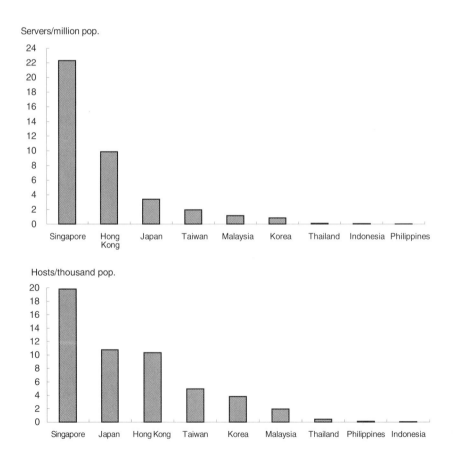

Source: Netcraft (servers) and Network Wizard (Internet hosts).

of the public sector and has fewer computers per capita than most Asian countries.

POLICY RESPONSES AND EVALUATION

The Asian Crisis triggered the realisation of the necessity to restore manufacturing competitiveness, and since 1998 the government has issued a number of programs and measures aimed at restructuring Thai industry.

Industrial Restructuring Master Plan

In June 1998, the National Committee for Industrial Development issued the Industrial Restructuring Plan. The plan focuses on upgrading Thailand's competitiveness through a set of strategies including allocating soft loans to 13 sectors, dispatching experts to provide technical assistance, and establishing funds and government organisations to support industrial development (Figure 4.12).[7] The implementation program budget allocation was US$1.19 billion.

Based on a breakdown of the budget, the restructuring plan emphasises upgrading production technology and machinery and relocating labour-

FIGURE 4.12
1998 Industrial Restructuring Plan for Thailand

1. Move towards production of high value-added products for middle to higher markets, with higher quality standards, by
   - upgrading technology and machinery as well as quality management
   - developing product design in line with market preferences
2. Improve efficiency in terms of production costs, streamline production process and improve delivery and quick response as well as improve management capability
3. Upgrade knowledge and production skills of industrial personnel
4. Create strategic alliances to penetrate and expand markets and enhance technology transfer
5. Reduce industrial pollution through the adoption of clean technology and industrial zoning policies
6. Disperse industrial employment to regional and rural areas

Source: MOI 1998.

intensive industries to outlying regions (Table 4.4). While it includes programs to improve productivity and upgrade labour skills and product design, it allocates only 9.1 percent of the budget to these activities.

Tariff Reform

In late 1999 the Cabinet announced a comprehensive reform of the tariff structure to enhance industrial competitiveness and meet international commitments. Under the ASEAN Free Trade Area (AFTA) agreement, import duties must be reduced to 0–5 percent on 1,190 items on January 1, 2000. Furthermore, under the Information Technology Agreement (ITA), 153 items will be exempt from import duties from January 1, 2000 and another 37 items from January 1, 2005. The reform also focuses on cutting tariffs on capital goods (machinery, mechanical appliances and parts, and electrical machinery, equipment, and parts) and on raw materials (inputs of pharmaceutical, food, chemical, plastic, and textile products). At the same time, the Cabinet removed the 10-percent import duty surcharge on items with a tariff rate over 5 percent. The tariff reform is estimated to cost the government approximately US$124 million a year in lost revenues.

SME Support Packages

Having been neglected for decades, SMEs suddenly gained recognition in a series of government support measures. A draft SME Promotion Bill was submitted to Parliament in June 1999. It provides for the creation of an SME Promotion Committee whose mandate is to recommend an SME Promotion Plan to the Cabinet, give incentives and other financial assistance to support SMEs, and direct the executive board of the SME Promotion Office. The bill will also set up an SME Promotion Fund to provide soft loans to SMEs for business start-ups and upgrading.

Independent of this bill, the Ministry of Finance initiated a package of financial support for SMEs. The package includes an allocation of nearly US$1 billion in credit for SMEs through specialised financial institutions and the Bank of Thailand. It also established a US$1 billion Venture Capital Fund, financed by structural adjustment loans from the World Bank, to invest in SMEs. The government also set up the Market for Alternative Investment (MAI), a special stock market with less stringent listing rules for SMEs.

TABLE 4.4
Allocation of the Industrial Restructuring Program Budget
(US$ millions)

	Loans to Private Sector for:		Allocation to Governmental Organisations for:			Total
	Investment	Hiring Experts	Compensation for Experts	Human Resource Development	Setting up Organisations	
Total allocation	960.0	27.9	45.2	90.2	68.5	1,191.8
1. Productivity improvement and process restructuring	0.0	19.2	19.2	20.5	5.0	63.9
2. Upgrading production technologies and machinery	375.0	1.8	1.8	2.4	5.0	386.0
3. Upgrading of labour skills	0.0	0.0	14.4	60.2	14.0	88.6
4. Incubating and strengthening small and medium industries	125.0	0.6	0.6	1.4	5.5	133.1
5. Product design and development and distribution channels	0.0	4.8	4.8	5.1	6.0	20.7
6. Relocating labour-intensive Industries to the regions	250.0	0.0	0.0	0.0	33.0	283.0
7. Attracting foreign investment in strategic industries	0.0	0.0	0.2	0.0	0.0	0.2
8. Relocating and containing hazardous industries	210.0	1.5	1.5	0.7	0.0	213.6

Source: MOI 1998.

Educational Reform

The National Educational Act was passed in 1999 to reform the educational system. The key component of the Act is the initiative to provide free basic education for every student through the upper secondary level from the year 2003. The Act also sets out an ambitious plan to decentralise educational administration by giving individual teachers and institutions more freedom to set their own curricula and mobilise their own resources. It also aims to introduce a quality assurance scheme through a school accreditation system. Finally, the Act promotes the use of information and other educational technologies in every school. If successfully implemented, the reform will gradually improve the quality of human resources and contribute to the long-term competitiveness of Thai industry.

Assessment and Policy Recommendations

Although the reform effort came late in the game, many aspects are laudable. At the same time, the efficacy of certain specific measures may be questioned and there remain many areas that have yet to be addressed.

The tariff reform will directly benefit manufacturers in a wide range of industries. For example, the textile industry will gain from lower tariffs on cotton and chemicals, while the electronics industry will gain from lower duties on copper cathodes. The reduced tariffs on capital goods will lower production costs for all sectors. At the same time, the removal of the import duty surcharge will reduce the degree of protection and encourage more efficient resource allocation. The tariff reform to comply with AFTA is an important step towards a comprehensive rationalisation of the tariff structure. By eliminating many distortions in the existing system it will prepare Thai industries to compete in a wider arena when full-scale trade liberalisation begins under the WTO commitments. Tariffs on non-AFTA products, however, remain high and continue to distort resource allocation in many industries.

While the educational reform program will undoubtedly raise the quality and productivity of Thai workers, it will be very costly. A recent study shows that the total increase in operating expenditure to implement the program will be as high as US$ 1.5 billion per year by 2010. This is equivalent to an increase about 63 per cent from the current operating cost in providing basic education service (Poapongsakorn and Tangkitvanich, forthcoming).

There are more questions about the effectiveness of the Industrial Restructuring and SME support programs than about the educational and tariff reforms. The program to provide soft loans to encourage industries to relocate to outlying regions lacks a basis in economic reasoning. If total production costs were actually cheaper in the regions, companies would relocate without the inducement of soft loans. A similar argument applies to soft loans to promote upgrading production technology and machinery. Without a clear economic rationale, such programs appear to be mainly politically motivated and more likely to promote resource misallocation than to improve competitiveness.

It is doubtful that the government programs to support SMEs will solve their financing problems. The Ministry of Finance's Venture Capital Fund is unlikely to succeed where experienced foreign venture capitalists have found it hard to make money. Similarly, it is not probable that the MAI will be able to attract investment by just relaxing its listing rules. Merely relaxing the rules would render the market much more risky for investors. Higher risks can be justified only if the listed SMEs generate higher returns than larger companies.

Government initiatives have so far overlooked certain critical areas that need to be addressed to fully restore the competitiveness of Thai industry. First, the programs have not focused sufficiently on ways to improve productivity, the critical element of competitiveness. Only a small portion of the Industrial Restructuring Plan budget allocation is to go toward improving productivity, upgrading labour skills, and improving product design. Moreover, nothing has been done yet to strengthen capability in science and technology. The way to cure Thailand's technological weakness, however, is not to simply put more government money into public research institutes. Instead, government should encourage these institutes to become more reliant on private funding in order to shift them away from supply-push R&D programs to demand-pull or market-oriented ones and to improve their productivity and accountability.

Another area that has not been touched by reform is the state monopolies. By introducing competition into infrastructure sectors, ending the state monopoly will improve the competitiveness of Thai industry across the board. For example, liberalising the telecommunication sector will boost Internet usage and catapult Thailand into the e-commerce bandwagon.

Regional co-operation on certain issues — some general and some sector-specific — will also lead to improved competitiveness for Thai industries. Co-ordination of investment policy would benefit Thailand as well as neighbouring economies. Southeast Asian economies are becoming involved in a costly zero-sum game, competing to offer similar investment incentives to multinational companies (Niclolas 1999). Regional co-operation in simultaneously lowering investment incentives would make each economy's FDI promotion efforts more cost-effective.

Another arena for regional co-operation is trade liberalisation. The difficulties in launching the new WTO round threaten a return to greater protectionism in world trade. Bilateral trade talks such as those between New Zealand and Singapore are also returning to vogue. With reciprocity, rather than MFN-treatment, as their key principle such arrangements can cause trade diversion and become stumbling blocks for trade liberalisation. An open regional trade arrangement such as APEC can restrain the forces for increased protectionism and bilateral agreements. The problem is how to make this regional forum work.

New industrial sectors such as e-commerce may prove to be productive areas for sector-specific co-operation among the regional economies. In fact, there is a need to harmonise laws and regulations, taxation, and standards in order to guarantee the free flow of goods and services traded by e-commerce. Regional co-operation on these issues could be a stepping stone towards global harmonisation.

Notes

[1] The authors thank Mr. Kiratipong Naewmalee for his excellent research assistance.
[2] The classification is adapted from OECD, 1987.
[3] Thailand ranked eleventh during 1970–79, eighth during 1980–89, and sixth during 1990–96.
[4] These categories correspond to the Boston Consulting Group's 'star', 'cash cow', 'question mark' and 'dog' categorisation of a firm's market position.
[5] The labour intensity of the knitting and weaving industries is due not to a lack of automation, but to the scale of production, as the industries consist of many small companies.
[6] An Internet host is a computer connected to the Internet with a domain name and an associated IP address. An SSL server is a computer that can set up a secure end-to-end link using the secure socket layer (SSL) protocol, a de facto standard protocol for e-commerce transactions.
[7] Organisations that have been established to date include industry-specific institutions such as the Textile Institute of Thailand, the National Food Institute, the Electronic and Electronics Institute, and the Vehicle Institute

and functional institutions such as the National Productivity Centre and the Industrial Design Institute. Examples of funds set up are the Fund for Venture Capital Investment and the Thailand Recovery Fund.

References

Bussayawit, Sunee and Sombat Saehae. 1996. *Impact of Tariff Reform on the Competitiveness of Thai Industries* (in Thai). Bangkok: Thailand Development Research Institute.

Colaco, Francis X. 1998. *Thailand's International Competitiveness: A Framework for Increased Productivity.* Conference on Thailand's Dynamic Economic Recovery and Competitiveness Volume II. Bangkok: Office of the National Economic and Social Development Board and World Bank, Thailand Office.

Foreign Investment Advisory Service (FIAS) 1999. *Thailand: A Review of Investment Incentives.* Washington, D.C.: FIAS.

International Organization for Standardisation (ISO). 1998. *The ISO Survey of ISO 9000 and ISO 14000 Certificates (Eighth cycle.)* <http://www.iso.ch>.

Kittikulsingh, Suthep. 1999. "The Textile Industry: Sunset or Just a Passing Dark Cloud". Unpublished manuscript.

Lall, Sanjaya. 1998. *Thailand's Manufacturing Competitiveness: An Overview.* Conference on Thailand's Dynamic Economic Recovery and Competitiveness Volume II. Bangkok: Office of the National Economic and Social Development Board and World Bank, Thailand Office.

Mallikamas, Vee and Kobsak Pootrakool. 1998. *Thailand's Balance of Payments and Financial Crisis: Export Competitiveness, Investment Efficiency, and Financial Fragility.* Conference on Thailand's Dynamic Economic Recovery and Competitiveness Volume II. Bangkok: Office of the National Economic and Social Development Board and World Bank, Thailand Office.

Middleton, John and Zafiris Tzannatos. 1998. *Skills for Competitiveness.* Conference on Thailand's Dynamic Economic Recovery and Competitiveness Volume II. Bangkok: Office of the National Economic and Social Development Board and World Bank, Thailand Office.

Ministry of Industry (MOI). 1998. *Industry Restructuring Master Plan: Executive Summary.* Bangkok: Ministry of Industry.

Niclolas, Stephen. 1999. "Japanese Multinationals in Thailand: The Impact of Incentives on the Location Decision." In Proceedings of the

International Conference in Commemoration of the 50th Anniversary of Thammasat University. Bangkok.

Organisation for Economic Co-operation and Development (OECD). 1987. *Structural Adjustment and Economic Performance*. Paris: OECD.

Poapongsakorn, Nipon and Somkiat Tangkitvanich. 1999. *Impacts of New Production Technologies on Labor: A Case Study on the Electronics Industries* (in Thai). Thailand Development Research Institute (draft).

————, forthcoming. *Financing the Educational Reform Program*. Bangkok: Thailand Development Research Institute.

Tangkitvanich, Somkiat. 1999. *The Status of E-Commerce in Thailand* (in Thai). Bangkok: Thailand Development Research Institute.

Tangkitvanich, Somkiat and Deunden, Nikomborirak. 1999. *The State of Competition in the Internet Market in Thailand* (in Thai). Bangkok: Thailand Development Research Institute.

Tinakorn, Pranee and Sussangkarn Chalongpob. 1996. *Productivity Growth in Thailand*. Bangkok: Thailand Development Research Institute.

United Nations Conference on Trade and Development (UNCTAD). 1999. *World Investment Report 1999: Foreign Direct Investment and the Challenge for Development*. New York and Geneva: United Nations.

UNIDO 1990. *Industrial Development in Thailand in the 1990s: Prospects, Constraints and Priority Areas for Technical Assistance*. Vienna: UNIDO Industrial Policy and Perspective Division.

5

Industrial Restructuring in Malaysia
Policy Shifts and the Promotion of New Sources of Growth

Vijayakumari Kanapathy

INTRODUCTION

The Malaysian economy recorded rapid growth from 1970 to 1997, with the exception of the brief recession of the mid-1980s. The economy grew by 8.3 percent between 1970 and 1980, slowed down somewhat to 5.9 percent between 1980 and 1990, but recorded unprecedented sustained high growth of about 9 percent from 1990 until it succumbed to the Asian financial crisis of 1997. The remarkable economic expansion was progressively led by manufacturing (Table 5.1). As a result, the manufacturing sector's share of GDP rose from 13.3 percent in 1970 to about 30 percent by 1997, while the sector's share of employment rose by 17 percent. Most notably, export of manufactured goods increased from a mere 12 percent of total exports in 1970 to 81 percent by 1997 (Table 5.2). The dominant position of manufacturing in the growth and development of the Malaysian economy is particularly evident from the pivotal role it has assumed in the current economic recovery from the nation's worst-ever recession. The economy contracted by 7.5 percent in 1998, but recovered quickly, expanding by 5.4 percent the next year.

The growth and structural transformation of the economy over the last three decades has occurred within the framework of a liberal trade and investment regime as well as the extensive use of so-called functional and selective industrial policies (Lall 1997). The overall approach to industrial development is anticipated to continue, but a shift towards more market-based policies is apparent in the industrial policy adjustments introduced

TABLE 5.1
Growth in the Economy and the Manufacturing Sector, 1970–99
(Percent)

| | Average Annual Growth | | |
	1970–1980	1980–1990	1986–1997
GDP	9.3	5.9	9.3
Manufacturing	12.0	9.3	12.4
Employment	3.7	3.2	4.2
Manufacturing	9.6	5.6	9.1
Exports	18.8	11.0	15.9
Manufacturing	25.9	22.2	21.1

Note: 1970–80 based on 1970 constant prices; 1980–90 based on 1978 constant prices; and 1986–97 based on 1987 constant prices.
Source: Calculated from Ministry of Finance, *Economic Report*, various issues; Department of Statistics 1999, *Malaysia Economic Statistics, Time Series,* Malaysia, Kuala Lumpur, December; and Bank Negara Malaysia, *Monthly Statistical Bulletin,* January 2000.

TABLE 5.2
Manufacturing Share in the Economy, 1970–97
(Percent)

	Share of GDP	Share of Total Exports	Share of Total Employment
1970	13.3	12.2	9.0
1975	16.4	21.8	11.1
1980	19.6	21.8	15.7
1985	19.7	32.2	15.2
1990	26.9	58.8	19.9
1997	29.9	81.0	26.4

Source: Calculated from Ministry of Finance, *Economic Report*, various issues; and Department of Statistics 1999, M*alaysia Economic Statistics, Time Series,* Malaysia, Kuala Lumpur, December.

since the late 1980s. A more pragmatic approach to policy interventions was adopted to adapt to Malaysia's rapidly changing comparative advantage and to cope with increasing global competition and revised regional and international rules and regulations governing trade and investment under AFTA and WTO. The recession of the mid-1980s brought to light the urgency to re-evaluate and redefine development strategies and policies. The effect was a broad shift from a relatively diffused policy approach to a more comprehensive and integrated strategy to foster industrial dynamism. The state withdrew from direct participation in production, and the private sector was assigned the lead role in industrial development. The state took on a more indirect and supportive role in spite of the continued targeting of industries. Hence, this phase of industrial restructuring witnessed the introduction of several new policy initiatives to redress fundamental weaknesses within the industrial sector, foster structural dynamism, and promote new sources of growth through a more focused and integrated approach to policy interventions.

The chapter examines these shifts in industrial development strategies and policies and highlights some of the future challenges and issues confronting policy makers in Malaysia. It briefly introduces the evolution of industrial development strategies and policies responsible for Malaysia's industrial dynamism and highlights some of the key success factors of the past that will continue to provide the underlying framework for future development. It also examines some of the fundamental weaknesses within the industrial sector that led to policy adjustments. Next, it shows how some of the new policy initiatives and new sources of growth complement existing strategies and policies within the context of a "Manufacturing ++" development strategy. Essentially, this involves a shift from an industry-based to a cluster-based development strategy to foster greater maturity and diversity of the industrial sector.

MAJOR THRUSTS OF INDUSTRIAL POLICIES
FROM 1970 TO THE 1990s

Most analyses of the evolution of industrial policies in Malaysia distinguish three phases of industrialisation since the 1970s. These are:

- Export-oriented industrialisation (EOI) based on export-processing zones (EPZs) in the early 1970s;
- A second-round of import-substituting industrialisation (ISI) based on heavy industries in the early 1980s; and
- Liberalisation and a second round of export push in the late 1980s and a sustained shift towards more market-oriented policies in the 1990s.

The key policy initiatives and their basic thrusts influencing Malaysia's industrialisation process are summarised in Table 5.3.

TABLE 5.3
Key Policy Initiatives in Malaysia's Industrialisation
from 1958 to the 1990s

	Major Policy Initiatives
Phase I (1958–1968)	
Import-substituting industrialisation	Pioneer Industries Ordinance, 1958 • Granting of pioneer status Tariff Advisory Board • Infant industry promotion though tariff protection
Phase II (1968–1980)	
Export-led Industrialisation via EPZs/LMWs	Investment Incentives Act, 1968 • Development of EPZs/LMWs • Export incentives
Promotion of public enterprises and *bumiputera* SMEs	New Economic Policy • State interventions through subsidies, quotas, and licensing • Industrial Co-ordination Act, 1975 • Establishment of public enterprises and promotion of *bumiputera* SMEs
Phase III (1981–1999)	
Second round of import-substituting Industrialisation through heavy industries — 1981	Formation of HICOM in 1981
Second round of export-push through liberalisation and deregulation — 1987	Promotion of Investments Act, 1986 • Foreign investment and export push through liberalisation of foreign equity and incentives tied to exports Tax reforms Review of heavy industries Privatisation of public enterprises Amendments to labour legislation to improve labour market flexibility
Focus on productivity-driven growth through emphasis on S&T and R&D as well as human resource development (HRD)	Industrial Master Plan, 1986–1995 Action Plan for Industrial Technology Development, 1990 Emphasis on HRD to improve quality of labour

continued on next page

TABLE 5.3 – cont'd

	Major Policy Initiatives
	• Mandatory training through the Human Resource Development Fund established in 1993. • Fiscal and financial incentives for expansion of education and training • Liberalisation of the education and training industry
Promotion of new sources of growth	Second Industrial Master Plan, 1996–2005 • Shift from industry-based to cluster-based industrial development approach Establishment of Multimedia Super Corridor, 1996

Export-oriented Industrialisation in the 1970s

Prior to the 1970s, Malaysia promoted specific industries primarily through tariffs and quotas and the provision of basic infrastructure, and these industries essentially produced for the domestic market. This initial ISI drive of the 1960s faced such inherent limitations as saturation of domestic market and failure to penetrate export markets. It also failed to absorb the economy's excess labour, leading to relatively high unemployment levels and subsequent political instability. Because of these circumstances export-oriented industries were promoted in the early 1970s through the Investment Incentives Act of 1968, the establishment of EPZs, and restrictions on labour unionisation to entice trans-national corporations looking for low-cost production sites abroad. Foreign firms in the EPZs employed low-wage labour to assemble imported raw materials and components for export. Electrical and electronics firms were the major producers in these zones, with some textile and garment factories.

The EOI drive through EPZs transformed the industrial sector into a significant economic activity. The contribution of manufacturing to GDP and employment rose by 7 percent within a decade, while exports rose by 8 percent (Table 5.2). By 1980, exports of electrical and electronic products and textiles and garments, located mostly within EPZs and licensed manufacturing warehouses (LMWs), accounted for about 60 percent of manufactured exports (Table 5.4). While the export-oriented development strategy was successful in terms of gross export earnings and overall employment generation, it had serious drawbacks for sustained industrial expansion.

Earnings from rapid export growth were limited because of the high import-intensity of exports. For instance, between 1972 and 1982 net foreign exchange earnings were as little as 10 percent of gross sales (Edwards 1995, p. 18). Employment expansion was significant and absorbed surplus labour, but it was mostly low-wage employment. Edwards (1995) noted that the average real wage in the manufacturing sector in 1978 was lower than in 1968. Little technology transfer or skill development took place and the EOIs developed in isolation as "export enclaves". Linkages between EPZ firms and the rest of the economy through the purchase of domestically produced raw materials and capital equipment were insignificant. Primarily to redress these weaknesses industrial policy focused on a second round of ISI based on heavy industries in the early 1980s.

ISI Based on Heavy Industries in the Early 1980s

The heavy industrialisation strategy was aimed at deepening and diversifying the industrial structure through the development of more local linkages, *bumiputera*-owned small and medium-scale industries, and indigenous technological capabilities. The heavy industries targeted under the programme included the national car project, motorcycle engine plants, iron and steel mills, cement factories, a petrol refining and a petrochemical project, and a pulp and paper mill. All of these industries require long gestation periods and heavy capital investment and hence were spearheaded by the public sector. A public sector agency — the Heavy Industries Corporation of Malaysia (HICOM) — was established in 1981 to lead the heavy industrialisation programme. Public development expenditure for heavy industries rose significantly from RM0.33 billion in 1981–85 to RM2.55 billion between 1986 and 1990, mostly financed through external borrowings (Table 5.5). Apart from enormous injections of public funds, the targeted industries were heavily protected through tariff and import restrictions and licensing requirements. For instance, the effective rate of protection for the iron and steel industry rose from 28 percent in 1969 to 188 percent in 1987. The level of protection for motor vehicle assembly and cement industries was so high that these industries operated at negative value added at free trade prices. In other words, they would not have survived without protection (Edwards et al. 1990).

TABLE 5.4
Gross Manufacturing Exports by Commodity Group, 1970–99

		1970	1975	1980	1985	1990	1995	1999
Food, beverages, and tobacco		18.3	13.7	8.2	6.2	4.4	2.5	2.1
Textiles, garments, and footwear		6.5	11.0	12.8	10.3	8.5	4.6	3.6
Wood products		14.4	10.4	7.4	2.9	2.9	4.2	3.7
Rubber products		2.8	2.2	1.3	0.9	3.3	2.2	2.0
Non-metallic mineral products		32.2	9.4	1.0	1.2	1.6	1.1	0.9
Chemicals, chemical and plastic products		3.3	1.2	3.0	4.9	4.0	4.5	4.4
Petroleum products		–	–	3.0	8.3	2.8	2.1	1.6
Iron, steel and metal manufactures		4.2	2.5	4.0	2.9	3.5	3.3	3.0
Electrical and electronic machinery		2.8	15.4	47.7	52.1	56.6	65.7	71.4
Transport equipment		11.1	13.6	3.5	4.5	4.1	3.6	1.9
Other manufactures		4.4	20.8	8.1	5.7	8.3	6.2	5.4
Total	%	100.0	100.0	100.0	100.0	100.0	100.0	100.0
	RM million	612	1,978	6,319	12,471	45,835	147,507	123,602

Note: For 1970 and 1975, petroleum products are combined with chemical products and transport equipment includes other machinery.
Source: Ministry of Finance, *Economic Report*, various issues

TABLE 5.5
Government Development Expenditures in
Heavy Industries by Plan Period

Five-Year Plan Period	RM million
1981–1985	330.61
1986–1990	2,553.1
1991–1995	567.7
1995–2000	354

Note: Figure for 1995–2000 Plan period refers to revised allocation.
Source: Government of Malaysia, *Five-year Development Plans*, Kuala Lumpur.

The performance of heavy industries in the early years was rather weak. Despite significant protection, the industries suffered severe financial losses due to lower-than-projected domestic demand and high operating costs. Many of Malaysia's targeted heavy industries also suffered from severe gluts on the world market. The recession of the mid-1980s and high external debt (Malaysia's external debt rose from 9.5 percent of GNP in 1980 to about 42.4 percent in 1986) forced the government to restructure and privatise many of the state-owned enterprises, including the heavy industries. The management of some of the heavy industries improved with privatisation and they began to penetrate export markets. The reorientation of strategies and policies with respect to heavy industries was part and parcel of an overall trend towards further liberalisation of the economy and rationalisation of industrial policies.

Liberalisation and Export Push from the Late 1980s

Macroeconomic adjustments and structural reforms to enhance the efficiency and competitiveness of the Malaysian economy followed the mid-1980s economic slowdown. The public sector was downsized through privatisation and mergers and there was general recognition of the private sector as the primary engine of growth. For the first time, industrial development was guided by a ten-year Industrial Master Plan (IMP), which provided the framework for the development of the manufacturing sector.

The First IMP (1986–1995) recommended the continuation of the export-led industrialisation strategy but emphasised the promotion of resource-based industries in which Malaysia had already developed a strong foundation with higher local content and the diversification of the non-resource-based industries. This strategy was pursued through further liberalisation of trade and investment, and substantial incentives were granted to encourage investment and exports. The incentive system under the IMP was tied to industries in which Malaysia had a comparative advantage and those products that were of strategic importance to the country, termed 'priority products'.

The 1986 Promotion of Investments Act replaced the 1968 Investment Incentives Act and provided a wider range of incentives for investments in manufacturing, agriculture, and tourism. Special incentives were targeted at export expansion and the development of small and medium-scale industries that were deemed essential to develop inter-industry linkages. Foreign equity guidelines were further relaxed to make it easier for foreign investors to own up to 100-percent equity, depending on export targets and other conditions. The scope of the Industrial Co-ordination Act of 1975 was relaxed so that only companies with more than RM2.5 million shareholder funds or engaging more than 74 full-time workers required operating licences. Previously the ceiling was RM250,000 or 25 workers.

The First IMP also stressed the importance of science and technology and human resource development to support the industrialisation process. It highlighted the critical need to prepare the workforce with industrial and technical skills and to develop indigenous skills in product design and production technology. Incentives were thus provided for training and for research and development.

Substantial labour market reforms were also introduced in the late 1980s and early 1990s to make Malaysia more cost-competitive and to facilitate industrial upgrading. In the second half of the 1980s, significant amendments were made to labour legislation to contain labour costs and to foster greater labour market flexibility. This does not necessarily imply that the labour market had been rigid prior to the wage reform measures. The primary elements of wage rigidity such as statutory minimum wage, high unionisation of the workforce, and strong role of unions in collective bargaining are not characteristic features of the Malaysian labour market.

These policy reforms and incentives made Malaysia more attractive as an investment centre, and the economy benefited tremendously from the outward-bound investment from Asian NIEs that were relocating their production bases. Direct foreign investment in manufacturing and selected sectors of the economy rose from only RM2.1 billion in 1987 to RM17.6 billion by 1990 (Table 5.6). Investment in Malaysia from Japan, Taiwan, South Korea, Hong Kong expanded significantly during this period. By 1990, these economies together accounted for about 70 percent of total foreign investment. Their share has fallen to around 40 to 50 percent in recent years as these economies completed the bulk of their structural adjustments.

The massive inflow of foreign investment into manufacturing following the liberalisation and deregulation measures resulted in significant structural shifts within the Malaysian economy. Manufacturing surpassed all expectations, becoming the leading sector in output, exports, and employment growth. By 1990, it accounted for about 27 percent of GDP,

TABLE 5.6
Investment in Manufacturing, 1985–99
(RM million)

Year	Foreign	Local	Total
1985	959	4,728	5,687
1986	1,688	3,475	5,163
1987	2,060	1,874	3,934
1988	4,878	4,216	9,094
1989	8,653	3,563	12,215
1990	17,629	10,539	28,168
1991	17,055	13,763	30,818
1992	17,772	10,003	27,775
1993	6,287	7,466	13,753
1994	11,339	11,612	22,951
1995	9,144	11,725	20,869
1996	17,057	17,201	34,258
1997	11,473	14,348	25,821
1998	13,063	13,289	26,352
1999	12,268	4,631	16,899

Notes: Foreign investment = foreign equity + estimated foreign loan (foreign share of total equity). Coverage includes licensed manufacturing projects (includes new projects and expansion/ diversification), small industries/exempted manufacturing projects, hotel agriculture, R&D and technical and vocational training institutes applying for incentives.
Source: Bank Negara Malaysia, *Monthly Statistical Bulletin*, August 2000.

about 59 percent of total exports, and about 20 percent of total employment (Table 5.2).

The uninterrupted high growth from 1986 transformed the labour market from a situation of high unemployment in the mid-1980s to severe labour and skill shortages by the early 1990s, with significant inflow of foreign workers. It was feared that the relatively easy access to low-skilled labour would retard industrial upgrading and trap the economy in low-skill equilibrium. Accurately estimating the number of foreign workers is difficult because of the high incidence of illegal entry and the many foreign workers overstaying or possessing forged documents. Based on the number of work permits issued, the number of foreign workers and their dependants in the country rose from 290,000 in 1990 to 650,000 in 1995 and to 730,000 by 1997. According to official estimates, there were about 1.7 million foreign workers in the country in 1997, including one million illegal or undocumented workers (Kanapathy 1999). In other words, foreign workers accounted for about 20 percent of the total labour force or 21 percent of all those employed. The significant presence of foreign workers helped to moderate wage growth, but even so, with unabated economic growth and full employment, wages grew in excess of productivity, impinging on profitability. Labour productivity as measured by value added per worker rose by 7.8 percent per annum between 1990 and 1993, whereas wages grew by 8.7 percent (Table 5.7). As a result, unit labour costs rose by about one percent, after declining about two percent between 1985 and 1990.

In addition, skill intensity in manufacturing was almost stagnant during the period of high growth, and the level of technical and tertiary education was insufficient to meet the growing demand for skilled workers. Skill intensity in manufacturing, as measured by the ratio of professionals, managers, technicians, and supervisors to the total workforce, rose by less than one percent, from 0.126 in 1983 to 0.132 in 1992 (Department of Statistics, *Annual Industrial Survey*, various issues). The World Bank attributed the sluggish growth in skill intensity mainly to supply constraints, while acknowledging demand constraints. It argued that the relative shortage of skilled workers resulted in high wage premiums and dampened investment in skill-intensive industries. And the high demand for less skilled workers was met by the relatively easy availability of foreign workers (World Bank 1995 pp. 16–18). Both supply and demand factors explain the almost stagnant or slow growth in skill intensity of the manufacturing sector. In other words, the labour market had reached a crossroads demanding a strategic shift towards higher value-added activities

TABLE 5.7
Wages, Labour Productivity, and Unit Labour Costs
(Ringgit)

	Labour Productivity	Average Annual Wage	Wages/Value Added
1985	25,438	7,605	0.299
1986	25,380	7,584	0.299
1987	25,720	7,478	0.291
1988	27,163	7,394	0.272
1989	29,497	7,650	0.259
1990	29,039	7,901	0.272
1991	31,875	8,610	0.270
1992	33,942	9,506	0.280
1993	36,426	10,155	0.279
1994	40,421	11,101	0.275
1995	42,913	11,850	0.276
1996	49,377	13,232	0.268
1997	55,769	14,475	0.260
		Average annual growth	
1985–90	2.7	0.8	−1.9
1990–93	7.8	8.7	0.9
1993–97	11.2	9.3	−1.7

Source: Computed using data from Department of Statistics, *Malaysia Economic Statistics, Time Series*, December 1999.

requiring greater capital-, skill-, and knowledge-intensity for sustainable growth. Industrial policy was fine-tuned to foster sustainable competitiveness by putting priority on human resource and technology development.

During the early 1990s, labour market policy attention diverted from job creation and fostering labour market flexibility to the expansion of education and training facilities to support industrial growth and restructuring. Although the state has traditionally been the main provider of education and training in Malaysia the widespread labour and skill shortages during the high growth phase made it apparent that the state could not meet the expanding demand for human resource development on its own. Several new policy initiatives were introduced to improve and expand education and training. There was a shift from a largely supply-driven approach to a more demand-driven approach. Elements of this shift include mandatory training by industry, liberalisation of the education market, greater incentives for the private sector to invest in education and training, and the forging of industry-institution links. With these far-reaching reforms, a comprehensive and dynamic education and skills delivery infrastructure has evolved in recent years offering more opportunities for workers and firms to invest in developing their skills. Meanwhile, the process of industrial restructuring itself has enhanced job prospects for skilled workers, encouraging a culture of lifelong learning.

Technology is perhaps the weakest link in Malaysia's industrialisation process. The technology capabilities of the manufacturing sector are not commensurate with its dominant position in terms of output, employment, and exports. This situation is somewhat reflected in poor productivity growth in manufacturing. Some of the more recent studies on productivity performance show negative or very low total factor productivity growth in manufacturing in the 1980s and early 1990s (Table 5.8).

The low level of technology development in Malaysia is largely the legacy of past policies that failed to provide state support for firms with potential for upgrading their technology capabilities. Foreign direct investment (FDI) was the principal mode of technology acquisition, but the investment incentives to promote FDI were tied to export and employment expansion, and not to technology development. Technology development was not given priority until the post-1985 industrial policy rationalisation. State support measures, including reform and expansion of public sector R&D institutions and infrastructure and introduction of a wider range of incentives for private sector R&D, brought about a more

TABLE 5.8
Estimates of Total Factor Productivity Growth
in Malaysian Manufacturing

Source	TFP Growth
Okamoto (1994) For the period 1981–1990	Annual TFP growth of –1.9 percent from 1981–1985 Annual TFP growth of 0.3 percent from 1986 to 1990
Tham (1996) For the period 1986–1993	Sources of growth from TFP was 0.1 percent from 1986–1993, compared to 10.3 percent from intermediate input growth and 0.3 percent from capital growth

comprehensive and dynamic policy and institutional framework for technology development (Table 5.9).

The mounting efforts to promote technology-based industrialisation have produced some positive results, but R&D expenditure is still far short of the national target of 1.6 percent of GDP. At present, R&D expenditure hovers around 0.3 percent of GDP, down from 0.6 percent in 1992 and 1994 (Table 5.10). The R&D expenditure rate in Malaysia is also way below that in Japan (2.8 percent) and in the first generation NIEs — Singapore (1.4 percent), South Korea (2.8 percent), and Taiwan: (1.9 percent) (Bank Negara Malaysia 2000, p. 65).

TABLE 5.9
Major Policy Support With Respect to
Industrial Technology Development

Key State Support Measures	Main Objectives
Fiscal Incentives Across-the-board tax incentives provided since 1984 for R&D activities that include double deduction for R&D expenses incurred, an industrial building allowance for buildings utilized for R&D activities and capital allowance for plant and machinery used in R&D.	To encourage R&D activities among private firms.
Pioneer status for new investment in selected high-technology activities that meet R&D intensity and other criteria were introduced in 1994. Other incentives were also tied to selected high-tech investment.	To induce companies to achieve R&D expenditure of one percent of sales revenue within a year. Also 7 percent total workforce must include science and technical graduates within one year
Technical Assistance MASTIC (Malaysian Science and Technology Information Centre) formed in 1992	A national S&T information center within MOSTE charged with collecting data through biennial national survey.
MIGHT (Malaysian Industry — Government Group for High Technology established in 1993	A consultative committee consisting of top government and business leaders to forge consensus on technology development priorities

continued on next page

TABLE 5.9 – cont'd

Key State Support Measures	Main Objectives
Financial Assistance	
IRPA (Intensification of Research in Priority Areas) introduced in 1986	To centralise management of public funds for R&D and set technology priorities
Industrial Technical Assistance Fund (ITAF) introduced in 1989	An R&D subsidy scheme that provides matching grants to SMIs for innovative projects.
Vendor Development Programme introduced in 1993 by Ministry of International Trade and Industry (MITI) and Ministry of Finance (MOF)	To raise technology capability of local SMIs to enhance linkage development. MNCs and large local companies sign agreement with MITI and designated banks to provide supplier firms with procurement contracts, technical assistance and subsidized finance.
Malaysian Technology Development Corporation (MTDC) established in 1993.	A public-private venture capital to commercialise public research institutes research findings. Two RM100 million matching grant funds allocated under the 7MP.
Khazanah Holdings established in 1994 as an investment arm of the MOF	To spearhead direct government investment in key strategic and high-technology areas.
Industry Grant Scheme introduced in 1996 under MOSTE	Provides matching grant funding for joint public-private R&D projects.
MESDAQ launched in 1996	An automated stock exchange for high-technology firms.
Establishment of Technology Parks	
Technology Park Malaysia established in 1988	To house and support private research facilities and technology intensive companies. Administers a RM10 million venture capital fund allocated under the 7MP.
Kulim High Technology Park Multimedia Super Corridor established in 1996	To attract technology-based foreign and local projects. To stimulate emerging IT development and research. A RM200 million multimedia matching grant scheme and a venture capital scheme for investment in MSC-status companies.

TABLE 5.10
R&D Expenditure as a
Share of GDP 1992–97

	R&D Expenditure/GDP %
1992	0.6
1994	0.6
1996	0.3
1997	0.3

Source: Ministry of Science, Technology and Environment (MOSTE).

Other critical problems include the low analytical capability and insufficient number of full-time staff in state agencies that disburse state support to identify the technology needs of the industry and their growth prospects. Recent changes have strengthened the system somewhat. In addition, the ambitious technology strategies of the state are not based on the realities and constraints faced by industry. State strategies tend to favour the creation of indigenous products and promote cutting-edge technologies, while the needs of industry are most pressing in the areas of quality improvement and technology mastery and adaptation (Felker 1999).

Despite the progress in industrial upgrading under the liberalisation and rationalisation of industrial policies since the late 1980s, critical problems continue to plague the industrialisation process. These include:

- low level of indigenous technology
- general lack of intra-industry linkages
- limited local content
- low level of domestic investment in export industries
- low level of value added activities

These pressing domestic constraints were compounded by rising global competition and resulted in Malaysia's re-evaluating its approach to development in the late 1990s. As a background to examining the revised approach to industrial development, the following section summarises the key elements of Malaysia's past industrial dynamism. These factors will continue to provide the underlying framework as the economy makes the transition to a higher level of industrialisation.

KEY ELEMENTS IN MALAYSIA'S INDUSTRIAL DYNAMISM
BETWEEN 1970 AND 1990

Several studies have acknowledged the central role of the state in Malaysia's past rapid industrial growth and development (Ismail and Meyanathan 1993, Edwards 1995, Jomo 1997, and Lall 1997). The state will continue to play a key role in restructuring industry. However, in order to foster competitiveness in the changing domestic and global environment of the twenty-first century, the state will now assume a more indirect and supportive role. Its principal function is to provide the necessary physical infrastructure, a transparent regulatory framework and a stable macro-economic environment to enable private enterprises to operate efficiently.

First, government policies have long supported the outward-orientation of the relatively small economy. Even prior to the 1970s, Malaysia was a leading exporter of resource-based products such as tin and rubber. It later expanded into timber and palm oil. The aggressive EOI drive, which opened EPZs and LMWs, strengthened the outward orientation of the economy. Selected products were produced for the domestic market under high tariffs and import restrictions, but overall the trade and investment regime during this period was fairly liberal. The export-oriented industrialisation drive coincided with the implementation of the New Economic Policy. The affirmative action policies to redress imbalances among ethnic groups involved both indirect interventions such as licensing, subsidies and quotas as well as direct participation of the state in industry. Numerous state enterprises were set up during the 1970s, mostly directed towards the domestic market. However, such interventions were implemented alongside an open policy towards trade and investment. In fact, MNCs dominated the EPZs and they operated in a virtually border-less economy. These "free zones" fostered the development of a critical mass of high-technology industries that form the basis of Malaysia's export success today.

Second, with the exception of short-lived inflationary pressure in the early 1970s and the recession in the mid-1980s, the government has maintained a fairly stable macroeconomic situation conducive to the growth of private enterprise and the preservation of socio-political stability. Malaysia also inherited a fairly developed and sophisticated institutional and legal framework, which minimised risks and the costs of doing business for private enterprises.

Third, the state committed to heavy investment in physical infrastructure to transform Malaysia into an attractive haven for foreign investment. Each of the five-year development plans gave priority to building an extensive system of transport and telecommunications facilities and public utilities. Industrial estates were opened beginning in the 1970s and sold or leased to private firms at subsidised rates. More recently, Malaysia has built world-class infrastructure that includes state-of-the-art airport and port facilities, highways, and telecommunications as well as science parks.

Fourth, education and human resource policies supported industrialisation. Malaysia's educated and disciplined, English-speaking workforce that commanded relatively low wages was an advantage in the initial EOI drive. The government's strong commitment to free basic education provided a ready supply of relatively skilled labour at competitive wages in the early stages of industrial development. In the late 1980s, when wages started rising and skill and labour shortages emerged, government policies gave priority to human resource development. Education and training opportunities, especially at higher levels, were expanded through increased public investment and liberalisation and deregulation of higher education. These policy and institutional changes have contributed to the development of a comprehensive and market-driven education and training infrastructure that supports lifelong learning.

Fifth, the state kept labour-management relations on an even keel through stringent labour legislation and close co-operation and co-ordination with labour and industry. Despite some stringent labour laws, labour standards have improved significantly in several aspects including wages and other benefits, safety, and security.

Finally, despite the mixed reviews it received, the government's 'Malaysia Incorporated' concept laid the foundation for building networks between business and government. A strong culture of consultation and co-operation between public and private sectors has developed since the early 1980s. Several channels and levels of communication have been forged over the last two decades between the public sector and private business to provide feedback on changing industry requirements and the problems faced by them.

NEW STRATEGIES AND APPROACHES TO INDUSTRIAL COMPETITIVENESS

Malaysia's industrial competitive strength has been built upon relatively low labour cost, sound physical and policy infrastructure, fairly educated workforce, availability of support services, and spearheaded by direct foreign investment. This has contributed to an industrial structure that is low in skill intensity and retained value added. These elements worked extremely well over the last three decades supporting the phenomenal growth of exports and employment.

The global and domestic environment is changing rapidly, however, calling for a different set of strategies to build new sources of competitive advantage. Malaysia's small population base and the rapid growth of relatively low-skilled jobs have contributed to wage escalation. Malaysian industry now has to compete with lower-wage newcomers, many of which have large domestic markets and are aggressively promoting themselves as low-cost export platforms. Not only does Malaysia have to compete with these new players to attract FDI, but also the investment flows are drying up as the Asian NIEs, which were the primary sources of FDI in the mid-1980s, complete the industrial restructuring that had been forced by the realignment of their currencies. This situation is challenging Malaysia's traditional reliance on FDI as the engine of growth.

Export growth in Malaysia, unlike in South Korea or Taiwan, was led by foreign investment. The failure to develop sufficient domestic linkages has resulted in the growth of industries with high import content of capital formation and industrial output. To nurture a more robust industrial sector and retain more value added in the economy Malaysia needs to avoid FDI that has low potential for linkages with the local economy and attract FDI that is conducive to developing indigenous supply capability. This presents a challenge for policymakers, because investing MNCs are not always sympathetic to such domestic development needs (MITI 1996).

The internal and external challenges that now confront the manufacturing sector mean that past industrial development approaches based on large-scale injections of capital to boost labour productivity are no longer viable. In the mid-1990s industrial policies were adjusted to focus on total factor productivity growth, which requires strong synergy among all factors of production. The essence of the new growth strategy was a shift from assembly-intensive manufacturing to an integrated, industry-wide approach encompassing both manufacturing and related services. Dubbed Manufacturing++ ('manufacturing-plus-plus') this revised strategy provides the framework for industrial development under the Second Industrial Master Plan, 1996–2000 (Second IMP).

Manufacturing++ Strategy and Cluster-based Approach to Industrial Dynamism

The Second IMP, formulated at a time of widespread labour and skill shortages and increasing global competition, focused on increasing productivity and competitiveness and built upon the foundations of the First IMP. With the Second IMP, however, industrial development strategy shifted from the traditional industry-based approach to a cluster-based approach. It emphasised development of industrial clusters, their key suppliers, and the requisite economic foundations such as human resources, technology, physical infrastructure, supportive administrative rules and procedures, fiscal and non-fiscal incentives, and business support services. It aimed to develop dynamic industrial clusters and strengthen industry linkages, while promoting higher value added activities.

Unlike the earlier more diffused approaches, the Manufacturing++ strategy is an integrated and co-ordinated approach to industrial development. It emphasises the full integration of manufacturing operations through the value chain to enhance industrial linkages and increase productivity and competitiveness. It involves changing the industrial structure from the predominance of basic assembly and production operations into more upstream activities such as research and design and product development as well as downstream activities such as distribution and marketing (Figure 5.1). The objective is to move into higher value added activities. Only industries that are able to develop the breadth and depth of their activities within the economy and establish regional or global linkages with related industries will be able to survive the competitive pressures in the global market place. The Manufacturing++ strategy entails not only moving along the value chain but more importantly shifting the value chain upwards through productivity growth.

FIGURE 5.1
The Value Chain

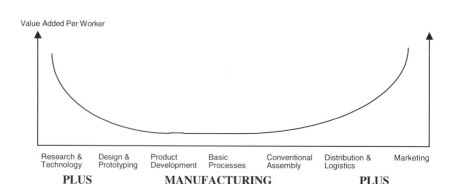

The Second IMP identified five strategic thrusts to counter the stiffer competition brought on by trade liberalisation and globalisation. These are:

- Global orientation — make firms world class manufacturers with global marketing capabilities.
- Enhance competitiveness of the manufacturing sector — deepen and broaden industrial linkages and enhance productivity through cluster-based development.
- Improve economic foundations — develop and manage human resources, acquire technology acquisition, and enhance the absorptive capacity, physical infrastructure, supportive administrative rules and procedures, fiscal and business support services.
- Develop Malaysian-owned companies — develop large Malaysian enter-prises geared towards regional and international markets.
- Increase information-intensive and knowledge-driven processes in higher value added activities — emphasise R&D, product design, marketing, distribution and procurement, and the use of information technology for electronic commerce.

The Second IMP continued the targeting approach of the First IMP by identifying eight industry groups involving 22 industrial clusters classified into three broad categories, e.g., internationally-linked, policy-driven, and resource-based industries (Table 5.11). The targeted clusters will be developed on a rolling plan. Targets for these industries will be set and periodically revised to accommodate changes in the domestic and global economy.

A new institutional framework was set up to implement the Second IMP. It is led by the Industrial Co-ordination Council, which consists of representatives of the public and private sectors. The state thus continues to play a strong supportive role in industrial development. Working groups for each of the clusters at the national, state, regional, and cluster levels also consult regularly with the private sector to obtain the feedback needed for successful implementation.

Promotion of New Growth Sectors

Malaysia expects to graduate into the post-industrial phase of development soon and is currently preparing for the transformation to a service-led economy. Even so, manufacturing is expected to retain a substantial role after the structural transformation, as it did within the economies of the

TABLE 5.11
Classification of Industries for Incentive Targeting

	Industry Group	Industry Cluster
Cluster-type		
Internationally-linked	Electrical & electronics	• Electrical & electronics
	Textiles & garments	• Textiles & garments
	Chemicals	• Pharmaceuticals
		• Petrochemicals
Policy-driven	Transportation	• Automobiles
		• Motorcycles
		• Marine transportation
		• Aerospace
	Material & advance materials	• Polymers
		• Metals
		• Composites
		• Ceramics
	Machinery & equipment	• Machinery & equipment
Resource-based	Resource-based	• Wood-based products
		• Rubber-based products
		• Palm oil- based products (food sector)
		• Palm oil-based products (non-food sector)
		• Cocoa & cocoa products
	Agro-based & food products	• Fish & fish products
		• Livestock & livestock products
		• Fruits & vegetables
		• Floriculture

Source: Second IMP (1996).

NIEs except Hong Kong. Under the Second IMP, manufacturing's share of GDP is expected peak at 38.4 percent. Based on the experience of many developed economies, the current manufacturing share at about 30 percent is generally regarded as the optimum growth level (Table 5.12). Hence, new policy initiatives to diversify into high value added services industries have been introduced.

Information technology (IT) and multimedia industries are being promoted as the new sources of growth. These two strategic sectors are instrumental in increasing efficiency, productivity, and competitiveness of the manufacturing sector and in realising the transition to a knowledge-based economy. The National Information Technology Agenda (NITA) formulated in 1996 provides the framework for the co-ordinated and integrated development of skills and infrastructure as well as IT-based applications. The Multimedia Super Corridor (MSC) was launched as a catalyst to the expansion of IT and multimedia industries. Similar to the way it promoted industries in the EPZs, to encourage the growth and development of IT and multimedia industries in the MSC, a government Bill of Guarantees grants key MSC infrastructure projects exemption from local ownership requirements, unrestricted employment of foreign knowledge worker and eligibility for tenders. Companies locating in the MSC are given pioneer status for up to 10 years or granted 100-percent investment tax allowance. As of December 1998, 195 firms including 88 local firms, had been approved for MSC status.

KEY CONCERNS AND CHALLENGES

Malaysia has witnessed some degree of natural and policy-induced industrial upgrading over the last decade. For instance, MNCs in the electronics industry have spawned local companies in such areas as metal fabrication, high-precision plastics, high-precision tooling parts, and mould and die production. Some of these local SMIs have graduated into multinational

TABLE 5.12
Composition of GDP, 1970, 1980 and 1997

	1970	1980	1997
Agriculture, livestock, forestry, and fishing	30.8	22.9	9.1
Mining and quarrying	6.3	10.1	7.3
Manufacturing	13.4	19.6	29.9
Construction	3.9	4.6	4.8
Electricity, gas & water	1.9	1.4	3.1
Transport, storage & communications	4.7	5.7	7.5
Wholesale, retail trade, hotels, and restaurants	13.3	12.1	15.0
Finance, insurance, real estate and business services	8.4	8.3	12.2
Government services	11.1	10.3	6.6
Other services	2.5	2.3	7.5
	100	100	100

Source: Ministry of Finance, *Economic Report*, various issues.

operations and some have formed joint-ventures with foreign technology firms to produce high quality parts and equipment. The development of such industries has not yet reached the critical mass for self-sustained industrial dynamism, however.

Availability of skilled labour presents a key challenge to upgrading Malaysia's manufacturing sector, which is still by and large shallow with considerable labour-intensive operations. There is concern that the shortage of skilled domestic workers coupled with the availability of foreign workers at competitive wages may discourage firms from investing in labour-saving, skill-intensive operations. (Currently, one out of every five workers in Malaysia is a foreigner.) At the same time, policymakers inherently fear that difficulties in recruiting workers could induce foreign firms to relocate to cheaper production sites in other countries.

Local industries will face serious competition when tariff and non-tariff barriers come down with the introduction of the Common Effective Preferential Tariff (CEPT) Scheme by the year 2003. Particularly affected will be heavy industries that currently operate under high tariffs and import restrictions such as the automotive industry. Malaysia's two national cars together account for about 80 percent of the local passenger car market. The local content, in terms of value, has risen to 70 percent for Proton and 50 percent for Perodua. For non-national car assemblers, the local content is between 30 to 40 percent (Ahmad and Singh 1999). Without the heavy protection the automotive industry will not be able to survive, due to the high cost of production. The recent financial crisis has further impacted adversely on the auto industry. Policymakers need to re-evaluate strategies with respect to heavy industries and strive to expand exports in order to meet the increasing competition from regional producers under AFTA (ASEAN Free Trade Area).

The shortage of critical skills, including creative talents and entre-preneurial capabilities, continues to plague the economy's transition to greater skill- and knowledge-intensive activities. Malaysia currently has a liberal policy with respect to the importation of critical skills in short supply. Continued reliance on foreign supply of skilled workers, however, will impinge on retained value added as well as raise concerns about equity. Moreover, the depreciation of the ringgit following the 1997 financial crisis has made it difficult for local firms to attract and retain skilled and talented foreign labour.

Perhaps the greatest challenge for Malaysia's industrialisation process is to raise the level of local technological capabilities to support self-sustaining industrial dynamism. Malaysia has to seriously address the mismatch between the immediate needs of industry and the state's ambitious goals to promote cutting-edge technologies. Moreover, it must recognise, nurture, and reward the creativity of its citizens to ward off the challenge of outward migration of talent in an increasingly globalised environment.

Finally, the accession of China into the WTO (World Trade Organisation) presents a potential challenge to Malaysia's efforts to attract foreign investment. While it will give Malaysian firms greater access to China's vast domestic market, it will also give international investors greater access to China's huge production potential and pool of skilled and unskilled labour.

CONCLUDING REMARKS

By and large, Malaysia's revised strategies and approaches to industrial development retain elements key to past industrial success. These include a fairly liberal trade and investment regime with strong emphasis on export growth and the provision of sound physical, legal, and institutional infrastructure as well as close consultation and co-operation between the public and private sectors. Although the state continues to target industries, these industries are spearheaded by the private sector. The state now assumes a more indirect supporting and facilitating role by providing the essential economic foundations for industrial competitiveness. The economic liberalisation and rationalisation of industrial policies since the mid-1980s have created a more market-friendly environment for industrial development.

Malaysia's transition to higher value added products and processes has not been easy because MNCs control both export production and technology. Industrial strategies and policies had to be continually revised to encourage the structural transformation of the manufacturing sector. Currently policies to upgrade the industrial structure focus on human resource and technology development. The Manufacturing++ concept and cluster-based approach to industrial development represent a more focused, integrated, and co-ordinated industrial policy. IT and multimedia industries are being promoted as new sources of growth to boost efficiency, productivity, and competitiveness.

Although the industrial sector is currently the leading growth sector, it has yet to reach a level of maturity that ensures self-sustained dynamism. Export growth is still based on assembly-intensive operations and is led by MNCs. Further efforts to upgrade Malaysia's industrial structure will take place in an increasingly competitive environment. The more immediate challenges to Malaysia's industrial expansion are posed by the CEPT, to be introduced by the year 2003, and the inclusion of China into the WTO.

References

Ahmad, Hasir Mahpodz and Paramjit Singh. 1999. "The Malaysian Auto Industry: Role of Policy in Industrial Restructuring." Paper presented at the Regional Conference on Industrial Restructuring in ASEAN, Kuala Lumpur, 26–27 October.

Bank Negara Malaysia. 2000. *Annual Report*. March, Kuala Lumpur.

Edwards, Chris, et al. 1990. "Protection and policy in the Malaysian manufacturing sector." *Policy Assessment of the Malaysian Industrial Policy Studies (MIPS) and the Industrial Master Plan (IMP)*. Volume 3. Report prepared for UNIDO and the Government of Malaysia. Kuala Lumpur, December.

Edwards, Chris. 1995. "Tariff and trade-related policies for Malaysian industrialisation." In *Managing Industrial Transition in Malaysia* ed. V. Kanapathy. Kuala Lumpur: Institute of Strategic and International Studies, Malaysia.

Felker, Greg. 1999. "Malaysia's Innovation System, Actors, Interest and Governance." In *Technology, Competitiveness and the State: Malaysia's Industrial Technology Policies* eds. K S Jomo and Greg Felker. London: Routeledge.

Ismail Salleh and S.D. Meyanathan. 1993. *The Lessons of East Asia: Malaysia, Growth, Equity and Structural Transformation*. Washington, D.C.: World Bank.

Jomo, K.S. et al. 1997. *Southeast Asia's Misunderstood Miracle: Industrial Policy and Economic Development in Thailand, Malaysia and Indonesia*. Oxford: Westview Press.

Ministry of International Trade and Industry. 1994. *Review of the Industrial Master Plan, 1986–1995*. Kuala Lumpur, December.

———. 1996. *Second Industrial Master Plan, 1996–2005*. Kuala Lumpur, November.

———. 1997. *Malaysia: International Trade and Industry Report 1996/97*. Kuala Lumpur, August.

Kanapthy, V. 1997. "Labour market issues and skills training: Recent developments in Malaysia." Paper presented at the PECC-HRD Task Force Meeting, Montreal, 30–31 May.

———. 1999. "The Financial Crisis and the Malaysian Labour Market:

Some Preliminary Observations." Paper presented at the PECC-HRD Task Force Meeting, Kong Kong, 15–16 May.

Lall, Sanjaya. 1997. *Learning from the Asian Tigers: Studies in Technology and Industrial Policy.* London: Macmillan Press Ltd.

Tham, S.Y. 1996. "Productivity and Competitiveness of Malaysian Manufacturing Sector." Paper presented at the Seventh Malaysia Plan National Convention. Kuala Lumpur, 5–7 August.

World Bank. 1995. *Malaysia, Meeting Labour Needs: More Workers and Better Skills.* Country Report. Washington, D.C.: World Bank.

PART II
Restructuring in Asia's Newly Industrialised Economies

6

Singapore: Towards a Knowledge-based Economy

Chia Siow Yue

INTRODUCTION

The Singapore economy grew at an average annual rate of over 8.5 percent from 1965 to 1997, before the regional financial and economic crisis of 1997–98. Having recovered from the crisis, the challenge facing the economy as it enters the twenty-first century is to sustain its record of nearly four decades of high economic growth.

Because Singapore is small and lacks a natural resource base, rapid economic development brought labour shortages and rising costs, and the economy has been losing its cost-advantage vis-à-vis other producers in the developing economies of East Asia. It has to continually upgrade into higher value added manufacturing and services and move up the value chain. Externally, globalisation and the information technology revolution are triggering the restructuring of corporations and national economies. Corporations are restructuring, downsizing, and relocating activities to optimise use of global resources, and are re-engineering job processes to harness new technologies. Knowledge-related activities have become central to creating national wealth and sustaining economic growth. By some estimates, more than 50 percent of the GDP in major OECD economies is now knowledge-based. As Singapore moves out of the low-wage, low-cost league, it has to compete with these OECD economies and their knowledge-based industries. Hence, Singapore faces an urgent need to address the issue of transforming towards a knowledge-based economy.

The OECD (1996) defines a knowledge-based economy as one in which the production, distribution and use of knowledge are the main drivers of growth, wealth-creation, and employment for all industries. In its most basic form the knowledge-based economy (KBE) should be qualitatively different from the industrial economy, where labour is a factor of production and competitive advantage comes from more resources, cheaper labour, and better machines. In the KBE, people and their ideas and capabilities are the key source of wealth and opportunities.

The emergence of the KBE is characterised by four changes — a rise in the residual component of labour productivity growth; the growth of investment in education; a rise in real stocks of intangible capital (education); and a decline in conventional capital share. The revolution in information and communications technology (ICT) is not synonymous with the emergence of the KBE, but the two are closely inter-related. Many features of the KBE are based on the increasing use of ICT. ICT gives the KBE a new and different technological base that radically changes the conditions for the production and distribution of knowledge as well as its coupling to the production system. The rise of ICT has spawned a host of new industries, created new areas of demand, and transformed the way we work and live. The KBE offers new possibilities for both individuals and nation states.

The 1998 Report of the Committee on Singapore's Competitiveness and the Economic Development Board's Industry 21 Master Plan set the goal for Singapore to become a globally competitive knowledge-based economy. In the coming years, Singapore's economy will be powered by knowledge-intensive and high value added manufacturing and manufacturing-related services and by exportable services. In support of this vision, Singapore has set in motion specific plans to transform key sectors to move Singapore up the value chain. While high-growth exportable products and services will drive the KBE, its proper functioning will depend on upgrading domestic-based industries. In addition to building capabilities in existing industries, the success of the KBE will require entrepreneurship and research to create new products, services, markets, and opportunities. Furthermore, investment in skills, knowledge, and creativity are necessary to ensure that Singapore's workforce has capabilities appropriate for a KBE.

This chapter examines the changing industrial structure of Singapore and the policy initiatives for the structural change towards the KBE.

CHANGING INDUSTRIAL STRUCTURE AND STRATEGIES

Changing Production and Employment Structures

As a city-state Singapore's pre-industrial economic structure was atypical, dominated by entrepôt trading rather than by agriculture or natural resources.

Since the 1960s, both manufacturing and services have been the pillars of the economic structure. The manufacturing sector's share of GDP began declining in the 1990s, reflecting the process of de-industrialisation. It reached a low of 23.0 percent before the onset of the regional financial crisis in 1997. In 1999 the goods sectors accounted for 35.9 percent of GDP, while the service sector accounted for 67.3 percent (Table 6.1). The manufacturing sector is dominated by electronics, chemicals and petrochemicals, and transport equipment, while the service sector is dominated by trade, finance, business services, and transport and communications. Traditional trade has been declining as a share of the service sector, while financial services and business services are growing rapidly.

Reflecting these changes in production structure, manufacturing's share of employment has been falling since 1980 and the shares of financial and business services have been rising (Table 6.2). The skill level of Singapore's workforce has been increasing. The proportion of administrative, managerial, professional and technical personnel rose from 18.0 percent of

TABLE 6.1
Composition of GDP by Sector, 1970–99
(Percent)

	1970	1980	1990	1995	1997	1999
Goods producing sectors	31.8	39.2	34.7	34.1	34.9	35.9
Manufacturing	19.9	29.1	27.1	24.7	23.0	25.9
Construction	6.7	6.4	5.4	7.5	9.5	8.0
Utilities	2.6	2.2	1.9	1.7	2.1	1.9
Other	2.6	1.6	0.4	0.2	0.2	0.2
Services producing sectors	64.3	62.3	66.3	69.0	67.5	67.3
Wholesale and retail trade	23.6	17.6	15.0	16.7	15.2	15.0
Hotels and restaurants	3.5	4.1	3.9	3.1	2.9	2.7
Transport and communications	10.5	14.0	13.2	12.0	11.3	11.4
Financial services	4.7	8.4	10.9	13.0	12.9	14.2
Business services	8.9	8.9	12.2	13.4	14.2	12.8
Other	13.1	9.4	11.1	10.7	11.0	11.1
Owner-occupied dwellings	2.8	2.4	4.2	3.5	3.3	3.6
Add: taxes and duties on imports	3.0	1.7	0.9	0.6	0.5	0.6
Less: imputed bank service charges	1.9	5.6	6.1	7.1	6.2	7.4
Total	100.0	100.0	100.0	100.0	100.0	100.0

Source: *Economic Survey of Singapore*, 1999.

TABLE 6.2
Composition of Employment by Industry, 1980–99
(Percent)

	1980	1985	1990	1995	1997	1999
Manufacturing	30.1	25.4	29.1	24.2	22.6	21.0
Construction	6.6	8.9	7.9	6.7	6.9	6.9
Commerce	21.3	23.5	22.0	20.4	21.8	21.2
Transport, storage and communications	11.2	10.1	9.5	10.7	11.5	10.8
Finance, insurance, real estate, and business services	7.8	8.7	10.9	14.6	14.9	16.0
Community, social, and personal services	0.0	0.0	0.0	22.1	21.3	23.1
Other services	23.1	23.1	20.6	1.2	1.0	1.0
Total	100.0	100.0	100.0	100.0	100.0	100.0

Source: *Singapore Yearbook of Statistics,* various years.

the workforce in 1980 to 40.3 percent by 1999 and the share of production workers and labourers declined from 46.3 percent to 29.1 percent over the same period (Table 6.3).

Competitiveness Factors

The *Global Competitiveness Report* of the Geneva-based World Economic Forum (WEF) and the *World Competitiveness Yearbook* of the Lausanne-based International Institute of Management Development (IMD) have consistently ranked Singapore as the world's most competitive or second most competitive economy in recent years (Tables 6.4 and 6.5).

Of the factor resources that gave Singapore its competitive advantages, only one, strategic location at the crossroads of international shipping and in a time zone straddling Europe and the Pacific, is an inherited factor. All the others are created factors. The initial competitive advantage conferred by Singapore's geographical location and natural harbour were buttressed by the free trade policy pursued by the colonial government and continued after political independence and by investment in world-class transportation and telecommunications infrastructure, facilities, and services. Extensive air, sea, and telecommunications networks link Singapore with major cities and ports in the region and around the world. Within only a 3-hour flying time radius are the ASEAN capitals, and in an 8-hour radius are

TABLE 6.3
Composition of Employment by Occupation, 1980–99
(Percent)

	1980	1985	1990	1995	1997	1999
Legislative, administrative, managerial	6.3	7.6	8.6	12.8	12.6	12.4
Professional	0.0	4.5	4.2	7.3	9.0	9.9
Technical and associate professional	11.7	9.9	11.5	15.8	17.5	18.0
Clerical	13.8	14.4	13.1	12.9	15.2	14.0
Service, shop, and market sales	14.6	15.4	13.8	12.3	12.5	13.1
Agricultural and fishery	1.6	1.1	0.3	0.1	0.1	0.1
Production, operators, cleaners, labourers	46.3	42.3	44.5	34.6	29.8	29.1
Other	5.8	4.7	4.0	4.2	3.3	3.4
Total	100.0	100.0	100.0	100.0	100.0	100.0

Source: *Singapore Yearbook of Statistics,* various years.

TABLE 6.4
WEF's National Competitiveness Balance Sheet
for Singapore, 1999
(Ranking out of 59 countries surveyed)

Assets	Rank	Liabilities	Rank
Overall	1		
Openness	2		
Average tariff rate	2	Foreign access to capital markets	31
Export position	2		
Government	1		
Tax evasion	1	Government influence	39
Government economic policies	1		
Government subsidies	1		
Composition of government spending	1		
Public sector competence	1		
Administrative regulations	1		
Inflation	1		
Value added tariff rate	2		
Government savings	2		
Tax system	2		
Government bureaucracy	3		
General government surplus	4		
Pension indicator	4		
Payroll tax rates	5		

continued on next page

TABLE 6.4 – cont'd

Assets	Rank	Liabilities	Rank
Finance	2		
Gross domestic savings	1	Share of domestic credit to private sector	31
Financial sector risk rating	3	Access to credit	32
Gross domestic investment	4	Bond markets	34
Banking sector assets	4	Domestic banks	39
		Change in gross domestic investment	43
		Entry into banking industry	52
Infrastructure	7		
Overall infrastructure	1	Private investment in infrastructure	38
Infrastructure investment	1		
Roads, air transport, ports	1		
Telephones and fax machines	4		
Cellular telephones	4		
Technology	2		
Math and science education	1	Internet for customer service	31
Technology licensing	1	Internet and supplier relations	45
Technology transfer	2		
Labour	1		
Unemployment insurance	1	Primary education enrolment	30
Labour-employer relations	1	Secondary education enrolment	40
Strikes	2		
Labour regulations	2		
Hiring and firing practices	2		
Labour tax wedge	2		
Work days lost to labour disputes	2		
Social welfare system	2		
Minimum wage regulations	3		
Unemployment rate	3		
Institutions	2		
Trust in politicians' honesty	1	Compensation for interference	30
Organised crime	1	Litigation against government	47
Additional payments	2	Litigation costs	48
Effectiveness of police force	2		
Forced contributions	3		
Irregular payments	3		
Institutional stability	3		
Government favourites	4		
Compliance	4		

Source: World Economic Forum (WEF), *Global Competitiveness Report, 1999.*

TABLE 6.5
IMD's National Competitiveness Balance Sheet for Singapore, 2000
(Ranking out of 47 countries surveyed)

Strengths	Rank	Weaknesses	Rank
Overall	2		
Domestic economy	8		
Gross domestic savings	1	Government final consumption	42
Companies and government	1	Gross domestic investment real growth	42
Restructuring of the economy	1	Cost of living comparisons	31
Real growth in private consumption	7	Gross domestic savings real growth	31
Customer sophistication	15	Total gross domestic investment	30
Internationalisation	2		
Current account balance %	1	Growth in exports of commercial services	46
Exports of goods %	1	Growth in direct investment stocks abroad	38
Trade to GDP ratio	1	Growth in direct investment stocks inward	35
Tourism receipts	1	Portfolio investments liabilities	26
Exports of commercial services	2	Direct investment flows abroad	19
Government	1		
Government economic policies	1	Employee's social security contribution rate	45
General government expenditure	1	Central government domestic debt %	41
Unemployment legislation	1	Effective personal income tax rate	31
Bureaucracy	1	Employer's social security contribution rate	30
Collected indirect tax revenue	3	Collected capital and property taxes	27
Finance	10		
Central bank policy	1	Foreign financial institutions	29
Insider trading	3	Access to local capital markets	29
Legal regulation of financial institutions	3	Interest rate spread	24
Venture capital	7	Access to foreign capital markets	13
Country credit rating	16	Value traded on stock markets	9
Infrastructure	13		
Environmental laws	1	Computers in use	39
Urbanisation	1	Computer power	35
Infrastructure maintenance and development	1	GDP and energy consumption	33
Sustainable development	1	Electricity costs for industrial clients	29
Labour regulations	2	Investments in telecommunications	28

continued on next page

TABLE 6.5 – cont'd

Strengths	Rank	Weaknesses	Rank
Management	**15**		
Industrial relations	11	Productivity in services	27
Process management	11	Labour productivity	22
Corporate credibility	21	Competence level	21
Employee training	2	Entrepreneurship	19
Overall productivity growth	7	Creation of firms	15
Science and technology	**9**		
Science and education	1	Securing patents abroad	35
Development and application			
of technology	1	Patents granted to residents	34
Science and technology and youth	2	Total R&D personnel nation-wide	
		per capita	16
Company-university co-operation	3	Total expenditure on R&D	
		per capita	16
Financial resources	3	Business expenditure on R&D	
		per capita	14
People	**5**		
Values of society	1	Total and current public	
		education expenditure	42
Educational system	1	Employment	42
Alcohol and drug abuse	1	Pupil-teacher ratio (secondary	
		education)	41
Economic literacy	1	Pupil teacher ratio (primary	
		education)	39
University education	1	Illiteracy	37

Source: International Institute of Management Development (IMD), *World Competitiveness Yearbook 2000*.

Beijing, Tokyo, Seoul, Taipei, and Hong Kong in the north, Sydney in the south, and New Delhi in the west. Singapore's seaport is the busiest in the world, and its airport carries a growing volume of air cargo and passenger traffic. Singapore is also being developed as an "intelligent island" with the comprehensive development of information technology infrastructure.

The quality of economic management and political governance are also a significant factor in Singapore's global economic competitiveness. Policies pursued since the mid-1960s created a strong macro-economic environment characterised by high savings and investment and low inflation. Savings rates exceeding 45 percent of GNP in recent years reflected the high rates of private compulsory savings under the Central Provident Fund and private voluntary savings, as well as the public sector's budgetary and operating surpluses. The low-inflation environment reflects prudent monetary and fiscal policies, a free trade policy that ensures access to world goods at world prices, and an efficient retail distribution system. Economic openness has contributed to economic efficiency and helped overcome the constraints of a small domestic market and a small resource base. Social equity has been maintained with rapid economic growth, full employment, low incidence of absolute poverty, and upward social mobility. Full employment and the Central Provident Fund provide a social safety net. In addition, subsidised public housing enables 85 percent of the population to enjoy home-ownership. Policy and practice have enabled Singapore to achieve social cohesion despite a multi-racial, multi-cultural and multi-religious population. Political stability and the probity and competence of the political leadership and bureaucracy are well known. Good governance helped Singapore escape the ravages of the 1997–98 regional financial crisis.

Effective harnessing of foreign direct investment (FDI) has been another important factor in Singapore's economic competitiveness. Up to 1990, Singapore was the largest recipient of FDI among Asian developing economies. FDI played a particularly crucial role in Singapore's pursuit of export manufacturing and the development of its financial centre. By adopting a liberal FDI policy regime and providing effective trading and financial infrastructure, Singapore enjoyed a first-mover advantage as a production base for MNCs looking for a location to produce the labour-intensive parts of the value chain. As labour costs in Singapore rose and the capacity for labour-intensive manufacturing in neighbouring countries improved, Singapore attracted FDI for higher value-added manufacturing and as regional headquarters for MNCs. International banks and other financial institutions were also crucial in the development of the Singapore financial centre. Singapore's success in attracting FDI despite its lack of natural resources and small domestic market may be attributed to the holistic approach — providing both an efficient business and comfortable living environment and attractive investment incentives.

Singapore has worked to develop the quality of its human resources to maintain economic competitiveness. To provide an industrial workforce Singapore revamped the educational system in the 1960s to emphasise technical and vocational education and established specialised industrial training institutes to turn out qualified technicians and craftsmen. The Skills Development Fund was established in the 1970s to support training to upgrade workers' skills using levies on employers. Tertiary education expanded rapidly to provide professionals and managers in science, engineering, business, and computing. To augment the small domestic labour pool, in recent years Singapore has been actively recruiting foreign talent for both the public and private sectors. English is the language of instruction in schools and universities as well as the language of government and business, facilitating the operations of foreign MNCs in Singapore and linking Singapore effectively with the global economy.

From Entrepôt to Manufacturing

In colonial times, Singapore's economic pillars were entrepôt trade and the British military base. By the late 1950s, though, Singapore's prospects as the regional entrepôt were uncertain because neighbouring countries had developed competing ports and begun trading directly. Moreover, in the late 1960s Britain announced the phased closure of the military base. After self-rule in 1959 and more particularly after political independence in August 1965, the Singapore government began a systematic effort to restructure and diversify the economy through industrialisation.

The industrialisation strategy was based on:

- strong government policy intervention, initially to jump-start industrialisation and increasingly to encourage specific types of investments and activities;
- continuing reliance on a free-trade regime and on FDI, particularly from U.S., EU, and Japanese MNCs, to spearhead export manufacturing, against the conventional models of industrialisation;
- investments in human capital and infrastructure to ease supply constraints and improve productivity;
- maintenance of a stable macro-economic environment and stable industrial relations; and
- lowering the burden of taxation for businesses through fiscal incentives.

Singapore faced several drawbacks as it tried to jump-start industrialisation. The small economy (581 sq km land area, 1.6 million population, and S$2 billion GDP) and the lack of natural resources precluded industries with scale economies and those based on local natural resources. Moreover high prevailing wages rates from entrepôt and military base activities were above levels for competitiveness in labour-intensive industries. Singapore had certain favourable conditions as well, including its strategic geographical location and excellent natural harbour and its well-developed transportation, communication, and commercial and financial infrastructure.

In addition, as a trading economy Singapore already had a sizeable literate and skilled labour force, trading and financial expertise, and capital resources, making the transition to an industrial economy easier than from an agrarian economy.

Singapore's initial import-substitution strategy of 1960–65 was premised on a Malaysian common market, but it shifted to export manufacturing spearheaded by foreign direct investment (FDI) when it seceded from the Malaysian Federation and became politically independent two years later. From 1967 to 1969 Singapore undertook to restructure institutions, expand tax incentives, create industrial estates, pass labour legislation to improve industrial relations, and restructure the education system to emphasise technical education and industrial training. The inflow of FDI surged between 1968 and 1973 and rapid industrial and GDP growth ensued. The manufacturing sector rose from 15 percent of GDP in 1965 to 28 percent by 1980. Labour-intensive industries such as textiles and garments, electronic components assembly, and ship repairing expanded rapidly and contributed to full employment by the early 1970s. As labour became scarcer and capital became more abundant, more capital-intensive processes and product lines emerged. As the stock of human capital grew, Singapore developed an advantage as a production base for human capital-intensive parts of the value chain.

By the 1970s Singapore had three major clusters of industry, all dependent on imported inputs and export markets. One industry cluster centred on petroleum refining using crude oil imported from the Middle East. Singapore's competitive advantage came from the large bunkering needs of its seaport and airport, its established entrepôt trade in petroleum, and its proximity to Asia-Pacific markets. When new refineries in the Middle East and in neighbouring countries came on-stream in the 1980s, Singapore upgraded its refinery operations and also developed a petrochemical complex. A second industry cluster was in shipbuilding and ship repair. This originated with the conversion of the British naval dockyards to commercial use. This and the legacy of engineering skills from the British naval base and the role of Singapore as a major port-of-call provided the initial locational conditions. A boom in petroleum exploration in Southeast Asian waters in the 1970s led to the growth of rig construction as well. Shipbuilding and ship repairing activities declined with waterfront shortages and rising labour costs in Singapore in the 1980s, resulting in major relocation of activities to elsewhere in the region.

The third industry cluster centred on electronics. In the 1960s American electronics MNCs were seeking offshore assembly and export platforms in East Asia, followed soon by European and Japanese MNCs. Singapore began courting them, offering low-cost, easily trainable young female labour, well-developed physical infrastructure, and generous investment incentives. Since then, the Singapore electronics industry has experienced dynamic growth as well as continual upgrading, restructuring from labour-intensive processes and products to production of computers and computer peripherals and components and further into semiconductors in response to changing costs and technologies. From the 1980s a large local and supporting industry supplying computer components and parts, facilitated by a growing pool of engineering expertise from the polytechnics and universities, emerged to service the foreign multinationals. Many MNCs established international purchasing offices to source their worldwide products and parts and components requirements from Singapore and the region. Singapore's well-developed logistics infrastructure provided efficient, timely, and low-cost delivery.

The tripartite National Wages Council, with representatives from the government, employers, and trade unions, was established to provide for orderly wage increases with the emergence of full employment in the early 1970s. Inflow of foreign labour was also liberalised. Worsening labour shortages and ensuing rising costs eroded Singapore's competitive advantage as a low-wage manufacturing base and necessitated a shift in industrial structure towards high-tech manufacturing and high value added services. Industrial restructuring policies were launched in the late 1970s, with parallel policies for accelerated wage increases and for automation, mechanisation, and computerisation. The restructuring programme was disrupted by the 1985–86 recession.

New Directions and Strategies for the 1990s

In 1985 the government convened the Economic Committee to review the progress of the economy and to identify new directions for future growth. The 1986 Economic Committee Report (ECR) focused on short-term measures to lead the economy out of the recession. For the longer term, the Economic Committee argued that Singapore needed to find a new niche because its niche as an offshore production centre for the developed world would have eroded by the 1990s. First, Singapore had to move beyond being a production base to being an international business centre and attract companies to establish operational headquarters to do product development, manage treasury activities, and provide administrative, technical, and management services. Second, Singapore had to become an exporter of services, not just Singapore-based activities such as tourism or banking, but also offshore-based activities. To accomplish this transition the ECR proposed strategies to ensure good fundamentals (good government, efficient infrastructure, education and training, free enterprise, flexibility), to maintain a high savings rate, to create a conducive business environment (competitive costs, low taxes, friendly regulations, good work attitudes), to depend on the private sector, to promote offshore activities, and to nurture both foreign MNCs and local companies.

Once recovery from the 1985–86 recession was assured, the Singapore government began to plan for the longer term. The Strategic Economic Plan (SEP) drawn up by the Economic Planning Committee and issued in 1991 provided an overview of the economic landscape over the next two to three decades. The SEP called for promoting and developing Singapore as a "total business centre" and developing high-tech and high value added manufacturing and services as twin engines of growth. It made two strategic proposals: evolving highly developed manufacturing and service clusters and upgrading the low productivity domestic sector. The cluster proposal adopted Michael Porter's framework for competitiveness — that business enterprises need access to various suppliers, qualified manpower, competency centres in relevant technologies, and efficient infrastructure and other services.

The key thrusts of the SEP were to develop an international orientation, to maintain international competitiveness, to develop manufacturing and service clusters, to spearhead economic redevelopment, to create a climate conducive to innovation, to enhance human resources, to promote national teamwork, and to reduce vulnerability. Strategies were grouped under the Manufacturing 2000 and International Business Hub 2000 Programmes. The Economic Development Board (EDB) was the lead agency to implement these programmes.

The Manufacturing 2000 Programme (M2000) affirmed the continuing role of manufacturing as a mainstay of the economy. The strategic goal was to sustain manufacturing at 25 percent of GDP and at 20 percent of national employment. These targets were only slightly below the sector's shares in the first half of 1990s. Policymakers wanted to avoid the kind of rapid industrial hollowing-out that was occurring in Hong Kong as industries relocated in droves across the border to Guangzhou. The model for Singapore's continued role as a manufacturing base was value-chain analysis, which saw modern manufacturing and services as integrated and complementary activities. In this view, industrial capability is an essential component of any advanced economy, providing the foundation for building advanced capabilities in science and technology, logistics, and operations management.

The key element of M2000 was the development of industry clusters and the programme had specific action plans for major sectors including electronics. The strategy was to upgrade capabilities across the value chain in each industry cluster, including product and process development, production, engineering, and strategic marketing. Based on detailed analysis of the value chain for various industries, the plan identified gaps in existing industry clusters and formulated initiatives and strategies to close them.

The plan for developing industrial clusters had two key components, the Cluster Development Fund and the Co-Investment Programme. The S$1 billion Cluster Development Fund was to promote strategic projects in manufacturing and services through equity participation in joint ventures and co-investment projects. The Co-Investment Programme involved government equity participation in joint ventures in three areas: new capabilities and supporting industries to fill critical gaps in industry clusters; developing local enterprises; and strategic investments in local companies and MNCs going regional. Investment partnerships with foreign MNCs recognise that traditional tax incentives offered by government may be inadequate in capital- and technology-intensive projects, and that government equity participation may be necessary to share in the capital requirements and risks. An example of this type of development is the semiconductor wafer fabrication industry, where EDB co-invested in SemiTech together with Texas Instruments, Hewlett Packard, and Canon.

The International Business Hub 2000 Programme focused on strategies to develop Singapore into a hub for business and finance, logistics and distribution, and communications and information. The basis for the hub strategy was the notion that key economic activities such as finance, shipping, air transport, telecommunications, and information are becoming concentrated in a few strategic nodes around the world. Each node acts as a hub providing services to the extended hinterland and linking it with the rest of the world.

Singapore seeks to secure the first-mover advantage as the business hub in the Asia-Pacific. Its competitive advantage as a regional trading, financial, transport, and telecommunications centre arises from its strategic location and its developed physical infrastructure and human resources, as well as its minimal restrictions on the movement of goods, services, and factors of production. Singapore has been providing trading, transhipment, storage, breaking of bulk, grading and processing, and financing since the nineteenth century as the entrepôt of Southeast Asia. As the region's economies industrialised, the entrepôt trade shifted from the two-way exchange of the primary products of Southeast Asia for western manufactures to two-way trade in manufactures and intra-industry trade. Because of its advantageous location for time-sensitive shipments Singapore became the hub for distribution and transhipment in the region. It also became a host to over 4,000 multinational corporations, many having divisions that perform regional headquarters functions.

Singapore emerged as a regional financial centre in the early 1970s with the establishment of the Asian Dollar Market collecting offshore funds for offshore lending. It ranks third after Tokyo and Hong Kong as an Asian financial centre. The assets of the Asian Currency Unit (ACU) peaked at US$557.2 billion in 1997, but shrank in 1998–99 as a result of the regional financial crisis. Over the years, the strategy has been to establish Singapore as a risk management centre with active foreign exchange trading, money market operations, and trading in capital market instruments, equities, and futures. Many foreign financial institutions have located in Singapore, including over 200 commercial and merchant banks, to enjoy its time zone advantage (straddling Asia and Europe), efficient transport and telecommunications facilities, a well-established financial regulatory framework, ready availability of professional manpower, attractive investment incentives, and political, economic, and financial stability.

TOWARDS A KNOWLEDGE-BASED ECONOMY IN THE 21ST CENTURY

The 1997–98 regional financial crisis heightened Singapore's awareness that it had lost competitiveness vis-à-vis the other economies in the region where currencies had devalued sharply. Cost-cutting measures in existing industries would only keep Singapore competitive in the short-term. Upgrading was hampered by Singapore's lack of the skills, technology base, and other capabilities of developed economies. Singapore must develop these capabilities in order to move up the value chain. In an increasingly challenging global environment characterised by intensified competition and rapid technological change, and facing severe domestic labour and resource constraints, Singapore must tap new sources of economic growth to maintain its competitive edge.

The current challenge facing Singapore is to transform into a knowledge-based economy. To become a KBE, Singapore will need human and intellectual capital to create, absorb, process, and apply knowledge, a strong technological capability, an entrepreneurial culture, an open cosmopolitan society attractive to global talent, and connections to other global knowledge nodes. To realise this vision requires a quantum leap in capabilities.

In May 1997, before the financial crisis took hold in the region, the Singapore government established the Committee on Singapore's Competitiveness (CSC) to assess Singapore's economic competitiveness over the next 10 years and to recommend strategies and policies. Together, the main committee, five industry subcommittees (manufacturing, finance and banking, hub services, domestic businesses, manpower and pro-ductivity), and a panel of resource persons comprising over 100 individuals representing the public, private, and academic sectors. As with the 1986 Economic Committee Report, the Competitiveness Report released in November 1998 contained both short-term measures aimed at recovery from the 1998 recession and measures intended to transform Singapore into an advanced and globally competitive knowledge-based economy. The Competitiveness Report recommended specific plans for key sectors, including manufacturing, finance, and telecommunications, to move Singapore up the value chain.

The eight recommended underlying strategies were:

- to maintain manufacturing and services as twin engines of growth;
- to strengthen the external wing to complement the domestic economy as a source of growth;
- to build world-class companies with core competencies to compete in the global economy;
- to nurture and strengthen local enterprises;
- to develop human and intellectual capital with cost-competitive and outstanding capabilities;
- to leverage on science, technology, and innovation as competitive tools;
- to optimise resource management by promoting alternative supply and efficient usage; and
- to use government as facilitator of the private sector by providing sound economic policies and regulatory environment for the conduct of business.

The major initiatives arising from the Competitiveness Report's recom-mendations are discussed below.

Manufacturing and Services as Twin Engines

Singapore has stressed maintaining manufacturing and services as twin engines of growth since the late 1980s. This strategy recognises the strong linkage between the two sectors and Singapore's need for a broad economic base to reduce its vulnerability. Also, Singapore needs to balance the global orientation of export manufacturing with the regional orientation of exportable services. Singapore's exportable services were more adversely affected by the 1997–98 regional financial crisis than its exports of manufactures because service exports were more dependent on regional demand.

In 1999 manufacturing investment commitments in Singapore show the following sectoral distribution: electronics, 42 percent in electronics, 33 percent in chemicals, 17 percent in engineering, 4 percent; general industries, and 4 percent life sciences. Services Investment commitments were distributed broadly, with 36 percent in infocomms (information and telecommunications) and media, 34 percent in headquarters services, 20 percent in logistics and supply chain management, and 10 percent in education and healthcare.

Manufacturing makes a large contribution to Singapore's GDP, employment, and foreign exchange earnings, as well as to technological progress, productivity improvement, and entrepreneurship. But Singapore can no longer remain a production base because of the growing problem of maintaining cost competitiveness. It seeks to become a location where foreign MNCs and local enterprises produce high value added products and to provide manufacturing-related and headquarters services to the region. It also seeks to move along the value chain into R&D, design, logistics, marketing, and sales.

Strategies recommended by the Competitiveness Report to develop the manufacturing sector included:

- integrating Singapore into the global economy to leverage on inter-national talent, knowledge, and technology;
- positioning Singapore as the premier regional hub to attract foreign MNCs and local enterprises to use Singapore as a production base for high value added products and to provide manufacturing-related services for their subsidiaries in the region;
- developing a strong external wing to overcome Singapore's small size and limited resources and distributing resource-intensive activities to the region;
- maintaining cost competitiveness by ensuring productivity growth;

- providing an entrepreneurial environment that tolerates business failures and allows freedom for the generation of ideas;
- embracing innovation to generate new businesses and growth;
- grooming world-class local and foreign companies in niche areas;
- having a balanced mix of manufacturing activities to provide economic resilience;
- building strong manufacturing capabilities in existing niche areas such as electronics and chemicals and emerging areas; and
- developing strong competencies in other parts of the manufacturing value chain, including R&D, design, logistics, marketing and sales.

For the services sector, the Competitiveness Report envisions Singapore becoming the premier Asian service hub by expanding existing financial services, international trading, transport and logistics, exhibition management, and tourism services as well as by developing new high-growth hub services such as healthcare, education, media, information and communications technology services, e-commerce and direct marketing. The Report recommended the following strategies:

- becoming the centre in Asia for knowledge- and skill-intensive and other high value added services in which Singapore has core competency;
- providing a business environment to attract top global service companies;
- having an externally oriented services sector focused on the international market;
- having a pool of local services companies with established niches in overseas markets;
- tapping the world market to attract creative manpower and talent;
- using ICT to enhance competency and overcome Singapore's physical and manpower limitations.

Following on the recommendations of the Competitiveness Report, the EDB launched Industry 21 (I21), a 10-year plan to develop Singapore into a vibrant and robust global hub of knowledge-driven industries in manufacturing and traded services with emphasis on technology, innovation, and capabilities. I21 encourages MNCs to locate more of their key knowledge-intensive activities in Singapore and encourages local companies to embrace more knowledge-intensive activities and become world-class players. I21 proposes five broad strategies:

- diversifying among and within industry clusters for a balanced and robust mix of industries and markets;
- building up world-class capabilities and global coverage;

- promoting innovation;
- developing local talent and attracting foreign talent; and
- creating a business-friendly environment and world-class infrastructure.

I21 identified electronics, chemicals, engineering, life sciences, education and healthcare, headquarters, communications and media, and logistics as industry clusters to be nurtured:

- To create a world-class electronics hub in Singapore by attracting global leaders with the latest product-design, manufacturing, and applications in semiconductors, infocomms products, data storage, and key modules and global leaders in the management of new products, applications, and markets.
- To nurture the chemicals industry cluster, I21 aims to make Singapore a world-class petroleum and petrochemicals hub based at a 3,200 hectare site located on Jurong Island with S$40 billion of capital investment targeted by 2010. Ten chemical plants came on-stream in 1999. The IT master plan for Jurong Island adds an e-business dimension to the chemicals cluster.
- I21 envisions a life science cluster with world-class capabilities in pharmaceuticals, medical devices, biotechnology, agri-biotech products, and food intermediates. Singapore is already a world-class manufacturing hub for pharmaceutical bulk activities. With several new projects in Tuas Pharma Park, biotechnology manufacturing output will double by 2005. The goal is to have 15 world-class companies and a regional centre for clinical trials and drug development by 2010. The EDB will invest in R&D and manpower development and nurture start-up companies through co-investment and venture capital in three dedicated investment funds, Singapore Bio-Innovations, Pharmbio Growth Fund, and Life Sciences Investments. More activities are also seen in R&D, product and process development, clinical trials, and manufacturing.
- Engineering has always supported the electronics and chemicals clusters. It now supports new fields such as optics, semiconductors, and pharmaceuticals and it promotes new business models to embrace e-capability. By nurturing engineering, I21 aims to generate growth potential for existing industry clusters and to improve the possibilities for creating new industries by developing multi-disciplinary capabilities and state-of-the-art technologies. Singapore will build on strengths in precision, process, and transport engineering and create synergy among disciplines. The target is to nurture five new industries and attract 20 global engineering centres and 50 manufacturing headquarters.

- To position Singapore as a world-class education and healthcare hub, I21's emphasis is on attracting world-class universities, executive learning centres, corporate training centres, and distance learning providers. To date, MIT, INSEAD, Wharton, Chicago Graduate School of Business, Georgia Tech, and Johns Hopkins have set up teaching and research facilities in Singapore. For the healthcare service cluster the plan envisions Singapore as the place for timely, reliable clinical trials and analysis. The strong cluster of education and healthcare companies will also support the life sciences industry.
- I21's goal for the infocomms and media cluster is to build Singapore into a global hub in Asia for the digital economy offering a wide range of initiatives and developments in telecommunications, IT, media, e-commerce, and the Internet. The telecommunications sector has been liberalised and more competition introduced into the local broadcast and print media industries. Parallel with efforts to strengthen the telecommunications infrastructure is the active promotion of software development, Internet builders, application service providers, portals, and intermediaries.
- I21 aims to build on Singapore's reputation as the premier location for MNCs to attract them to base regional and business headquarters. Singapore offers political and social stability and excellent infrastructure to allow MNCs to manage regional or international operations effectively, spearhead new developments, and undertake high value added activities. From 1997 to 1999, 75 companies received the HQ incentive, creating high-value jobs and transferring technology, management, and marketing expertise.
- By nurturing a logistics and supply-chain management cluster, I21's vision is to develop Singapore into a leading integrated logistics hub for the Asia-Pacific region. The strategy is to build up supply chain capabilities by getting third-party logistics players, cargo airlines, value-added distributors, and manufacturers to locate their supply chain centres for Asia in Singapore. These companies provide world-class logistics services, and enhance manufacturers' global supply chains. A 23-hectare Free Trade Zone Logistics Park has been established at Changi Airport and an 80-hectare Chemical Logistics Hub on Jurong Island.

In addition to the industry cluster programme, five other programmes under I21 aim to support the manufacturing and service sectors:

- The World Class Companies/Promising Local Enterprises Programme aims to build at least 50 local knowledge-based enterprises that offer world-class products, services or capabilities by 2010. EDB works closely with potential companies on financial resources for mergers and acquisitions, resource support, image building, technology acquisition, strategic alliances, and business partnerships. This programme complements the EDB's Promising Local Enterprises programme, which aims to develop at least 100 local enterprises, each with an annual turnover of $100 million, by year 2005.

- The International Business Programme aims to build an external economy that enhances and is strongly linked to Singapore's domestic growth. EDB supports and nurtures local companies with strong overseas growth plans through schemes to develop their manpower and market capabilities.
- The Innovation Programme aims pro-actively to identify and promote innovation projects for each industry cluster, to introduce innovation systems and practices in companies, to expand the innovation infra-structure, and to intensify innovation awareness. Through innovation capability development programmes, innovation will be undertaken at the national level through a concerted multi-agency effort.
- The Resource Development Programme encompasses the planning, development, and optimisation of the use of Singapore's manpower, land, utilities and housing resources to support industrial growth. The International Manpower Programme supports companies in their international manpower needs. Industrial land policies support the dynamic and changing needs of the economy.
- The Co-investment Programme aims to strengthen partnerships between foreign MNCs and promising local enterprises in key industry clusters, through equity co-investment within and beyond Singapore. The EDB manages the Cluster Development Fund and the Venture Capital Fund (VCF), aimed at developing new capabilities, technology projects, and innovative start-ups to fill critical gaps in the industry clusters. Since 1985 the EDB has engaged in direct venture capital (VC) investment activities to grow the VC industry and support industry cluster development and regionalisation and to promote innovation and entrepreneurship. Venture capital funds had grown to S$10.2 billion by 2000. The VCF is also leveraging on partnership with global VC funds and government agencies to invest in more young companies in Singapore and abroad.

Paralleling the EDB's work, the Trade Development Board (TDB) is promoting and marketing Singapore's total trade capabilities through its trade regulation, facilitation, and promotion functions. An open global trading environment is critical for ensuring Singapore's prosperity. As regulator, TDB monitors foreign trade policies and their impact on Singapore's trade, recommends trade policy responses, and participates in international trade negotiations. As facilitator, TDB helps Singapore leverage its advantage in information technology (IT) and position it as a centre for e-business. It seeks to build on Singapore's IT infrastructure to facilitate trade transactions and further business efficiency through IT applications. As trade promoter, TDB leads Singapore's participation in international fairs and exhibitions and sectoral missions to targeted overseas markets. As part of the vision of Singapore as an e-commerce hub, TDB is attracting companies to set up regional e-commerce trading centres in Singapore, with a target of 25 companies over the next five years under the Approved Cyber Traders scheme. This scheme is similar to those for international traders and oil traders, that has attracted over 130 companies to do their international trading activities from Singapore.

Outward Investment and Regionalisation

Singapore began the drive to create an external wing in 1993, pushed by the increasing constraints of space and labour at home and pulled by the burgeoning business opportunities in the booming East Asian region. Besides allowing Singapore's increasingly abundant capital to earn higher rates of return, outward investments would bring spillover benefits from increased trade flows through Singapore, consolidation of Singapore's headquarters function, development of domestic technology, know-how, and R&D, and tapping of foreign expertise.

The government believes its role is to facilitate regionalisation by providing basic infrastructure. It makes bilateral agreements with countries that interest Singapore's private sector, encourages government-linked companies (GLCs) to partner with private-sector companies in larger scale projects, disburses various regionalisation financial schemes to assist companies venturing abroad, and establishes bilateral business councils as a means of networking and exchanging business information. The EDB facilitates the efforts of Singapore companies to diversify in the region through tax incentives and grants, risk-sharing partnerships, and other broad-based support mechanisms, including the Overseas Enterprise Incentive and the INTECH scheme, which trains Singapore managers for overseas postings.

Singapore government initiatives extend to promoting ASEAN growth triangles and overseas industrial parks. The ASEAN southern growth triangle links the infrastructure, capital, and expertise of Singapore with the natural and labour resources of Johor (in Malaysia) and Riau (in Indonesia). Singapore government agencies also play an active role in establishing overseas industrial parks, which offer one-stop services facilitating investor approvals, licences, employment, and other requirements for start up operations. By mid-1999, investment commitments in eight overseas industrial parks reached S$14 billion with potential to create more than 114,000 jobs. The Batamindo Industrial Park and Bintan Industrial Estate in Indonesia have created 74,000 direct jobs in production, supervision and management as of 1998. The International Tech Park in Bangalore, India was launched in 1994, commenced operations in the second half of 1998, and 28 investors had started operations by the end of 1999. The Vietnam Singapore Technical Training Centre set up in August 1997 supports the Vietnam Singapore Industrial Park and human resource training needs in Vietnam.

With the regional initiatives, factor income from abroad increased. The contribution of foreign operations to value added in the Singapore economy averaged 11–12 percent a year, and 20 percent of the total sales of overseas manufacturing affiliates was shipped back to Singapore. However, the regional financial crisis exposed the downside of this strategy. Singapore businesses that had expanded into the region were badly affected by the sharp contraction of demand in host markets, currency volatility, and non-performing loans, resulting in some companies having to trim or even shut down their regional operations.

Nevertheless, outward investment remains crucial for Singapore's continued development. The indigenous private sector is still weak and it takes time to develop a critical mass of world-class Singaporean companies with a global reach. Regionalisation will have to remain a strategic pillar, and Singapore firms need to position themselves to take advantage of opportunities when the regional economies recover. Both GLCs and private companies that have the resource capacity are encouraged to continue investing in the region's economies, especially because these economies have liberalised their FDI policies, opening up formerly closed sectors and allowing for mergers and acquisitions to re-capitalise their financial and corporate sectors. But to reduce the vulnerability of Singaporean corporations to future adverse developments in the region, the Competitiveness Report also recommended a broader global dimension to the external wing strategy as well.

Strategies to develop the external wing recommended in the Competitiveness Report included:

- generating linkages between overseas affiliates and the home economy through trade flows through Singapore;
- consolidating Singapore's headquarters, high-tech operation and R&D functions;
- pooling the resources of Singapore companies venturing overseas, particularly by forming clusters and tie-ups to maximise collective leverage;
- promoting strategic flagship projects;
- promoting tripartite co-operation, enhancing Singapore's role as a partner for foreign investors into the region;
- developing globally- and regionally-minded managers and investors; and
- tapping foreign talent to overcome domestic manpower constraints.

Domestic Enterprises

Unlike the other Asian Newly Industrialised Economies (NIEs), Singapore's industrial strategy neglected domestic enterprises, until recently. From the mid-1960s, Singapore focused on foreign MNCs to spearhead export manufacturing and exportable services. It did not abandon its long-standing free trade policy to protect domestic manufacturing and nurture domestic entrepreneurs. As a result, after more than three decades of industrialisation, Singapore's indigenous entrepreneurs have only a marginal role in export manufacturing and have limited capacity to venture abroad.

Since the mid-1980s, the EDB has been promoting SMEs in supporting industries and linking them with foreign MNCs to facilitate technology transfer and market networking, particularly in the electronics industry. Earlier on, there was a dearth of local industrial entrepreneurs to reliably supply quality parts and components to foreign MNCs. Industrial and FDI policies had no local-content requirements to pressure foreign MNCs to source locally. By the 1990s, a sizeable local supporting industry emerged, with local contract manufacturers producing parts and components to supply foreign MNCs. Massive government investment to raise the stock of human capital, particularly in engineering, business management, and information technology, created a pool of technically savvy entrepreneurs. In addition, the EDB's Local Industry Upgrading Programme (LIUP) gave more capital subsidies to raise a pool of local entrepreneurs. Many top-

and middle-level managers once employed by Singapore-based MNCs eventually established their own businesses and became subcontractors. Foreign MNCs were encouraged to source components and parts locally, based on their trust in these former employees.

Except for a handful of large GLCs, the bulk of domestic enterprises are small- or medium-sized. SMEs comprise over 90 percent of business establishments, employ half the workforce, and contribute a third of value added. But productivity of SMEs is only about half that of non-SME establishments. The poor productivity performance is due to several structural weaknesses — weak entrepreneurial culture, insufficient management know-how and professionalism, shortage of professional and technical manpower, insufficient use of technology, outmoded, unproductive methods of operation, limited ability to tap economies of scale, and small domestic market. However, Singapore has come to realise that building local enterprises is important for its sustained development and economic depth and resilience.

As noted earlier, the EDB aims to build at least 50 local world-class, knowledge-based enterprises in product, service or capability by 2010, to serve MNC clients or to create their own niche markets. These business entities will be professionally managed and they will have excellent process and customer service management, capabilities to create new knowledge technology to develop high value added products and services, and the ability to compete globally. To develop the type of world-class, knowledge-based enterprises targeted under the I21 World Class Companies Programme, the Competitiveness Report recommended leveraging off the capabilities of existing GLCs. This would help local enterprises to overcome inadequacies in skilled manpower, R&D capability, capital and financing, and market networks for access to regional markets. These companies will complement those from the EDB's Promising Local Enterprises (PLE) programme which aims to develop at least 100 local enterprises, each with an annual turnover of $100 million, by the year 2005 through its co-investment programme.

The 1988 SME Master Plan marked the first co-ordinated national effort to upgrade SMEs and promote entrepreneurship. Its aims were to nurture a business environment that promotes entrepreneurship and innovation; to increase market efficiency by encouraging information exchange and provision of information about new methods and opportunities; to promote best practices in business through easy access to consultancy, technology adoption, and training; and to encourage local enterprises to go international. The SME Master Plan had five underlying thrusts: technology adoption, application and innovation; business planning and finance; human resource management; productivity improvement and training; and international marketing and business collaboration.

A decade after the 1988 SME Master Plan and a plethora of SME-assistance schemes under several government agencies, SMEs remain a problem in Singapore. Local enterprises accounted for more than 60 percent of value added by supporting industries in the manufacturing sector where local SMEs are active in transport engineering, electronic contract manufacturing, and precision engineering. More problematic are the majority of SMEs concentrated in the service sector. They serve domestic consumers in commerce, construction and real estate, and community, personal, and social services, and they operate on a relatively small scale and shielded from international competition, resulting in low productivity.

In the knowledge-based economy, SMEs need to keep pace with the rest of the economy. Firm size is not critical in the KBE; what is needed is the expertise to undertake knowledge-intensive activities, the ability to innovate, and the enterprise to identify and capitalise quickly on commercial opportunities. SMEs need to build up distinctive competencies, exploit and harness technology and knowledge, and establish strategic alliances with customers, suppliers, and competitors. The Competitiveness Report recommended the following strategies to strengthen local enterprises:

- consolidate and pool resources among local enterprises to achieve synergy and competitiveness, such as through linking private-sector companies with GLCs to take advantage of the latter's size, financial resources, core capabilities and experience in venturing abroad;
- improve the supply of engineering and managerial manpower through expanded education and training facilities;
- promote innovation and technology, such as through government provision of funding and facilities and incentives for commercialisation of innovation, acquisition of technology, and technological upgrading;
- build indigenous products and brand names; and
- increase international and regional orientation.

The latest effort to build up the capabilities of Singapore's SMEs is detailed in the SME 21 Report, which appeared in 2000. According to the report, SMEs are needed in the KBE — as a source of entrepreneurship and innovation, as a base of strong supporting industries and strategic partners for foreign SMEs and MNCs, as manufacturers of high value added products and global providers of professional services, and as robust domestic service sectors enhancing the quality of life. The SME21 Report specifies three strategic goals as part of a 10-year strategic plan:

- To nurture innovative high-growth SMEs with the capacity to compete globally on a sustained basis so that a steady stream of Singapore SMEs reaches world-class status. These SMEs will produce innovative products and services, use ICT to add value to new products and services, develop and use brands to increase the knowledge-component of their products, and have superior distribution channels. The target is to treble the number of local SMEs with more than $10 million in sales turnover to 6,000 by 2010.
- To enhance the productivity of SMEs and improve land and labour resource utilisation by restructuring, revitalising, and upgrading SMEs in the domestic service sector, particularly retail trade. The target is by 2010 to double annual labour productivity in the retail sector from $28,000 to $56,000, which is 70 percent of the national productivity level.
- To create a knowledge-based, pro-enterprise environment that inculcates the appropriate mindset for business, encourages entrepreneurship and innovation, and eliminates barriers to organisational growth. A key enabling factor is e-commerce, which will open up vast opportunities and remove the traditional barriers to SME growth. The target is to quadruple the number of local SMEs with e-commerce transactions from 8,000 to 32,000 by 2010.

The SME 21 Report recommends several programmes to achieve these three goals. Broad-based programmes include promoting entrepreneurship; financing growth; facilitating market access; strengthening local talent; accelerating e-commerce; and promoting Singapore as an SME hub. Recommended sector-level programmes include facilitating collaborative partnerships and strategic alliances and upgrading domestic service sectors. Enterprise-level programmes cover developing entrepreneurs and employees, managing for business excellence, harnessing technologies and knowledge for growth, and designing new business models for competitive advantage. The SME 21 plan is being implemented jointly by the government, chambers of commerce, industry associations, and the private sector. A multi-agency SME 21 Implementation Committee led by the Singapore Productivity and Standards Board (PSB) has been formed to oversee the implementation of the recommendations.

Local and Foreign Manpower

Lack of land and natural resources has forced Singapore to focus on human resources as the engine of economic growth. The pool of human talent remained limited up to the 1980s, not only because of Singapore's small population base but also as the legacy from neglect of education during the colonial era and the immediate post-independence years. According to the 1990 population census 61 percent of the non-student population had not completed secondary education and only 14 percent had upper secondary and tertiary education. Near 40 percent of the current workforce is still without secondary education. About 40 percent of these workers are still relatively young, aged 40 or under.

By 1998 the skill profile of the workforce had improved considerably, with 34 percent skilled, 28 percent semi-skilled, and 38 percent unskilled. But more top-end professional, managerial, technical and specialist personnel will be required in the future. Official projections show that over the next 10 to 15 years, 65 percent of jobs will require a post-secondary education (25 percent degrees, 20 percent diplomas, 20 percent post-secondary certifications), 20 percent will require at least a secondary education, and 15 percent of jobs will require only a primary education or below. The EDB is aiming to attract new investments that require at least a post-secondary education for two out of three jobs in manufacturing and three out of four jobs in the exportable services sector. The National Computer Board expects 90 percent of IT jobs in Singapore to require at least a good polytechnic/university qualification. Singapore faces a serious mismatch of skills and structural unemployment unless workers are re-trained and their skills upgraded. On the bright side, the proportion of the workforce comprised of skilled workers has been increasing. Among new workforce entrants, 80 percent have at least post-secondary and diploma qualifications.

For the KBE, the Singapore workforce must be able to meet the changing needs of industry and enterprises and have the know-how to create new products, markets, and wealth. There is need to nurture a workforce with the skills, quality, and mindset to support the demands of the New Economy. As Singapore makes the transition to the KBE, its manpower faces four challenges: to develop expertise, innovation, and entrepreneurial capabilities that will enhance competitiveness and enable Singapore to stay ahead in the rapidly changing economic environment; to support growth industries with the appropriate quality and quantity of manpower resources; to minimise structural unemployment; and to ensure that Singapore workers can be engaged in meaningful jobs in which they realise and develop their capabilities to the fullest and achieve a good quality of life.

The Competitiveness Report recommended a two-pronged manpower strategy consisting of upgrading the domestic workforce and augmenting the domestic labour pool with foreign talents. To upgrade the domestic workforce, Singapore needs to encourage life-long learning for lifetime employment and to continue harmonious industrial relations through closer co-operation among the government, employers, and trade unions. Funds for education and training have grown rapidly in the past two decades. In particular, government expenditures on education tripled and enrolment in polytechnics and universities more than doubled from 1987 to 1997. At the end of the 1990s, 60 percent of the relevant age cohort were receiving polytechnic and university education.

Singapore has been recruiting foreign manpower to augment its limited domestic workforce. Employment of foreign workers has increased rapidly. Foreign manpower accounted for over 20 percent of the workforce with 80,000 employment pass holders and more than 450,000 work-permit holders in 1998. The trend seems to be a growing dependence on low-skilled foreign labour. In making the transition to the KBE Singapore needs to ensure that foreign manpower contributes to upgrading the profile of Singapore's workforce. Dependence on unskilled foreign workers needs to be reduced and their distribution across economic sectors rationalised. Hence, the EDB is spearheading a systematic policy of recruiting foreign talent. This emphasis has met resistance from some Singapore citizens who are concerned over the "crowding out" effect, particularly for better-paying jobs. The government has gone to great lengths to explain that the foreign talent pool will enable Singapore to remain competitive and that a larger economic pie means an absolute gain for all Singaporeans.

The Manpower 21 (M21) Report lays out the blueprint for Singapore's manpower development in the 21st century. It recommends six manpower strategies:

- To identify and enhance the short- and long-term fit between manpower demand and supply through integrated manpower planning. The Report recommends forming a National Manpower Council to oversee national manpower strategies and targets and an enhanced Manpower Information System to provide relevant and timely labour market information.
- To provide lifelong learning for lifelong employability through a comprehensive in-employment education and training framework. The framework includes a National Skills Recognition System to define

and recognise skill competencies; an enhancement of the existing Skills Development Fund and tax incentives for employers and workers; and a network of One-stop Career Centres to provide training and career information and counselling. University education must equip students with problem-solving skills for the modern workplace, invest in high-tech, cutting-edge research, and develop programmes for continuing education and worker training. The onus is on universities to teach students to "learn to learn". They must also be analytical, creative, entrepreneurial, and possess good problem-solving and inter-personal skills. The issue of creativity and innovation in Singapore is being debated publicly, with critics arguing that a dominant government and Asian values are inhibiting factors. The education system and curriculum in both schools and universities are undergoing a major revamp to encourage greater creativity among students.

- To augment the domestic talent pool with immigration. The "Contact Singapore" scheme is being expanded to attract high-end international talent. In 1998 alone, the EDB facilitated the entry of more than 3,500 professionals, technicians, and skilled personnel and 19 recruitment missions abroad involving 38 organisations. Singapore is establishing an Internet site for recruiting international talent, developing programmes to enable talents to work in overseas operations of Singapore companies, and cultivating a wide network of "Friends of Singapore". At the same time, a foreign manpower management system has been established to review the allocation and deployment of low-skilled foreign workers among the economic sectors.

- To transform the work environment. The nature of work, the workplace, and workplace practices need realignment for the KBE. The M21 Report recommends flexible work arrangements and job re-design to keep pace with the nature of knowledge-based work and to increase participation rates of women and older people. It also advocates adopting best practices in human resource management and development and improving safety and health at the workplace.

- To develop a vibrant manpower industry comprising learning providers, manpower management services, and manpower recruitment and deployment services.

- To redefine partnerships to enlist all stakeholders at the national, industry, and community levels in realising the vision and recom-mendations.

Science, Technology, and Innovation

While Singapore has depended heavily on foreign MNCs introducing advanced and sophisticated technology and know-how through the FDI process, it has reached a developmental stage where it must also develop its own science, technology, and innovation capabilities. Serious efforts to develop such capability began in the 1990s. In 1991 a National Technology Plan was launched with strategies for developing technology infrastructure, encouraging private sector R&D activities, as well as formulating a human resource plan to complement the science, technology, and innovation needs. In 1996 the National Science and Technology Plan (NSTP) continued the core strategies of the earlier plan and sought to increase the development of research institutes and centres, gross expenditures on R&D (GERD), the number of research scientists and engineers (RSEs), and the number of patents introduced. The Innovation Programme was launched in 1995 to enhance innovation awareness, introduce new innovation systems and practices in companies, expand innovation infrastructure, and launch a national innovation framework for action.

Despite a decade of such efforts, Singapore's R&D thrusts remain modest in absolute terms, reflecting the economy's small size and strong services orientation. Total R&D expenditure reached S$2.5 billion in 1998. GERD reached 1.8 percent of GDP. Private R&D spending accounted for 62 percent of national GERD, with spending concentrated in the electronics industry followed by engineering, chemicals, and IT and communications. Compared to the private sector's S$1.6 billion spending on R&D, public research institutes and centres spent S$351 million, higher education institutions spent $306 million, and the government sector spent S$300 million. In 1998, 0.66 percent of the labour force or 19,007 workers were engaged in R&D and R&D investment commitments stood at S$890 million with the majority in microelectronics, advanced IC development, semiconductors, multimedia, consumer electronics, PC communications, Internet-based product development, biotechnology, and medical devices. R&D expenditures and manpower in Singapore are small in absolute size and their shares of GDP and total employment are still behind those of South Korea and Taiwan and many advanced industrial countries. On the positive side, Singapore's high-tech domestic exports reached S$66.1 billion in 1999, accounting for 65 percent of non-oil domestic exports. Furthermore, over half of recent student admissions into polytechnics and universities are in science and engineering courses.

The Competitiveness Report made several recommendations on how to improve Singapore's science, technology, and innovation position:

- Focus R&D on areas where Singapore has already demonstrated reasonable capability and that have eventual economic relevance. Possible areas include software development, data storage, and biotechnology.
- Target R&D funding to ensure continual competitive capabilities to industry. Limit government role to providing co-financing and tax incentives and grants. Persuade foreign MNCs to locate some R&D activities in Singapore. Deepen the technological capabilities of local universities in upstream and strategic research.
- Make capabilities developed in universities and research institutes available to the private sector through industry assistance schemes to enable local enterprises upgrade their technological level. Encourage universities and research institutes to set up spin-off companies to commercialise new technologies and innovation, especially through joint ventures with the private sector. Use government grants and tax incentives to promote entrepreneurship and technology acquisitions from abroad.
- Continue to secure technology transfers through linkages with global technology centres while pursuing indigenous technology development. Government to facilitate technology transfer by initiating contacts with overseas technology centres, acting as an information-gathering house, and setting up overseas business and technology incubator centres.
- Enhance R&D manpower through joint collaboration with overseas research programmes; programmes to strengthen the effectiveness of the existing technical workforce, including use of innovation; and a mechanism to attach potential technopreneurs to business development units of MNCs abroad.
- Create an environment conducive to intelligent risk-taking and entrepreneurship, including acceptance of failure as a learning process, to nurture creativity and innovation.

The Technopreneurship 21 (T21) initiative was announced in April 1999 specifically to boost development of technopreneurship in Singapore. It recommended strategies to promote start-ups and harness new products, services, and markets through entrepreneurship and applied research. A Technopreneurship 21 Ministerial Committee supported by a working group from the public and private sectors was established to oversee the effort. The T21 plan's four broad thrusts aim to develop: a pro-enterprise environment, a conducive physical infrastructure, a venture investment infrastructure, and education:

- Specific measures to create an environment favourable to enterprise include adopting a qualified employee stock option scheme to encourage equity ownership; revising bankruptcy laws to promote responsible risk-taking; allowing high-tech start-ups to tender for government projects; relaxing work pass and long-term social visit pass rules to facilitate foreigners starting technopreneurial businesses in Singapore; and allowing technopreneurs to use their residential premises as offices.
- To provide physical infrastructure conducive to entrepreneurial high-tech business, a Science Hub will be developed in the Buona Vista area. The integrated development will encompass industrial, R&D, commercial, social, recreational, and residential uses.
- To build up Singapore's venture investment infrastructure, a US$1 billion Technopreneurship Investment Fund (TIF) has been established. The TIF will co-invest with the private sector to provide seed money for technopreneurial start ups, to draw venture capital into Singapore, and to develop strategic linkages and networks with other top-tier venture capital companies worldwide. The TIF is co-managed by the National Science and Technology Board (NSTB) and the Government of Singapore Investment Corporation Special Investments. To date, it has invested US$237 million in a total of 14 funds. The NSTB also initiated two other venture co-investment programmes (the Business Angel Fund and the Venture Investment Support for Start-Ups) to stimulate early-stage investments in promising start-up companies. Under the Technopreneur Investment Incentive scheme, companies and individuals are allowed tax deductions on losses from selling qualifying shares or liquidating investments in approved start-ups.
- Effective in 2003 the National University of Singapore and Nanyang Technological University will supplement the GCE A-Level examinations with a reasoning test, project work, and extra-curricular activities in determining admissions. This move will reinforce and complement the ongoing reorientation of the education system to ensure that the next generation of university graduates will be able to contribute effectively to the growth of the KBE.

The National Science and Technology Board is building a knowledge infrastructure to facilitate technology development. The 13 research institutes and centres supported by the NSTB have achieved economic impact by developing technologies jointly with industry, by training R&D

manpower, and by transferring know-how to industry. To date, these research institutes and centres have spun off a total of 35 high-tech start-ups.

Singapore is pushing for further development in information technology (IT) both to enable business and to position itself as an IT hub in the Asia-Pacific region. In 1992 the National Computer Board (NCB) released the IT2000 Report which envisioned Singapore as an Intelligent Island, with an advanced National Information Infrastructure (NII) connecting computers in virtually every home, office, school, public library, community club, factory, and workplace, and linking government, business, and people in cyberspace. The major thrusts of IT2000 were intensified development of ICT-related manpower, improved quality of life, improved personal and community communications, and competitive advantage using the NII.

The key vehicle for making Singapore an intelligent island is Singapore ONE, an island-wide broadband infrastructure of high capacity networks and switches for multimedia applications and services, which was launched commercially in June 1999. Users have access to entertainment, news, education, online shopping, and other e-commerce services, video-conferencing, and government transactions, as well as fast Internet. At end-1999, Singapore ONE offered a total of 180 applications, and had 100,000 users. As a city-state with world-class physical infrastructure and adequate financial resources, Singapore has little difficulty in developing nation-wide IT infrastructure. What is problematic is achieving the quantity and quality of IT manpower targets.

The Competitiveness Report recommended that as IT is a key technology and to become an IT hub, Singapore should initially focus on the following areas:

- Communications and media: Singapore's educated, multilingual, multi-cultural background gives it a competitive edge as the content gateway to both the East and the West. To that end, Singapore should attract creative talents from around the world and improve enforcement of intellectual property rights protection. Singapore ONE can be used to jumpstart the local multimedia and broadband industries.
- IT innovation: Singapore should position itself as a test bed where new and innovative products and services are created, customised, and tested before export.
- E-commerce: E-commerce is expected to present tremendous business opportunities and impact on such sectors as logistics, transportation and financial services. The government is already setting up the infrastructure to establish Singapore as an e-commerce hub.

In December 1999, reflecting the global convergence of information technology and communications, the NCB and the Telecommunications Authority of Singapore (TAS) were merged to form the Infocomm Development Authority of Singapore (IDA). To position Singapore as an infocomm hub with a thriving knowledge-based digital economy, IDA formulated the Information and Communications Technology 21 Master Plan (ICT 21). The three strategic thrusts of ICT21 are: to develop ICT as a major growth sector; to leverage on ICT to boost the competitiveness of key economic sectors; and to prepare Singapore for the information society of the future.

In January 2000 the government unveiled a programme for liberalisation of the telecommunications sector to ensure that Singapore remains competitive. It accelerated by two years the timetable for full competition in the sector, to 1 April 2000, and immediately lifted the existing 49-percent direct and indirect foreign equity limits for public telecomms service licences. IDA is to adopt a liberal policy when assessing new entrants and in general it will not restrict the number of new licences issued except where there are spectrum limitations. The government followed the liberalisation by measures to support ICT development, including changes to the legal and policy environment, assistance to promising local enterprises and SMEs, development of a strong broadband network and introduction of an ICT manpower development programme.

Financial Sector Development

A key pillar of the knowledge-based economy is a robust financial sector to finance domestic development and provide competitive exportable financial services. Singapore has been pursuing a regional financial centre strategy since the early 1970s. With the rapid changes in the global financial industry, falling regulatory barriers, advances in IT, and mergers and acquisitions among financial institutions, global financial markets are becoming increasingly integrated. To thrive as a financial hub, Singapore needs to at least keep pace, if not be ahead of the curve, and quicken the pace of market development and innovation. The thrust of financial sector reforms in Singapore is not like the financial reforms in countries ravaged by the regional financial crisis. The lead agency, the Monetary Authority of Singapore (MAS), is taking steps to provide a more conducive regulatory environment and become more pro-active in promoting the financial sector.

Singapore's stringent system of prudential regulation and supervision helped the financial sector come through the 1997–98 regional financial crisis relatively unscathed. Nevertheless, markets were becoming concerned that over-regulation of the financial sector in Singapore, particularly compared to Hong Kong, had slowed Singapore's development as a financial centre. This led Singapore to recognise that it needed to liberalise further in order to retain its competitive position in this sector. MAS shifted from a "one-size-fits-all" regulation to a risk-focused supervisory approach, focusing on systemic risk rather than the risks of individual institutions or transactions. The new approach entails monitoring and examining institutions for compliance with guidelines and assessing the adequacy of internal controls and risk management systems. It gives stronger and better-managed players greater leeway. MAS is also promoting more disclosure and transparency in the financial market to enable investors to make informed decisions.

A five-year liberalisation programme for the domestic banking sector was launched in May 1999. The aims are to move towards a more open and competitive environment to spur the development of local banks to strengthen the banking system, to provide Singaporeans with quality banking services, and to enhance Singapore's position as an international financial centre. The government warned that local banks will become progressively marginalised if they do not undertake positive changes. The programme to liberalise the banking sector has four elements:

1. Implementing a 5-year liberalisation package: MAS will implement a 5-year programme to liberalise access by foreign banks to Singapore's domestic market. A new category of full banking licence known as Qualifying Full Banks (QFBs) has been introduced and MAS planned to issue up to 6 QFBs over the 1999–2001 period; incumbent foreign full banks not awarded QFBs will retain their existing privileges. MAS will also increase the number of restricted banks, and give offshore banks greater flexibility in Singapore Dollar wholesale business.
2. Improving corporate governance: Unlike the lack of protection for Singapore's manufacturing sector, the government has protected and nurtured the local banks and enabled them to grow to their present size and strength. However, to survive in the new liberalised environment, local banks have to increased emphasis on efficiency, quality of service and shareholder returns; most importantly, they must strengthen corporate governance, attract leadership talent endowed with the necessary autonomy to make professional management decisions. The local banks need to institute systems for ensuring appointment of capable individuals to their boards and key posts — MAS requires all local banks to appoint

Nominating Committees within their boards to ensure the appointment of the most competent individuals to their boards and key posts; the majority of board members must be Singapore citizens or permanent residents and comprises mainly independent directors.

3. Lifting the 40-percent foreign shareholding limit: MAS lifted the 40-percent limit on foreign investors' total shareholding in local banks. It viewed that the requirement for Nominating Committees and for board members to comprise a majority of Singapore citizens and permanent residents are adequate to ensure national control.

4. MAS will review all regulations concerning local banks so as to give them greater flexibility in their operations without compromising on prudential objectives.

Areas of major revision of bank supervision requirements included:

• Capital adequacy ratio (CAR) requirement: MAS had required local banks to maintain a CAR of 12 percent, comprised entirely of Tier-1 (equity) capital, compared to the 8-percent CAR required by the BIS, with 4 percent each of Tier-1 and Tier-2 capital. As a result Singapore banks are overcapitalised, which raises their cost of funds and lowers their return on equity. Effective December 1998, the requirement for local banks was reduced to a minimum of 10 percent Tier 1 capital, while the remaining 2 percent may be Upper Tier 2 capital (comprising perpetual cumulative preference shares and subordinated debt which satisfy strict qualifying conditions). The definition of Tier 1 capital is also widened to include equity-like capital instruments in line with BIS recommendations.

• Internal models for computing market risk capital: Effective December 1998, MAS allowed banks to use internal models to calculate market risk capital, giving them an incentive to improve their risk-management systems. In March 1999 MAS sent guidelines on the use of internal models and back-testing to the five local banks.

• Disclosure standards: MAS prescribed a minimum disclosure standard for banks and merchant banks, taking into account the recommendations of the Committee on Banking Disclosure.

• Prudential guidelines on asset securitisation: In line with its plan to develop the securitisation market, MAS prepared a set of prudential guidelines for asset securitisation activities by financial institutions.

• Minimum cash balances (MCB) of finance companies: To align with the July 1998 reduction in banks' minimum cash balance, the MCB

requirement for finance companies was reduced from 6 percent to 3 percent in December 1998.
- Common risk framework: Innovations in technology and business products have obscured the distinctions among banking, securities, and insurance activities and international regulatory and supervisory practices are converging towards a consistent risk-focused approach at a consolidated enterprise-wide level. MAS is developing a common risk framework.

Apart from these measures to build a strong and competitive banking industry, measures have been taken to strengthen other parts of the financial industry in order to enhance Singapore's overall position as a financial centre. For example,

- Measures to develop the securities industry include enhancing the competitiveness of the Stock Exchange of Singapore (SES), de-mutualising and merging SES and the Singapore International Monetary Exchange (SIMEX), and making capital market funding more transparent, efficient, and flexible by establishing more flexible listing requirements for growth enterprises and more flexible rules on foreign listings in Singapore dollars, by reducing capital requirements for securities firms; freeing commission fees, and by allowing free access to stock exchange trading by January 2002.
- To develop the debt market, restrictions on borrowing in Singapore dollars are being relaxed to enable foreign players to issue Singapore-dollar denominated bonds. An approved Bond Intermediary scheme is established to encourage the origination, placement, and management of debt issues in Singapore. To create a more liquid market for government bonds, issuance of Singapore government securities has increased and the maturity profile extended to 10 years.
- Measures for the fund management industry include increasing access to the large pool of Central Provident Fund (CPF) funds and government funds farmed out by the MAS and the Government Investment Corporation. Tax incentives and more flexible licensing requirements are intended to attract more foreign fund managers to Singapore.
- Measures for the futures industry include revising the requirements for futures brokers and abolishing the minimum commission structure.
- Measures for the insurance industry include reducing capital requirements for captive insurers; granting blanket approval for captives to write certain non-inhouse risks; enhancing the regulatory framework for

investment-linked policies under the CPF investment scheme; and reviewing insurance and financial reinsurance regulations.

CONCLUSION

Domestic constraints on growth and a rapidly changing external environment have forced Singapore, a small and highly open city-state, to restructure its economy more frequently than larger and less open economies.

Since the early 1960s the government has been an active leader in initiating and directing change. To that extent, economic restructuring in Singapore has not been market-driven but government-directed, although the restructuring was in response to changing domestic and external circumstances. This reflects not only the strength of the government sector but also the weakness of the domestic private enterprise sector. The weak domestic sector is attributed in part to the dominance of foreign multinational corporations and government-linked companies in the economy and to the slow process of transforming the traditional domestic entrepreneurial class steeped in trade and real estate into industrial entrepreneurs and technopreneurs.

The situation is changing. In the 1990s a second generation of domestic entrepreneurs emerged, who are better educated and more tech-savvy than their predecessors, reflecting the fruits of the educational investments of the past three decades and the managerial and technical expertise acquired by a generation of Singaporeans working for foreign MNCs. The dominant role of the government in directing restructuring reflects the high quality of Singapore's political leadership and its bureaucracy. Facilitated by its long stay in power, the political leadership has been forward-looking and strategic in planning. Nevertheless, restructuring was not entirely a top-down matter. The numerous official restructuring committees and pro-grammes have always had broad-based input from the private sector, professionals, and academia to create synergies among planners and implementers and constituents.

Having escaped being ravaged by the regional financial crisis and the ensuing burden of rebuilding, Singapore is fortunate in having the leadership and financial resources to chart a course towards a knowledge-based and digital economy to take advantage of the opportunities offered by accelerating globalisation and technological revolution. Domestic resource constraints, however, necessitate that Singapore continues to leverage on external resources and external markets to achieve its economic vision.

References

Chia Siow Yue. 1998. "Singapore: Advanced Production Base and Smart Hub of the Electronics Industry." In *Multinationals and East Asian Integration*, eds. Wendy Dobson and Chia Siow Yue. Canada and Singapore: IDRC and ISEAS.

Committee on Singapore's Competitiveness. 1998. *Report*. Singapore: Ministry of Trade and Industry. November.

Department of Statistics. *Yearbook of Statistics Singapore*. Singapore: Department of Statistics. Various years.

Economic Committee. 1986. *The Singapore Economy: New Directions*. Singapore: Ministry of Trade and Industry, February.

Economic Development Board. *Yearbook*. Singapore: Economic Development Board. Various years.

Economic Planning Committee. 1991. *The Strategic Economic Plan: Towards a Developed Nation*. Singapore: Ministry of Trade and Industry.

International Institute of Management Development. 2000. *The World Competitiveness Yearbook 2000*. Lausanne: International Institute of Management Development.

Ministry of Labour. 1999. *Manpower 21: Vision of Talent Capital*. Singapore: Ministry of Labour.

Ministry of Trade and Industry. 2000. *Economic Survey of Singapore 1999*. Singapore: Ministry of Trade and Industry.

Organisation for Economic Cooperation and Development (OECD). 1996. *The Knowledge-Based Economy*. Paris: OECD.

Productivity and Standards Board. 2000. *SME 21: Positioning SMEs for the 21st Century*. Singapore: Productivity and Standards Board.

World Economic Forum. 1999. *The World Competitiveness Report 1999*. Geneva: World Economic Forum.

7

Economic Restructuring of Hong Kong on the Basis of Innovation and Technology

Edward Chen and Raymond Ng

INTRODUCTION

Hong Kong experienced perhaps the most severe economic downturn in its recent economic history following the outbreak of the 1997 Asian financial crisis. The economy contracted sharply by 5.1 percent in real terms in 1998 and rebounded to grow moderately by 2.9 percent in 1999. The unemployment rate has been on the increase, from 2.2 percent in 1997 to a record high of 6.2 percent in 1999. Arguably, Hong Kong's small size and extreme outward orientation have rendered the economy particularly vulnerable to adverse external economic shocks. Nonetheless, the apparently robust economy suffered from certain structural weaknesses that made the downward adjustment more severe than it otherwise would have been.

The Hong Kong economy has undergone a drastic structural shift since the early 1980s, and it has now become extremely service-oriented. This heavily skewed industrial structure greatly increased the concentration risk. The rapid increase in land, labour, and other operating costs in Hong Kong since the 1970s worsened the international competitiveness of its manufacturing industry, which is dominated by the production of labour-intensive light consumer goods. To maintain their cost advantage, manufacturing firms took steps to restructure their operations and relocate labour-intensive production processes to China, while keeping the more sophisticated processes and headquarters operations in Hong Kong. The rapid growth in outward processing activities in turn created strong demand for transportation, financial, managerial, and related services, which further accelerated the process of industrial restructuring. In addition, the finance and real estate industries dominated the equity market and the economy as a whole. This added to concentration risk too and exposed the economy to adverse interest rate movements and investor sentiment, increasing macroeconomic instability.

Hong Kong is well known for its positive, non-intervention approach to industrial policy (Haddon-Cave 1980). Hong Kong policymakers are reconsidering this long-followed laissez faire strategy, however, since other Asian emerging economies, which in general have more active industrial policies and more balanced industrial structures and have diversified into technology-intensive industry, outperformed Hong Kong in recovering from the recent economic turmoil. The policymakers need to examine the economy's resource base and competitive advantage and identify the direction for industrial restructuring. Economic and industrial policies should be adopted to facilitate the upgrading of Hong Kong's manufacturing and service industries to rebuild international competitiveness and promote sustainable economic growth in the long run.

The government has seemingly switched to a more active industrial strategy, having announced in 1998 an ambitious plan to develop Hong Kong as a knowledge- and innovation-based economy and to promote high technology and value-added industries. The Commission on Innovation and Technology has been appointed to examine the strengths and weaknesses of Hong Kong's technology and resource base and to recommend appropriate technology and industrial policy measures to reshape the resource base and competitive advantage accordingly. New economic opportunities such as the development of a cyberport, a Chinese medicine centre, and a Disney theme park are also being explored. The recommendations in general call on the government to more actively provide infrastructure and financial support for R&D activities and to invest in development of human resources.

This chapter examines the direction and strategy for industrial restructuring in Hong Kong, specifically the government's attempts to transform Hong Kong into a knowledge- and innovation-based economy and to facilitate the development of technology and knowledge-intensive industry. It begins by examining economic restructuring trends in Hong Kong over the past two decades. It then reviews the recent literature on the role of government policy in industrial and technological development. After a brief review of past industrial policy in Hong Kong it discusses the government's current plan and strategy to promote knowledge- and technology-intensive industry.

ECONOMIC RESTRUCTURING IN HONG KONG

The structure of the Hong Kong economy has shifted dramatically in the past two decades to become extremely service-oriented. The industry sector contracted sharply from 31.7 percent of GDP in 1980 to 15.2 percent in 1998 and manufacturing industry, in particular, contracted even more sharply, from an average 22.6 percent of GDP in the first half of the 1980s to as low as 6.6 percent during 1996–98 (Table 7.1). In contrast, the service sector expanded rapidly from 67.5 percent of GDP in 1980 to 84.7 percent in 1998. Within the service sector, the finance industry's share of GDP rose from an average of 19.1 percent in the first half of the 1980s to an average of 25.6 percent in 1996–98. During the same period, the share of commercial and trade services expanded from 21.3 percent to 25.4 percent, community and personal services expanded from 15.2 percent to 18.5 percent, and transport and storage services grew from 7.8 percent to 9.4 percent of GDP.

The drastic decline in Hong Kong's manufacturing industry and the expansion of the service sector are reflected in the changing pattern of exports (Table 7.2). As domestic merchandise exports decreased, Hong Kong again emerged as a re-export oriented economy. While domestic goods exports averaged 48.9 percent of total goods and services exports in the first half of the 1980s, this share dropped to a record low of 12.1 percent during the period 1996–98. The share of re-exports more than doubled, from an average of 29.2 percent of total exports of goods and services during 1981–85 to 71 percent in 1996–98. Service exports also gained relative to domestic exports. The ratio of services to domestic merchandise exports increased from an average of 44.9 percent for 1981–85 to 140 percent in 1996–98. From HK$29.2 billion in 1980, service exports grew by eight times to reach HK$264.7 billion in 1998, while domestic goods exports expanded by only 1.8 times during the same period.

The massive relocation of manufacturing industry to China in the 1980s and early 1990s was largely responsible for this industrial hollowing-out. The manufacturing industry in Hong Kong was dominated by the production of light consumer goods with low technology content. Also, the small size of most firms in the industry kept them from conducting R&D or upgrading to higher technology activities. With local land and labour costs surging, manufacturing firms in Hong Kong took steps to restructure and relocate labour-intensive production processes across the border to Mainland China where cheaper land and labour were abundant. By moving their production

TABLE 7.1
Ratios of Selected Industries' Output to GDP, 1980–98
(Percent)

	Industry		Services				
	Total	Manufacturing	Total	Wholesale, retail, import/ export trade, restaurants & hotels	Transport, storage & communications	Finance, insurance, real estate & business services	Community, social & personal services
1980	31.7	23.7	67.5	21.4	7.4	23.0	12.1
1981	31.8	22.8	67.5	20.3	7.4	23.9	12.9
1982	30.0	20.8	69.3	20.0	7.7	22.5	15.2
1983	31.9	22.9	67.5	20.4	8.2	17.6	16.0
1984	32.2	24.3	67.3	23.1	7.8	15.6	15.4
1985	29.9	22.1	69.6	22.8	8.1	16.0	16.7
1986	30.3	22.6	69.2	22.3	8.2	17.0	16.0
1987	29.4	22.0	70.3	24.3	8.6	17.9	14.5
1988	27.6	20.5	72.0	25.1	9.1	18.9	13.9
1989	26.7	19.3	73.1	25.0	8.9	19.5	14.1
1990	25.3	17.6	74.5	25.2	9.5	20.2	14.5
1991	23.1	15.4	76.7	25.9	9.6	22.7	14.9
1992	20.9	13.6	78.9	26.1	9.7	24.4	15.1
1993	18.5	11.2	81.3	27.0	9.5	25.8	15.7

continued on next page

TABLE 7.1 – cont'd

| | Industry | | Services | | | | |
	Total	Manufacturing	Total	Wholesale, retail, import/export trade, restaurants & hotels	Transport, storage & communications	Finance, insurance, real estate & business services	Community, social & personal services
1994	16.4	9.2	83.4	26.2	9.7	26.8	15.9
1995	16.1	8.3	83.8	26.6	10.1	24.4	17.3
1996	15.5	7.2	84.4	26.7	9.8	25.1	17.6
1997	14.7	6.5	85.2	25.4	9.1	26.2	17.9
1998	15.2	6.2	84.7	24	9.3	25.6	19.9
Average							
81–85	31.2	22.6	68.2	21.3	7.8	19.1	15.2
86–90	27.9	20.4	71.8	24.4	8.9	18.7	14.6
91–95	19.0	11.5	80.8	26.4	9.7	24.8	15.8
96–98	15.1	6.6	84.7	25.4	9.4	25.6	18.5

Source: Census and Statistics Department, Hong Kong SAR Government, 1999, *Estimates of Gross Domestic Product 1961 to 1998*.

TABLE 7.2
Hong Kong's Export Pattern, 1980—98

	Total Goods and Services Exports		Domestic Merchandise Exports		Re-exports		Services Exports		
	Amount HK$ million	Growth rate %	Amount HK$ million	Share of Total %	Amount HK$ million	Share of Total %	Amount HK$ million	Share of Total %	Ratio to domestic exports
1980	127,407		68,171	53.5	30,072	23.6	29,164	22.9	42.8
1981	157,494	23.6	80,423	51.1	41,739	26.5	35,332	22.4	43.9
1982	167,739	6.5	83,032	49.5	44,656	26.6	40,051	23.9	48.2
1983	207,006	23.4	104,405	50.4	56,294	27.2	46,307	22.4	44.4
1984	277,810	34.2	137,936	49.7	83,504	30.1	56,370	20.3	40.9
1985	296,202	6.6	129,882	43.8	105,270	35.5	61,050	20.6	47.0
1986	348,344	17.6	153,983	44.2	122,546	35.2	71,815	20.6	46.6
1987	470,306	35.0	195,254	41.5	182,780	38.9	92,272	19.6	47.3
1988	604,051	28.4	217,664	36.0	275,405	45.6	110,982	18.4	51.0
1989	697,656	15.5	224,104	32.1	346,405	49.7	127,147	18.2	56.7
1990	782,195	12.1	225,875	28.9	413,999	52.9	142,321	18.2	63.0
1991	926,973	18.5	231,045	24.9	534,841	57.7	161,087	17.4	69.7
1992	1,114,305	20.2	234,124	21.0	690,829	62.0	189,352	17.0	80.9
1993	1,261,827	13.2	223,027	17.7	823,223	65.2	215,577	17.1	96.7
1994	1,410,681	11.8	222,092	15.7	947,921	67.2	240,668	17.1	108.4
1995	1,609,762	14.1	231,657	14.4	1,112,470	69.1	265,635	16.5	114.7

continued on next page

TABLE 7.2 – cont'd

	Total Goods and Services Exports		Domestic Merchandise Exports		Re-exports		Services Exports		
	Amount HK$ million	Growth rate %	Amount HK$ million	Share of Total %	Amount HK$ million	Share of Total %	Amount HK$ million	Share of Total %	Ratio to domestic exports
1996	1,694,106	5.2	212,160	12.5	1,185,758	70.0	296,188	17.5	139.6
1997	1,751,532	3.4	211,410	12.1	1,244,539	71.1	295,583	16.9	139.8
1998	1,612,314	-7.9	188,454	11.7	1,159,195	71.9	264,665	16.4	140.4
Average									
1981–85	221,250	18.9	107,136	48.9	66,293	29.2	47,822	21.9	44.9
1986–90	580,510	21.7	203,376	36.6	268,227	44.4	108,907	19.0	52.9
1991–95	1,264,710	15.6	228,389	18.7	821,857	64.2	214,464	17.0	94.1
1996–98	1,685,984	0.2	204,008	12.1	1,196,497	71.0	285,479	16.9	140.0

Note: Figures in italics are percentage shares of total exports of goods and services.
Source: Census and Statistics Department, Hong Kong SAR Government, 1999, *Estimates of Gross Domestic Product 1961 to 1998*.

bases to a low-cost location, they were able to improve their cost position and maintain competitiveness without diversifying into the production of capital- or technology-intensive goods. The wholesale relocation of production to China in turn brought about drastic growth in Hong Kong's re-export and out-processing activities and created huge demand for transportation, managerial, banking, and other trade-related services. China's Open Door policy, adopted in 1978, also fuelled demand for such services, pushing Hong Kong to become a commercial and financial centre and a regional hub for headquarters to co-ordinate manufacturing and other business activities in Mainland China and in other Asian emerging markets.

Economic growth requires continuous upgrading from traditional labour-intensive industries to industries with high knowledge- or technology-content. Continual increases in value added are needed in order to cover the rising costs of production and to warrant higher standards of living for the workforce. In Hong Kong, value added by the industrial sector averaged a much smaller percentage of gross output than value added by the service sector during the years 1981 to 1996 (Table 7.3). (Value added is the sum of compensation to employees and gross operating surplus.) Nonetheless, industry's share increased gradually from 30.4 percent in 1980 to 33.5 percent in 1990 and further to 38.7 percent in 1996. The profit margin of the industrial sector also improved moderately, as compensation to employees declined from an average of 65.1 percent of value added during 1981–85 to 58.8 percent during 1991–96 (Table 7.4). For manufacturing, the average value-added share of gross output dropped from 28.1 percent in the first half of 1980s to 27.5 percent during 1986–90, and then improved gradually to 29 percent during 1991–96 (Table 7.3). Employee compensation fell from an average of 65.4 percent of manufacturing value added in the first half of 1980s to 56.6 percent during 1991–96 (Table 7.4). The service sector has been more profitable than manufacturing, with higher added value and a lower share of employee compensation. Nonetheless, value-added share of gross output in the service sector declined slowly, and the profit margin also narrowed as the share of employee compensation gradually increased. Finance has been the most profitable service industry, with value-added averaging 73.6 percent of gross output from 1981 to 1996 and employee compensation accounting for an average of 33.2 percent of gross output.

The process of industrial restructuring in Hong Kong could be seen as an attempt by local manufacturing firms to maintain their competitiveness and profitability by relocating production to China. Given the limited

TABLE 7.3

Value Added as a Share of Gross Output, by Industry, 1980–96

(Percent)

	Industry		Services				
	Total	Manufacturing	Total	Wholesale, retail, import/export trade, restaurant, and hotel	Transport, storage and communications	Finance, insurance, real estate and business services	Community, social and personal services
1980	30.4	27.3	62.8	61.7	45.8	83.7	61.1
1981	31.1	27.6	60.3	59.9	44.6	81.2	58.1
1982	32.9	28.9	59.3	57.0	44.1	78.3	60.8
1983	31.4	27.6	57.6	56.1	44.8	73.3	59.7
1984	31.3	27.9	57.9	57.9	43.3	71.9	60.1
1985	32.1	28.5	57.6	55.2	44.6	70.5	60.8
1986	31.5	27.7	57.8	54.0	45.3	71.9	61.5
1987	30.7	26.9	58.7	55.6	49.7	71.8	61.7
1988	30.3	26.4	58.3	53.9	51.6	72.4	60.7
1989	31.8	27.6	57.2	51.6	50.0	72.0	59.8
1990	33.5	28.8	55.1	48.3	49.8	70.8	59.9
1991	33.9	28.7	55.6	49.0	52.8	72.7	61.5
1992	35.1	29.5	58.7	55.2	52.5	75.0	61.8
1993	35.8	29.3	57.8	54.3	50.9	75.3	59.5
1994	36.9	29.3	58.2	53.4	52.7	74.1	59.3
1995	36.2	28.1	57.9	54.2	52.7	72.7	59.7
1996	38.7	29.2	58.5	55.5	52.5	72.9	60.3
1981–85	31.8	28.1	58.5	57.2	44.3	75.0	59.9
1986–90	31.6	27.5	57.4	52.7	49.3	71.8	60.7
1991–96	36.1	29.0	57.8	53.6	52.4	73.8	60.4

Source: Census and Statistics Department, Hong Kong SAR Government, 1999, *Estimates of Gross Domestic Product 1961 to 1998.*

TABLE 7.4
Employee Compensation Share of Value Added, by Industry, 1980–96
(Percent)

	Industry		Services				
	Total	Manufacturing	Total	Wholesale, retail, import/export trade, restaurant, and hotel	Transport, storage and communications	Finance, insurance, real estate and business services	Community, social and personal services
1980	70.7	71.2	38.7	41.9	48.3	18.4	77.5
1981	67.0	66.1	40.4	45.6	48.0	20.6	73.6
1982	66.9	66.9	44.4	48.8	52.3	24.3	75.9
1983	63.1	63.6	47.5	49.9	49.7	33.3	74.8
1984	62.4	62.7	46.9	45.1	48.6	36.0	75.9
1985	66.3	67.7	49.1	49.7	49.4	38.9	75.4
1986	62.7	63.1	48.4	49.6	47.1	36.4	77.4
1987	60.9	60.1	46.0	45.5	42.7	34.8	78.3
1988	60.3	59.0	45.4	46.2	41.2	34.8	77.5
1989	60.3	59.0	47.1	49.0	44.3	36.1	79.2
1990	60.6	58.6	49.1	51.5	46.8	37.1	80.4
1991	59.6	57.2	49.2	52.6	43.6	34.4	81.6
1992	58.4	55.3	48.3	51.5	44.9	31.8	83.3
1993	59.1	56.8	48.4	52.0	45.8	30.3	83.5
1994	58.2	57.4	47.0	52.0	44.9	30.7	81.5
1995	58.9	56.9	49.9	53.7	46.6	35.0	82.1
1996	58.3	55.4	49.5	51.0	46.1	36.4	82.4
1981–85	65.1	65.4	45.7	47.8	49.6	30.6	75.1
1986–90	61.0	60.0	47.2	48.4	44.4	35.8	78.6
1991–96	58.8	56.5	48.7	52.1	45.3	33.1	82.4

Source: Census and Statistics Department, Hong Kong SAR Government, 1999, *Estimates of Gross Domestic Product 1961 to 1998.*

technology base as well as managerial and financial resources for conducting R&D, it was not to Hong Kong's advantage to try to transform into the production of high-technology and capital-intensive industries. Instead, Hong Kong diversified into the more profitable and higher value-added service industry. The economic success of Hong Kong lay in its entre-preneurial and managerial expertise and its ability to respond and adjust quickly to new market opportunities.

THE ROLE OF GOVERNMENT POLICY IN INDUSTRIAL DEVELOPMENT

Innovation and technology have long been seen as crucial sources of economic growth. Conventional development theory emphasises the role of technological improvement in offsetting diminishing returns to production and boosting the output that can be produced with fixed amounts of capital and labour. Economists have made substantial efforts to measure the contribution of technological progress to output growth and to learn about the mechanism through which technology advancement affects growth. In a pioneering effort Solow (1957) focused on the portion of measured economic growth that is not explained by growth in labour and capital inputs. He attributed this unexplained residual growth, or growth in total factor productivity, to technological improvement. Despite its crudeness, Solow's model laid the foundation of many later studies. In particular, considerable attention has been paid to examining the relative importance of embodied and disembodied technological progress in boosting economic growth. Disembodied technological progress contributes to output growth independently of capital accumulation, whereas embodied technological change affects output by enhancing, for instance, the quality or efficiency of capital accumulation. It is crucial to distinguish between these two types of technological change as sources of growth in order to interpret correctly the total factor productivity growth.

One important implication of the Solow model of economic growth is that government policies do not have any permanent impact on the rate of economic growth although they can raise the rate of growth temporarily, as an economy moves to a higher level of income. Endogenous growth theories, in contrast, hypothesise that government policies *can* influence the long-term rate of growth (Romer 1986 and Lucas 1988). Endogenous growth models presume that the returns to capital can continue to increase. Any government policy that increases the rate of investment in the economy will permanently raise the rate of growth. This is because economic growth hinges on knowledge, and knowledge depends on investment. Lucas (1988) placed sole importance on human capital. He assumed that the rate of economic growth depends on time individuals spend accumulating skills, i.e., investment in human capital. Any policy that leads to a permanent increase in an economy's accumulation of human capital per person will increase the long-term rate of growth. In the Solow model, on the other hand, diminishing returns to capital eventually result in negative capital accumulation when the amount of investment falls short of depreciation.

The importance of government policy in industrial development has conventionally been argued in terms of the divergence between private and social benefits to investment in R&D and human capital, and in industrial restructuring. Mansfield et al. (1977) present a framework to measure the social benefits of innovation. When innovation shifts an industry's cost and supply curves downward, the social benefits of the investment in the new technology are the sum of the increase in consumer surplus due to lower prices and the resources saved by producing with the new technology. The social benefits will increase further as other firms imitate the innovation. According to their estimates for seventeen product and process innovations, social rates of return on average have been remarkably high. The median social rate of return they estimated was about 56 percent, which is much higher than the median private rate of return of about 25 percent.

The divergence between private and social returns resulting from the existence of spillover benefits suggest that private markets tend to under-invest in R&D and human capital. Firms cannot appropriate fully the benefits generated from their innovations, as technical knowledge spills over to other firms without compensation to the innovating firms. The problem of appropriability combined with the risky nature of R&D inhibit private sector investment in technology and innovation. Technical risks arise from uncertainty about outcomes and technical performance of innovations, especially during the early phases of R&D. Investment in technology and innovation may also entail significant market risk because of the long time until innovators finally gain from the commercialisation of R&D results. Furthermore, individual firms may lack the unique facilities or diversity of talent to undertake certain R&D investments.

Market failure such as this justifies a government role in supporting investment in R&D. Because the market-determined level of investment is socially sub-optimal, government should invest actively in such activities that would otherwise be under-invested. Many technologically advanced countries have long followed an active science and technology policy based on this rationale, using direct funding programmes and fiscal incentives (tax reduction or tax credits for R&D expenditure) to encourage private sector R&D activities. The post-war science and technology policies of the United States and Japan illustrate two distinct approaches to building science and technology capacity. In the United States, federal support for basic research by universities expanded rapidly after the 1945 Vannevar-Bush report "Science: The Endless Frontier" selected the university as the centrepiece of post-war science policy. This was so despite the fact that most government-funded research was related to defence, space, and atomic energy technology. The university-based research system has become the key part of the U.S. national technology network and a major source of innovation. In contrast, in post-war Japan, the Ministry of International Trade and Industry (MITI) was responsible for carrying out industrial and technology policies and was the major source of government funding for R&D. Government-funded R&D was mainly conducted in the form of large, on-going projects. MITI also strategically focused on funding applied R&D in a limited number of large technology firms. Importantly, the government promoted a system of research associations, which were non-profit, project-specific groups established to conduct government-led joint R&D projects. By 1989 Japan had a total of 168 such research associations (Sumita and Namiki 1997).

Referring especially to industrial restructuring in East Asia, Smith (1995) argues that government industrial policy generally fits into one of two categories: functional or selective intervention. Functional intervention is aimed to correct market failure without favouring any particular activity or industry, while selective intervention is designed to favour a certain activity or industry in order to overcome sub-optimal resource allocation. For the former, the government tends to invest in broad-based institutional and infrastructure support for R&D and human resource development and to deregulate trade and investment regimes to promote competition and create new opportunities. Selective intervention, on the other hand, is usually firm- or industry-specific and uses trade, financial, fiscal, or investment policies as incentive instruments to direct private sector resource allocation to targeted activities. Direct government investment and ownership may sometimes be adopted to develop the strategic industry. Importantly, both approaches tend to identify high-technology industry as the strategic sector based on its potential to generate beneficial external economies and exports.

This policy-driven growth argument implies a straightforward strategy for economic restructuring in developing economies. In addition to conventional, sector-neutral measures to provide adequate infrastructure, an investment-friendly environment, a well-educated workforce, a free economy, and a well-functioning financial market, to promote optimal growth the government should also adopt a science and technology policy to develop the economy's technology and knowledge base. First of all, it should invest in public R&D and perhaps more importantly provide institutional and infrastructure support to encourage private sector R&D activities. Developing economies with a low technology base should perhaps focus on applied technology R&D and on enhancing their ability to absorb, upgrade, and commercialise technologies imported from advanced countries. Second, the government should work to develop the economy's human resources and to ensure that the education and training system meets the fast-changing skill requirements. It should give special attention to ensuring an adequate supply of well-educated professionals with technology-specific training and with the ability to digest, absorb, and diffuse modern technology. The government should also encourage the workforce to continuously upgrade its knowledge and skills. Finally, the government should ensure that the economy can tap into external advances in technology. It should provide institutional support and infrastructure so that imported technology is effectively assimilated, adapted, diffused, and acquired for commercial utilisation. In particular, it should ensure the availability of appropriate human resources and R&D infrastructure, which are crucial to the transfer and absorption of advanced technology. The government should also attempt to attract inward FDI in technology-based industry, for instance, by providing proper infrastructure and an environment conducive to rapid industrial and technological development and by actively improving the industry's capacity to absorb more sophisticated technology. The eventual aim should be for industry to become capable of generating new technology on its own.

Underlying currents in the international economy are pushing policymakers to adjust and re-focus their R&D and industrialisation policies designed to foster competitive advantage. The increasing integration of the global economy (with rapidly growing multinational corporations adopting cross-border production, sourcing, and marketing strategy) poses a major challenge to the conventional wisdom on economic growth and restructuring. Advances in transportation, telecommunication, and information technology have lowered the transactions and operating costs associated with physical distance. Liberalisation of trade and investment regimes in many developing countries has removed barriers to international trade and capital flows. These changes in turn are encouraging firms to move toward more fragmented production and supply structures and to seek out international suppliers. Ultimately, these changes are impelling firms to take a global perspective, locating the various parts of the production process according to the factor price, productivity, or other technology-based advantages of each location, if they are to achieve efficiency and sustain profit growth.

These developments challenge the traditional view that large scale brings economic advantages. Economies of scale achieved through standardised and mass production (i.e., so-called 'Fordism') have been edged out by the advantages of flexible manufacturing systems characterised by the networking of small, specialised, and innovative production units (Teubal et al. 1995). In addition, following the rapid growth of the IT industry and the integration of the global economy, size no longer seems as important a factor in the growth prospects of an economy or a firm. In fact, some small countries such as Ireland, Israel, New Zealand, and Singapore have already achieved rapid development in the information technology industry. Advances in electronic commerce and Internet technology facilitate access to market and technical information anywhere in the world, independent of size. These advances also facilitate the formation of industrial alliances and the efficient exchange of information between suppliers and purchasers. Smaller firms can now develop their own competitiveness by flexibly applying production technology to produce customised products that cater to the needs of individual customers or differentiated products for multiple markets. More importantly, inter-nationalisation of production chains facilitates the transfer of knowledge and technology and extends sourcing and marketing linkages to smaller, developing economies. These economies are now in a stronger position to leapfrog development in certain industries even if they lack a technology and industry base. The dramatic transformation of Ireland from an agriculture-based to a technology-based economy (and a leading exporter of computer software) is a perfect example. Therefore developing economies may not need to follow the conventional course of economic development or industrialisation.

The strategy for government support of R&D and innovation may also need to be revised in the face of the new economic paradigm. Up to now, R&D has generally tended to be large scale, aimed at achieving radical technology breakthroughs. Moreover, largely due to limited foreign competition, new technologies used to enjoy a long technology and market life cycle and hence to entail relatively low risk. Innovators had relatively more control of the market. Now, particularly since most advanced and emerging countries have already adopted a technology-based growth strategy, global competition has intensified, and this has greatly shortened the technology life cycle. Innovators are forced to focus R&D efforts on less risky and shorter-term (but on-going) projects, such as process-innovation or minor production improvement, for example, which generate results that can be commercialised quickly. Technology advances are more likely to come as incremental improvements instead of major changes, and maintaining economic competitiveness depends on continuously improving innovative capacity. Thus, a government should, among other things, adopt a human resource development strategy that focuses on encouraging a creative and technologically sophisticated workforce. Such a strategy should also encourage people to work smarter and pursue life-long education and training. To engender such a quality, the government should consider removing the traditional distinction in education between arts, humanities, and science disciplines and focusing the education system on development of the whole person. This is particularly crucial as industrial restructuring has already proceeded toward increasing knowledge- (or perhaps wisdom-) orientation.

The traditional path of economic restructuring, moving from manu-facturing- to service-orientation may also need to be reconsidered. Particularly in the case of Hong Kong, the production process is highly fragmented with substantial processing and sourcing taking place outside the economy. A significant proportion of Hong Kong's service industry, including transportation, telecommunication, accounting, managerial, and other professional services, is tied to manufacturing activities that are located elsewhere. In addition, major real property developers, including Cheung Kong Holding Limited, Henderson Company Limited, Sun Hung Kai Properties Limited, and New World Development Company Limited, have already diversified into Internet-based and e-commerce businesses. Thus, to a large extent, Hong Kong's manufacturing and service sectors have already been integrated, and it is no longer practical or accurate to draw a distinction between them. Therefore policymakers should adopt an integrated approach to industrial and technology policies. They should support particularly manufacturing-related service R&D based on a wide range of information and Internet technology. The new technology should help manufacturers add value at the service stage of the vertical supply chain.

INDUSTRIAL POLICY IN HONG KONG

The industrial policy of Hong Kong can best be described as a strategy of "maximum support but minimum intervention". The Hong Kong government has long adopted a laissez faire strategy for industrialisation. Unlike many Asian high-performing economies, the government has not selected any strategic industry for development and has therefore played a minimal role in allocating resources. Industrial support was generally indirect, primarily aimed to ensure the adequacy of infrastructure and factor inputs (especially industrial land) and an institutional environment conducive to competition and private investment in physical capital (e.g., an open and market-oriented economy, a low and simple tax system, and a well-developed financial market). Nonetheless, the government intervened to a certain extent on the microeconomic level through its considerable control over the supply (and hence price) of land. For example, the government assisted targeted industries by offering land in industrial estates through private treaty instead of public auction.

In Hong Kong the public sector has had very limited direct involvement in R&D and it has provided minimal support for private-sector R&D activities. Public support for industry concentrated on developing education, infrastructure, and institutions that indirectly promoted all industries. The government has made special efforts to provide training and technical services to support the upgrading of traditional industry. The Industry and Technology Development Council was established in 1992 to replace the former Industry Development Board and the Committee on Science and Technology to advise on Hong Kong's industrial and technology policy. The Industry Department facilitates the development of manufacturing industry by promoting inward investment, improving access to relevant technologies, encouraging applied R&D activities, and conducting research on market trends. The Hong Kong Trade Development Council is responsible for promoting trade and the service sector. Its major functions include exploring new export markets, providing information to local manufacturers and traders about foreign buyers, and working closely with them to upgrade the quality and design of their products. The Hong Kong Productivity Council acts as an agent for technology transfer and productivity enhancement. It provides a variety of training programmes, industrial and management consulting, and technical support services. The Vocational Training Council provides technical education and industrial training. It runs a New Technology Training Scheme, which provides financial assistance for employers to train their technicians and managerial staff.

Since the early 1990s the government has increased its efforts to boost the technological and technical capacity of Hong Kong's manufacturing industry. The Industry and Technology Development Council was established largely to ensure that Hong Kong could respond promptly to the fast-changing technological environment and to enhance the vital connection between industry and technology. The Hong Kong Industrial Technology Centre Corporation was established in June 1993 to facilitate technological innovation and the application of new technology in domestic industry. It provides incubation programmes for start-up technology-based business, technology transfer services, and product design, development, and support services. The government also took steps to expand tertiary education and postgraduate training to meet increasing manpower needs. It established the Open Learning Institute in 1990 and the Hong Kong University of Science and Technology in 1991. Polytechnics and other colleges were upgraded to university status providing more degree programmes.

The government is committed to developing Hong Kong as an innovation-driven and knowledge-based economy with the focus on technology and knowledge-intensive industries. As the economy transformed from a manufacturing base to become heavily biased towards the service sector, its resource base and comparative advantage also became biased toward services. The goal of making Hong Kong competitive in knowledge- and technology-intensive industry calls for drastic measures to actively re-shape the technology and resource base of the economy.

In a knowledge-based economy the key input to production is intangible capital, such as knowledge and human capital, rather than labour or physical capital. Hence, improvements in productivity and economic growth depend on increasing this intangible capital, that is they depend on the capacity to innovate and to create and accumulate knowledge. Knowledge-intensive industry such as information technology becomes the strategic industry, while raising the knowledge content of traditional industries also becomes a policy objective. Hong Kong should concentrate, in particular, on the technology and knowledge content of such services industries as banking, insurance, and brokerage with the support of advances in information technology and the increasing popularity of Internet usage.

In contrast to these objectives, the existing technology stock and resource base for high-technology industry in Hong Kong is weak, and the economy seriously lags behind in technological development. Although Hong Kong remains one of the most competitive economies in the world, its technology competitiveness has weakened in recent years. According to a study of technology competitiveness in 46 countries, Hong Kong fell from an overall rank of 10 in 1992 to 25 in 1998 and its overall competitiveness was below the average for the group of countries in the study (Table 7.5). In R&D investment Hong Kong dropped from a ranking of 15 in 1992 to 29 in 1998, in scientific environment it dropped from 9th place to 23rd, and in technology management if fell from 6th to 11th place. On the other hand, between 1992 and 1998 Hong Kong's ranking in intellectual property protection rose from 27 to 23. Hong Kong's weakness in technology development can be attributed in part to the fact that the manufacturing industry was dominated by small firms and by the production of labour-intensive light consumer goods. Such producers were not likely to undertake R&D activities. Moreover the government did not have an active technology development policy and it consistently invested fewer resources in R&D than did other advanced economies or NIEs (Table 7.6).

Hong Kong also lacks a resource base of scientists and engineers to support technology development. Hong Kong has fewer scientists and researchers than other countries. For every 10,000 workers Hong Kong has only 10 scientists compared to 80 in Japan, 78 in the United States, 57 in Taiwan, and 45 in Singapore (Chen 1999). Despite heavy investment in education and expanded tertiary education in the 1990s, students enrolling

TABLE 7.5
Hong Kong's Ranking on
Selected Technology Competitiveness Factors, 1992–98
(Ranking out of 46 countries surveyed)

	1992	1993	1994	1995	1996	1997	1998
Overall	10	10	19	19	20	18	25
R&D Resources	15	17	21	21	19	18	29
Technology Management	6	6	13	16	16	18	17
Scientific Environment	9	9	17	17	22	20	23
Intellectual Property	27	26	27	27	29	23	23

Note: Lower rank indicates greater competitiveness.
Source: International Institute for Management Development, *The World Competitiveness Yearbook*, various issues, cited in X. Chen, 1999, p. 15.

TABLE 7.6
Ratio of R&D Expenses to GNP in Selected Economies, 1990–96
(Percent)

	1990	1991	1992	1993	1994	1995	1996
Australia	1.37	–	1.57	–	–	–	1.38
Canada	1.46	1.51	1.55	1.59	1.57	1.52	1.64
China	0.68	0.66	0.63	0.57	0.48	0.49	0.48
Hong Kong	–	–	–	–	–	–	0.26
Indonesia	–	–	–	–	–		0.08
Japan	3.04	3.00	2.95	2.88	2.84		3.33
South Korea	1.87	1.93	2.08	2.30	2.58	2.69	2.81
Malaysia	–	–	0.38	–	0.33	–	0.23
Mexico	–	–	–	0.24	–	–	0.26
New Zealand	–	–	–	–	–	–	0.90
Philippines	–	–	–	–	–	–	0.14
Singapore	0.86	1.04	1.18	1.08	1.11	1.15	1.35
Taiwan	1.66	1.70	1.78	1.76	1.80	1.81	1.85
Thailand	–	–	–	–	–	–	0.11
U.S.A.	2.82	2.84	2.78	2.64	2.54	2.45	2.42

Source: Australian National University, cited in *Capital*, August 1998, No. 129, p. 74.

in Hong Kong universities tend not to focus on science and engineering subjects. According to official statistics, in 1997 business administration programmes accounted for 24.6 percent of total enrolment and social and arts subjects accounted for 32.7 percent. In comparison, biological, physical, and mathematical sciences accounted for 10.6 percent of total enrolment and computer science, information technology, and engineering and technology together accounted for 22.8 percent. The rapid growth of Hong Kong's service sector attracted a significant share of talented students away from physical science or engineering, and even many science and technology graduates chose to work in the booming, dynamic service sector.

On the other hand, Hong Kong already has a well-developed infra-structure, an educated and hard-working workforce, and a favourable business environment with a developed financial market and an open, competitive economy. With cautiously designed and properly implemented technology and human resource development policies, Hong Kong will be in a strong position to leapfrog to become a knowledge and technology-based economy. Particularly, in view of the more scale-neutral competition and the shift in industrial advantage toward small-scale production units, the small and medium-sized enterprises (SMEs) that predominate in Hong Kong could even be a source of competitive advantage and industrial dynamism. According to official statistics, in June 1999 the more than 280,000 SMEs in Hong Kong accounted for over 98 percent of total business establishments and employed about 60 percent of the workforce. The majority of SMEs were in the import and export sector. These SMEs have long been crucial suppliers of parts and components to the global market. They have already developed entrepreneurial talents and international linkages, and adopted flexible production and marketing techniques.

STRATEGY FOR INDUSTRIAL RESTRUCTURING

The Hong Kong government established the Commission on Innovation and Technology in March 1998 to examine the feasibility of various policies to promote high-technology and knowledge-intensive industries in Hong Kong. Based on the Commission's recommendations the government announced a plan to develop Hong Kong as a centre for innovation and technology with a focus on information technology, fashion and design, multi-media-based information and entertainment services, and bio-technology especially related to Chinese medicine. The Committee's recommendations included reforming government institutions related to formulation and implementation of technology policy, providing infrastructure facilities for R&D, investing in human resource development, and fostering an innovation and technology culture. Specifically, the Commission recommended establishing a cross-bureau policy group to set and co-ordinate technology and related policy. A standing advisory body and a common secretariat with full-time science advisors should support the policy group. The Committee also recommended merging the Hong Kong Science Park, Hong Kong Industrial Estates Corporation, and Hong Kong Industrial Technology Centre Corporation. Together, these reforms should enhance the government's ability and efficiency to introduce and co-ordinate various technology development and human resource programmes.

Investment in R&D Infrastructure and Private Sector R&D Activities

The relative underdevelopment of Hong Kong's technology resources is the expected outcome of the government's past stance toward technology investment and the economic nature of such investment. The Hong Kong government has not had a comprehensive long-term plan for technology development and it has provided very limited support for R&D activities. Without public support, R&D and other knowledge-creating activities tend to be under-invested, since investment in new technology or knowledge represents a typical case of market failure, as discussed above. Now, the government has committed to expanding infrastructure to support R&D activities and incubator programmes to promote high-technology industry, especially among small firms. It launched an Innovation and Technology Fund replacing the Industrial Support and Services Support Funds to stimulate private-sector interest in R&D and to encourage various activities that promote an innovation and technology culture, such as conferences and training programmes. Specifically, the Innovation and Technology Fund (ITF) runs a HK$250 million University-Industry Collaboration Programme, which is a matching grant scheme to encourage collaborative research between industry and academia. The collaboration will encourage industry to conduct R&D by making greater use of the available research resources of universities, and it will establish a network for technology creation and transfer. The ITF also operates a HK$500 million Small Entrepreneur Research Assistance Programme (a technology incubator programme) to assist small entrepreneurs undertaking commercial R&D at the pre-market launch stage.

In order to improve the infrastructure for R&D activities, the government is building a Science Park at Tai Po in the New Territories to provide land and premises especially for high technology firms and activities. The park will provide a focal point and create an environment to attract overseas technology firms to invest in Hong Kong and to stimulate growth of local technology-based business. The first phase, estimated to cost HK$3.3 billion, will be in operation by 2001. The government is also building an Applied Science and Technology Research Institute (ASTRI), located in the Science Park, to provide technological infrastructure for mid-stream R&D. ASTRI will play an important role in facilitating technology transfer and technological human resource development. It will also help to attract R&D professionals from overseas to work in Hong Kong and to encourage industry-university collaboration. In addition, the government should adopt measures to facilitate the inflow of technological expertise from China to allow Hong Kong industry to draw on the Mainland's human and other resources on basic research. Hong Kong should focus on mid- to down-stream applied research and play a strategic role in commercialising research results for the Mainland.

The government has begun to partner with the private sector in order to promote Hong Kong's information technology industry. For example, in March 1999, the government launched a cyberport project through a private agreement with Pacific Century Cyberworks Ltd. The project aims to provide the infrastructure appropriate for promoting the strategic information technology industry in order to attract foreign technology companies to invest in Hong Kong, to expand the pool of talent and expertise, and to facilitate technology transfer. As a way to upgrade and diversify the tourist industry, the government got Disney Enterprises to agree to build a theme park in Hong Kong. It is also working on other opportunities to promote technology-intensive industry, such as a Chinese medicine centre. In addition to fostering the transfer of technical knowledge, attracting MNEs in the technology sphere to Hong Kong could create horizontal and vertical linkages that would open commercial opportunities for local firms through parts supply or logistics support, for instance. Local emerging technology firms that find it difficult to compete in international markets could also form strategic alliances with large multinational corporations to take advantage of their marketing networks.

In addition to pursuing steps such as these, Hong Kong should establish a national innovation network with the combined effort of the government, industry, and academia. This tripartite collaboration is crucial for pooling and synthesising the wide-ranging talents and expertise of the network participants. These include the skill base and market insights of industry and the research capabilities and intellectual stock of universities. The government should be the catalyst, facilitating technology development and technology transfer through a clearly articulated strategic vision and both short- and long-term plans and targets for technology development. A civil service with a higher level of professional expertise in technology development could be a better facilitor. The government should take the initiative by evaluating the economy's existing technology level, identifying emerging areas of technology advancement, and introducing appropriate policies to close the identified technology gaps. It should also introduce mechanisms to enhance communication and information exchange among policymakers, industry, and academia in order to keep track of the latest technology developments and market changes. Finally, it should support specific R&D activities that will help SMEs to upgrade production and delivery systems, enhance design capability and quality control, and develop new customers and markets.

Human Resource Development Strategy for Technology-based Growth

The government is committed to reforming the education and training system in order to produce the sort of workforce required by a knowledge economy. In addition to promoting creativity, language and communication skills, information technology, and analytical thinking, it is important to inspire young people to pursue science and technology studies and to develop a culture of the whole-person and life-long learning. School curricula and assessment systems should be reformed to support these aims, and the government has issued a consultation paper with proposals for reform. For secondary education the proposals include removing the streaming of natural science and humanity disciplines, phasing-out vocational schools, and emphasising multifaceted intelligence assessments rather than subject-based examinations. For tertiary education, the government proposes to develop a credit transfer system for universities and post-secondary educational institutions to allow students more flexibility, choice, and mobility among programs in order to encourage cross-disciplinary learning, and to improve post-graduate programs for specialised training. In addition, to encourage private firms to take on graduate students to work on specific R&D research projects, the ITF instituted a Teaching Company Scheme under which it pays half the students' salaries and the participating universities provide guidance.

The government should take serious steps to encourage university graduates to pursue graduate degrees in science and engineering research and it should consider providing more scholarships for post-graduate study (locally and overseas). It should also examine the feasibility of establishing a graduate division within ASTRI, with faculty and students perhaps involved in ITF-funded research projects. In addition to an adequate supply of workers with higher education and training in science and engineering, technological improvement demands an adaptable and trainable skilled labour force that can adjust to new technologies and production processes. Firms should provide both continuous pre-service and on-the-job-training. The government should also encourage a culture of life-long learning and trainability among the workforce. In addition to providing better infrastructure for technical and vocational training, the government should provide more fiscal incentives to encourage continuing studies, in-house training programmes, and government re-training programmes. As it will take time for Hong Kong to upgrade the scientific skills of the local population, in the short run the government should amplify its efforts to attract overseas talents in order to immediately boost Hong Kong's intellectual capital and energise the technology sector. Overseas professionals with exposure to and experience in technology-based industry or R&D could bring in new knowledge, technology, and management skills, and they could identify the market gap for future development. The government has already launched a scientist importation scheme by relaxing immigration restrictions on Mainland talents working in Hong Kong.

In the long term, education reform should promote liberal arts education, which emphasises development of the whole person and offers flexible courses of study that combine the arts, humanities, and science disciplines. Many graduates of liberal arts colleges in the United States pursue higher degrees in mathematics and science. According to Stephen Lewis, Jr., President of Carleton College, of the 100 tertiary educational institutions in the United States with the highest percentage of graduates earning PhDs in science and mathematics, 61 were liberal arts colleges. Furthermore, certain American liberal arts colleges, including Carleton, consistently lead the large universities in the number of graduates going on to obtain PhDs in all fields of science and mathematics and particularly in physics, astronomy, and chemistry.

Mobilise Financial Resources for Innovative and High-technology Industries

The ability to raise and channel adequate financial resources to fund business start-ups and expansion is crucial to promoting R&D activities and high-technology industry. Compared with large enterprises, small firms tend to have less financial resources and to find it more difficult to raise capital, through public listing or bank lending for instance, to invest in R&D. Hong Kong needs to pay particular attention to the funding needs of small and medium-sized enterprises because they have dominated the manufacturing industry. In addition to the Small Entrepreneur Research Assistance Programme already mentioned, the government started an Applied Research Fund Scheme to provide equity capital to promising local technology ventures. Launched in November 1998, the HK$750 million fund is operated by three private venture-capital firms that have market and management expertise. The government also established a Growth Enterprise Market at the stock exchange to help emerging technology companies raise equity capital.

Equally important to meeting the financing needs of technology start-ups are efforts to encourage venture credit lending by banks and a private sector venture capital market for technology-based industries. In general, Hong Kong banks are inexperienced with venture capital issues and lack expertise in risk and return evaluation of high-technology projects. Traditional practice in the banking sector requires loans to be fully secured by real property collateral. The sharp decline in property prices following the 1997 Asian financial crisis further constrained small firms from securing bank credit. Above all, small technology firms are in an unfavourable position because their assets are mostly intangible ones, such as innovative ideas and business potential. The government should encourage banks to revise their lending practices to provide more unsecured loans to high-technology companies based on their intangible assets or their investment in machinery and equipment. It could help introduce a venture loan insurance scheme to diversify the risks of such lending.

Bank credit and other debt financing can play only a limited role in funding young technology firms due to their pronounced technical and commercial risks. Equity is the obvious preferred private fund-raising vehicle for such firms. Reform of the financial market should address market imperfections and the funding needs of a technology-based growth strategy. The government should consider enlarging incubation programmes and other forms of funding assistance (e.g., venture capital or subsidised loans) to start-up technology firms. The government should also strive to get more qualified emerging technology firms to list in the Growth Enterprise Market. This would give the market a more balanced structure and attract wider participation among institutional investors.

CONCLUSION

The course of industrial restructuring in Hong Kong can be characterised by a shift from the production of low-technology, light consumer goods to production of high value-added services. Instead of developing their own product-based advantage or diversifying into technology-based industry, local producers have upgraded their business activities by actively relocating geographically and becoming involved in outward processing activities in China. The slow pace of technological development in Hong Kong should be attributed to the small size of most manufacturers and to the government's laissez faire policy, which did not favour R&D activities with special infrastructure or financial support.

In the late 1990s the government switched to a more active industry and technology policy. It committed to developing Hong Kong as an innovation and knowledge-based economy. This transformation is a great challenge because the economy's comparative advantage and resource base have become so skewed toward the service industry. The government has formulated various R&D and human resource development policies that assist smaller firms, promote entrepreneurship in technology-based industry, encourage applied research and mid-stream R&D, and establish a network of technology creation and transfer among the government, industry and academia. These programs are appropriately focused and, with proper implementation and co-ordination, they should raise the economy's knowledge- and resource-base as well as its innovative capacity. This strategy and the scale of government involvement must be monitored continually, however, to ensure that they remain appropriate and sufficient to make Hong Kong competitive as an innovative, knowledge-based economy.

The government's technology policy should be market-based and focused on the traditional industries in which Hong Kong has already accumulated a stock of knowledge and other production and marketing expertise. It should help traditional industries re-structure toward higher knowledge-content products and developing product-based advantages perhaps supported by advances in information technology. Hong Kong should concentrate on mid- to down-stream applied research and take a strategic role in commercialising pure research results from Mainland China. As important as upgrading technology is the need to re-shape the human resource base and intellectual stock. While waiting for the effects of educational reforms and training programs on indigenous human resources, Hong Kong should seek out and attract talent from overseas and Mainland China. In this regard, the government should increase its financial support for collaborative projects with overseas research centres and programmes to bring overseas scientists to work in Hong Kong on a short-term or project basis.

References

Akyuz, Yilmaz, Ha-joon Chang, and Richard Kozul-Wright. 1999. "New Perspectives on East Asian Development." In *East Asian Development: New Perspectives*, ed. Yilmaz Akyuz, pp. 4–36. London: Frank Cass.

Archibiugi, Daniele and Simona Iammarino. 1999. "The Policy Implications of the Globalisation of Innovation." In *Innovation Policy in a Global Economy*, eds. Daniele Archibiugi, Jeremy Howells, and Jonathan Michie, pp. 242–271. Cambridge: Cambridge University Press.

Bartholomew, Susan. 1997. "The Globalisation of Technology: A Socio-culture Perspective". In *Technology, Innovation and Competitiveness*, eds. J. Howells and J. Michie, pp. 37–62. Cheltenham, UK: Edward Elgar.

Brooks, Harvey. 1996. "The Evolution of U.S. Science Policy." In *Technology, R & D, and the Economy*, eds. B.L.R. Smith and C. E. Barfield, pp. 15–48. Washington, D.C.: Brookings Institution and American Enterprise Institute.

Cantwell, John. 1999. "Innovation as the Principal Source of Growth in the Global Economy." In *Innovation Policy in a Global Economy*, eds. Daniele Archibugi, Jeremy Howells, and Jonathan Michie, pp. 225–271. Cambridge: Cambridge University Press.

Capital. 1998. "The Future of Hong Kong's High Technology Industry" (in Chinese). August, pp. 72–78.

Census and Statistics Department. 1999. *Estimates of Gross Domestic Product 1961–98.* Hong Kong: Hong Kong SAR Government.

Chen, Edward K.Y. and Kui-wai Li. 1996. "Industrial Policy in a Laissez-faire Economy: The Case of Hong Kong." In *Industrial Policies in East Asia*, eds. S. Masuyama, D. Vandenbrink, and S. Chia, pp. 91–120. Singapore: Institute of Southeast Asian Studies and Nomura Research Institute.

Chen, Huailiang. 1999. "Lessons from a High Technology Town-Ireland" (in Chinese). Singapore *United Morning Post (Lianhe Zaobao),* 28 November.

Chen, Xiuzhen. 1999. "How to Enhance Hong Kong's Technology Competitiveness" (in Chinese). *Hong Kong Economic Journal Monthly,* no. 263 (February): 15–20.

Chiu, Stephen W.K., K.C. Ho, and Tai-lok Lui. 1997. *City-States in the Global Economy: Industrial Restructuring in Hong Kong and Singapore.* Boulder, CO: Westview Press.

Commission on Innovation and Technology. 1999. *Final Report.* Hong Kong: Hong Kong SAR Government.

Education Commission. 1999. *Review of Education System: Framework for Education Reform.* Hong Kong: Hong Kong SAR Government. September.

Edwards, Ron. 1999. "Information Technology: The Key to Global Growth." *World Trade*, 12(7): 68–71.

Ein-Dor, Phillip, Michael D. Myers, and K.S. Raman. 1997. "Information Technology in Three Small Developed Countries." *Journal of Management Information Systems*, 13(4): 61–89.

Freeman, Christopher. 1987. *Technology Policy and Economic Performance*. New York: Science Policy Research Unit, University of Sussex.

Haddon-Cave, Phillip. 1980. "Introduction: The Making of Some Aspects of Public Policy in Hong Kong." In *The Business Environment in Hong Kong*, ed. D. Lethbridge, pp. xi–xix. Hong Kong: Oxford University Press.

Hercowitz, Zvi. 1998. "The 'Embodiment' Controversy: A Review Essay." *Journal of Monetary Economics* 41(1): 217–24.

International Institute for Management Development. 1997. *The World Competitiveness Yearbook*. Switzerland: International Institute for Management Development.

Jones, Ronald W. and H. Kierzkowki. 1999. "Horizontal Aspects of Vertical Fragmentation." Paper presented at the International Conference on Global Production: Specialisation and Trade. Co-sponsored by Centre for Asian Pacific Studies, Lingnan University, Hong Kong. 25–27 October.

Laio, Xiangkun. 1999. "Can Hong Kong Develop as a Knowledge-based Economy?" (in Chinese). *Hong Kong Economic Journal Monthly*, 270 (September): 18–22.

Leyden, Dennis Patrick and Albert N. Link. 1993. *Government's Role in Innovation*. Boston: Kluwer Academic Publishers.

Liang, Winston W. and W. Michael Denny. 1997. "Upgrading Hong Kong's Technology Base." In *The Emerging Technological Trajectory of the Pacific Rim*, ed. Denis Fred Simon, pp. 256–74. New York: M.E. Sharpe.

Lucas, Robert E. 1988. "On the Mechanics of Economic Development." *Journal of Monetary Economics*, 22(1): 3–42.

Mansfield, Edwin. 1996. "Contribution of New Technology to the Economy." In *Technology, R&D, and the Economy*, eds. B.L.R. Smith, and C. E. Barfield. Washington, D.C.: Brookings Institution and American Enterprise Institute.

Mansfield, Edwin, J. Rapoport, A. Romeo, S. Wagner, and G. Beardsley. 1977. "Social and Private Rates of Return from Industrial Innovations." *Quarterly Journal of Economics*, 91 (May): 221–40.

ORiain, Sean. 1997. "The Birth of a Celtic Tiger." *Association for Computing Machinery*, 40(3): 11–16.

Romer, Paul M. 1986. "Increasing Returns and Long-Run Growth." *Journal of Political Economy* 94(5): 1002–37.

Ruttan, Vernon. W. 1998. "The New Growth Theory and Development

Economics: A Survey." *The Journal of Development Studies,* 35(2): 1–26.

Rycroft, Robert W. and Don E. Kash. 1999. "Innovation Policy for Complex Technologies." *Issues in Science and Technology,* 16(1): 73–79.

Smith, Heather. 1995. "Industry Policy in East Asia." *Asian-Pacific Economic Literature,* 9(1): 17–39.

Solow, Robert M. 1957. "Technical Change and the Aggregate Production Function." *Review of Economics and Statistics,* 39(August): 312–20.

Sumita, Makoto and Fujio Namiki. 1997. "Industrial Policy in Japan." In *Industrial Policies in East Asia,* eds. S. Masuyama, D. Vandenbrink, and S.Y. Chia, pp. 21–52. Singapore: Institute of Southeast Asian Studies and Nomura Research Institute.

Tassey, Gregory. 1997. *The Economics of R&D Policy.* London: Quorum Books.

Teubal, M., D. Foray, M. Justman, and E. Zuscovitch. 1995. *Technology Infrastructure Policy.* London: Kluwer Academic Publishers.

United Nations Conference on Trade and Development (UNCTAD). 1999. *World Investment Report 1999.* New York and Geneva: UNCTAD.

Virmani B.R. and Kala Rao. 1997. *Economic Restructuring, Technology Transfer, and Human Resource Development.* London: Response Books.

Warr, Peter G. 1994. "Comparative and Competitive Advantage." *Asian-Pacific Economic Literature,* 8(2): 1–14.

8

Taiwan as the Asia-Pacific Regional Operations Centre
Its Significance and Prospects

Kai Ma

INTRODUCTION

From the middle of the 1980s to the late 1990s the Asia-Pacific region exhibited a sparkling picture that attracted attention from people all over the world. The developing countries including Mainland China to the north and Thailand, Malaysia, and Indonesia in Southeast Asia showed extraordinarily high growth rates. Their situation in the decade up to the outbreak of the financial crisis in the summer of 1997 was both extraordinary in their own development history and admired by almost all other regions.

The region has been subject of many studies aimed at identifying the exact factors that push countries into rapid growth. Before the financial crisis, many countries around the world asked the more practical question of how they could accommodate themselves to this economic dynamism so they could prosper along with the rising stars. The answer that a group of Taiwan's scholars and bureaucrats came up with was to make the island the operations centre for the Asia-Pacific region. In 1995 the Taiwan administration announced a major national target with the slogan 'Making Taiwan the Asia-Pacific Regional Operations Centre' (APROC). Despite this bold announcement, few local people know the exact meaning of the term APROC. Project officials in the government claim that it means nothing more or less than the decade-old policy of market liberalisation and internationalisation. If so, the APROC is not worth the publicity efforts at home and abroad, and entrepreneurs will not continue to take it seriously. The bureaucratic slogan must hide a deeper significance that should be analysed to connect the words with the current position of

Taiwan's economy and Taiwanese industries in the increasingly global economy.

The first section of this chapter examines the APROC as defined by government officials. The next section describes the economic development of the Asia region over the last decade as a 'megatrend' and relates this trend to Taiwan's experience from 1957 to 1986. Although the relationship needs to be established by further empirical studies, the idea of the connection is outlined here to introduce Taiwan's role as the APROC. The subsequent section describes the mission and chances of Taiwan in the Asia-Pacific region under this megatrend. It discusses what Taiwan needs in order to fulfil this role successfully and makes some suggestions about the future structure of the regional and world economies.

OFFICIAL DEFINITION OF THE APROC

The idea of making Taiwan the APROC was first officially advocated in 1993 by Vincent Siew, who was chairman of the Council for Economic Planning and Development. In a so-called economic revitalisation program aimed at boosting Taiwan's economy, he proposed a long-term goal to make Taiwan an operations centre for the Asia-Pacific region. Although the concrete details of the regional operations centre were not spelled out, the main idea was that based on its strategic geographic location and economic background, Taiwan could be made a highly open and liberalised economy, so that personnel, funds, information, and merchandise could flow in and out freely. Taiwan could become a manufacturing centre, a financial centre, and a transportation centre for the region, a perfect location choice for international enterprises as their Asia-Pacific regional base.

In order to promote this long-term goal, the revitalisation program included a short-term project to establish an "Asia-Pacific regional operations zone" as a scaled down experiment for the much more ambitious APROC plan. The original reasoning behind the APROC was quite simple. The burgeoning of economic strength in the Asia-Pacific region since the mid-1980s has made it the world's production base. Any company that fails to establish itself in the area faces the greatest danger and, hence, many companies will have to set up operations centres to take care of their business activities in the Asia-Pacific region. With its strategic location, a strong manufacturing base, and well-developed trade and investment network, Taiwan stands out as the ideal candidate to host regional operations for international businesses and to be their gateway to the dynamic East Asian market. The operations zone proposal got no attention at all and the entire economic revitalisation program was soon forgotten.

In 1995, however, the new Premier Lien announced that the primary goal of his administration was to establish the APROC, which would be a great reengineering mission to be carried out in three stages lasting beyond the year 2000. The concrete details of the APROC plan were spelled out for the first time with the help of the consulting firm, McKinsey and Company. With the underlying theme of promoting liberalisation and internationalisation of Taiwan's economy, the APROC was defined as a set of six centres: a manufacturing centre, a financial centre, a telecommunications centre, a media centre, a maritime transportation centre, and an air transportation centre. Thus, the faint idea hidden in the 1993 economic revitalisation program took on a clear and specific structure.

The choice of the six specific centres was harshly debated. Some critics of this structure doubted Taiwan's potential to compete with Hong Kong and Singapore as a regional financial and transportation centre. Some argued that Taiwan was too ambitious in aiming to develop all six centres all at once with limited resources. A heavy blow came from Michael Porter of Harvard Business School when he was invited by Premier Lien to give a talk on the APROC. Porter bluntly stated that the six-centre plan was inappropriate and that Taiwan should aim at developing only one, a science and technology centre. Since then, although official documents still refer to six centres, the APROC project has mainly focused on liberalisation and internalisation, the old tune of the 1980s. Nevertheless some entrepreneurs and scholars still advocate building Taiwan into a "science and technology island" as a new theme playing along with the old tune.

Certainly, Taiwan should work toward liberalisation and internalisation; the whole world has been moving in this direction for decades. The question is why give this policy a fancy new label like APROC? Were bureaucrats simply trying to mislead the public by promising something imaginative, something able to boost the economy into a new era? If APROC is not just an empty slogan, then it must encompass some concrete activities to lead Taiwan into a new mode. Yet, when officials chose this title and claimed that in essence it meant no more and no less than liberalisation and internalisation, they gave no hint of such specific plans. We must dig out and examine the concrete contents of the APROC idea to understand its significance and to evaluate whether it offers a realisable blueprint for Taiwan to follow into the twenty-first century to re-engineer its economic destiny.

TAIWAN AND THE DEVELOPMENT MEGATREND IN EAST ASIA

During the decade up to 1997 Taiwan's economy was undergoing a dramatic restructuring at the same time that many Asian economies were surging. In only a few years' time Taiwan's export-processing industries, which had pushed the economy energetically forward since the second half of the 1950s by taking advantage of its comparative advantage in cheap labour, were exiled to neighbouring countries such as Thailand, Malaysia, and Mainland China, as Taiwan lost its comparative advantage to those economies. The industries that remained in Taiwan had to fill the gap so that the economy did not collapse. The restructuring of the Taiwan economy and the flourishing of the Southeast Asian economies appear to be closely connected because they occurred simultaneously and involved related activities. In this section we examine the connection more closely.

Taiwan 1957–1987

Taiwan's economy grew at an average rate of around 9.2 percent per year from the 1950s until the 1990s. The growth spurt began with a surge of foreign investment to Taiwan's export-processing industries. Over US$1 million of investment came from Japanese firms in 1958. The amount doubled by 1962, and stood at US$16 million a decade later. American firms acted even more quickly. As early as 1960 U.S. investment, which comprised almost all of private foreign investment in Taiwan, stood at around US$14 million, it surpassed US$35 million in 1965, and reached US$109 million in 1970. Taiwan's exports and imports increased rapidly along with FDI. The US$195 million of exports in 1961 was exactly double the amount in 1954. Exports exceeded US$330 million in 1963, and topped US$1 billion before the end of the 1960s. Imports surged even faster than exports, rising from less than US$300 million in 1960 to over US$800 million in 1967. During the 1960s when FDI, exports, imports, and GNP all grew at a rapid pace, the trade deficit reached US$165 million, the highest level in five decades.

Taiwan's Export-oriented Development Strategy

Many factors contributed to Taiwan's extraordinary achievement, but the dominant one must be the adoption of an export-oriented development strategy. The economy's brilliant performance from the late 1950s to the late 1980s almost exactly coincided with that strategy.

Around 1960, the capital-scarce Taiwan economy faced a serious situation. The import-substitution policy had saturated the domestic market for industrial products and the growth rate of the manufacturing sector had dropped to 3.5 percent from double-digit rates. Manufacturing firms competed viciously to protect their market share and they called on the administration to bar new entrants to certain industries. Also, Taiwan needed to find a new source of foreign exchange to settle its swelling trade deficit, because U.S. aid was scheduled to end in the early 1960s.

The only hope was to increase exports, but rice and sugar were the only domestic products competitive in international markets. Taiwan had virtually no comparative advantage in any manufactured goods because it lacked capital and technology. It did have surplus labour due to the improving efficiency of the agricultural sector, however, and world demand for unskilled labour was outpacing supply because advanced economies were booming and because low-cost workers in developing economies were isolated from the world market by communist regimes or government policies. Taiwan took advantage of the shortage of unskilled labour by adopting an export-oriented development strategy. In lieu of exporting surplus workers, Taiwan mobilised their productivity by attracting foreign firms to set up local assembly lines and export the finished products. In 1954 it exempt export goods from taxes and in 1957 it made low-interest loans available as an additional incentive to export firms. The real momentum came with the 1958 reform in the trade and exchange systems and the "19-Point Program of Economic and Financial Reform" that began the following year. The surge of foreign investment turned the economy around.

Taiwan's strategy depended on markets in developed countries. Exports to the United States almost doubled from only US$5 million in 1957 (3.5 percent of total exports) to US$9.7 million the next year, and they increased rapidly every year from then on. Exports to the United States exceeded US$115 million in 1966, totalled US$278 million in 1968, and reached US$1.25 billion in 1972 (42 percent of total exports). Moreover, imports increased even faster than exports because Taiwan's export-processing industries depended on advanced economies for machinery, critical parts, and intermediate products. Imports from Japan increased sharply in 1958, when Japan started FDI in Taiwan. They reached US$149 million in 1964 and had increased ten-times by 1973. Machinery was the largest category of imports. Besides leading to an increase in imports, Taiwan's focus on processing and assembly industries meant that local producers retained only a small portion of the final value of exports. The bulk of value added went to the up-stream suppliers of equipment, parts, and materials, who were mostly in Japan. The division of labour was of course conducive to Taiwan's rapid growth, yet it was Japan that enjoyed the greatest share of the benefits.

Restructuring of Taiwan 1987–97 and Relocation to East Asia

In the late 1980s the Taiwan economy faced a new and critical situation. Internal and external pressure led Taiwan to turn away from export-oriented development based on export-processing and to pursue economic liberalisation and industrial upgrading. Under strong pressure from the United States, the currency appreciated from 40 NT dollars per U.S. dollar in 1985 to around 26 NT dollars per U.S. dollar less than four years later. As a result, imports flooded the domestic market as import-substitution policies were weakened. At the same time, the Labour Standards Law passed in 1984 stimulated harsh confrontation between employers and employees. Environmental movements forced firms to undertake higher expenditures for pollution control. A boom in the stock and real estate markets lured thousands of workers from many industries to quit their jobs to earn easy money. It caused labour costs to escalate and simultaneously caused a severe labour shortage. The coincidence of these events took away the competitive edge of Taiwan's export-processing firms. The thirty-year momentum of export-oriented development finally waned, and Taiwan was suddenly pushed into a new era.

The growth momentum did not die, however, it simply migrated to other Asian economies. Although many Taiwanese producers went out of business, many others looked in neighbouring countries for more favourable locations in which to operate. Direct investment from Taiwan to Southeast Asia and Mainland China increased dramatically in the late 1980s (Table 8.1). According to local government statistics, Taiwan's investment in Thailand rose from US$300 million in 1987 to US$842 million the next year and it reached a peak of US$871 million in 1989. Similarly, Taiwan's investment in Malaysia soared from US$47 million in 1987 to US$815 million in 1989 and peaked at about US$2.4 billion in 1990.

Southeast Asia's Export-Oriented Strategy and a Megatrend

During the 1980s many Asian economies initiated export-oriented development strategies similar to Taiwan's. As the first to do so, Thailand

TABLE 8.1
Taiwan's Investment in ASEAN and Mainland China, 1987–99

	Thailand		Malaysia		Philippines		Indonesia		Mainland China	
	US$ million	Number	US$ million	Number	US$ million	Number	US$ million	Number	US$ million	Number
1987	5.4	5	5.8	5	2.6	3	1.0	1		
1988	11.9	15	2.7	5	36.2	7	1.9	3		
1989	51.6	23	158.6	25	66.3	13	0.3	1		
1990	149.4	39	184.9	36	123.6	16	61.9	18		
1991	86.4	33	442.0	35	1.3	2	160.3	25	174.1	237
1992	83.3	23	155.7	17	1.2	3	39.9	20	247.0	264
1993	109.2	19	64.5	18	6.5	12	25.5	11	3,168.4	9,329
1994	57.3	12	101.1	17	9.6	10	20.6	12	962.2	934
1995	51.2	15	67.3	13	35.7	17	32.1	8	1,092.7	490
1996	71.4	9	93.5	12	74.3	20	82.6	13	1,229.2	383
1997	57.5	13	85.1	13	127.0	11	55.9	22	4,334.3	8,725
1998	131.2	23	19.7	14	38.8	6	19.5	15	2,034.6	1,284
1999	112.7	12	13.7	10	29.4	9	7.3	5	1,252.8	488

Source: Investment Commission, Ministry of Economic Affairs, R.O.C. *Statistics on Overseas Chinese and Foreign Investment, Outward Investment, Outward Technical Co-operation, Indirect Mainland Investment, Guide of Mainland Industry Technology*.

enjoyed quick success similar to Taiwan's earlier experience. In the 1980s the Thai Board of Investment aggressively solicited export-oriented FDI, supported by a depreciation of the exchange rate. About 1986, Thailand adopted measures to improve the domestic investment environment and provide tax exemptions and subsidies to FDI in order to develop export-processing industries and utilise its abundance of cheap labour. Malaysia followed Thailand in 1987 and soon began to share in the same success. Between 1986 and 1988, the Malaysian government committed to relaxing state-led industrialisation and providing tax incentives for manufacturing exporters, including promulgating an Investment Act. Canton Province in Mainland China joined this club around the same time, adopting a similar strategy and India also undertook significant economic reforms to welcome FDI.

Foreign direct investment (FDI) poured into the Southeast Asian economies. In Thailand, FDI more than tripled between 1980 and 1988. In Malaysia, FDI approvals jumped from the modest level of around US$0.3 billion in 1980 to US$2 billion in 1988. Exports grew rapidly along with FDI. Thailand's annual exports doubled from around US$7 billion in the first half of the 1980s to US$15.8 billion in 1988, and they exceeded US$20 billion the next year. Thai exports jumped to US$32.5 billion in 1992 and reached a record high of US$54.3 billion in 1995. Malaysia's experience was similar. Malaysia's exports rose from US$11.7 billion in 1987 to US$20.8 billion the next year, and they almost doubled to US$40.7 billion in 1992. They peaked in 1996 at US$79.6 billion, almost seven times their 1987 value. Imports expanded as fast as exports. Thailand's imports rose from around US$10 billion during the first half of the 1980s to over US$40 billion in 1992 and reached almost US$69 billion in 1996.[1] Malaysia's story is similar. Imports increased from around US$13 billion in the first half of the 1980s to almost US$40 billion in 1992, and doubled to US$79.8 billion just four years later.[2]

Southeast Asia's pattern of export-oriented development strategies, rising FDI, exports, and imports, and rapid economic growth replicated the earlier experience of Taiwan. Similar to Taiwan, these economies focused on the export-processing industries. Labour-intensive export-processing industries such as garments, footwear, toys, and electronics became the most dynamic industries in East and Southeast Asia, and these economies became the world's assembly line. In its influential study, *The East Asian Miracle,* the World Bank credited the active promotion of manufactured exports, more precisely, the export-processing industries, in addition to high investment rates and human capital endowments for the rapid growth of these economies.

Also as Taiwan had done, these economies imported intermediate inputs from more developed economies. Moreover, just as producers of upstream parts and equipment in Japan benefited from the growth of export-processing industry in Taiwan, so would suppliers of inputs to the Southeast Asian economies benefit from the growth of export-processing there. Importantly, these economies significantly increased their imports from Taiwan after Taiwanese producers began relocating production facilities in the late 1980s. For example, in 1987 the year after it started to receiving FDI from Taiwan, Thailand's imports from Taiwan (US$425 million) increased 52 percent (Tables 8.1 and 8.2). Thailand imported more than US$1.1 billion from Taiwan in 1989 and over US$2 billion in 1993, 4.9 times the amount in 1987. Similarly, Malaysia's imports from Taiwan increased 66 percent from 1987 to 1988, 54 percent from 1988 to 1989 and 58 percent from 1989 to 1990. They passed US$1.1 billion in 1990, and reached US$1.67 billion in 1993. Indonesia, the Philippines, and Mainland China had similar patterns of FDI and imports from Taiwan. Taiwan's exports to these Southeast Asian economies consisted almost entirely of manufactured goods, a large part of which was machinery and equipment (Table 8.3), the same items that Japan had exported to Taiwan during the 1960s and 1970s.

The model of FDI-driven, export-processing oriented growth was repeated in Indonesia, the Philippines, and Mainland China in the same period and it was repeated in Vietnam, India, and Cambodia soon after. These economies all showed a similar pattern that as soon as they opened the doors to foreign direct investment to develop the export-processing industries, their imports, exports, and growth rates all rose rapidly. Indeed, this pattern could be called the driving force, or 'megatrend', of the Asia-Pacific region.

THE PROSPECTS FOR THE ASIAN ECONOMIES AND THE ROLE OF TAIWAN

When these other Asian economies applied the export-oriented development strategy, conditions were different than they had been for Taiwan. First, unlike Taiwan, the economies of Southeast Asia are not alone. By 1992, almost every Asian economy had adopted an export-oriented strategy and doors are wide open to FDI and intermediate products in almost every country in the region from Mainland China to India. Second, while the

TABLE 8.2
Taiwan's Trade with ASEAN and Mainland China, 1987–99
(US$ millions)

	Thailand		Malaysia		Philippines		Indonesia		Mainland China	
	Exports	Imports	Exports	Imports	Exports	Imports	Exports	Imports	Exports	Imports
1987	424.6	200.4	272.1	729.0	459.7	194.4	445.5	567.2	1,227	289
1988	753.7	341.9	451.1	943.4	601.4	242.3	632.6	613.4	2,242	479
1989	1,110.2	390.2	694.8	887.5	778.1	238.5	934.1	706.2	2,897	587
1990	1,423.6	448.0	1,103.6	1,003.0	811.4	236.3	1,245.8	921.6	3,278	765
1991	1,444.9	586.1	1,464.9	1,409.4	848.0	235.3	1,207.2	1,234.3	4,667	1,126
1992	1,809.6	824.6	1,600.3	1,829.2	1,023.3	305.2	1,214.8	1,407.3	6,288	1,119
1993	2,019.0	973.0	1,671.8	1,938.9	1,031.1	364.8	1,284.5	1,624.0	7,585	1,104
1994	2,440.2	1,108.8	2,224.2	2,326.9	1,222.5	460.7	1,433.0	21,14.4	8,517	1,292
1995	3,071.7	1,485.3	2,898.6	2,953.7	1,653.6	623.2	1,868.9	2,150.4	9,883	1,574
1996	2,789.6	1,671.7	2,953.7	3,565.2	1,931.2	840.3	1,955.3	1,884.5	9,718	1,582
1997	2,562.1	1,926.9	3,035.5	4,228.3	2,242.5	1,374.6	2,133.8	2,184.7	9,715	1,744
1998	1,925.8	1,967.7	2,285.9	3,623.0	1,934.3	1,823.0	1,048.9	2,101.1	8,365	1,655
1999	2,104.5	2,383.4	2,848.1	3,882.0	2,611.4	2,172.5	1,298.6	2,291.4	8,175	1,628

Source: Ministry of Finance, R.O.C., *Monthly Statistics of Exports*, Taiwan Area, the Republic of China, various issues.

TABLE 8.3
Composition of Taiwan's Exports to ASEAN Countries, 1981–91
(Percent)

	Machinery and Transportation Equipment					Manufactures				
	1981	**1985**	**1988**	**1990**	**1991**	**1981**	**1985**	**1988**	**1990**	**1991**
Singapore	32.12	25.76	47.16	51.96	51.86	88.97	85.10	94.83	96.82	95.86
Malaysia	32.45	35.47	49.93	52.78	52.78	91.44	89.50	95.20	97.23	97.38
Thailand	40.80	26.55	51.24	45.04	45.04	89.09	72.68	91.18	91.57	93.09
Indonesia	40.53	38.51	41.87	45.25	45.25	80.73	82.12	85.43	92.33	93.13
Philippines	18.50	14.70	26.74	26.55	26.55	71.63	86.81	89.64	93.33	93.60
Total	33.01	27.40	42.59	46.72	46.72	84.32	83.74	92.00	94.55	94.91

Notes: Machinery and Transportation Equipment is SITC code 7; Manufactures includes SITC codes 5, 6, 7, 8. Figures are ratios of exports of listed products from Taiwan to ASEAN (excluding Brunei) over Taiwan's total exports.
Source: OECD.

shortage of cheap labour on the world market and the fact that Taiwan was a virtual monopsonist (except for Hong Kong and Singapore) for three decades were critical to Taiwan's success, cheap labour is no longer scarce in the 1990s. The available supply of cheap labour on the world market now amounts to about three billion workers compared to the few million in past decades. Thailand, Malaysia, and Canton temporarily benefited for a few years from their position as relative early-comers in the supply of lower wage labour. But harsher competition among economies with surplus labour diminished their advantage bit by bit and shifted the competitive edge to developing countries with even lower wages. The outburst of the Asian financial crisis in Thailand and Malaysia in 1997 was simply a dramatic culmination of this miserable process. The crisis clearly indicates that the trend for the other East Asian economies is not as smooth as the pattern of Taiwan's experience.

The Asian economies face a different world economic structure than Taiwan faced at a similar point in its development. In the late 1990s the international division of labour between assemblers and up-stream producers that once involved mainly Taiwan and Japan now includes a much larger number of economies in the Asia-Pacific region and extends well beyond the region. Asian economies with a combined population in the billions now compete with each other to play the role of low-wage assembler of labour-intensive export products that Taiwan filled in the 1950s. Moreover, as they accepted FDI to develop their export-processing industries these Asian economies became linked to worldwide markets as the globalisation movement progressed in the last decade. Their huge supply of cheap labour will affect the world economic order, the global labour and capital markets, and economies within as well as outside of the region. Each country has to find a role and a place in this framework and take advantage of the megatrend to the greatest extent possible.

In order to succeed in export-oriented development based on export processing industries, East Asian economies need more than technology, capital, parts, and materials. They need

- entrepreneurs to connect the ever-increasing cheap unskilled labour to sophisticated manufacturing and marketing techniques. Industrial and commercial technologies have progressed so quickly that they are beyond the reach of newcomers to handle directly.
- mediators to transfer not-too-advanced technologies from the more advanced countries to the assemblers. (The way the Japanese entre-preneurs around 1960, transferred the not-too-advanced technologies

and facilities to Taiwan to help develop Taiwan's export-processing industries).

- access to low-cost, appropriate machinery, parts, and material inputs. If up-stream producers locate too far away from the export-processors the transportation cost is too high, either in time or money. Up-stream firms that lack experience are inefficient in the manufacturing and transporting businesses.

- entrepreneurs to develop commodities to suit market demand, to promote and market these products, to improve technologies, to rationalise production procedures, and to procure inputs. Such entrepreneurs effectively minimise transactions costs and expand world demand for processed products to accommodate the expansion of supply.

At one time, Japanese entrepreneurs filled all these roles for Taiwanese export processors. Indeed, Japan could be described as the operations centre for Taiwan's export-processing industries. With abilities accumulated over four-decades of experience Taiwan is aiming to step into the position that Japan had in the 1950s. Taiwan aims to be the provider not only of up-stream materials, equipment, and parts, but also of know-how, marketing channels, brand names, financial support, and technologies. The role of regional operations centre is even more necessary and certainly more important today, when billions of people are competing to take Taiwan's place as export-processor. In short, Taiwan wants to be the APROC. This is the fundamental sense in which Taiwan aims to be the APROC.

Any economy that relies on export-processing industries to drive development has a strong motive to substitute domestically sourced parts and materials for up-stream inputs produced abroad. Such substitution not only allows the country to capture more added value and save time wasted in transportation, but also it enhances economic sovereignty and promotes the upgrading of the industrial structure. But it is difficult for such an economy to develop domestic upstream industries for two reasons. First, an economy that relies on the labour-intensive export-processing industries must lack capital and skilled personnel that are needed by capital- and technology-intensive up-stream industries. Processing industries do not add sufficient value to allow an economy to accumulate the minimum capital and technology required for up-stream industries, unless it has a large enough market share of exported goods to generate relatively abundant profits. Second, it takes time to establish up-stream industries. It takes a lot of time to acquire sophisticated know-how, to train appropriate personnel, and to climb up the ladder from the production of parts and material that are relatively simple in technical know-how and much less capital-intensive. Only if a country can stick to this course for a sufficiently long period can it reach a relatively high level and rely upon up-stream industries to support the upgrading of the economy.

Starting from the end of the 1950s to the end of the 1980s, Taiwan worked hard step-by-step to substitute locally made products for imported parts and material. Both quality and technology have improved continuously. Fortunately for Taiwan, its position as the sole supplier of low-cost labour-intensive goods for 30 years provided the extra resources it needed to invest in physical and human capital to upgrade from very low-end export-processing industries to more capital-intensive and technology-intensive up-stream ones.

After 1986, when more and more developing countries in East Asia with much cheaper labour began competing to create export-processing industries, Taiwan lost the industries that had supported the economy so vigorously. Taiwan's manufacturing output and export value continued to grow. The up-stream industries that were supporting domestic down-stream partners are now supporting down-stream processors throughout East and Southeast Asia. Taiwan has automatically moved into the role of a regional operations centre since then, and is growing stronger along the time.

There is another dimension to the role of regional operations centre. The production procedure can be divided into many stages, from acquiring materials, hiring labour, establishing the factory, designing the appropriate process, to the research and development in technologies, know-how, to the design and marketing of the products. These activities do not need to be carried out in a single location or by a single firm. The mission of a capable entrepreneur is to locate each input (the labour, material, technical equipment) at the lowest cost, with greatest efficiency.

During the last decade, when Taiwanese export-processing enterprises shifted production to Thailand, Malaysia, Canton and other developing countries in East and South Asia, they typically continued to handle all their operations except the actual processing in Taiwan. In other words, these entrepreneurs made Taiwan their regional operations centres. As more and more entrepreneurs in the up-stream industries in the electronics and information industries join this group, they together are making Taiwan an important APROC.

Facing this energetic reshuffling situation, Taiwan's prospects for becoming a true and/or significant APROC depend on a number of factors. First Taiwan needs to strengthen the necessary conditions, such as the competitiveness of its up-stream manufacturing industries, the expansion and improvement of marketing channels, and the soundness and efficiency of its financial system. Second, it must offer as sufficient and efficient infrastructure as do Singapore, Hong Kong, and Japan. Third, Taiwan's decision-makers must have a proper understanding of the future of the Asia-Pacific economy. They must recognise that the way to fully utilise Taiwan's comparative advantages as the APROC is to allow more capital and firms to move to cultivate the neighbouring economies. Last, but not least, Taiwan's decision-makers have to predict the impact of such a revolutionary leap onto the future structure of the world economy in the century to come. The over-supply of cheap labour, the increasing scarcity of physical and human capital, the collapsing labour costs, the declining prices of processed products are all woven into a new web that covers the entire world. Most of what we know today will change significantly in the coming years. Without correct foresight, not only would Taiwan's chances to become the APROC be slim, but also Taiwan's own economic prospects would be dim.

CONCLUSION

Although the term "making Taiwan the Asia-Pacific Regional Operations Centre", the brainchild of scholars and bureaucrats, is not well defined, the phenomenon it describes is the natural outcome of the economic progress in Taiwan and in the Asia-Pacific region over the last half-century. The development strategy followed by Taiwan for almost three decades from the late 1950s has a significant connection to this phenomenon. On one hand it forced Taiwan to relocate production facilities to neighbouring economies. At the same time it helped Taiwan to upgrade from a major supplier of labour-intensive export-processing products to supplier of parts, equipment, and material for down-stream export-processing industries and to offer operations headquarters functions.

As the export-oriented strategy spread to almost all the developing economies in the Asia-Pacific region during the 1990s, a megatrend encompassing half of the world's population emerged. This megatrend will continue to play out in the rest of the world for many decades to come. Through its physical location at the centre of the Asia-Pacific region and its structural position in the megatrend of regional economic development, Taiwan has already become an APROC. Taiwan must use this position effectively so it can enjoy a new era of development as glorious as the three decades following the late 1950s.

Notes

[1] At the same time, Thailand's trade deficit increased to US$8.2 billion in 1992 from less than US$3 billion in 1982. Many analysts have cited Thailand's US$15 billion deficit for 1996 as one cause of the currency crisis.

[2] Malaysia's trade deficit rose from almost zero in the first half of the 1980s to more than US$2.3 billion in 1991. Although the imbalance was smaller than in Thailand Malaysia's trade deficit reached almost US$4.2 billion in 1995.

References

In English:

Borensztein, E., J. De Gregorio, and Lee Jong-Wha. 1995. "How Does Foreign Direct Investment Affect Economic Growth?" Working Paper No. 5057. National Bureau of Economic Research (NBER).

Chiu, Lee-in Chen. 1997. "Toward an Interregional Integration of Habitat, Production and Ecosystem: Developing Taiwan into a Regional Operations Centre." *Industry of Free China* 41–78.

Chou, Tein-Chen. 1985. "The Pattern and Strategy of Industrialization in Taiwan: Specialization and Offsetting Policy." *The Developing Economics* 23(2): 138–57.

Choudhury, Masudul Alam. 1999. "Global Megatrends and the Community." *Asian Economic Review,* 41(1): 43–58.

Collins, S. M. and B. P. Bosworth. 1996. "Economic Growth in East Asia: Accumulation versus Assimilation". *Brookings Papers on Economic Activity* 2: 135–203.

Gunasekera, H. and Don B. H. 1989. "Intra-industry Specialization in Production and Trade in Newly Industrializing Countries: A Conceptual Framework and Some Empirical Evidence from East Asia." *World Development* 1(8): 1279–87.

Hill, H. and P-C. Athuborala. 1998. "Foreign Investment in East Asia." *Asian-Pacific Economic Literature* 12(2): 29–50.

Manning, Chris. 1999. "Labor Markets in the ASEAN-4 and the NIEs." *Asian-Pacific Economic Literature* 13(1): 50–68.

Radelet, S. and G. Sachs. 1998. "The East Asian Financial Crisis: Diagnosis, Remedies and Prospects." *Brookings Papers on Economic Activity.* Vol. 1: 1–90.

Ranis, Gustav, ed. 1992. *Taiwan: From Developing to Mature Economy*. Oxford: Westview Press.

Schive, Chi. 1994. "Regional Operations Center and the ROC Economy in the 1990s." *Industry of Free China* April: 43–53.

Siew, Vincent C. 1994. "The Changing Role of Taiwan in East Asian Economic Grouping." *Industry of Free China* April: 23–27.

Smith, H. 1995. "Industry Policy in East Asia." *Asian-Pacific Economic Literature* 9(1): 17–19.

World Bank. 1993. *The East Asian Miracle: Economic Growth and Public Policy*. New York: Oxford University Press.

In Chinese:

Ma, Kai. 1994. "The Retrospect and Prospect of Taiwan's Economy." *Economic Outlook*, 9(1): 59–64.

————. 1995. "Making Taiwan the APROC: Dream Comes True." *Economic Outlook* 10(5): 10–15.

Pang, L. W. 1996. "An Evaluation of the Prospects of Three International Financial Centres: Taipei, Hong Kong and Shanghai." *Industry of Free China* December: 19–34.

Tu, Jen-hua and Chi Schive. 1995. *Theory and Practice of an Asia-Pacific Regional Operations Centre*. Taipei: Hua-Tai Publishing.

9

Industrial Upgrading of Korea
Process, Prospects, and Policies

Cheonsik Woo

"... no time to be wasted. The window of opportunity would not be open for long"[1]

INTRODUCTION

For more than four decades the Korean economy expanded at a remarkable rate, dramatically transforming from a poverty-ridden agrarian base into a modern industrialised economy with OECD membership.[2] Since its initial take-off in the early 1960s, reform and restructuring programs appropriate to different stages of development more or less succeeded in facilitating Korea's industrial transition to sustain high growth. The 1997 Asian financial crisis rekindled debate over the extent of Korea's past success and raised doubts over whether Korea can sustain its growth momentum with continuous industrial upgrading in face of the formidable challenges of the "knowledge-based economy". Indeed, despite a dramatic recovery from the nearly debilitating impact of the crisis, the Korean economy is still highly vulnerable, with many remaining structural problems. The traditional source of Korea's strong economic growth — successful mobilisation of capital and labour — is depleting fast, while learning from or adopting foreign technologies is becoming increasingly difficult.[3]

After five decades of industrialisation, Korea now resembles the major advanced economies in its basic industrial profile. But with industrial activities heavily concentrated in low to medium value added industrial activities such as processing and production, Korea remains behind these economies in the quality of its industrial structure. Except for a few elite firms that belong to *chaebol* in select fields such as semiconductors and automobiles, Korean firms lack their own basis of competitiveness that is adequate ensure their survival in the ever-accelerating wave of open, innovation-based, global competition.

Korea must surmount huge obstacles to retain growth momentum in the medium term and to become a competitive, knowledge-based economy with sound fundamentals in the long term. Although the need is urgent, there is no clear vision or cogent view about how to upgrade the competitiveness of Korean industries. Most agree that Korea should find new comparative advantages in high value added technology- and knowledge-intensive industries, but there is no consensus about which those industries are and what the government needs to do. Most agree that traditional interventionist policies that artificially funnel resources are neither desirable nor feasible, but Korea lacks the institutional mechanisms, policy guidelines, and incentives to help the majority of mediocre, non-innovative firms escape the 'incompetence-trap'.

In order to make headway toward an innovation-based, high-productivity economy with a solid and robust industrial and innovation base Korea needs to capitalise on its existing strengths. What are the potentials of Korean industry and what policies are needed to realise them? These are the central questions of this chapter. A brief review and assessment of Korea's industrialisation process to date provides a background for the main section which characterises and assesses Korea's industrial basis today from a dynamic, comprehensive perspective. It highlights the limits and potential of Korean industries in the context of the rising trends of global competition and co-operation and discusses the basic direction of industrial upgrading as well as the requisite policy measures. The analysis especially stresses the importance of promoting small- and medium-sized companies. It concludes with a practical proposal for establishing a cluster of firms in the machinery industry — both to upgrade this core industry to compete in the environment of the twenty-first century and to provide a new model of industrial and regional development for other Korean industries to follow.

REVIEW OF KOREA'S INDUSTRIALISATION PROCESS

The Take-off Phase: 1961–1972[4]

With virtually no domestic economic resources to draw on, Korea relied mainly on foreign aid to finance the reconstruction and stabilisation programs that followed the partition and Korean War. Until the 1960s industrial policy was mainly inward looking, encouraging import-substitution in non-durable consumer-goods industries. Korea abruptly switched to an outward-looking, export-oriented industrialisation and growth strategy in 1962. The growth rate soared immediately to 9.1 percent in 1963 and the economy entered a prolonged period of high growth and rapid industrialisation.

Under this strategy, most other policy objectives were aligned with or subjugated to the goal of export-promotion and the government undertook a sequence of reforms of exchange rate, currency, budget, and tax system policies. Domestic market protection was high in industries without strong export prospects and low in industries with international competitiveness. The government introduced a complex system of incentives to promote exports. An important aspect of Korea's success in this phase was the deliberate concentration on industries with relatively low capital requirements, such as clothing and wigs, which had favourable and rising international demand. Exports rose sharply, while the industrial structure was solidifying and diversifying into such light manufacturing industries as clothing, footwear, and electronics. Strong export performance helped Korea overcome the constraints of its relatively narrow domestic market and the growth rate averaged 8.9 percent from 1963 to 1972.

The Heavy and Chemical Industry Promotion Phase: 1973–79

In 1973 Korea shifted from this general export-promotion strategy to a strategy biased toward the heavy and chemical industries (HCIs). Under the HCI drive, the government took the initiative in introducing sector-specific import-substitution while reinforcing and modifying the existing export incentive programs to favour the selected HCIs.[5] A rapid increase in domestic wage rates, increased global competition in traditional export markets, and adverse changes in global political and economic environments called for deepening Korea's industrial structure around HCIs such as chemicals, basic metals, general machinery, shipbuilding, and electronics.[6] The government introduced a broad range of interventionist policy instruments, including special tax treatment and most notably, preferential access to credit through policy loans to support the large-scale, risky investments required by HCIs.[7] These policies, especially the special credit support, led to a dramatic expansion of fixed capital formation in the targeted industries, which exhibited rapid growth and high profitability despite relatively low rates of return.

During the 1970s under the HCI-biased development strategy Korea created comparative advantage in more capital-intensive industries, whether physical or human capital. The export ratio of the heavy and chemical industry sector rose from 7.4 percent in 1970 to 19.3 percent in 1980. The sector's share of total output almost doubled between 1970 and 1975 and it continued to rise. By 1980 heavy industry's share of total output surpassed the share of light industry.[8] Nevertheless, neglected industries such as textiles managed to survive, and indeed continued to drive export performance in the latter half of 1970s, when much of the heavy-chemical sector lumbered with excess capacity. Despite a slowdown in export growth, the Korean economy grew at an average annual rate of 8.9 percent in the 1973–79 period. It is now widely agreed that this high growth was largely due to expansionary aggregate demand policies and heavy foreign borrowing not to the HCI strategy, however. The over-ambitious HCI drive is seen to have caused serious economic problems such as inter-sectoral resource misallocation, external debt, and serious distortion of the private-sector decision process.[9] Regardless of its cost, the HCI strategy did achieve many of its original policy objectives; the industrial structure shifted markedly toward the heavy and chemical industries. Under the impetus of the HCI drive, the Korean economy made strong progress in upgrading its export structure from labour-intensive to capital- and skill-intensive products, with capital-intensive products such as ships and steel gradually replacing light manufactured products as its major export portfolio.[10]

Rationalisation and Liberalisation Phases: 1980s Onward

By 1979, the Korean economy faced grave structural and macroeconomic problems such as escalating inflation, faltering exports, and over-capacity in the HCIs. In the early 1980s the new government started various institutional and structural reform programs and established a new direction for industrial policy, concentrating on technology- and skill-intensive, rather than capital-intensive, industries.[11]

The shift toward a more sector-neutral and market-oriented approach to industrial policy was clearly articulated in the Fifth Five-year Development Plan (1982–86). Through an array of financial and import liberalisation programs, the government gradually reduced its role in credit allocation, terminating policies that awarded HCIs preferential interest rates and credit access. Flexibility in interest rate management, introduced in 1984 and reinforced by deregulation in 1988, allowed financial intermediaries to determine their own lending rates within a given range. The tax reform of 1981 also greatly reduced the scope of special tax treatment for key industries.

Despite the general thrust toward neutrality, however, the government bypassed competitive solutions for the most part. Instead, it continued to take an active role in restructuring distressed industries, supporting the development of technology, and promoting competition. In its rationalisation efforts, for instance, the government would not let troubled firms go bankrupt for fear of enormous financial losses to the banking sector and their social and economic repercussions. Numerous rationalisation programs were thus staged under the initiative and tight supervision of the government via forced mergers, mandatory capacity reduction, and a general support for commercial banks. These massive government-directed restructuring operations engendered unfortunate side effects, particularly a serious moral hazard problem in private businesses.[12]

The reorientation of industrial policy that began in 1979 took root by the mid-1980s. Most troubled businesses in shipbuilding, shipping, and overseas construction, which had been plagued by over-capacity and financial distress, were successfully bailed out or rationalised without grave repercussions on the economy. Also there was a big turnaround in Korea's external balance around 1986 due largely to a fortuitous change in three external conditions (known now as 'the 3-lows').[13] With the completion of the five-year liberalisation program (1984–88), trade protection was significantly lowered by the end of the 1980s.[14] Foreign direct investment, one of the most tightly controlled areas of Korea, also began to increase sharply after 1984. Through the mid 1980s, Korea regained its growth-momentum and, helped greatly by resounding export performance in the second half of the decade, achieved an average growth rate of 9 percent for the 1980s.

During this period Korea greatly enhanced its overall technological capacity. Intervention in technological development emphasised the establishment of institutions to train scientists and engineers and to conduct basic and applied research. Under the Fifth Five-year Development Plan (1982–1986) national science and technology investment was increased from 0.9 to 2 percent of GNP and the Sixth Plan raised Korea's science and technology (S&T) spending ratio to 2.5 percent by 1991, roughly comparable to spending by OECD members. The government budget supported general research and scientific training, as well as special research centres for energy and resources, machinery, electronics, telecommunications, and chemicals. In addition, the National Project for Research and Development (1982) was established to fund public and public-private joint R&D projects in the high-technology fields of electronics, fine chemicals, and engineering. With the help of these programs, and new tax incentives under the Technology Development Promotion Act — strengthened in 1981 — private R&D expenditures expanded rapidly, and a number of private research centres were established.

In sum, over the four decades from 1960 Korea transformed in stages from emphasis on light industry to heavy and chemical industries and to a greater technology base. Strong capital accumulation and growth in labour inputs, in which the government played a pivotal role as manager and nationwide resource mobiliser, underpinned this transformation. Toward the mid 1990s, the limits of such an input-driven, statist model of development began to loom in symptoms such as mounting trade deficits, rampant credit growth by financial institutions, and overextended, highly leveraged *chaebol*. Nonetheless, Koreans seemed optimistic about the future of their economy until 1996.[15] This attitude changed drastically in the turmoil and virtual collapse of the economy that followed the onset of the financial crisis in 1997. With the faltering of the mainstay industries and *chaebol* many came to see Korea's future as bleak. Korea's development paradigm is now at a crossroads. Korean industry must continue its transformation to provide a solid base for an innovation-based, high-productivity economy. This upgrading will take place in the context of rising trends of global competition and co-operation. In the remainder of this chapter we examine Korea's industrial structure from a comprehensive, dynamic perspective to identify the future direction of transformation and recommend policy measures appropriate for Korean industry to realise its potential.

INDUSTRIAL UPGRADING: NEW CHALLENGES AND PROSPECTS

Profile of Korean Industries and Direction of Upgrading

In the course of managing the crisis, the upgrading of Korean industry as a whole emerged as a hotbed of debate. As many of Korea's 'traditional' thrust industries, including the flagship electronics and automobile industries, slid into a deep slump, their potential for future growth came to be seriously questioned. At the same time interest in the more cutting-edge technology industries such as bio-engineering, aerospace, and new materials, as well as a group of other promising 'new' industries was heightened.

Considering the experiences of the major advanced economies, we should not expect industrial upgrading in Korea to be based on exciting new high-tech industries, however. Rather, it will be based on old established industries. Six industries have long formed the basis of the industrial sectors of the leading world economies, the United States, Germany, Japan, France, UK, Italy (hereafter, designated the G-6).[16] In 1994, these six industries — electrical/electronics, transportation equipment, chemicals, machinery, textiles/apparel, and scientific equipment — together accounted for 55 to 60 percent of total manufacturing value-added and employment in the G-6 nations and for 70 to 90 percent of their total manufacturing exports (Figure 9.1). Even in the United States and the UK, where fast changing industries such as bio-engineering and new materials play a vital role precipitating technological innovation in the major industries through

FIGURE 9.1
Value Added Share of Major OECD Economies by Industry

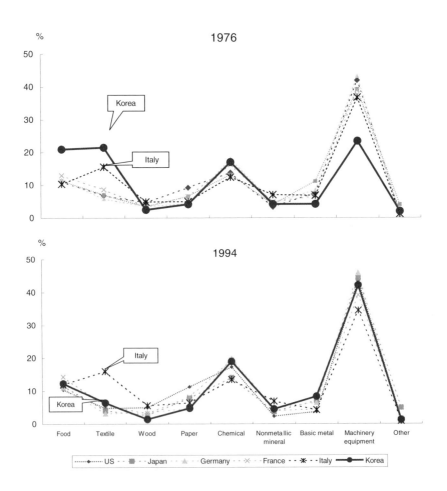

new intermediate goods or technological spillovers, cutting-edge technology industries have only a small share of value added and employment. In Korea as well, these new cutting-edge technology industries, which are all in their infancy at present, will gain their share gradually, in line with the overall upgrading of the six mainstream industries.

Over the past decades of industrialisation Korea's overall industrial profile has come to resemble that of the major advanced economies. The composition of Korea's output differed markedly from that of the G-6 nations in 1976, but by 1994 the discrepancy had completely gone (Figure 9.1). Moreover, the value added and export shares of the six major industries in Korea's economy (62.3 percent of value added and 82 percent of exports) lie in the normal range of the G-6 economies. It is worth noting that the industrial profiles of the G-6 economies today are virtually isomorphic to the ones they exhibited in 1976. In view of the speed and extent of change occurring in the technology and economic environment today, though, it unlikely that Korea's future industrial evolution will follow the same trajectory that the G-6 economies followed to date. Nevertheless, we speculate that Korea's industrial structure will not change drastically in the next ten years, since Korea currently lags considerably behind the G-6 economies in level of development and since their overall industrial profile has remained stable over the past two decades.

Despite the similarity in output structure there is a qualitative gap between Korea and other advanced economies, as indicated by differences in labour productivity and trade structure. Average labour productivity for the manufacturing sector in Korea stands at about half the level in Japan and also falls behind the levels in the United States, Germany, and France by substantial margins (Table 9.1). For individual industries, the gap in labour productivity between Korea and the best-performing country ranges from a low of 37 percent in the textile/apparel industry to a high of 71 percent in the electrical/electronic industry.[17]

Looking at export structure, the textile/apparel industry's share of exports in Korea is unusually high compared to most other economies (Table 9.2). Moreover, although Italy's export share in this industry is also high, Italy exports mainly high-quality, fashionable items whereas Korea exports low-end commodity items. Likewise, Korea's high export share in the electric/electronics industry is comparable to the share in Japan, but again Korea's exports in this category consist largely of final assembly products that are less technologically sophisticated than Japan's exports.

The weakness in Korea's trade structure is better illustrated by the pattern of specialisation (Table 9.3). Although chemical products and

TABLE 9.1
Index of Labour Productivity by Manufacturing Industry
in Selected Economies, 1995
(US Manufacturing = 100.0)

	US	Japan	Germany	France	UK	Italy	Korea
Manufacturing	100.0	122.6	99.7	107.3	57.2	68.0	62.2
Major Industries Sub-total	106.4	119.2	104.0	109.2	55.6	64.9	59.7
Textile/Apparel	48.2	39.5	58.2	67.2	36.5	45.5	19.9
Chemicals	155.4	174.1	160.3	169.0	88.6	93.6	87.1
Machinery	98.7	123.9	84.1	85.6	50.2	75.2	49.9
Electric & Electronics	123.0	125.2	85.5	106.3	44.5	74.7	79.4
Transport Equipment	107.3	146.1	109.4	98.5	53.9	67.0	63.3
Scientific Equipment	85.4	123.4	69.9	106.6	51.2	72.9	42.3

Note: Data for Italy and UK are 1994.
Source: OECD, OECD STAN Database, 1999.

TABLE 9.2
Composition of Manufacturing Exports by Industry
in Selected OECD Economies, 1994
(Percent of total manufacturing exports)

	US	Japan	Germany	France	UK	Italy	Korea
Textiles and apparel	3.6	1.8	4.9	6.2	5.1	18.0	18.9
Chemical products	16.3	10.3	18.5	20.4	21.1	13.2	12.4
Machinery	19.1	21.0	16.9	10.8	17.4	18.2	7.5
Electrical and electronics	15.5	23.7	11.2	9.9	11.9	8.2	28.9
Transport equipment	20.3	26.5	21.5	20.5	15.0	10.4	13.6
Scientific equipment	5.0	5.9	3.8	1.3	4.3	2.0	1.1
Major industries subtotal	79.9	89.1	76.9	69.1	74.9	70.0	82.5

Source: OECD, OECD STAN Database, 1997.

machinery account for 6.5 and 6.0 percent of Korea's exports respectively, Korea's overall trade position in these two industries is significantly in deficit, while all G-6 countries post a substantial surplus (except Italy in chemicals). Actually, the industries in which Korea runs a trade surplus, such as computers/office machines and telecommunication equipment, are ones in which all G-6 nations except Japan are in a deficit position.

TABLE 9.3
Patterns of Trade Specialisation by Industry in
Selected OECD Economies, 1995
(Percent)

	US	Japan	Germany	France	Italy	Korea
Chemical products	0.20	0.17	0.24	0.11	–0.29	–0.21
Rubber and plastic products	–0.04	0.63	0.17	0.13	0.27	0.43
Drugs and medicines	0.07	–0.45	0.21	0.11	–0.04	–0.44
Basic metals	–0.31	0.45	0.12	0.05	0.17	0.06
Machinery and equipment	0.02	0.72	0.44	0.06	0.45	–0.51
Electrical and electronic equipment	–0.18	0.55	0.13	0.06	0.10	0.32
Office and computing machinery	–0.28	0.39	–0.26	–0.19	–0.12	0.16
Communication equipment	–0.30	0.51	–0.00	–0.01	–0.23	0.49
Motor vehicles	–0.37	0.72	0.31	0.07	0.01	0.68
Aircraft and shipbuilding	0.52	0.58	0.21	0.50	0.23	0.16
Scientific equipment	0.02	0.42	0.20	–0.08	–0.10	–0.47
Textiles, apparel, and leather	–0.64	–0.59	–0.28	–0.16	0.45	0.53
Other	–0.27	–0.65	–0.20	–0.13	–0.56	–0.53

Note: Trade specialisation coefficient defined as (exports – imports)/(exports + imports).
Source: OECD, *Foreign Trade by Commodities*, 1995.

The qualitative deficiency of Korean industries eventually translates into a gap in knowledge-intensity, which in turn can be explained in terms of the composition of various activities comprising the chain of value-creation. Figure 9.2 illustrates the fundamental difference in value-creation structure between Korea and an advanced economy. For the purpose of exposition, products are divided into high value added (high-end) and low value added (low-end) goods. The value-chain is broken into five component activities according to knowledge-intensity, ranging from product design (the most knowledge-intensive) to production (the least knowledge-intensive).[18] Compared to advanced economies, Korea concentrates more on low-end products and less knowledge-intensive activities, such as production and simple adaptation or improvement of products or processes.

Figure 9.2 may be a stylised representation of Korea's development gap but, seen in conjunction with the previously discussed stability in the industrial profile of the G-6 nations, it has a crucial implication about the essence and direction of Korea's industrial upgrading. In the figure Korea's position today corresponds to the position of the advanced nations two or three decades ago. What occurred in the advanced nations over a long

FIGURE 9.2
Characterisation of Gap in Knowledge-Intensity

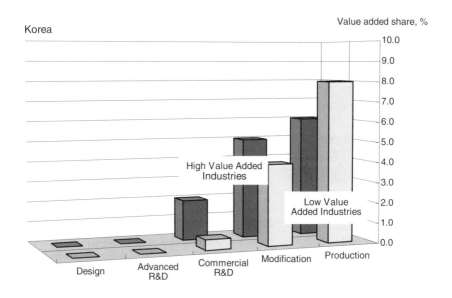

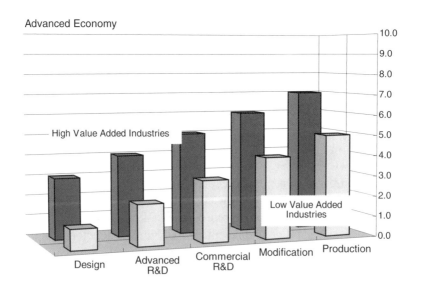

period was a gradual upgrading of traditional mainstay industries, characterised by sequential shifts toward more knowledge-intensive, higher value-added activities within and across industries. Accumulation of knowledge and technological capabilities is essentially a cumulative and gradual process, and so is an economy's evolution toward a more knowledge- and technology-intensive, advanced structure. Considering the obvious chronological lag in Korea's industrialisation, it may be then quite natural for a substantial qualitative gap to exist between Korea and the G-6 nations for now. The present gap implies that there is still room for the traditional type of industrial upgrading to take place in Korea, until it reaches a level of development comparable to the G-6 economies today. Given the far-reaching and ever-deepening impacts of globalisation and information and communications technology (ICT), upgrading in Korea will take place in a more complex and volatile dynamic context than it did in these advanced economies. Regardless of the exact mechanism and process, however, one thing is clear. There is no tectonic shift in industrial structure and advancement. The thrust and focus of Korea's industrial upgrading need to be on, not off, the existing mainstream industries.

Korean Industries in a Global and Dynamic Context

The process and outcome of industrial upgrading in Korea will vary across industries, depending particularly on the competitive base of domestic firms and the competitive structure of global markets. It is convenient to distinguish two groups of industries based on the competitiveness of global markets (Table 9.4):

- global, high-technology industries, such as electronics, fine chemicals, and automobiles, in which a few leading multinational enterprises (MNEs) maintain substantial oligopoly power and
- local, medium-technology industries, such as machinery and textiles/apparel, in which innovative small- and medium-sized enterprises (SMEs) lead the market by producing highly differentiated or specialised products.[19]

Responding to the trends of integrating markets, accelerating techno-logical change, and intensifying competition, leading MNEs in global industries have escalated their efforts to extend important dimensions of their business activities around the world. Their strategic thrust is to locate each functional business element in the most suitable site/firm and to tap and link together the tangible and intangible assets at each location to

Table 9.4
Characteristics of Major Industries

		Global, High-tech Industries (Electronics, Automobiles, Chemicals)	Local, Mid-tech Industries (Machinery, Textiles/Apparel)
Characteristics	Market structure	Oligopoly among leading MNEs – Highly dynamic	Led by innovative SMEs – Stable monopolistic competition in a highly differentiated market
	Lead nations	• Automobiles: US, Germany, Japan, France, Italy • Electronics: US, Japan • Chemicals: US, UK, Germany	• Machinery: US, Germany, Japan • Textiles & apparel: Italy, France
	Source of competitive advantage	Economies of scale in R&D and production – Individual core competence – Global R&D network	Economies of agglomeration – Collective innovation in local networks of clusters
Globalisation	Globalisation of firm	Intensifying and deepening – Intra-firm, global division of labour – Global network of R&D and sourcing – Multi-domestic strategy	Limited – Intricate local division of labour – Local network – Traditional export
	Trade Pattern	Increasing intra-firm and intermediate product trade Decreasing inter-regional trade	Typical inter-regional product trade Some intra-regional trade in intermediate products
	Linkage with home country	Weakening (low/mid value-added activities out-sourced)	Robust (core activities integrated into a region)
Developing Countries	Overall position	Passive participants – Competition to attract MNEs – Produce low-end products and parts	Import high-quality products Export commodity products and parts
	Prospect of advancement	Low/modest (absolute gap in capital & technology)	Very low (difficulty building innovative clusters)

optimise the division of labour within the firm around the world. As MNEs pursue this strategy, both the number of cases and the value of inter-regional foreign direct investment (FDI) has increased sharply, and so have inter-regional M&A activity and strategic alliances among leading companies. Consequently, the overall performance and industrial profile of national economies has come to depend to some extent on the decisions by MNEs on where to locate their R&D, production, marketing, and outsourcing functions.

In contrast, globalisation has not occurred to this extent in the mid-tech industries and the dominant mode of international transaction in these industries remains traditional product trade. R&D requirements for these industries are relatively low, and markets are segmented along highly differentiated product lines. Accordingly, there is no impending incentive or pressure for individual firms to pursue scale economies (in R&D and production) through globalisation. Typically, several innovative SMEs that lead the market in some mid-tech industrial product locate together somewhere in Europe.[20] They comprise a unique regional innovation system and collectively maintain their competitive position in high value added market segments, producing highly differentiated fashion or specialty products. Because each firm's competitiveness stems from collective assets concentrated in a specific region, these firms tend to remain 'local', with all core dimensions of innovative activities existing within the regional boundaries.

If we look simply at the present level of productivity, Korean industry and Korean firms may not appear to have a very promising future. We know that there is a productivity gap between industries in Korea and in the most advanced (G-6) economies. At the individual firm level, Korean companies do not have a solid base of competitiveness from which to withstand fierce international competition. Even Korea's small circle of vanguard companies are seriously behind their foreign competitors with respect to business portfolio, financial structure, core competence, and globalisation. Indeed, Korea's industrialisation process to date was certainly input-driven, rather than productivity driven. Growth accounting studies attribute at most 40 percent of Korea's growth to pure improvements in total factor productivity.[21] Moreover, the latest study by Yoon and Lee (1998) suggests that while investment during the early 1990s continued to increase as fast as in the 1980s, TFP growth slowed sharply, with some industries, such as chemicals and home electrical appliances, exhibiting negative growth.[22]

To make a balanced assessment of the potential of Korean industries and firms, however, we need to look at dynamics as well as static levels. Korea's potential appears brighter in light of recent efforts to accumulate innovative and technological capabilities and their associated industrial performance. Recent critics of Korea's low productivity tend to neglect the persistent trend of productivity catching-up. Manufacturing productivity has continued to rise faster in Korea than in any of the leading economies, resulting in a steady narrowing of the productivity gap (Table 9.5). For instance, although labour productivity in Korea's manufacturing sector was just about 30 percent of the level in the United States in 1980, it stood at 46 percent in 1990 and reached about 63 percent by 1996.

Much, but not all, of Korea's productivity catching-up is ascribable to capital deepening (input-driven). Although capital accumulation itself contributes to TFP growth through learning-by-doing absorption of embodied technologies, maintaining persistent growth in productivity requires more systematic efforts to enhance technological know-how. Since the mid 1980s, facing rapidly rising wages, mounting pressure from second-tier NICs, and increasing difficulty in acquiring foreign technology, Korean companies stepped up sharply their indigenous R&D efforts. Business R&D expenditure, which started to pick up in the early 1980s, continued to rise steeply throughout the 1990s, and so did the total number of R&D personnel and corporate R&D centres (Tables 9.6 and 9.7).[23]

In fact, R&D records and market performance suggest that in the late 1980s, a significant number of Korean companies started to shift from the typical investment-driven stage to the innovation-driven stage. Most noteworthy were the efforts of leading firms in certain industries such as electronics and automobiles. With global technological advances accelerating, many major corporations began to move from 'imitative' towards 'defensive' R&D positions, which made it imperative for them to assimilate R&D-intensive and system-oriented technologies. They established extensive networks of in-house laboratories and pursued a more active overseas R&D strategy. On top of acquiring advanced technology in major industries through FDI, they set up R&D facilities near pockets of innovation in the United States, Japan, and Europe in order to monitor frontier technological changes as well as to tap high calibre scientists and researchers (Table 9.8). In addition, they resorted to M&A to gain access to cutting-edge technologies.

Tangible outcomes of this vigorous effort started to show up in the mid 1990s. In 1996, Korea ranked eighth in the number of U.S. patent registrations and seventh in the number of foreign-owned R&D laboratories

TABLE 9.5
Labour Productivity in Korea Relative to the U. S. Level, 1980–95
(Percent)

	Manu-facturing	Textiles and Apparel	Chemical Products	Basic Metals	Electrical/Machinery	Electronics	Shipbuilding	Motor Vehicles
1980								
PPP	42.7	47.7	42.1	48.6	37.3	36.8	119.3	31.1
NER	30.3	33.9	29.9	34.5	26.5	26.1	84.7	22.1
1990								
PPP	60.8	62.4	39.3	127.2	57.7	57.0	106.4	75.3
NER	46.2	47.4	29.9	96.7	43.9	43.3	80.9	57.2
1995								
PPP	77.7	51.7	70.0	152.1	63.9	80.7	152.2	63.3
NER	62.2	41.4	56.0	121.7	50.6	64.6	121.8	50.7
Productivity growth rate	8.2	4.3	8.0	9.6	10.1	13.6	8.2*	

Note: PPP denotes productivity based on Purchasing Power Parity Exchange Rate, NER denotes comparison based on nominal exchange rate. Growth rate of productivity measured in real-value added terms. *denotes productivity growth for transportation equipment.
Source: OECD, OECD STAN Database, 1997.

TABLE 9.6
Evolving R&D Profile of Korea, 1980–95

	1980	1985	1990	1995
R&D expenditures				
GDP share (%)	0.77	1.58	1.95	2.61
Government share (%)	64.0	25.0	19.0	16.0
R&D/Sales (%)	0.50	1.51	1.96	2.72
Research scientists and engineers				
Number	–	19,000	70,500	100,500
% in manufacturing	–	89.2	89.9	86.2
Number of R&D centres/labs	54	183	996	2,270

Note: Numbers of scientists and engineers for 1990 and 1995 refer to 1989 and 1994.
Source: Ministry of Science and Technology, *Report on the Survey of R&D in S&T*, various issues.

in the United States. All major Korean automobile makers had acquired the capability to design and develop their own mid-sized models. In electronics, cases of successful new product development increased in such fields as DRAM and TFT-LCD, and Korea's lag behind the world leaders in the timing of commercialisation was substantially reduced or even reversed. Most significant, strategic alliances between Korean companies and leading foreign companies became frequent, showing that Korean companies were sophisticated enough to enter the global market based on their own technological assets.

Despite these considerable improvements, Korea is far behind the advanced economies in both the level and scope of its technological capabilities. In industries such as machinery, heavy equipment, shipbuilding, and petrochemicals, technological gains have been largely confined to production or process improvement, while product design and basic project engineering remain in the infancy stage. Even in Korea's technological vanguard fields, such as electronics, the technological capabilities of Korean leaders only extend as far as commercial product development (commercialisation) and not to applied or generic research capabilities possessed by the global leaders. In fact, Korea's technological dependency actually increased in the course of the technological upgrading of Korean industries (Table 9.9). As more Korean companies moved into production of more technically sophisticated products, they had to import more advanced and expensive foreign technologies, resulting in a persistent increase in the technology trade deficit.

TABLE 9.7
R&D Expenditures of Major OECD Countries

	Increase in R&D spending 1991–96	1996 R&D Expenditures US$ billions	R&D Share of GDP %		R&D Share of Sales %		Government Share of R&D Expenditures %
			1992	1996	Total	Manu-facturing	
United States	2.83	184.7	2.78	2.54	2.8	2.93	33.6
Japan	1.83	138.6	2.94	3.00	2.8	3.4	26.5
Germany	1.39	53.1	2.48	2.26	4.03	–	37.3
France	2.68[4]	35.9[1]	2.42	2.34[1]	4.8[2]	–	43.6[1]
UK	3.63[4]	22.6[1]	2.18	2.05[1]	–	–	36.4
Korea	21.21	13.5	2.08	2.79	2.4	2.8	22.1

Note: [1] 1995   [2] 1994   [3] 1993   [4] Increase for 1990–95.
Source: Ministry of Science and Technology, *Report on the Survey of R&D in S&T,* 1997.

TABLE 9.8
Overseas R&D Centres of Korean Firms, 1995
(Number of centres)

	US	Japan	Europe	Russia	Total
Electrical/ Electronics	15	8	7	1	31
Motor Vehicle	4	3	2	–	9
Other	5	1	4	1	11
Total	24	12	13	2	51

Source: Reproduced from Table 5-4-3 STEPI (1998).

The backward technical level of Korean firms may partly reflect some serious shortcomings in their basic business orientation and past strategy, but it may reflect more the disadvantage of being a late-comer still in the middle stage of corporate evolution. Just as technological progress is a continuous and cumulative process, so is a firm's evolution toward a higher stage of technological development. Korean firms accumulated a set of technological assets commensurate with their stage of development and evolution under the regime of nationalistic industrialism. Now, the advent of global competition and alliance capitalism (Dunnings 1997), fundamentally changed the meaning of an individual firm's or economy's technical standard, as well as the paradigm of its technological evolution. The adequacy of Korea's technological assets is to be tested in conjunction with its other indigenous assets, where the central theme is how much strategic value they would fetch in the global market, especially in relation to the globalisation strategies of the world leaders.

Korea's Locational Advantages

Context and Hypothesis

Despite the severe economic setback spawned by the 1997 financial crisis, many experts predict that East Asia as a whole will resume its growth momentum and emerge as one of the largest world markets by early in the twenty-first century.[24] No only will the region's market grow larger, but the mode of international and intra-firm interactions in the region will change as well. The share of Asia in global trade and investment flows has increased drastically over the past 20 years or so. More noteworthy is the sharp increase in trade flows *within* Asia. Increasing *intra*-regional trade

TABLE 9.9
Characteristics of Korea's Technology Trade, 1990–97
(US$ million, percent)

	Trade Volume			Major Import Products						Major Source Countries					
	Imports	Exports	Imports minus Exports	Electrical and Electronics		Machinery and Equipment		Chemicals and Petroleum Products		United States		Japan		EU	
	$US mil	$US mil	$US mil	$US mil	%	$US mil	%	$US mil	%	$US mil	%	$US mil	%	$US mil	%
Volume of trade	1,200	630	−1,137	601	50.1	232	19.3	138	11.5	633	52.8	360	30.0	177	14.8
Growth rate															
1990–97	12.1	33.3	11.3	15.3		10.7		−0.7		16.2		5.8		8.3	
1994–97	23.7	13.7	24.5	17.8		31.3		24.1		28.4		14.2		33.8	

Source: Reconstructed from Tables II-62 and II-63, Korean Industrial Technology Association (KITA), *Annual Report on Industrial Technology*, 1998.

in lieu of traditional *inter*-regional trade has been a global trend since the early 1980s. But intra-regional trade in Asia has surged markedly, with its share of global trade more than doubling between 1980 and 1995 (Table 9.10).[25]

The trend increase in intra-regional trade in Asia (from 6.4 percent of world trade in 1981–85 to 12.0 percent in 1991–95) indicates that the Asian market has become mature and diverse enough to develop a more intricate and sophisticated intra-regional division of labour, involving a greater variety of goods and services geared to region-specific demands. As the rewards to firms with a presence in the region increase, MNEs, especially U.S. and European MNEs engaged in global industries, will reinforce and upgrade their Asia strategy so that they can better respond to and capitalise on the new challenges and opportunities of the Asian market.

By and large, the competitive advantages of Western MNEs in respect to their Asian manufacturing business overlap in highly knowledge-intensive activities, such as advanced research or engineering of technologically sophisticated products. They will continue to perform most of these activities at the global 'centres of excellence' located in the Europe, Japan, or the United States. The optimal intra-firm, global division of labour for each MNE is to combine these activities with some medium value added activities encompassing production, after-service, and local adaptation located in the Asia region.

Although most Korean firms are not competitive enough to survive direct head-to-head competition with the leading MNEs, they do have indigenous assets that can complement the Asia strategy of these MNEs.

TABLE 9.10
Patterns of World Trade Flows by Region, 1981–85 and 1991–95
(Percent)

	1985				1991–95			
	EU	NAFTA	Asia	Import Total	EU	NAFTA	Asia	Import Total
EU	18.1	3.4	1.9	34.0	24.1	3.3	3.4	33.8
NAFTA	3.6	7.1	3.5	18.5	3.4	7.3	4.4	17.8
Asia	2.3	5.3	6.4	18.2	4.5	6.8	12.0	26.0
Export Total	35.7	20.9	17.6	100.0	39.1	20.0	23.8	100.0

Note: Asia refers to 38 countries excluding Middle East area.
Source: IMF, *Direction of Trade Statistics*, Yearbook.

In essence, the single national entity Korea commands a fair degree of the locational advantages of East Asia in a wide range of industrial activities of interest to MNEs. Korea's specific locational advantage compared to other East Asian economies including Taiwan, Singapore, and ASEAN, surely will differ from industry to industry.[26] Nevertheless, in the medium-to high-tech industries and business services, Korea has considerable advantage over all the ASEAN and neighbouring economies in terms of skilled manpower including R&D personnel, related and supporting industries, and 'relevant' market size (Table 9.11).[27] In addition, Korea may find a natural advantage in its physical proximity to China's colossal market (especially the northeastern coastal area). Of course, proximity may not prove to be much of an asset for Korea in some consumer markets. China could easily out-compete Korea and attract a range of low-to-mid value-added business activities based on its low labour costs. Nevertheless, with a longer history of industrialisation Korea has an advantage in some mid-to-high valued added areas in which quality and reliable provision of skills, parts, and institutional support count more.

Korea seriously lags behind Japan in the quality of technicians and engineers, let alone in endowments of other science, technology, and industrial resources needed for highly advanced industrial activities such as advanced research and engineering. Yet, wages of mid-level technicians and engineers are substantially lower in Korea than in Japan, making Korea an advantageous place for some mid-level, relatively cost-sensitive activities.

The locational advantages of Korea, Japan, and China are compared roughly in Table 9.12. More research is needed to identify the exact functional areas in which Korea has advantages in individual industries. Nevertheless, Korea's most pronounced advantage is probably as a production site for mid-to high-end products of virtually all 'global' industries, including electronics, automobiles, petrochemicals, and heavy machinery and equipment. In addition, Korea may have a modest advantage in some skill- and experience-intensive activities such as local adaptation of products or processes, which also applies to most global industries.

Recent Trend in Inward FDI

The latest trend in inward FDI partly testifies to Korea's locational advantages in these areas. Although FDI inflows to Korea increased steadily since 1993, they remained quite limited until the second half of 1998 when they started to surge. Total inflow in 1998 reached US$8.89 billion,

TABLE 9.11
R&D Personnel in East Asia and Other Economies, 1997

	US	Germany	Japan	Korea	Taiwan	Singapore	China	Malaysia
Total number (1,000s)	962.7	459.11	891.8	135.7	98.6	12.1	588.7	4.4
Ratio to Korea (Korea = 1)	9.37	2.25	6.62	1.00	0.59	0.07	5.73	0.02
Number per 10,000 population	37.29	56.24	70.93	29.80	45.65	32.26	N/A	2.05

Note: Korea is for 1996.
Source: IMD, *The World Competitiveness Yearbook,* 1999 and Andersson, 1999, for China.

TABLE 9.12
Summary of Locational Advantages of Japan, Korea, and China

	Japan	Korea	China
Advanced research (generic/applied)	◎	×	×
Commercial research and basic engineering	◎	×/Δ	Δ/×
Product/process adaptation and improvement	◎/O	O/Δ	×
Production (mid to high-end product)	Δ	◎	Δ
Production (low to mid-end product)	×	Δ	O

Note: ◎ indicates a strong advantage, O denotes an advantage, Δ means neutral, and × denotes a disadvantage.

exceeding half of the total volume of inflows from 1991 to 1997.[28] The trend continued in 1999, with the final figure reaching US$15.54 billion.

The composition of FDI inflows in terms of source countries and recipient businesses also changed (Table 9.13). While investment from the United States and Japan has been predominant for a long time, investment from the EU region, especially from the Netherlands, Germany, and France, increased sharply. In 1998, the EU countries' combined share of investment into Korea exceeded 50 percent. Japan's share of FDI into Korea has been falling since the mid-1980s, with a marked decline in 1998. Entering 1999, however, investment from Japan bounced back sharply.

By sector, FDI into Korea has become more diversified and nuanced (Table 9.14). The share of the services sector has risen steadily, shifting the balance away from a manufacturing-centred structure. While consumer-oriented businesses such as restaurants and hotels once led this trend, the focus of service sector investments is shifting toward finance, telecommunications, and other business services. In the manufacturing sector, chemicals, electrical and electronic equipment, transport equipment, and machinery continue to absorb a majority of incoming FDI. A noteworthy trend is a prominent increase in FDI into the food processing, paper and lumber, and machinery industries. In general, the motives behind inward FDI into Korea appear to have matured and diversified. Until recently, the dominant form of FDI was so-called market-oriented FDI to penetrate the domestic market.[29] Since the Asian Crisis the number of investments of a more strategic nature has been growing, with a host of leading MNEs, including Japanese firms, using Korea as platform for their Asian or even global strategies.

TABLE 9.13
Amount and Composition of
Korea's Inward FDI by Source, 1981–98

	1981–1985	1986–1990	1991–1997	1998
		Amount, US$ millions		
United States	375.9	1,005.2	2,182.0	1,450.3
Asia	304.7	1,996.3	3,288.9	877.2
Japan	263.2	1,850.2	1,733.3	413.6
Europe	109.0	598.3	4,615.9	2,662.5
Germany	24.2	165.2	761.5	643.8
France	9.1	63.5	814.3	352.7
Netherlands	8.8	107.2	1,338.4	1,218.3
Total	832	3,704.2	10,452.0	5,155.6
		Share of Inward FDI, %		
United States	45.17	27.14	20.88	28.13
Asia	36.62	53.89	31.47	17.01
Japan	31.63	49.95	16.58	8.02
Europe	13.09	16.15	44.16	51.64
Germany	2.91	4.46	77.29	12.49
France	1.09	1.71	7.79	6.84
Netherlands	81.06	2.89	12.81	23.63
Total	100.0	100.0	100.0	100.0

Source: Reconstructed from Kim 1999.

Of course, it is too early to tell whether these changes herald a new long-term trend. The upsurge in FDI volume over the past two years could prove to be transitory, induced only by the sharp depreciation of the won as well as severely depressed asset prices. Indeed, with the portfolio of businesses for sale (M&A targets) in Korea running out, inbound FDI may level off eventually. On the other hand, the recent upsurge could prove to be the start of a longer-term trend in FDI. If so, the legal and institutional shake-up regarding inbound FDI will have been the critical reason for the change. Once one of the most closed economies in the world, Korea is now free of obvious barriers to incoming FDI, thanks to the thorough liberalisation measures taken in the course of managing the crisis. Most legal barriers were removed or eased (restrictions on ownership share and business area, for instance), administrative procedures were simplified, and even hostile M&As by foreigners were legitimised.

TABLE 9.14

Amount and Composition of Inward FDI by Sector, 1981–98

(US$ million, percent)

	Amount				Share of Inward FDI			
	1981–85	1986–90	1991–97	1998	1981–85	1986–90	1991–97	1998
Agriculture and fishing	2.5	20.4	35.8	162.8	0.31	0.55	0.34	3.16
Mining and quarrying	1.4	4.5	19.9	21.3	0.17	0.12	0.19	0.42
Manufacturing	593.0	2,277.6	6,104.0	2,831.6	71.26	61.49	58.40	54.92
Food	42.6	154.9	663.9	629.8	5.12	4.18	6.35	12.22
Textile and clothing	8.2	53.6	199.8	6.7	0.99	1.45	1.91	0.13
Paper and lumber	15.8	25.0	335.3	446.7	1.90	0.68	3.21	8.66
Chemicals	114.1	415.2	1,388.8	429.1	13.72	11.21	13.29	8.32
Fertiliser	1.2	0.3	0.7	0.3	0.14	0.01	0.01	0.00
Medicines	47.3	135.3	234.1	119.6	5.68	3.65	2.24	2.32
Petroleum	5.6	49.7	684.3	0.9	0.68	1.34	6.55	0.02
Ceramics	3.2	42.0	196.5	243.3	0.39	1.14	1.88	4.72
Metals	24.3	39.4	71.3	5.8	2.91	1.06	0.68	0.11
Machinery	22.8	265.1	571.0	534.8	2.74	7.16	5.46	10.37
Electrical and electronics	174.7	616.5	865.8	231.7	21.00	16.64	7.90	4.49
Transport equipment	125.9	437.5	825.8	154.0	15.13	11.81	7.90	2.99
Other manufacturing	7.3	43.0	66.6	28.6	0.88	1.16	0.64	0.55
Services	235.2	1,401.8	4,292.2	2,139.8	28.26	37.84	41.07	41.51
Electricity and gas	0.0	0.0	26.1	0.0	0.00	0.00	0.25	0.00
Construction	40.2	9.0	101.3	5.4	4.83	0.24	0.97	0.11
Wholesale and retail	15.0	5.0	690.0	519.6	1.81	0.14	6.60	10.08
Trade	0.2	55.5	701.7	243.0	0.02	1.50	6.71	4.71
Restaurants	0.1	4.1	67.3	6.2	0.02	0.11	0.64	0.12
Hotels	76.6	887.1	573.7	0.0	9.20	23.95	5.49	0.00
Transport and storage	7.0	6.6	160.1	4.2	0.84	0.18	1.53	0.08
Finance	78.7	313.6	1,191.1	471.4	9.46	8.47	11.40	9.14
Insurance	1.0	76.7	181.3	73.1	0.12	2.07	1.73	1.42
Other services	31.4	44.2	597.9	816.1	3.77	1.19	5.72	15.83
Total	832.1	3,704.2	10,452.0	5,155.6	100.0	100.0	100.0	100.0

Source: Reconstructed from Kim 1999.

Remarks

Even if Korea's locational advantages do attract investment in a broad range of business activities, the economy's prospects also depend on who will manage and control those activities. It is reasonable to expect foreign MNEs to control a substantial part of these activities, in which case Korean firms will assume a subordinate or supporting role. But a more reciprocal partnership relation should develop in areas where Korean firms possess some independent technological or managerial assets that complement the global strategy of foreign MNE's. In Korea's technological frontier fields such as semiconductors and displays (TFT-LCD, PDP, and the like) the engineering acumen and commercialisation ability of Korean firms will be a main attractive factor and various forms of strategic alliances with foreign MNEs will continue to spring up. Korean firms should also retain some autonomy in other industrial fields such as automobiles and heavy equipment, although the specific types of relationships with MNEs will differ (Figure 9.3).

FIGURE 9.3
Conceptual Characterisation of the Positions of MNEs
and Domestic Firms in Korea

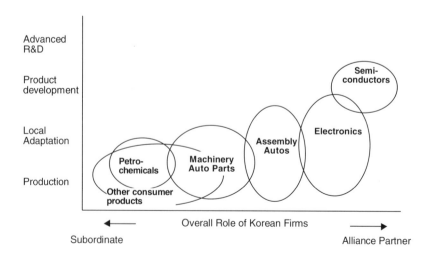

In the automobile industry, for instance, no Korean company, including leader Hyundai, has the ability to cope with the escalating global competition on its own. In their desperate search for survival strategies Korean automobile companies need to note that besides their well-regarded production techniques, they possess a unique set of managerial assets and know-how that can perfectly complement the strategies of foreign MNEs, especially in emerging markets. These assets could be highly valued by global leaders such as GM, Ford, and Volkswagen, which lack a competitive position in emerging markets, especially China and India, comparable to that of their Japanese counterparts (Table 9.15). Despite the strategic value of establishing a presence in the emerging markets, the global leaders are not likely to attempt full-scale penetration of these markets independently, because the overall business environment is too challenging. As alliance partners with the MNEs, Korean automobile makers would bring the substantial volume of investment they already have in place in the region and, more importantly, their managerial know-how and determination to maintain a physical presence for the long term.[30]

Challenges and Policy Responses

Prospects and Challenges

Korea's future industrial upgrading can be accomplished in two steps that have different basic strategy and different policy goals. First, over the coming ten years or so, Korea needs to solidify its present competitive advantages and gradually expand its areas of competitiveness, drawing on present 'core' competencies and locational advantages within an East Asian regional division of labour. After securing its position as a regional production platform for high-end products and a regional innovation site for an array of advanced activities, such as advanced engineering and basic research beyond commercialisation, Korea then may move to become a 'centre of excellence' that can support and self-generate advanced scientific and technological tasks such as applied research and advanced system engineering.

Although Korea may ultimately attain this goal, it will not happen automatically. Korea must overcome two obstacles in the coming decade for the first step to succeed. They are feeble market and framework conditions and un-competitive SMEs, especially in the machinery industry.[31] According to the *World Competitiveness Report* for 1998, Korea lags most seriously behind other advanced economies in the framework conditions

TABLE 9.15
Asian Market Shares of Major Automobile Companies, 1995
(Percent)

	China	India	Taiwan	Thailand	Indonesia	Malaysia	Philippines	Overall Asia Share
Japanese companies	24.4	36.2	58.0	89.9	95.3	92.3	87.9	54.3
Toyota	0.7	0.3	17.0	27.9	25.5	7.7	29.1	10.7
Nissan	–	0.7	11.9	15.4	0.5	6.0	14.7	4.9
Mitsubishi	1.7	0.8	18.7	12.5	19.2	51.4	24.9	11.5
Honda	–	–	7.2	4.8	1.3	3.9	9.2	2.4
Mazda	–	0.5	1.0	4.1	0.8	1.0	6.0	1.2
Suzuki	9.9	33.9	1.2	0.6	18.5	1.0	–	11.0
Isuzu	4.1	–	–	20.8	11.2	3.2	1.7	5.9
Daihatsu	8.0	–	0.2	0.7	6.5	17.5	0.5	–
US companies	1.8	–	–	2.0	1.2	2.5	–	4.9
Ford	–	–	–	0.9	0.7	2.1	–	3.0
European companies	15.7	–	–	6.1	3.2	5.1	0.8	9.0
VW/Audi	14.1	–	–	0.6	–	0.1	–	5.4

Note: Asian share is combined share in seven nations.
Source: Abrenica 1997.

of the labour market, the financial market, corporate governance, the public sector, and the regulatory system (Table 9.16). Besides inflicting turbulence and turmoil, the Asian Financial Crisis benefited Korea by driving it to greatly upgrade outdated framework conditions through across-the-board reforms in all major trouble areas. These reform efforts are ongoing and we do not know how successful they will ultimately be. Certainly, however, with the opening of the economy, including the financial sector, to foreign MNEs, the institutional framework will emerge from the crisis more sober and robust than in the pre-crisis closed economy.

Transforming Korea into an innovation-driven advanced economy with a solid self-regenerating industrial foundation will require more than the improvement of framework conditions. To re-invigorate and re-orient the economy Korea will need foreign MNEs to bring in capital, technology, and essential soft assets, such as managerial know-how, work practices, and new rules based on 'global standards'. With the continued upgrading of the economies in Asia, the MNEs in Korea will gradually move up to more technologically demanding, higher value added activities, such as

TABLE 9.16
Korea's Rank on Selected Competitiveness Factors

	Competitiveness Factor	Rank
Internationalisation	• Protectionism	46
	• Culture	46
	• Government procurement	45
	• Incentives for inward FDI	42
Government	• Regulation	46
	• Legal frame	45
	• Transparency	43
	• Policy-making	40
Finance	• Presence of foreign institutions	46
	• Access to foreign markets	45
	• Capital cost	45
	• Central bank	44
Corporate	• Governance	46
	• Venture firms	43
	• Labour relations	43
	• Image	42

Note: Rank is Korea's ranking out of 46 nations surveyed with higher ranking indicating greater weakness.
Source: IMD, *World Competitiveness Yearbook*, 1998.

advanced research and production of state-of-the-art products. To attract and retain these activities, Korea will need a much more advanced science and technology (S&T) infrastructure and a substantive pool of SMEs with high technical capabilities. Despite recent progress, there are still relatively few SMEs with innovation potential in Korea, and their R&D capabilities are quite limited. R&D efforts in Korea are highly concentrated among large-sized firms and around the two pillar industries, electronics and automobiles (Table 9.17). Even with the best possible outcome from the ongoing structural reforms, the performance of SMEs is unlikely to improve markedly because of the grave elements of market failure intrinsic in the SME sector. The limited technical capacity of SMEs will eventually become a challenge to upgrading the economy.

The locational advantages of the economies in Asia, including Korea, are extremely volatile, especially because of the rapid maturing and industrialising of China's economy. Proximity to China could be a great advantage in terms of market access, but it could easily also prove to be a great disadvantage if Korea does not overcome the deficiencies in its SME sector and framework conditions to keep ahead of China. Without great improvement over the next ten years, Korea's attraction to foreign MNEs will decline fast. Most new FDI into East Asia will head to China. Even worse, a substantial part of the core industrial activities that now are located in Korea, including activities of Korea's indigenous flagship companies, will relocate to China.

Promoting SMEs: the General Problem

The employment and output shares of Korean SMEs in manufacturing have increased consistently over the past two decades (Table 9.18). There also has been considerable structural upgrading of the SME sector as a whole, with the share of low-tech, labour-intensive products declining in place of the shares of mid- to high-tech products with greater technology and skill content (Table 9.19).[32] In line with such structural upgrading, the number of SMEs conducting some form of R&D has increased explosively, as has the number of in-house R&D facilities and research personnel (Table 9.20). Though yet small in number, innovative and proactive SMEs with technical competence have started to emerge.

Despite this progress, innovative SMEs that have an independent and sustainable competitive base are rare. Most SMEs in Korea are engaged in the production of technologically unsophisticated parts and components under a passive subcontract relationship with larger companies. Accustomed

TABLE 9.17
Composition of R&D Investment by Industry and Size of Establishment
(Percent)

	Total	5–99 employees	100–299 employees	300–999 employees	1000+ employees	Share of Sector's R&D by 1000+ Establishments
All sectors	100.0	3.5	5.4	9.7	81.4	81.4
Manufacturing	84.5	2.8	4.6	7.3	69.8	82.6
Principal industry subtotal	77.9	2.5	4.2	6.3	64.9	83.3
Electrical/electronics	36.6	0.9	1.5	1.6	32.6	89.1
Transport equipment	25.9	0.1	0.5	1.9	23.4	90.3
Scientific instruments	0.7	0.2	0.3	0.1	0.1	14.3
Chemical products	10.0	0.7	1.1	1.8	6.4	64.0
Machinery	3.6	0.5	0.5	0.7	1.9	52.8
Construction	5.0	0.0	0.0	1.0	4.0	80.0
Transportation, storage, telecommunications	3.7	0.0	0.1	0.5	3.1	83.8

Source: Ministry of Science and Technology, *Report on the Survey of R&D in S&T*, 1997.

TABLE 9.18
Evolution of SMEs in Korea's Manufacturing Sector

	1980	1985	1990	1995	SME % of Manufacturing Total			
					1980	1985	1990	1995
Number of establishments	29,779	42,950	67,679	95,285	96.9	97.5	98.3	99.0
Employees (thousand)	1,000	1,368	1,864	2,034	49.6	56.1	61.7	68.9
Value-added (billion won)	4,168	10,059	31,432	73,808	35.2	37.6	44.3	46.3
Productivity differential	55.0	47.2	45.8	39.4				

Note: Productivity differential indicates productivity of SMEs as a percent of productivity in companies with 300 or more employees.
Source: National Statistical Office, *Basic Survey on Korea's Manufacturing Sector*, 1998.

TABLE 9.19
Structural Changes in Korean Manufacturing
(Percent of total value-added)

	Manufacturing Total					SMEs				
	1975	1980	1985	1990	1995	1975	1980	1985	1990	1995
Embodied technology										
High-tech	10.7	12	15.7	19.1	22.7	6.5	10.2	12.6	14.8	13.4
Mid-tech	17.7	22.4	23.1	30.1	30.9	20.2	24.0	25.7	29.2	31.3
Low-tech	71.6	65.6	61.2	50.8	46.4	71.3	65.9	61.7	56.0	55.3
OECD S&T classification										
Resource-intensive	39.6	33.1	28.8	24.9	22.9	39.8	32.1	28.9	25.1	25.3
Labour-intensive	26.3	24.6	22.5	18.8	16.0	29.1	31.6	31.5	28.8	25.9
Specialised supplier	9.1	11.5	16.0	21.3	26.9	8.8	10.0	12.8	17.6	19.6
Scale-intensive	21.3	26.9	28.7	30.9	30.3	18.8	21.5	21.2	23.0	24.0
Science-based	3.7	3.9	4.0	4.1	3.8	4.0	4.8	5.5	5.4	5.1

Source: Reproduced from Woo and Lim 1998.

to low-cost competition for undifferentiated products in a sheltered market, they remain relatively uninterested in sérious innovation and R&D. Very few SMEs conduct any R&D (7.4 percent of SMEs in 1996), and they invest only a tiny amount of resources for systematic R&D (Table 9.20).[33] Even among the leaders, innovations centre around minor modifications of products or processes based on imported or borrowed technology. SMEs rarely come up with more significant process innovations or product developments that incorporate new technological concepts.

In consequence, most Korean SMEs are in great peril. Their ultimate basis for competitiveness — that is, their sheltered markets, subcontracts with leading domestic companies, and production cost advantage — are quickly eroding and they face such adverse forces as market liberalisation, globalisation of parent companies, and relentless catching-up of the NIEs, especially China. Moreover, most SMEs in Korea lack the ability to capitalise on changes that favour SMEs, such as the increased demand for differentiated products and the easier, lower cost access to information through, for instance, the Internet.

Korea needs a creative new approach to realise the imperative to upgrade its SMEs. Even first-tier OECD member economies still find nurturing innovative SMEs a top policy challenge, and there are no universally applicable best policy measures yet. The backbone of Korea's SME policy at present remains to redress the disadvantages of SMEs' vis à vis larger businesses through direct resource support and market protection. The experiences of many advanced countries as well as Korea clearly testify that such redemptive and protective measures are not sustainable and in fact run counter to the long-run interests of SMEs by undermining the incentive to build up the capability to respond independently to changes in

TABLE 9.20
R&D by SMEs in the Manufacturing Sector

	1980	1985	1990	1993	1996
SMEs conducting R&D					
Number	2,982	5,630	6,758	5,645	7,084
Percent of all SMEs	10.0%	13.1%	10.0%	6.4%	7.4%
R&D/Sales	0.13	0.22	0.25	0.42	0.34

Source: Small and Medium Industry Promotion Corporation, *Major Statistics of SMI*, 1996.

the business environment.[34] Korea needs to foster a business environment conducive to the innovative activities of proactive SMEs and to develop institutional components and arrangements to stimulate co-operative networking.

For SMEs, networking constitutes the best and the most economic mode of absorbing new scientific and technological information. A primary reason for the paucity of innovative SMEs in Korea and their limited R&D capacity is the lack of formally organised networks and other specialised sources serving a similar function. The form of network most relevant to Korea at this time is the local network comprised of a group of potential innovators clustered in a specific geographic area (industrial district). Local networking can bring huge efficiency gains when combined with the spatial agglomeration economies of innovative firms with interrelated business interests. Many regions in Korea are home to such agglomerations of industry, but because they import core components and key facilities from abroad, they are no more than specialised production areas. They are devoid of the intricate local linkages, extensive long-distance connections, and regional developmental dynamics that define local networks.

Promoting SMEs: the Case of the Machinery Industry

The general machinery industry illustrates the importance of and the key policy issues related to developing local networks in an industrial district. As a result of fast expansion since the mid 1980s, the general machinery industry became one of Korea's 'core' mid-tech industries, accounting for 7.8 percent of GDP and 6.2 percent of manufacturing exports in 1996 (Tables 9.21 and 9.22). Domestic firms built up technological capacity through learning-by-doing, stepped up R&D efforts, and effective absorption of advanced technologies from Japan, the United States, and Germany.[35]

The general machinery industry is in a perilous situation today, however, as the market environment becomes more challenging. Despite considerable progress, the accumulated technological capability of domestic firms is insufficient, and the majority of SMEs are engaged in joint-production of low-end machinery and commodity-type parts and components.[36] The technology level for R&D, design, and new product development is low by international standards, even among the leading Korean SMEs (Table 9.23). Many small machinery firms have managed to survive under the shelter of the so-called 'Import Source Diversification Program', but the recent phasing out of such protective measures leaves them on their own to handle unchecked competition from Japanese producers.[37]

TABLE 9.21
Evolution of Korea's Machine Industry, 1986–96

	1986	1991	1993	1996
Production (US$ millions)	4.948	24.110	25.017	51.921
Share of domestic manufacturing (%)	5.1	8.5	7.8	–
Share of world production (%)	1.1	4.5	4.6	–
Exports (US$ millions)	1.663	3.838	4.912	10.736
Imports (US$ millions)	4.847	12.69	11.321	26.463
Trade balance (US$ millions)	–3.184	–8.852	–6.409	–15.727
Overall trade balance (US$ millions)	4.206	–6.980	1.86	–15.306
Domestic market share (%)	40.0	61.5	63.9	60.8
Exports/production (%)	33.6	15.9	19.6	20.6

Note: Domestic market share of domestic producers = (production – exports) / (production + imports – exports).
Source: Reproduced from Woo and Lim 1998.

TABLE 9.22
Characteristics of the General Machinery Industry
by Firm Size, 1993
(Percent)

	5–9 Employees	20–99 Employees	100–299 Employees	300 + Employees
Production share	16.9	30.7	15.5	36.9
Employment share	28.1	37.4	13.6	20.9
Establishment share	72.6	24.8	2.0	0.6
Productivity differential 1993	53	65	85	100
Productivity differential 1983	49	62	79	100

Note: Productivity differential indicates productivity of SMEs as a percent of productivity in companies with 300 or more employees.
Source: National Statistical Office, *Survey on Korean Manufacturing Sector,* 1993.

Although this new market environment poses a grave threat to many individual domestic firms in the machinery industry, it may also present the opportunity for the industry as a whole to pursue a new mode of industrial development. The rapid expansion of the Asian market (ASEAN and China) for those mid-quality machine products in which Korean companies have a comparative advantage is the source of opportunity.

Table 9.23
Comparison of the Machinery Industry
in Korea and Germany, 1993
(Percent)

| | Employment Share | | Relative Productivity | |
	Germany	Korea	Germany	Korea
Number of employees				
20.99	18.9	36.3	59.8	23.9
100.299	24.1	15.5	67.4	30.8
300.499	13.0	6.1	69.6	29.6
500 or more	44.1	42.2	100.0	59.5

Note: Relative productivity indicates productivity of firm size category relative to productivity of German firms with 500 or more employees.
Source: Reproduced from J.K. Park 1997.

Although Korean companies do not have the advanced skills and technologies to compete in the major OECD market for spearhead products such as automation facilities and CAD/CAM, they can stay competitive in lower quality, more price-sensitive products for which there will be increasing demand from many Asian nations. The small domestic market has been a critical constraint to the emergence of specialised machine makers in Korea. The rapid expansion of the Asian market will ease that constraint and create the opportunity for innovative Korean firms to upgrade their competitive base against an ample, yet unoccupied market.

A new policy approach and stalwart policy leadership are called for if this opportunity is to lead to the upgrading of Korea's entire machinery sector. Firms in the machine industry tend to interact closely at the local level, exchanging tacit knowledge about production processes and components and also providing markets for each other. Because network externalities at the local level are so crucial, SMEs in the machine industry tend to locate in industrial districts. Countries with a strong machine industry have industrial districts with innovation networks, the representative model of which is Baden-Würtemburg, Germany.

Korea has some specialised industrial districts where several firms produce machines and machine components, but neither the resident firms nor the local public sector have taken the initiative to form innovative network linkages.[38] In principle, the development of innovation networks requires action at the local level, and the initiative to develop a dynamic industrial district needs to be led by some local champion, whether it is an individual firm or a public authority. Such a local initiative or leadership is unlikely to spring up in Korea in the foreseeable future. First, the few innovative Korean firms that could be active networking participants are spatially dispersed across disjoint regions. If it is necessary to agglomerate innovative firms in a single industrial district in order to achieve a critical mass, then the central government should take on the task to create such a precondition.

Second, in addition to the spatial agglomeration of existing firms, the new type industrial district is an intricate institutional complex involving diverse modes of business transaction, interest co-ordination, and private-public partnership, but no Korean firm or public authority has a practical vision for such an industrial complex. Rather than Korea attempting to develop such vision by trial and error, it might be less costly to call on established leaders with extensive, in-depth operational experience to set up such an industrial district. Specifically, the complex of machinery industry firms in Baden-Würtemburg presents a promising place to find such leaders. Indeed German entrepreneurs would likely find this an attractive opportunity, considering the rapidly growing market in China (and in other Asian NIEs) and the mounting pressure from their Japanese competitors. Given the present locational advantages of Korea over China as discussed earlier, German machinery and machinery-related companies seeking a location for new regional business platforms in East Asia should find Korea attractive.

In order for Korea to get the most out of this situation, it needs to attract not just individual German firms, but an entire cluster of German machinery companies as a collective unit. To accomplish this requires a strong, concerted scheme of incentives. A policy initiative at the local government level would not suffice. The central government, in close consultation with local governments, needs to assume an active role in this precedent-setting endeavour.

It may take more than a decade to establish a machinery industry complex in Korea. Getting all basic institutions and core interface arrangements in place calls for collaborative initiatives and co-ordinated, systematic efforts by the central government, regional authorities, and businesses. In its formative stage the district will surely not be as effective as established ones in other advanced nations due to deficiencies in the quality of participants, external linkages, and collective intangible assets. Nonetheless, successful launching and gradual phasing-in of a machinery industry district could be an epochal event for the entire Korean economy.

It would give a big boost to Korea's arduous endeavour to foster a competitive machinery sector. In addition, it could have a huge diffusion effect by providing a model of industrial and regional development that could be emulated by other stagnant industries such as textiles and apparel and fine chemicals.

Although 'innovation' has become a buzzword in Korea these days, neither the practical meaning nor the impending policy implications of this word appear to be properly understood. Put bluntly, the gist of 'innovation' is collaborative networking among various parties subjected to common competitive pressure. Accustomed to input-driven growth and input-based competition most Koreans perceive innovation, instead, as a kind of individual output that merely requires more individual ingenuity or more stand-alone R&D effort. Although pouring in more R&D resources will surely make the Korean economy somewhat more innovative, there is a clear limit to a purely input-based model of innovation. Probably the greatest expected payoff of the new model of industrial district would come from the culture of collaborative and synthetic networking that it would create. At the present critical stage of industrial upgrading and evolution the Korean economy badly needs to build this kind of networking environment.

Notes

1   MOST/STEPI, OECD *Review of Korea's Science and Technology* (review version), 1995.
2   The conventional view that Korea's success in attaining rapid and equitable growth was somehow 'miraculous' has been challenged recently by a cadre of so-called 'contrarian scholars', who contend that Korea (and Singapore) simply experienced Soviet-style, input-based growth driven by massive state-led mobilisation of labour and capital over a protracted period. The conventional view is well represented in *The East Asian Miracle* (World Bank 1993), and the contrarian view by Krugman (1994). For a comprehensive discussion of the issue of the role of the Korean government, especially the debate over Korea's trade regime in theoretical and empirical literature, see Rodrik (1995). A lucid review can be found in Yoo (1996).
3   The contribution of capital and labour inputs to growth is destined to disappear over time, and a stage of relatively weak growth will naturally set in in due time. According to the base-scenario of KDI's long-term growth projections, Korea's growth potential will slow down to 5.5

percent for 2000–10 period, and it will decline further to 4 percent in the following decade (Table A9.1).

4 Scholars differ on the classification of Korea's industrialisation process. The classification that we adopted for this chapter is supported by many including Park (1994). See Table A9.2.

5 Yoo (1996) contains an interesting characterisation of the nature of Korea's trade policy during the HCI phase.

6 See Park (1994) for a discussion how external factors might have motivated the HCI drive and Yoo (1996) for a succinct differentiation of the HCI drive from the general export-promotion policy of the 1960s.

7 For a general evaluation of all these fiscal and credit policies, see World Bank (1993).

8 There were some differences among heavy industries. The chemical industry and primary metal manufacturing lost ground slightly in the 1980s after recording substantial gains in the 1970s, whereas the share of the metal products and machinery industries continued expanding even in the 1980s. The share increase was particularly substantial in the general machinery, electrical machinery, and transportation equipment industries. The shares of the electronics and transportation industries were even higher than the share of textiles in the early 1980s.

9 A comprehensive and rigorous study of the HCI drive can be found in Stern et al. (1995). Park (1994) takes a positive view of the role of the HCI drive while Yoo (1996) argues that the misguided policy hampered Korea's industrialisation process.

10 Even so, textiles and garments still occupied the largest share of exports.

11 The basic tenet of this rationalisation program was laid down by the Comprehensive Stabilisation Program, announced in 1979 under President Park. These policy efforts and the enactment of the requisite laws brought major reforms in four areas including financial liberalisation (deregulation in 1984 and 1988), realignment of the industrial incentive system (Industrial Development Law, 1986), promotion of competition among domestic and foreign firms (Fair Trade Law, 1981), and trade and capital market liberalisation (Import Liberalisation Program, 1983, and Revised Foreign Capital Inducement Act, 1984).

12 Government interventions reduced the incentive for private industry to undertake positive adjustment programs and they encouraged firms to wait for public rescue. Distressed companies could postpone adjustment until the rescue, hoping that their share in the final merger or cartel would be an improvement over scaling down or a private merger proposal. Surely it is too early to assess the overall effect of the

Annex Table 9.A1
Growth Accounting and Long-term Growth Projections
(Percent)

	1972–1982	1982–1992	1992–2000	2000–2010			2010–2010		
				Base	Low	High	Base	Low	High
Actual Growth	7.1	9.5							
Cyclical factor	-0.7	1.3							
Potential Growth	8.1	8.1	7.2	5.5	5.0	6.0	4.0	3.5	4.4
Inputs	5.2	4.4	3.8	2.7	2.6	2.8	1.9	1.8	2.0
Labour	3.2	2.5	1.9	1.0	1.0	1.0	0.4	0.4	0.4
Capital	2.0	1.9	1.9	1.7	1.6	1.8	1.5	1.4	1.6
Productivity	2.9	3.7	3.4	2.8	2.4	3.2	2.1	1.7	2.4
Resource reallocation	0.7	0.9	0.7	0.5	0.4	0.6	0.2	0.2	0.3
Scale economies	1.5	1.8	1.5	1.1	1.0	1.2	0.7	0.5	0.7
Technology	0.7	1.0	1.2	1.2	1.0	1.4	1.2	1.0	1.4

Note: Base denotes base growth scenario; low means low growth scenario; and high refers to high-growth scenario.
Source: KDI.

Annex Table 9.A2
GDP Growth by Phase of Industrialisation
(Percent)

	Take-off 1963–1972	HCI Drive 1973–1979	Rationalisation 1980–1989	Liberalisation 1990–1995	1963–1995
GDP growth rate	8.93	8.87	9.00	7.48	8.47
Per capita GDP	6.46	7.14	7.70	6.51	6.79

Source: National Statistical Office, *National Income Accounts of Korea.*

rationalisation programs during this period, but some (Park, 1994, for instance) argue that they were economically justified by the extent of the market imperfections that prevailed at the time.

[13] The '3-lows' are: low interest rate, low yen (appreciation of yen against US dollar), and low oil prices.

[14] With the completion of the program, the import liberalisation ratio increased from 80 percent in 1983 to over 95 percent. About three-quarters of the items remaining under restriction were primary products, food and beverages. Together with the lower quantitative import restrictions, the average nominal tariff rate was gradually lowered from 24 to 13 percent between 1983 and 1989.

[15] Despite some reservations voiced from inside and outside Korea and especially remarks by the group of so-called 'contrarians' demystifying the East Asian Miracle (see, for instance, Krugman 1994) the prevailing sentiment until 1996 was that Korea had made all requisite adjustments and preparations to stay on a super-growth track for a prolonged period. Such optimism appeared to be justified by Korea's astonishing industrialisation history itself and further vindicated by the extraordinary economic performance in 1994–95, which most Koreans belatedly came to acknowledge was due to the worldwide boom in the semiconductor market, especially DRAMs.

[16] Four of the six major industries (electrical/electronics, transportation equipment, machinery, and scientific equipment) are grouped together under the 'machinery and equipment' category in Figure 9.1.

[17] International comparisons of productivity, especially comparisons of levels, are tricky. Here, in order to deliver the key message of this chapter clearly using a consistent data set, the comparison is made using nominal exchange rates, nominal value-added, and without controlling for labour hours.

[18] The five categories are: product design, advanced research (generic/applied research and advanced engineering), product development, adaptation/modification, and production.

[19] The high-tech and mid-tech classification here differs from the usual OECD classification. Global high-tech industries in this paper correspond to the OECD's high- and medium-high tech industries categories, while local mid-tech industries correspond to the OECD's medium-low tech category.

[20] Some of the best known examples are Emilia Romana of Italy (textiles/apparel) and Baden-Wuertemberg of Germany (machinery and motor vehicles).

[21] The quality and results of these sources-of-growth studies vary, depending on the period covered, methodology, and data set used. Although some studies claim that the TFP growth factor in Korea is as low as 9 percent, it appears that reasonable numbers lie somewhere in the 20–35 percent range.

	Kim-Lau (1994)	Young (1995)	Collins-Bosworth (1996)	Kim-Park (1988)	Yoon-Lee (1998)
Period covered	60–90	66–90	60–94	66–83	(70–95)
TFP/VA growth	16.0	21.3	26.3*	36	28.4

Note: * measured in total output.
Source: Reconstructed from Yoon and Lee (1998).

[22] According to Yoon and Lee (1998), the slowing-down of TFP has occurred in about two-thirds of the 27 industrial branches encompassing almost all of Korea's major export industries. The productivity decline was most pronounced in the mid-tech industries such as machinery and petrochemicals.

[23] While growth in R&D investment remained stagnant in almost all advanced economies during the 1990s, R&D expenditure in Korea increased more than 20 percent a year during at least until the 1997 crisis. The R&D-GDP ratio in Korea rose steeply from 2.1 percent in 1992 to 2.8 percent by 1996. Another notable aspect of Korea's R&D efforts is the overwhelming role of the private sector. Nowadays in Korea, the proportion of government-funded R&D investment, which was as high as 80 percent in the early 1980s, is in the range of 18–23 percent.

[24] In its latest forecast of the world economy up to 2020, WEFA (1999) predicted that Asia, excluding Japan, will continue to lead the world growth with an average annual growth rate of 5.8 percent (5.3 percent for Korea), followed by Latin America (4.2 percent), Europe (2.2 percent), the U.S. (2.2 percent), and Japan (1.9 percent). For the 10-year period until 2010 WEFA predicted that China and India will lead Asia's growth (7.4 percent), followed by the ENIEs group (Indonesia, Thailand, Philippine; 6.0 percent), and by the four Asian tigers (Korea, Singapore, Taiwan, and Hong Kong; 5.6 percent).

[25] Forecasting world trade flows by regions until 2020, one research institute in Japan predicted in 1996 that East Asia will grow into the

single largest trading region of the world by 2020, surpassing EU in both export and import shares. In addition, the study forecasted that the intra-regional trade share in East Asia will keep growing to take up about 20.4 % of global trade flows, and that the shares of inter-regional trade involving Asia will dwindle eventually.

[26] One rough method to gauge the locational advantages of East Asian nations in different industries is to compare each economy's distribution of R&D workers across industries. According to analysis by Andersson (1999) Indonesia's locational advantages appear in food products, wood/paper/textile products, and chemicals; Malaysia's are in electrical/electronics products; Singapore's in electrical/electronics and services; Thailand's in services; and Korea's in chemicals, electrical/electronics, and transportation equipment.

[27] Concerning overall R&D capacity, Andersson (1999, p. 135), for instance, states: "Looking at the level of research and development, especially Korea but also Taiwan are well on par with the most developed countries in the world, whereas the other Asian countries lag behind. ... In absolute terms, China is a major player in several respects."

[28] In terms of notified volume. Executed volume was US$5.16 billion.

[29] Until the mid 1980s, low-cost labour was the main advantage of investing in Korea. As wages increased after the mid-1980s, an increasing proportion of FDI was made to penetrate attractive domestic markets.

[30] The alliance between Hyundai and Renault for joint venture production in Malaysia may be a case in point. The unique managerial advantage of Korean carmakers in the emerging market was pointed out by McDermott (1996).

[31] From a mid- to long-term perspective, Korea's backward S&T infra-structure may be another principal hindrance. To stay focused and short, this chapter does not address the S&T issue.

[32] The output composition of manufacturing SMEs is similar to that of the manufacturing sector overall. In 1995, for instance, machinery and equipment industry produced the largest share of valued-added by SMEs (35.7%), followed by textiles and clothing (16.0%), chemicals (14.7%), and food processing (10.3%). As in the manufacturing sector as a whole, SMEs in heavy and chemical industries far outweighed those in light manufacturing in activities (62.4% vs. 37.6%) — although by a somewhat smaller margin (73.4% vs. 26.6%). The SME sector has undergone a discernible structural change toward HCIs over 1985–95. The shares of relatively high value-added sectors such as machinery

and equipment have increased substantially while the shares of the traditional SME sector such as textiles and clothing have dwindled. The speed and extent of structural progress in the SME sector are still less than in the manufacturing sector overall. For instance, while the machinery and equipment industry's share in total manufacturing value-added increased from 30.6 percent to 45 percent, its share of value-added by manufacturing SMEs increased from 25.4 percent to 35.7 percent. This implies that SMEs have lagged somewhat behind large firms in the structural transition to high value-added industries.

33 Although more than 7 percent of SMEs are reportedly engaged in some R&D, more than 60 percent of firms conducting R&D spend less than 3 percent of their revenue on R&D. For SMEs as a whole, total R&D spending is as little as 0.3 percent of total turnover.

34 The popular perception that direct government intervention is required to rectify the disadvantages of SMEs has long been an ideological cornerstone of Korea's SME policy. The amended 1982 Constitution, for instance, states that the 'protection' and 'promotion' of small businesses shall be the government's 'responsibility' and 'duty'. Korea started to switch to a more market-logic policy in the late 1980s, emphasising the selective nurturing of innovative groups, but the backbone of SME policy has not changed that much.

35 In the 1990s, some leading domestic firms started to form technical alliances with foreign companies to gain design capability and to localise core parts and components. For instance, Daewoo Heavy Industries allied with Kawasaki Heavy Industries to develop its own industrial robot model and it collaborated with Toshiba to develop a sophisticated 32-bit CNC device for its CNC lathes and machining centres, which are currently for sale.

36 Exports have increased steadily, but as imports of high-end products continued to increase sharply to keep pace with facility investments in the manufacturing sector, the trade deficit in general machinery remains huge and rising. In 1996, the deficit in this industry reached $13.9 billion, which in turn amounted to 91 percent of Korea's total trade deficit that year.

37 There also has been a naturally protected low-end market due to proximity to users, cheap cost of production, and the language barrier. This market is gradually fading away too. With the advance of transportation and communication, foreign firms are at near parity in terms of speed of getting access to users' needs and the cost of A/S service. Most of all, the low price market which has been dominated by

domestic machine producers will be challenged by cheap machines from the second tier NICs such as China and Malaysia as well as those from some transition economies in Eastern Europe such as the Czech Republic, Poland, and others.

[38] Though firms are located in the same district, the linkages and interactions among the resident firms are quite limited because they import most core components and technologies from abroad.

References

Abrenica, Joy V. 1997. "The Asian Automotive Industry: Assessing the Roles of State and Market in the Age of Global Competition." *Asia-Pacific Economic Literature.*

Andersson, Thomas. 1999. "Policies for Knowledge-Based Industries in the Asian Economies." Paper presented at the APEC Seminar on The Promotion of Knowledge-based Industries in the APEC Region. June 17–18, Seoul. (pp 123–144 of the Conference volume).

Institute for Management Development (IMD). 1998. *The World Competitiveness Yearbook.* Lucerne: IMD.

Kim, Linsoo. 1997. *Imitation to Innovation: The Dynamics of Korea's Technological Learning.* Boston: Harvard University Press.

Krugman. Paul. 1994. "The Myth of Asia's Miracle." *Foreign Affairs.* 73(6).

Korea Federation of Small Business. 1995. *The Survey Report of Technology in Small Firms.* Seoul: Korea Federation of Small Business, Ministry of Trade and Commerce.

Korea Development Bank. 1997. *Industry in Korea.* Seoul: Korea Development Bank.

McDermott, M. 1996. *South Korea's Motor Industry: New Global Competitor? Economist Intelligence Unit Report.* London: EIU.

Nordicity Group Ltd. 1996. *Regional/Local Industrial Clustering: Theory and Lessons from Abroad.* Ottawa: National Research Council Canada.

Organisation for Economic Co-operation and Development (OECD). 1996a. *Globalization of Industry: Overview and Sectoral Reports.* Paris: OECD.

———. 1996b. *Networks of Enterprises and Local Development: Competing and Co-operating in Local Productive Systems.* Paris: OECD.

———. 1997. *Globalization and Small and Medium Enterprises.* Paris: OECD.

Park J.K. 1994. "Industrial Policies for Industrial Restructuring." KDI Policy Monograph series 94-01. Seoul: Korea Development Institute.

————. 1997. *The Long-term Trend of the Industrial Structure and the Policy Direction for Small Firms* (in Korean). Seoul: Korea Development Institute.

Porter, M. E. 1990. *The Competitive Advantage of Nations*. New York: Free Press.

Rodrik, Dani. 1995. "Trade and Industrial Policy Reforms." In *Handbook of Development Economics* ed. Behrmann and Srinivasan. Amsterdam: Elsevier.

Lee, K., ed. 1998. *National Innovation System of Korea* (in Korean). Seoul: Science and Technology Policy Institute (STEPI).

Stern J., J. Kim, D. Perkins, and J. Yoo. 1995. *Industrialization and the State: The Korean Heavy and Chemical Industry Drive*. Seoul: KDI and HIID.

Wharton Economic Forecasting Associate (WEEA). 1999. *World Economic Outlook, Twenty Year Extension*. Eddyston: WEFA Group.

World Bank. 1998. *East Asia: The Road to Recovery*. Washington, D.C.: World Bank.

Woo, C.S. 1998. "Human Capital and Economic Development of Korea." KDI Working Paper No 9801. Seoul: Korea Development Institute.

———— and C.S. Lim 1998. "Promoting SMEs in Korea: Mandate for a New Approach." Paper presented at University of Hawaii-KDI Conference on Korea's Transition to a High Productivity Economy. 6–7 February, Hawaii.

Yoo, J. H. 1996. "Challenges to the Newly Industrialized Countries: A Reinterpretation of Korea's Growth Experience." KDI Working Paper Series No. 9608. Seoul: Korea Development Institute.

Yoon, C. H. and J. H. Lee. 1998. *Technology Capability and International Competitiveness of the Korean Manufacturing Industries* (in Korean). Seoul: Science and Technology Policy Institute (STEPI).

PART III
Industrial Restructuring in the Two Large Asian Economies

10

China's Industrial Restructuring in the Twenty-First Century[1]

Wu Zhengzhang

Since the start of reform and opening-up, China's national economy has been developing at an unprecedented and sustained high rate. China's industrial structure is upgrading in the course of industrialisation, but there are still structural problems due to the economic system and geographical disparities. Deflation in China after the Asian financial crisis made such structural distortions an even more pressing issue. China needs a clear understanding of the existing problems and the challenges to readjustment for the twenty-first century in order to optimise the industrial structure and put national economic development on a healthy path at a sustained, fast rate.

The first part of this chapter reviews the changes in China's industrial structure over the past two decades. The second part discusses the major problems with China's current industrial structure and the third part describes the expected challenges in the twenty-first century. The last part gives some policy suggestions for industrial restructuring in the coming century.

CHANGES IN INDUSTRIAL STRUCTURE OVER THE LAST TWO DECADES

Changes in Three-sector Structure

After China launched reforms and opened its doors to the outside world, the process of industrialisation apparently accelerated. From 1979 to 1998 GDP increased at an average annual rate of 9.7 percent. Primary industry grew at 5.1 percent per year on average whereas the secondary and tertiary industries grew at average rates of 12.0 and 11.2 percent, respectively. The different growth rates of the three sectors resulted in striking changes in

China's industrial structure. These changes largely followed the evolutionary rule that governs industrialisation of all countries in the medium-term, that is, the share of value-added of primary industry decreases, whereas the shares of secondary and tertiary industries increase. In China, from 1978 to 1998 the primary sector fell from 28.1 percent of GDP to 18.4 percent while the share of the tertiary sector rose from 23.7 to 32.9 percent (Table 10.1).

In several ways these changes in industrial structure clearly reflect state policies and the government's strong influence over economic activity. First, the contribution of cultivation to total agricultural output value decreased dramatically. In 1979, under the policy that emphasised self-sufficiency in grain supply, crop cultivation contributed as much as 80 percent of agricultural output, compared to animal husbandry which accounted for 15.0 percent, forestry, 3.4 percent, and fisheries, 1.6 percent. By 1998, however, cultivation represented a mere 58.0 percent of primary sector value added while the shares of animal husbandry, forestry, and fisheries had risen to 28.6, 3.5, and 9.9 percent respectively. Farmers' control over agricultural production decisions increased and they could tailor their output to the market.

Second, the shares of light and heavy industry have become more rational. In order to relieve the severe shortage of consumer goods at the end of the 1970s, government policy gave top priority to light industry, and consequently its share of secondary sector output rose significantly, from 43.1 percent in 1978 to 50.2 percent in 1982. Industries producing

TABLE 10.1
Total Value Added and Distribution by Sector, 1978–98

	GDP 100 million yuan	Primary Sector %	Secondary Sector %	Tertiary Sector %
		Share of GDP Value Added from:		
1978	3,264	28.1	48.2	23.7
1981-85 avg.	6,445	31.4	44.2	24.4
1986-90 avg.	14,510	26.2	43.2	30.6
1991-95 avg.	37,625	20.9	46.9	32.2
1998	79,396	18.4	48.7	32.9

Source: China Statistical Yearbook 1980–99.

consumer commodities developed swiftly in all parts of the country, and by the end of the 1980s China had largely eliminated the quota system for consumer goods. At present, daily necessities, by and large, tend to be over-supplied. Since the beginning of the 1990s, the government has spent more on basic industries and infrastructure facilities and the heavy industrial sector has resumed its development momentum (Table 10.2).

Third, the tertiary sector, including finance, insurance, and other service industries, is increasing dramatically. Since the 1980s the government has attached much importance to this sector, which is the largest contributor to value added and employs the greatest number of workers. Within the tertiary sector the shares of transportation and telecommunications, and of commerce slipped, while the share of the finance and insurance industries increased (Table 10.3).

TABLE 10.2
Light and Heavy Industry Contribution to
Industrial Sector Output, 1978–98
(Percent)

	1978	1982	1990	1995	1998
Light industries	43.1	50.2	49.4	47.3	49.3
Heavy industries	56.9	49.8	50.6	52.7	50.7

Source: *China Statistical Yearbook* 1980–99.

TABLE 10.3
Composition of Tertiary Sector Value Added, 1978–97
(Percent)

	1978	1980	1990	1995	1997
Transportation and communication	20.1	21.2	19.7	17.0	16.5
Commerce	30.9	22.1	24.4	27.5	26.7
Finance, insurance	9.0	9.0	21.2	19.4	19.7
Real estate	5.7	5.9	5.6	5.9	5.5
Other	34.3	41.8	29.0	30.2	31.6

Source: *China Statistical Yearbook* 1980–99.

Changes in Ownership

Since China's reform and opening-up began in the late 1970s, the government has adopted a series of proactive policies to encourage and support the development of the non-public economy. This has brought great changes in the ownership structure of the economy.

Public Economy

The public economy's place in the national economy has diminished over the last two decades, although it still far outweighs the non-public economy's share. In 1997 the public economy, which includes state- and collective-owned enterprises, accounted for just over three-fourths of GDP, although this was 23.3 percentage points lower than its share in 1978 (Table 10.4).[2] Output of state-owned enterprises amounted to 3,129.6 billion yuan (including 486 billion yuan attributed to partially state-owned enterprises) and the output of collective-owned enterprises was 2,538 billion yuan (including 165.7 billion yuan produced by partially collective-owned enterprises).[3] The output of state-owned enterprises fell from 56.2 percent

TABLE 10.4
Composition of Output by Type of Ownership,
1978 and 1997
(Percent of GDP)

	1978	1997
Public economy	99.1	75.8
State-owned enterprises	56.2	41.9
Mixed ownership enterprises in which state holds controlling share	n.a.	6.5
Collective-owned enterprises	42.9	33.9
Mixed ownership enterprises in which collectives hold controlling share	n.a.	2.2
Non-public economy	0.9	24.2
Total	100.0	100.0

Note: State- and collective-owned enterprises may be owned jointly with foreign firms or entrepreneurs from Hong Kong, Macao, or Taiwan. Output of those in which the state or collective has a controlling share is counted under the public economy. The non-public economy includes individuals and households as well as share-holding corporations and enterprises funded by foreigners or by entrepreneurs from Hong Kong, Macao, or Taiwan.
Source: China Statistical Yearbook.

of total GDP in 1978 to 41.9 percent in 1997 and the output of collective-owned enterprises dropped from 42.9 percent to 33.9 percent. Despite this diminished role, the public economy retains absolute preponderance in basic natural monopoly industries such as railways, post and telecommunications, water, electric power, coal, and gas as well as in such sectors such as civil aviation, finance, insurance, and education.

Non-public Economy

The fast-growing non-public economy, which includes private Chinese-owned as well as foreign-owned companies and companies based in Hong Kong, Macao, or Taiwan, has become an important part of the national economy. It accounted for almost one-fourth (24.2 percent) of output in 1997 compared to under one percent in 1978 (Table 10.4). Not only has the total amount of output by the non-public enterprises increased significantly, but also non-public enterprises account for a significant share of output in many industrial sectors. The non-public economy contributed over half (53.8 percent) of total value added in the wholesale and retail trade and restaurant industries in 1997. The industries with the next largest output contributions by the non-public economy were agriculture (27.5 percent) and manufacturing (21.2 percent). Even in the transportation and post and telecommunications industries, where state and collective enterprises' presence is greatest, the non-public economy contributed more than 10 percent of industry output.

The distinctive feature of the change in ownership in China has been the shift from a single type of ownership — by the state — to a system with various types of ownership. Such diversity is conducive to effective allocation of social resources, to competition among enterprises, and to improved economic efficiency.

Changes in Employment Structure

Since 1978 employment in China has been expanding through three main channels:

- vigorous development of the tertiary sector in size and area;
- structural readjustment of ownership so that collective and private economies have absorbed a great number of workers;
- adherence to market-oriented reform with market levers to allocate labour.

In 1998 employment stood at 699.57 million persons, up 74.2 percent (401.52 million) since before the reform and opening-up began in 1979. Employment in cities and townships increased even more dramatically. In 1998 employment in cities and townships (206.78 million people) was 117.3 percent above the level 1978. The employment mix changed in two significant ways.

Rapid Growth of Secondary and Tertiary Sector Employment

Employment in the secondary and tertiary sectors grew very fast. In 1978, 70.5 percent of total employment was in the primary sector, 17.3 percent in the secondary sector and 12.2 percent in the tertiary sector. By 1998 the primary sector share had dropped to 49.8 percent, while the share of the secondary sector had risen to 23.5 percent and the share of the tertiary sector had more than doubled to 26.7 percent (Table 10.5).

Rapid Increase in Non-public Economy Employment

Employment outside of the public economy increased rapidly after the public economy was established as the leading sector in a system with several coexisting sectors. The non-public economy quickly absorbed a growing number of workers. By the end of 1998, joint-stock economic entities employed 4.1 million workers, economic entities with investment from foreign business, Hong Kong, Macao, or Taiwan employed 5.87 million, and private and household entities employed 78.24 million. The

TABLE 10.5
Total Employment and Distribution by Sector, 1978–98

	Total Employment 100,000 people	Share of Total Employment in:		
		Primary Sector %	Secondary Sector %	Tertiary Sector %
1978	4,015.2	70.5	17.1	12.2
1980–85 avg.	4,670.5	65.8	19.3	14.8
1986–90 avg.	5,552.9	60.1	21.9	18.0
1991–95 avg.	6,637.5	56.2	22.3	21.6
1998	6,995.7	49.8	23.5	26.7

Source: *China Statistical Yearbook* 1980–99.

increase in non-public economy employment was even more apparent in cities and townships (Table 10.6).

In a nutshell, China's industrial structure changed significantly during the two decades of reform and opening-up that accelerated the industrialisation and transformation from a socialist planned economy to a market-oriented economy which brought the economy to a new stage of development.

MAJOR PROBLEMS IN THE EXISTING INDUSTRIAL STRUCTURE

While restructuring has effectively reduced industrial disparity in China over the past two decades, the industrial structure today is still far from complete compared with that of other economies at a similar stage of development and it has not reached the targets for domestic economic growth and reform.

Reliance of Agriculture on the Natural Environment and Resource Constraints

In the late 1970s introduction of the contract responsibility system that linked remuneration to output was the beginning of the shift from a socialist planned economy to a market-oriented economy. This reform set productive forces loose, greatly boosting agricultural output and the rural economy. As a basic industry, agriculture has played an important role in

TABLE 10.6
Distribution of Urban Employment by Economic Sector, 1978 and 1998
(Percent)

	Share of Urban Employment in:			
	State- and Collective-owned Enterprises	Share-holding Corporations	Enterprises funded by foreigners, Hong Kong, Macao, or Taiwan	Individual and Household Enterprises
1978	99.8	n.a.	n.a.	0.2
1998	79.6	2.0	2.8	15.6

Source: *China Statistical Yearbook* 1980–99.

sustaining the stable and healthy development of the national economy. However, China's agricultural sector — with individual households as the typical production unit and grain as the major product — relies too heavily on the natural environment and it is constrained by the available natural resources.

There are three principal problems. First, basic agricultural infrastructure is inadequate and the capacity to withstand disaster is diminishing. Although the state has stepped up efforts to support agriculture, funds earmarked for basic agricultural facilities are limited. Many such facilities operate above capacity, thus straining their ability to cope with natural disasters. The second problem is that the amount of arable land has decreased drastically in recent years because of urbanisation and industrialisation. From 1990 to 1995 the total amount of land under cultivation decreased 455,000 hectares. China currently has only 0.08 ha per capita of arable land, roughly one-third the world average. The third problem is that the condition of land resources and the ecological environment are deteriorating as a result of heavy reliance on chemical fertilisers and pesticides to increase grain output.

Over-capacity in Low Value Added Processing and Similarity in Industrial Structure among Regions

As economic reforms decentralised decision-making and gave local governments and enterprises more autonomy over investment, the general processing industry developed very quickly, at an average 21.6 percent per year from 1990 to 1995. With a growth rate 7.2 percentage points higher than the growth rate of such basic industries as energy and raw materials, general processing has reached a state of excess capacity. According to the Third General Survey of Industries, in 1995 more than half of the 900 major industrial products was turned out by enterprises that were operating below 50-percent capacity. Capacity utilisation was only 43.4 percent among manufacturers of washing machines, 34.5 percent for manufacturers of industrial bearings, and 13.3 percent for makers of photographic film. At the same time that the processing industry has surplus capacity, high-tech and high-quality processed items are in short supply, and demand has to be met by imports.

Excess capacity in low value added processing is manifested in the lack of geographical specialisation and duplication of industrial activities in many locations around the country. For example, according to the Third General Industrial Survey, in 1997 TV sets were produced in 29 different provinces and regions, refrigerators and washing machines were made in 23 different areas, and items such as textiles, plastics, bicycles, motors, and chemical fibres were produced in more than 20 different locations. According to one estimate, the industrial composition of the eastern, central, and western parts of China is correlated as closely as 93.5 percent, and the correlation is even higher among cities and regions within provinces.

Slow Growth of the Tertiary Sector and Burgeoning Sectors

The growth of the tertiary sector has been decelerating since the 1990s. The average growth rate for 1991–95 was 10 percent per year, which is not only below the 17.4 percent annual growth rate of the secondary sector but also lower than the 12 percent annual average growth of GDP during the same period. China is falling behind other countries in the tertiary sector's share of value-added in GDP. At 32.8 percent in 1998, the tertiary sector's share in China was 10 percentage points or more below the share in other Asian countries at similar levels of development, including India (42.1 percent), Thailand (49.7 percent), Malaysia (43.8 percent), and Indonesia (41.4 percent).

Furthermore, China's tertiary sector still focuses on traditional commerce and service trade. There are three main reasons why China lags far behind the developed countries in finance, insurance, information, consulting, and technology. First, industrialisation in China is still at the stage when the secondary sector is expanding and the market for tertiary products is sluggish. Second, the government still exercises control over or monopolises certain emerging segments of the tertiary industry. Third, some industries in the tertiary sector require a high level of knowledge, service, and management, which China cannot yet provide.

Delayed Progress in Industrial Technology

China's industries are technologically backward and productivity is low, across the board in primary, secondary, and tertiary sectors. Only 30.3 percent of economic growth during the 1978–90 period came from technological progress and around 35 percent in the 1990s. In comparison, 50 to 70 percent of the growth of developed countries during the 1980s was due to technological progress.

China's slow progress in industrial technology is mainly due to two factors. One is the stagnant scientific and technological system. In China, basic and applied research are divorced from commercial production and there is a low rate of application of scientific and technological achievements. The other is the lack of spending on scientific and technological research. In 1997 China invested 39.4 billion yuan, or 0.6 percent of GDP, in R&D far below the share in developed countries and in newly industrialised economies such as Korea (2.79 percent in 1996) and Singapore (1.35 percent in 1996). Besides, scientific and technological input is not directed toward enterprises. In 1997 only 42.9 percent of China's total R&D expenditures went to enterprises, well below the 60 percent average for developing countries.

Over-diversification of the State-owned Economy

Although non-state economies have made remarkable gains over the past two decades, the pattern of state involvement extending to all sectors remains essentially unchanged from the traditional planned economy. The state's limited capital is diluted among too many enterprises and industries, with over 60 percent of the state's current operating capital in such competitive industries as manufacturing, construction, trade, and restaurant and beverages. According to the Third General Industrial Survey, 63 percent of the total value of fixed assets of independent-accounting industrial enterprises is in large-sized enterprises and 35 percent is in small and medium-sized enterprises. Thus, the state invests more than one-third of its assets in numerous small and medium-sized enterprises, while it does not invest sufficiently in many sectors for which government should be responsible, such as infrastructure, education, and high technology.

Inefficient Industrial Structure

Inefficiency of China's industrial structure is seen in two main aspects: enterprises are too small and co-ordination among industries is too limited. Only a few of the existing state-owned enterprises have attained the minimum economic scale required by modern technology. This is true even in such leading industries as automobiles, steel, chemicals, and other industries that apparently have scale economies. As a result, state-owned enterprises are not competitive either at home or abroad. According to statistics for 1997, as much as 56 percent of total capital investment went to small-scale capital construction projects. For example, recipient iron and steel plants and cement plants had average production capacity of 34,000 tons and 88,000 tons respectively, and the annual output of recipient carmakers was below 10,000 vehicles. Moreover, there is a lack of co-ordination among industries. The propensity of state-owned enterprises to be vertically integrated and autonomous deprives the economy of the benefits of an efficient division of labour and co-ordination among various manufacturing industries. Instead, state-owned enterprises compete excessively with each other, and this further weakens their international competitiveness.

CHALLENGES OF INDUSTRIAL RESTRUCTURING IN CHINA IN THE NEW CENTURY

Economic Globalisation and Entry into the WTO

The world economy is rapidly moving in the direction of globalisation and regional conglomeration, and this trend will accelerate in the twenty-first century. After two decades of reform and opening-up, China is integrating with the world economy. Investment from abroad amounts to US$40 billion or more per year, and reliance on foreign trade ((imports + exports)/GDP) approaches 40 percent. China's entry into the WTO will create a relatively stable external environment for economic development, induce co-operation and participation in the international division of labour, protect rights and interests through multilateral dispute settlement mechanisms, and broaden enjoyment of the advantages of liberal international trade and investment. From analysis of a sectoral input-output model the Development Research Centre of the State Council estimates that China's entry into the WTO will boost economic growth. In the long run, liberal trade and investment will help optimise the distribution of resources, upgrade industry, and improve welfare for the whole nation by allowing full use of both foreign and domestic markets. At present, though, China is a developing country with wide disparities among sectors and regions and a yet incomplete market mechanism. The WTO requirement to open the domestic market means that certain industries will face the pressure of external competition for the first time. If it must open its markets too widely, too quickly, China faces the possibility of many bankruptcies of factories in less competitive sectors and resulting high unemployment. For this reason, the government's active approach to negotiating WTO entry aims to co-ordinate the timing of the liberalisation of trade and investment as much as possible with the restructuring of industry. This means that China will have to address the structural economic problems discussed above during the early years of the new century.

Population and Employment Pressure

With the world's largest population, China has a huge number of workers, and ensuring adequate employment opportunities and an appropriate employment structure are constant problems. Natural population growth creates continual pressure to expand employment. The labour force increased an average of 12.5 million people per year in the first five years of the 1990s and it is expected that the increase was 14.5 million people per year in the second half of the decade. According to official estimates the labour force will increase 13 million per year on average in the first 10 years of the twenty-first century.

Disguised unemployment or under-employment adds to employment pressure. Vigorous development of township enterprises and increased agricultural productivity have created a huge surplus of rural labour. From 1979 to 1998 more than 240 million rural labourers flocked to towns and cities for jobs. Surplus rural labour is expected to reach 165 million in 2000 and to surpass 300 million people in 2010. Moreover, continuing enterprise reform and restructuring in cities will certainly result in a great number of workers being laid off from SOEs. Thus, at the start of the twenty-first century, China faces employment pressures arising from population growth and industrialisation, on one hand, as well as pressure to increase capital density as a channel to improve the country's economic efficiency and competitive edge, on the other. It will be a difficult task to address the needs of both the capital-intensive and labour-intensive economies.

Resource and Environmental Constraints

Population growth and acceleration of urbanisation and industrialisation are straining China's resources and environment in six areas.

- Accelerating desertification. Currently, 27.3 percent of China's total land area is desert. The increase in desert area drastically reduces useable land area and soil fertility, depletes the natural environment, and destroys conditions for agricultural production.
- Worsening soil erosion. Areas of soil erosion make up 38.2 percent of China's total land area.
- Decreasing forest resources. Cutting and consumption far in excess of new growth are drastically reducing forest resources.
- Diminishing water resources. With only 2,300 cubic meters of fresh

water per capita China's resources are only one-fourteenth the world average. Eighteen provinces and regions, with 30 percent of China's land and 60 percent of the population, are on the verge of severe water shortage.

* Deteriorating air quality. The major source of air pollution is coal, which makes up more than 75 percent of energy consumption. Smoke dust and sulphur dioxide account for as much as 90 percent of total emissions.
* Depleting mineral and energy resources. Mines and deposits of some major energy resources that support industrialisation are in short supply, and some are even on the verge of exhaustion.

Intensive operation and inefficiency are the reasons for China's too rapid consumption of resources and its heavy pollution of the environment. According to one survey, 70 percent of pollution originates from the secondary sector, and this sector will continue to develop as China proceeds to industrialise. Balancing industrialisation with effective utilisation of resources and protection of the environment poses a severe challenge for readjusting China's industrial structure in the next century. Failure to address these issues properly will have a direct impact on the sustainable development of the national economy.

POLICY CHOICES FOR INDUSTRIAL RESTRUCTURING IN THE TWENTY-FIRST CENTURY

Strategic Reshaping of the State-owned Economy

In 1998, based on two decades of experience with reform and opening-up, the Chinese government adopted special measures to reshape the state-owned economy and deepen the reform of state-owned enterprises (SOEs). These measures illuminated the strategic direction for industrial restructuring in the twenty-first century. This direction can be summarised as follows:

* Reshaping the state-owned economy should be integrated with industrial upgrading and carried out under the principle of "dos and don'ts, advances and withdrawals". The state-owned economy must remain dominant in certain major industries and key areas and at the same time gradually withdraw from competitive sectors. Specifically, the state-owned economy will hold a controlling position in areas that: 1) involve state security (arms manufacture, coinage); 2) are natural monopolies

(railways and electric power); 3) provide important public goods and services (ports, expressways); and 4) are backbone or key industries (information technology and high-tech industries). In other sectors and areas, concentration and capital reorganisation and restructuring can improve the quality of state-owned economic entities. The government will in principle not inject any more investment into competitive industries.

• Deepening SOE reform will involve:
Continuing efforts to move toward a modern enterprise system, to step up privatisation of state-owned enterprises, to actively explore and test effective models for management of state-owned assets, to turn medium and large-sized SOEs into independent, market-oriented legal entities.

Improving SOEs' mix of assets and liabilities and gradually reducing the social burdens on SOEs as macroeconomic and financial conditions permit.

Accelerating technological progress and industrial upgrading of SOEs and revamping traditional industries by introducing advanced technology and market-oriented operating mechanisms.

Continuing strategic reorganisation of SOEs to make the most of the market mechanism to cultivate large-scale enterprises and complexes, while relaxing control over small and medium-sized enterprises.

The strategic reshaping of the state-owned economy has determined the orientation of industrial restructuring at the macro level, and the reform of SOEs has provided the micro-foundation for industrial restructuring. Overall, the state-owned economy is expected to increase in absolute size in terms of value added, as SOEs become more efficient and better managed. However, the state-owned economy's share of the national economy will decrease, and its presence in different industries will be determined on a more rational basis.

The withdrawal of the state-owned economy from competitive areas has created a rare opportunity for the non-public economy. China's practice has proven that non-public economic entities, especially private entities, are sources of high growth and absorbing surplus labour. Although the non-public economy has developed remarkably in the last two decades, it has not yet reached its full potential. In 1998 the National People's Congress adopted a revised draft of the Constitution that established the status of private economic entities. In the next century non-public, and especially private, economic entities will expand greatly and become an important force for industrial restructuring and upgrading.

The government must take several steps to create an adequate environment for the non-public economy. First, it must strengthen the legal system. The government should accelerate adoption of legislation regarding private economic matters so that the legitimate rights and interests of private enterprises have legal protection. Second, the government should improve the competitive environment by putting private enterprises on an equal footing with SOEs. It should allow private enterprises more room to operate and expand, and treat them the same as other economic bodies in such matters as personnel, financing, taxation, land use, and importing and exporting. Third, the government administrative system for private economic entities should be changed from the current multi-department system to a single-level administration. Fourth, the government should provide for a system of pension, unemployment, and health and medical care services that is independent of enterprises.

Positive Stance toward Continued Opening-up

Opening-up to the outside world is one of China's long-term state policies. At the beginning of the 1990s China instituted large cuts in import duties, lowering the total tariff level to 17 percent. It reduced the number of items under non-tariff restriction from 1,530 to around 500, of which 146 are the electrical machinery category. This is roughly similar to the level of tariff protection enjoyed by producers in Japan in the early 1970s. The government has undertaken to further readjust the tariff structure downward to 10 percent by the year 2005.

Given the ongoing economic and technological globalisation, the Chinese government is fully aware that it cannot restructure industry with the country's doors closed. It intends to actively pursue the current open policy. In order to attract more foreign investment, encourage import of advanced technologies and equipment, heighten the utilisation of foreign capital, and boost industrial restructuring and technological progress, the government has recently formulated some new measures. These measures are designed to encourage foreign investors to develop technology and innovation and expand local procurement; to give greater financial backing to foreign-funded enterprises; to encourage foreign business people to invest in the central and western areas; and to further improve the management of and service to foreign-funded businesses.

China's strategic economic restructuring and deepening of SOE reform represent an unprecedented opportunity for foreign investors. Domestic demand for foreign funds is surging. Strategic restructuring of the state-owned economy aims to concentrate state-owned assets in a few key sectors while withdrawing them from most other industrial sectors. This withdrawal may involve either transfer of physical assets or sale of equity. It is estimated that the ongoing reorganisation of SOE capital (assets) will require a total of 2 to 2.6 trillion yuan. Domestic sources alone cannot provide such a huge amount of funds, and foreign investment can be an important supplement. There are significant opportunities for foreign investment in the industries from which the state-owned economy is withdrawing (including general manufacturing and a considerable portion of the commercial and service sector), in the transfer of SOE equity, and in the reform of small and medium-sized SOEs, which are currently reorganising through merger, leasing, contractual operation, auction, and joint-stock co-operation. Such foreign investment typically takes one of five forms: full acquisition, majority ownership, purchase of a small number of shares, operation on a contract or lease basis, or establishment of a proprietary business after the state withdraws from the sector. Full acquisition and majority ownership by foreign investors are only permitted in sectors from which the state has already withdrawn.

The environment for foreign investors will continue to improve. Establishing a modern enterprise system and clearly defining property rights will make it feasible for foreign investors to acquire SOEs. Adopting a comprehensive social security system will address concerns over the social and employment consequences of allowing foreign businesses to acquire SOEs. The financial condition of SOEs will improve as their asset-liability mix adjusts and their social burden is reduced. All of these changes will reduce the costs and risks faced by foreign investors, and this in turn will increase the expected and realised gains from investment.

Cultivation of Talent and Technological Innovation

Faced with fierce international competition and domestic resource constraints, the government has come to understand that the only way to achieve industrial restructuring is through technological upgrading and accelerated scientific advances. On the one hand, existing high-technologies must be adopted to renovate and upgrade traditional industries and on the other, development of new technologies and industries must be accelerated. Specifically, this approach includes the following five points:

- First, the pace of the scientific and technological revolution in agriculture should be advanced to speed up innovation and popularisation of key technologies. China must rely upon technological innovation in agriculture including breakthroughs in agricultural gene projects, ecological resources, and water-saving farming methods, to solve the problem of feeding the more than one billion Chinese people in the next century.

- Second, new equipment, technology, craft, and management know-how should be widely applied to infrastructure, basic industries, and processing industries. To compete in domestic and international markets, traditional industries must integrate electronic information technologies and new materials in order to develop new, higher quality products with added value.

- Third, the scientific content of the tertiary sector should be increased. Development of such new service sectors as e-commerce and e-media and the quick and wide application of new technology to telecommunications, banking, consulting, and trade should be promoted.

- Fourth, the application of technology to critical problems of sustainable development including resource development and utilisation, ecological preservation, and environmental protection should be intensified. At the same time the production of clean energy and related technologies and industries should be developed extensively.

- Fifth, high-tech industries should be vigorously developed to cultivate new sources of economic growth. Top priority should be given to industries that have production applications or market potential and those that use Chinese intellectual property and have strong development potential, such as fibre-optic information, software, ecological engineering, and new energy and materials.

Technological innovation in these key areas and application of scientific and technical achievements to production will raise China's overall technological level, its national strength, and its international competitive edge. To accomplish these goals, the government will have to

- Intensify efforts to reform the science and technology system. It should enable enterprises to engage in technological innovation to improve their capacity to upgrade, and it should turn the majority of scientific and technological institutions into enterprises and speed the application of their achievements to production as much as possible.

- Encourage the rapid development of a pool of talented people with the spirit of scientific and technological innovation.

- Earmark more funds for science and technological development, provide financial support and favourable fiscal treatment to enterprises, cultivate a capital market to support the development of high-tech industries, and gradually establish a venture capital mechanism and expand venture capital funds for science and technology.

• Encourage civil scientific and technology enterprises, which are uniquely effective in translating scientific and technological advances into practical applications. By the end of 1998, there were 70,000 such enterprises in China, with a total staff 4 million.

Increasing the Role of Enterprises and the Market

With the inertia from China's planned economic system, industrial restructuring in the 1980s was accomplished mainly by administrative means and force of the plan. Under the socialist market economy that is taking shape since the late 1990s industrial restructuring has come to depend more on the market mechanism in three ways. First, the number of entities making investment decisions has diversified and the government has relaxed restrictions on the activities of investors and left investment decisions largely up to economic means. Second, the conditions of demand and supply for the most part determine what and how much an enterprise should produce. Third, the pricing system has been greatly improved so that prices are market-driven, and the price signal has become an important lever regulating demand and supply.

As industrial restructuring has come to be guided mainly by market forces rather than by central planning, the government has been replaced by enterprises as the main restructuring body. Changing the industrial structure depends more upon the investment activities of enterprises, the depth and speed of their technological innovation, and the incomes and demand of urban and rural residents. As a matter of fact, in recent years, the speed of development in competitive industries and the merger or bankruptcy of enterprises are no longer determined by administrative and planning authorities but by market demand and supply as well as by the competitive strength of individual enterprises. With strategic reshaping of the national economy and continued reform of SOEs and government organisations, enterprises and the market mechanism will play an even greater role in industrial restructuring in the twenty-first century.

Government Role in Industrial Restructuring

In a market economy, enterprises are the main body to engage in industrial restructuring but this does not deny a role for government. Its role is primarily to direct investment and provide enterprises with favourable systems, environment, and policy. At the same time, although rescue of failing industries is difficult and the social cost of restructuring is rather high, the government can still support and rectify in cases of market failure. The Chinese government's role in industrial restructuring in the twenty-first century will be largely through fiscal and financial policy.

Fiscal Policy

In keeping with the state industrial policy and strategic development program, the government will continue policies favourable to investors, and it will try to increase input in basic industries and infrastructure facilities such as agriculture, energy, transportation, essential raw and processed materials, and water conservation projects. These industries generally require a large amount of long-term investment with relatively low return. Although they are critical to sustaining economic development, they will not attract civil capital without special policy support. Therefore, to improve the basic living conditions for investors and residents and to realise sustainable and stable economic growth these sectors require government fiscal input. When there are many different types of investors and state financial resources are limited, government expenditures are a way to attract and channel social funds to infrastructure construction. Apart from direct investment, the government can channel enterprises' surplus funds to this sector through such other incentives as interest rate discounting, tax reduction, and accelerated depreciation.

Financial Policy

At present, China has a significant accumulation of financial assets with 6 trillion yuan in household savings deposits and 3 trillion yuan in enterprise deposits. Moreover, the market value of stocks has reached 10 percent of GDP. It should implement policies to direct these financial assets to support industrial restructuring and upgrading. Key state industries should have access to long-term financing, while the capital markets should allocate financing to new and improved industrial technologies based on the efficiency and cost of various projects. Furthermore, China should explore ways to allow venture capital funding for industrial upgrading and high-tech development. High-tech industrial development should have access to venture capital and stock market funding, and financial risk should be reduced in order to enable small and medium-sized high-tech enterprises to realise sustained investment and development.

Notes

[1] I am indebted to Mr. Zhang Xiaoji for many valuable and constructive suggestions.

[2] The public economy includes enterprises that are partially or wholly state- or collective-owned.

[3] The other owners include foreign firms and entrepreneurs from Hong Kong, Macao, or Taiwan.

References

Li Guoping and Yu Wenhua. 1999. "Investigation of China's Basic Countermeasures for Industrial Restructuring in the Midst of Transfer of International Industries" (Chan ye guo ji zhuan yi zhong zhong guo chan ye jie gou cong zu de ji ben dui ce tan tao). *China Soft Science* (Zhong guo ruan ke xue). February.

Li Yixue. 1999. "Problems and Countermeasures in China's Industrial Technological Progress" (Zhong guo chan ye ji shu jin bu de wen ti he dui ce). *Management World* (Guan li shi jie). January.

Wang Maokui. 1992. *Review and Forecast of China's Economic Development (1979–2020)* (Zhong guo jing ji fa zhan de hui gu yu qian zhan 1979–2020). China Fiscal and Economic Publishing House (Zhong guo cai zheng jing ji chu ban she). February.

Wu Zhengzhang. 1998. "Restructuring and Optimising Regional Economies" (Qu yu jing ji jie gou tiao zheng yu you hua). *Grand Reshaping — Six Major Problems in China's Economic Restructuring* (Da tiao zheng). China Development Publishing House (Zhong guo fa zhan chu ban she). January.

Zhuang Jian. 1991. "Review and Rethinking of China's Economic Restructuring" (Zhong guo jing ji jie gou tiao zheng yu fan shi). *Financial and Trade Economy* (Cai mao jing ji). January.

11

Restructuring Strategy of Japan's Service Sector in the Twenty-First Century

Hisashi Ono

INTRODUCTION

Despite a prolonged economic recession, Japan is still the second largest economy in the world and it plays a central role in the Asian economy in trade, foreign direct investment, and official development assistance (ODA). During the post-war period Japan's economy expanded by enhancing production capability to become a so-called manufacturing economy. Japan's automobile and consumer electronics industries are world leaders and they are strong global competitors. On the other hand, its service industries such as telecommunications, transportation, and finance are far behind the global top runners. "Strong manufacturing and weak services" describes the overall situation of Japanese industry in the global economy today.

As an economy matures, the industrial structure changes, and employment and value-added increase in the service sector while they decrease in the manufacturing sector. In fact, Japanese manufacturing companies have already moved a substantial portion of their production facilities to other places in the Asia region. The service industries must create jobs in Japan to absorb their workers as well as new entrants to the labour force. Furthermore, with the globalisation of capital, goods and services, and information, the service industries can no longer remain purely domestic. Although human resources and logistics depend on domestic participants, the global movement of capital and information breaks down national borders. Japan's service industries have been less exposed to global competition than its manufacturing industries and their management has become less efficient. Foreign-owned companies are moving into Japan's service sector, and Japanese companies are losing their positions in high value added industries such as telecommunications, the Internet, and insurance.

Entering the twenty-first century, Japan's service sector must build its own core competence to meet increasing competition. Japanese households have more than US$10 trillion saved at banking institutions. Domestic companies can tap into this vast buying power by selling services and attracting investment — if they offer something different, like the foreign-owned companies that have begun doing business in Japan.

This chapter focuses on Japan's service sector, within which some industries are doing well and others are not. It emphasises the necessity for change in the management system and for deregulation in order to restructure the service sector to cope with globalisation and to exploit new information technologies. The first part of the chapter examines the current situation and the challenges facing Japan's service sector. The second part discusses the strategy that the service industries should adopt to restore their vitality and competitiveness. The chapter concludes with policy recommendations.

CURRENT STATUS OF THE SERVICE SECTOR IN JAPAN

In 1997 services comprised 67.7 percent of Japan's GDP value added compared with 24.3 percent for manufacturing (Table 11.1). The service sector's share of the economy is roughly the same in Japan as in the United States (67.9 percent of GDP value added) and higher than in Germany (58.1 percent of GDP value added) or the UK (62.0 percent). Real estate and wholesale and retail trade are the two service industries with the largest share of value added. The service sector accounts for 72.0 percent of total employment in Japan compared with 80.7 percent in the United States. Wholesale and retail trade alone accounts for almost one-fourth of total employment in Japan and personal, community, and other services for about another one-fourth. The construction industry has a larger share of employment in Japan than in the United States, Germany, or the UK. On the other hand, financial services has a smaller share of employment in Japan than in these three other advanced economies.

Services are not Driving the Economy

In the United States and Europe the service industries are driving economic growth, but that is not the case in Japan. Low growth rates in the finance,

TABLE 11.1
Composition of Value Added and Employment by Sector in Japan, the United States, Germany, and the UK
(Percent)

	Share of Value Added				Share of Employment			
	Japan	U.S.	Germany	UK	Japan	U.S.	Germany	UK
Manufacturing	24.3	17.0	23.6	18.5	22.0	16.1	23.7	18.7
Services	67.7	67.9	58.1	62.0	72.0	80.7	70.7	78.8
Construction	9.7	4.1	5.5	2.3	10.4	6.4	9.1	7.0
Wholesale & retail	12.2	15.7	8.9	13.4	22.5	20.7	17.4	20.2
Finance, insurance	5.0	7.8	5.2	2.1	8.8	11.4	10.4	14.3
Real estate	13.6	11.5	8.6					
Transportation & communication	6.6	5.8	5.0	7.2	6.3	5.9	5.4	6.4
Utilities	2.9	2.6	2.5	2.0	0.5	1.2	0.9	0.7
Other services	17.7	20.4	22.1	14.9	23.5	35.1	29.5	30.2

Source: Value added: Bank of Japan, *Comparative Economic and Financial Statistics Japan and Other Countries, 1999*. Employment: Bureau of Labour Statistics, U.S. Department of Labour; Bureau of Economic Analysis, U.S. Department of Commerce; and Ministry of Labour of Japan.

insurance, and telecommunications industries have restrained overall GDP growth in Japan compared to the United States, Germany, and the UK (Table 11.2). As the *Economist* (27 November 1999) put it:

> In Europe and America, service industries such as information technology and finance have become engines of growth as manufacturing has moved offshore. In Japan, they have been hobbled by restrictive regulations. Small, entrepreneurial companies have a hard time of it. Instead, capital and labour stay locked up in big companies, which try to diversify into new, "growth" industries, but rarely succeed.

High Unit Costs

One source of weakness in the service sector can be seen by comparing value added per employee in Japan and other countries. Overall and in the manufacturing sector, value added per employee is similar in Japan and the United States (Table 11.3). In every service industry except trade, on the other hand, value added per employee is higher in Japan than in the United States. The discrepancies are particularly large for the construction and utility industries. In the context of minimal competition in Japan, these differences imply that service industry costs in Japan are higher than in the United States, not that service industries in Japan are more productive than in the United States.

TABLE 11.2
Average Annual Growth Rates in
Selected Advanced Economies, 1987–97
(Percent)

	Japan	United States	Germany	UK
GDP	3.0	5.1	6.3	5.8
Manufacturing	1.2	3.9	2.7	3.8
Finance and insurance	0.0	8.2	6.7	7.3
Transportation, storage, and communication	2.5	5.4	5.0	5.1

Source: Bank of Japan, *Comparative Economic and Financial Statistics Japan and Other Countries, 1999.*

TABLE 11.3
Value Added per Employee in Japan
and the United States by Sector
(Million yen)

	Japan	United States
Total	7.7	7.6
Agriculture, forestry, fishing, and mining	2.7	7.4
Manufacturing	8.6	8.2
Services		
Construction	7.2	5.0
Wholesale & retail	4.2	5.9
Finance, insurance real estate	16.4	13.1
Transportation & communication	8.1	7.6
Utilities	45.0	16.4
Other services	5.8	4.5

Note: Converted at ¥120.99=US$1 average exchange rate for 1997.
Source: Bank of Japan, *Comparative Economic and Financial Statistics Japan and Other Countries, 1999.*

Lack of Global Presence

Japan's service industries also are relatively inactive outside of the domestic economy, although this was not always the case. At one time, Japan's general trading companies, or *sogo shosha,* were active throughout the world. During the 1980s, Japanese financial institutions expanded their overseas branches. The major activity of these overseas branches was not to do financial businesses with local companies, however, but to lend to sovereign borrowers and financial institutions overseas, and since the bursting of the bubble economy they have been closing these overseas branches. The service industries' inactivity outside Japan is manifest in the service trade deficit, which is the largest in the world (Table 11.4). Particularly worrisome is the deficit in information services. Japan has carried a trade deficit in information services since the late 1980s, at the same time that the United States was carrying a large surplus in this industry. This explains Japan's weak position in the emerging information-based economy.

According to the Organisation for Economic Co-operation and Development such strategic business services as computer software and information processing services, R&D and technical testing services, marketing services, business organisation services (management consulting and recruiting

TABLE 11.4
Japan's Trade in Services, 1992–97

	Japan Receipts US$ billions	Japan Payments US$ billions	Japan Balance US$ billions	Japan Service Trade Balance/GDP %	US Service Trade Balance/GDP %
1992	49.07	93.03	–43.96	–1.18	1.54
1993	53.22	96.30	–43.08	–1.01	1.42
1994	58.3	106.36	–48.06	–1.02	1.40
1995	65.27	122.63	–57.36	–1.12	1.45
1996	67.72	129.96	–62.24	–1.35	1.85
1997	69.3	123.45	–54.15	–1.29	2.14

Source: *International Financial Statistics*, International Monetary Fund

TABLE 11.5
U.S.–Japan Trade in Strategic Business Services
(US$ billions)

		1994	1995	1996	1997
Computer services	Imports from US	18.1	17.7	29.0	28.8
	Exports to US	2.0	2.2	2.7	4.1
Management consulting	Imports from US	6.2	6.8	10.0	14.0
& public relations	Exports to US	1.7	2.8	3.5	5.0

Source: OECD *Strategic Business Services*, 1999, p. 138.

services), and human resource development services are essential to business progress, firm competitiveness, and growth (OECD 1999). Japan's 21 percent share of world trade in these strategic business services is less than half that of the United States (49 percent). Japan imports key business services such as computer services, management consulting, and public relations from the United States (Table 11.5).

Competitiveness Factors

The Institute for Management Development (IMD) in Lausanne, Switzerland ranked 47 countries and regions on the basis of factors that contribute to international competitiveness. In the Institute's *World Competitiveness Yearbook* for 1999, Japan ranked at the bottom or next to the bottom on eight individual factors, including entrepreneurship and creation of new businesses (Table 11.6). Japan's weakness in entrepreneurship and new business creation is a critical disadvantage to enhancing the service sector. As the success of Yahoo and Amazon.com demonstrates, new services come from entrepreneurship.

Low Diffusion of Information Technology

In other economies, Internet-based e-commerce is a driving force of new service business, but in Japan inadequate information infrastructure for consumers is holding back the service sector. Internet penetration and e-commerce volume are far lower in Japan than in the United States (Tables 11.7 and 11.8). During the 1990s, investment in information technology in part supported the long up trend in the U.S. economy. In Japan, on the other hand, the rate of IT investment was much lower, and the economy suffered slow or negative growth (Table 11.9).

TABLE 11.6
World Competitiveness Yearbook Rankings for Japan, 1999

Competitiveness factor	Japan's rank out of 47
Overall	16
Input factors	
Science and technology	2
People	13
Infrastructure	20
Internationalisation	21
Government	23
Finance	25
Management	26
Domestic economy	29
Selected individual factors	
Cost-of-living comparisons	46
Companies and the government	46
Tourism receipts	46
Financial institution transparency	46
Public sector contracts	47
Immigration law	47
Creation of firms	47
Entrepreneurship	47

Source: IMD, *The World Competitiveness Yearbook 1999*.

TABLE 11.7
Internet Usage in Selected Countries

	% of population
U.S.	37
Canada	36
North Europe	33
Australia	31
UK	15
Germany	10
Japan	10
France	8

Source: Henry et al., *The Emerging Digital Economy II.*
U.S. Department of Commerce, 1999.

TABLE 11.8
Volume and Composition of Electronic Commerce Transactions in Japan and the United States, 1998 and 2003*

	1998			2003*	
	Japan	**U.S.**		**Japan**	**U.S.**
Volume of transactions			¥ billion		
Business-to-consumer	65	2,250		3,160	21,300
Business-to-business	8,620	19,500		68,400	165,300
Share of e-commerce			%		
Business-to-consumer	0.02	0.4		1.0	3.2
Business-to-business	1.5	2.5		11.2	19.1

Note: Exchange rate US$1 = ¥120
*Projected
Source: Ministry of International Trade and Industry.

TABLE 11.9
IT Share of Private Machinery and Equipment Investment, Japan and United States, 1990 to 1997
(Percent)

	1990	**1991**	**1992**	**1993**	**1994**	**1995**	**1996**	**1997**
Japan	7.3	7.3	6.8	8.6	10.4	12.4	12.5	12.5
United States	13.3	14.3	16.4	17.1	18.6	22.9	28.3	33.9

Source: Ministry of Posts and Telecommunications, *White Paper on Telecommunications, 1998.*

IMPEDIMENTS TO THE GROWTH OF THE SERVICE SECTOR

Although Japan has undertaken some deregulation of service industries, the dynamism and competitiveness of the service sector are still impeded by government regulation and its consequences and by the incentives of the traditional management and corporate systems.

Over-regulation

A distinctive and long-standing feature of Japan's service industries is an absence of competition. Banking, telecommunications, construction, insurance, transportation, and utilities have all operated in a highly regulated domestic environment and they have been heavily protected from foreign competition. Regulations established after World War II when Japan was a developing country remained in place for many years after the economy attained an advanced stage of development. At one time, regulated interest rates were necessary to support the small banks that provided financing to small, local businesses; a domestic telecommunications monopoly was needed to build up a nation-wide telecommunications infrastructure; and a highly regulated motor vehicle inspection system was needed because of the low quality of Japanese cars. Much of Japan's problem today results from the fact that such regulation of the service sector did not change as companies and markets matured.

These problems are compounded by restrictions on entry (and exit) that limit competition. For example, permission is given to open new banking establishments only in locations that are served by few banks. This means that even if a bank could be very competitive in an area and push out inefficient competitors, the branch application will not be approved. It also reduces the pressure on existing banks to manage their business efficiently. In transportation, the government regulates the number of taxi licenses and airline routes. In utilities, deregulation of electricity generation began in March 2000, but the newly independent power producers may only sell to large-volume (more than 2,000 kw), high-voltage (above 20,000 V) users, not to small businesses and households.

Protection from Foreign Competition

Some service industries were both protected from foreign competition and closed to foreign companies. Inward foreign direct investment in Japan's telecommunications, construction, and transportation industries has been low relative to value added or employment (Table 11.10). Furthermore, the closed local distribution networks made it difficult for foreign companies to access Japanese consumers. With the advent of information technology, global logistics networks, and the Internet, however, it is no longer possible to continue maintain the service sector as a domestic market.

High Prices

One consequence of regulations that limit competition is that service industry prices are relatively high in Japan. For example, electricity costs more than 20 yen per kilowatt-hour in Japan compared to around 10 yen per kilowatt-hour in the United States. An *Economist* survey on Japan (1999) reported transport in Japan five times as expensive as in America and average warehouse rent ten times that in Britain. A report by Japan's Economic Planning Agency (EPA) compared the prices of certain basic services in Tokyo with those in other major cities around the world (Table 11.11). In most categories of personal services, including house rent, delivered pizza, movies, and golf fees, costs in Tokyo were significantly higher than in other cities.

Local telephone service in Tokyo appears to be relatively inexpensive (Table 11.11). For example, a local call from a public telephone in New York costs 25 cents, or about 30 yen, compared to only 10 yen in Tokyo. However, local telephone companies in the United States offer fixed rates for local calls. Moreover, Japan's lower cost for local telephone service is offset by higher prices for long distance service. In the United States major long distance carriers have rates as low as 10 cents per minute to any location in the country. In comparison in 1998, a three-minute call between Tokyo and Osaka during business hours cost 90 yen, after falling from 400 yen in 1988. Unlike the United States where fees are largely determined by the market, Japanese government policies make long-distance users subsidise local telephone service and NTT's fee structure is subject to approval by the Ministry of Post and Telecommunications.

The high cost of telecommunications is seen as the main obstacle to diffusion of the Internet in Japan. In areas where Internet service is provided through cable television companies subscribers pay about ¥6,000 per month for unlimited Internet use. Where access is through the telephone lines, however, the cost of using the Internet for two hours per day can amount to more than ¥12,000 per month because NTT charges on a per-minute basis even for local calls. To stimulate Internet usage, Japan needs to introduce flat-rate local telephone charges as well as to expand use of

TABLE 11.10
Inward Foreign Direct Investment by Industry, 1989–98
(100 million yen)

	1989	1990	1991	1992	1993	1994	1995	1996	1997	1998
Manufacturing	1,561	2,283	2,577	2,081	1,836	2,054	1,412	3,111	2,674	3,126
Services (non-manufacturing)	2,296	1,763	3,319	3,225	1,750	2,273	2,284	4,595	4,108	10,278
Telecommunications	32	30	136	63	32	30	53	21	33	168
Construction	11	13	31	0	1	4	1	0	3	14
Wholesale & retail	732	1,065	1,073	1,554	1,005	1,135	679	1,664	996	1,759
Finance & insurance	235	159	1,203	190	40	687	1,001	273	1,616	4,569
Services	186	384	737	1,067	240	374	491	2,360	888	3,181
Transportation	64	18	35	25	51	8	12	10	4	61
Real Estate	904	35	94	307	107	32	16	265	482	416
Other	132	59	11	18	274	3	32	2	87	111
All Industries	3,857	4,046	5,896	5,306	3,586	4,327	3,697	7,707	6,782	13,404

Source: Ministry of Finance.

TABLE 11.11

Comparison of Service Sector Prices in Selected Cities, 1998

(Tokyo = 1.00)

	New York	London	Paris	Berlin	Geneva
Electricity	0.68	0.81	0.94	0.97	1.11
Transportation	0.92	1.19	0.96	1.03	1.09
Local phone call	1.12	0.94	1.06	1.25	1.03
House rent	0.72	1.02	0.70	0.88	0.66
Delivered pizza	0.75	0.96	0.69	0.40	0.85
Golf fees	0.19	0.24	0.36	0.29	0.38
Movie	0.56	0.70	0.55	0.47	0.76
Haircut	1.08	0.58	0.80	0.72	1.19

Note: Similar, not identical, items are chosen in each city. Exchange rates are from IMF *International Financial Statistics*, annual average for 1998: US$1 =¥130.90 yen, £1= ¥216.83, 1FFr = ¥22.19, 1DM = ¥74.39, 1SFr = ¥90.29.

Source: Economic Planning Agency of Japan, *Price Difference Survey*.

the cable television network.[1] In July 2000, NTT agreed to reduce the fee to connect to its network by 22.5 percent over three years. This will have a big impact on Internet use in Japan.

Traditional Management System and Service Sector Business Model

A second set of impediments to the service sector comes from the inability of the traditional management system to support service industries in an environment of globalisation and information technology. Here, management system refers to human resource management, corporate finance, corporate governance, and use of information technology (IT), all of which are key factors defining the competitiveness of companies in the service sector.

Local history, culture, and institutions all influence management systems. The distinctive characteristics of Japan's management system are attributed to cross-share holding among affiliated companies, main-banks, lifetime employment, and seniority-based wages (Table 11.12). This system worked well when the country was trying to recover from the devastation of World War II, but it is less suited to Japan's situation as an economic giant in a global market at the beginning of the twenty-first century. For example, cross-shareholding encourages internal investment to satisfy stockholder

TABLE 11.12
Increase in Consumer Surplus Attributed to Deregulation
(100 million yen)

	Cumulative to Fiscal 1998	Increase from previous year	
		1997	1998
Domestic telecommunications	38,555	8,530	8,222
International telecommunications	2,623	169	141
Domestic air transportation	3,575	1,997	737
Automobile registration and inspection	6,122	1,005	424
Electricity	17,138	1,258	6,816
Oil products	14,492	2,122	2,182
Stock brokering	3,185	1,185	509
Gasoline	132	0	51
Total	85,822	15,266	19,082

Note: Includes only industries accumulating over ¥10 billion in consumer's surplus. Other examples include ¥3.1 billion consumer surplus generated through deregulation of the taxi business.
Source: Economic Planning Agency, "Economic Impact of Recent Deregulation", January 2000.

expectations of long-term appreciation. This was advantageous when Japan lacked technology, capital, and international competitiveness and it was effective in helping Japan to catch up with the advanced economies. But because cross-shareholding also lessens the pressure on companies to focus on shareholders' interests, return on equity for Japanese companies is low by international standards. Moreover, to compete effectively in the era of globalisation and information technology, Japanese companies need to choose business partners on the basis of particular strengths rather than because of their affiliation with a certain business group or *keiretsu*.

The traditional management system and management tools can no longer create value in Japan's service sector. The finance system based on bank borrowing does not serve the financing needs of start-up businesses because bank loans require collateral, which new companies lack, and because they are more costly than direct finance in the capital market. Japanese financial institutions have not provided enough resources to venture businesses in the way that the "angels" and venture capitals have in the United States. Lack of appropriate financing contributes to the paucity of new business start-ups in Japan.

The incentives of the lifetime employment system, including steady promotion and seniority-based wages, discourage workers from changing companies. Most of Japan's top college graduates still accept employment under traditional conditions at large companies. Although one-third of new hires change jobs within three years, job changers are at a disadvantage in terms of pension and promotion at their new companies.

Today, management practices are becoming standardised around the world, especially in finance, accounting, and use of information technology. The Internet allows consumers to compare services and prices easily, investors to move money globally, and multinational companies to act across national borders. Therefore, Japan's management system must be able to withstand competition from foreign-owned companies that have their own management systems and to be attractive and transparent to foreign customers and investors. Japan must adopt such management tools as information technology and merger and acquisitions to restructure the service sector so that it becomes more efficient and offers better value to consumers.

DEREGULATION AND RESTRUCTURING IN PROGRESS

The service sector in Japan is moving to become a driving force in the economy and to create new jobs to replace lost manufacturing jobs. Regulatory reforms and deregulation instituted by the government have brought some important changes in the markets of service industries. Other changes are taking place as a result of restructuring efforts by the private corporate sector.

Regulatory Reform and Deregulation

The Japanese government began deregulation in finance, telecommunications, and retail trade in the 1970s (Figure 11.1). During the 1990s deregulation increased competition from foreign firms in some service industries. Inward investment in retail and wholesale trade has remained steady at around ¥100 billion per year since 1989, but foreign companies have been entering the finance and insurance industry since the start of the Big Bang financial deregulation in 1998. Inward foreign direct investment in telecommunications is just beginning, as illustrated by the 1999 acquisition of IDC, one of Japan's new international carriers, by Cable and Wireless of the UK.

Entry of foreign firms already has brought enormous change to the service sector. In the retail industry, for example, the entry of one foreign company, Toys'R'Us, changed the entire toy market, driving out traditional small toy shops, reducing toy prices, and expanding the number of items for sale. In finance, the entry of U.S. banks has improved services dramatically. For example. after Citibank first introduced 24-hour ATM service it then spread throughout the industry. Automobile insurance premiums decreased about 30 percent in certain categories as a result of the entry of U.S. insurance companies such as American Home Direct that introduced detailed risk analysis and telephone sales in place of the traditional agency. U.S. telecommunications giant AT&T's value-added services subsidiary, AT&T Jens Corporation, pioneered commercial Internet use in Japan with its Internet access, website facilities, and management and consulting services. It also offers low-cost (¥15 per minute) Internet phone services to subscribers anywhere in Japan. .

The deregulation of the service industries has benefited the Japanese public. The Economic Planning Agency calculated that from 1990 to 1998 deregulation generated ¥8.5 trillion per year in consumer surplus due to lower prices and greater demand (Table 11.13). A large portion of this amount came from the deregulation of the telecommunications industry. For fiscal 1998 alone, consumer surplus increased an estimated ¥1.9 trillion, equivalent to 2.3 percent of national income.

Corporate Restructuring

"*Risutora*"(restructuring) has become a buzzword in the Japanese business community. The basic strategic concept of Japanese companies today is to get rid of low-performing assets and put resources into promising businesses. For growth companies must strive to differentiate themselves from their competitors in terms of cost, quality, convenience, and flexibility. Innovation, M&A, and capital market financing are the keywords for the service sector's growth strategy. Over the past several years, Japanese companies have been restructuring in one of three ways: reducing costs and economising on resource use; becoming involved in M&As; and focusing on specific business domains.

Cost Reduction

In 1999, 15 major Japanese banks announced a 14-percent reduction in employment, a decrease of 20,000 employees. The Mizuho Financial

FIGURE 11.1
Deregulation Measures Affecting Japan's Service Sector

	Measure	Date Adopted	Impact
Air transport	• Routes that can be served by more than one airline increased	1986	→ Increased competition
	• Regulation of airfares and restrictions on entry relaxed	1996	→ New carriers
			→ Lower fares
			→ Discount fares
Construction	• Regulation of standards and inspection relaxed		→ Increased construction
Corporate restructuring	• Business laws changed	1997	→ Holding companies allowed
			→ Increased merger & acquisition activity
			→ Exchange of shares
			→ Corporate split-up
Electric utilities	• Competitive tenders required	1995	→ New pricing system
	• Cost calculation method changed		
	• Entry to production partially liberalised	2000	→ Independent power supplier for industrial users
Insurance	• Business entry liberalised	1996	→ Lower prices
	• Commissions on fire and auto insurance rates liberalised	1998	→ Greater variety of products

continued on next page

FIGURE 11.1 – cont'd

	Measure	Date Adopted	Impact
Banking	• Interest rates and services liberalised	1993	→ Diversified interest rates and services
	• Foreign exchange transactions liberalised		→ 24-hour ATM service
	• Cross-entry liberalised	1998	→ Telephone/Internet banking
		1999	→ Entry to financial business from other sectors
Securities brokering	• Commissions on equity transactions liberalised	1998	→ Diversified commissions
			→ Internet transactions
Tele-communications	• Monopoly on local service and domestic and international long distance services reduced and then terminated	1985	→ New entrants
	• Tariff and business entry liberalised		→ Foreign entrants
	• Equipment lease abolished		→ Lower prices
	• NTT and KDD privatised		
Wholesale/Retail Distribution	• Establishment of large stores, opening times, and closing days liberalised.	1990s	→ More large stores, discount stores
	• Retail distribution of liquor gradually relaxed	1989	→ Longer hours
	• Retail price maintenance on cosmetics and general medicine removed	1997	→ Increased competition
			→ Lower prices
	• Construction of gas stations liberalised	1990	→ Increased competition
	• Restrictions on petroleum import lifted	1996	→ Increased competition

Source: Nomura Research Institute and OECD, *Regulatory Reform in Japan.*

TABLE 11.13
Characteristics of Management Systems in the United States, Germany, and Japan

	United States	Germany	Japan
Dominant ideology:	Free enterprise liberalism	Social partnership	Techno-nationalism
Political Institutions:	• Liberal democracy • Divided government • Interest group liberalism	• Social democracy • Weak bureaucracy • Corporatist legacy	• Developmental democracy • Strong bureaucracy • Reciprocity between state and firms
Economic institutions:	• Decentralised, open markets • Un-concentrated, fluid capital markets • Antitrust tradition	• Organised markets • Tiers of firms • Dedicated, bank-centred, capital markets • Certain cartelised markets	• Guided, closed, bifurcated markets • Bank-centred capital markets • Tight business networks • Cartels in sunset industries
Corporate governance	• Short-term shareholding; • Managers highly constrained by capital markets; • Risk-seeking, financial-centred strategies	• Managerial autonomy except during crises; • Little take-over risk; • Conservative, long-term strategies	• Stable shareholders; • Network-constrained managers; • Take-over risk only within network; • Aggressive market-share-centred strategies

continued on next page

TABLE 11.13 – cont'd

	United States	Germany	Japan
Corporate financing	• Diversified, global funding; • Highly price sensitive	• Concentrated, regional funding; • Limited price sensitivity	• Concentrated, national funding; • Low price sensitivity
Independent board oversight of management	Limited	Formally, limited; informally, can be extensive, especially in crisis	Extensive
Monitoring by financial institutions	Weak	Strong	Moderate, but can be strong in crisis
Monitoring by non-financial shareholders or affiliates	Weak	Moderate	Strong
Monitoring by individual shareholders	Weak	Weak	Can be strong
Hostile take-overs	Common	Rare	Rare
Inward direct investment	Liberal; No constraints	Liberal; Tacit constraints	Resistant; Formal and informal constraints
Outward direct investment	Broadly supportive Manufacturing, finance, services	Neutral Manufacturing, wholesale trade	Selectively supportive Wholesale trade

Source: Doremus et al. *The Myth of the Global Corporation*, pp. 17, 58, 76, and 140.

Group, which was formed in 2000 with the merger of the Industrial Bank of Japan, Daiichi Kangyo Bank, and Fuji Bank, plans to cut 7,000 employees by 2005. In October 1999 the Sumitomo Mitsui Banking Corporation announced plans to reduce personnel by 9,300 and to close 260 domestic branches by March 2004.[2] Nomura Securities cut its staff by 660 employees by centralising back office operations during fiscal year 1999. In the retail industry, the venerable Mitsukoshi Department Store plans to cut employment by 600 through voluntary resignations.

Mergers and Acquisitions

M&As accelerated the change in industrial structure. M&A activity by Japanese corporations picked up considerably in 1999. There were 1,160 cases and the total disclosed amount was ¥6.7 trillion, twice the amount in 1998.[3] In two major deals of 1999, Japan Tobacco (JT) acquired RJR Nabisco and Renault acquired Nissan Motors. In telecommunications, AT&T and BT bought Nippon Telecom at a cost of ¥640 billion, UK's Cable and Wireless bought International Digital Communications (IDC) for ¥55 billion, and NTT bought Philippine Long Distance Telephone Company for ¥87.5 billion (Figure 11.2).

Other Factors for Change

Increased Foreign Ownership

As share prices have fallen during the long recession in Japan, foreign companies have come to view Japanese companies as affordable and they see this as an opportune time to build up their presence. By acquiring Japanese companies foreign firms gain access to an existing customer base and support network, which saves the time and expense of establishing these business foundations.

New Sources of Financing

The outlook for financing of Japanese start-ups improved with the November 1999 opening of MOTHERS (Market of the Highly Emerging Enterprises), a stock market for emerging companies. The financing situation for new businesses should improve further with the formation of a number of new private equity businesses. Mitsubishi Corporation, Marubeni Corporation, Mitsui Corporation, and Industrial Bank of Japan

FIGURE 11.2
Major Japan-related M&A Activity in 1999

Type of Purchase	Acquirer	Acquiree	Price ¥ billion
Foreign acquisition of Japanese company	AT&T (U.S.) and British Telecom (U.K.)	Japan Telecom	220
	Cable & Wireless (U.K.)	International Digital Communications (IDC)	55
	General Growth Properties Group	Daiei Ala Moana Shopping Centre (Hawaii)	97
Japanese acquisition of foreign company	NTT	Philippine Long Distance Telecommunication Company	87.5

Source: *Nihon Keizai Shimbun*, 25 December 1999.

have each established private equity funds with foreign partners, including U.S.-based Ripplewood Holdings.

New Business Models

Overall, Japan's service sector must adopt new business models appropriate to the era of globalisation and information technology. Management must utilise IT, innovation, and performance-based human resource management. Efficiency is paramount to improving profitability, so firms must cut sales, general, and administrative expenses without skimping on customer satisfaction. Besides reducing costs, service firms need to develop customer-orientation, flexibility, and differentiated services in order to expand sales and maximise corporate value. In addition, they must improve accounting and corporate governance to assure transparency for investors. Japanese service industries should enhance their business capability. Domestic companies should tie up with the leading companies in the global market in order to obtain international competitiveness.

Japanese firms need to take the following steps to adapt to globalisation and the penetration of international management standards:

- sell off low-performing subsidiaries and assets
- introduce performance measurement and evaluation
- use the Intranet

- adopt corporate governance that emphasises ROE
- choose and focus business domain, customers, and regions
- give control to shareholding companies to facilitate business restructuring
- diversify financing
- support incubation of entrepreneurial firms
- use M&A.

Labour relations in Japan are diversifying under the influence of the recruiting and human resource management styles of foreign-owned companies. Some companies, such as Matsushita Electric Industrial, have introduced prepayment of retirement bonuses to young employees, and other companies, such as Park24, Japan's largest provider of metered hourly parking, have introduced stock option incentive systems to attract talented employees.

Successful Service Companies

Some Japanese service companies have been growing even during the prolonged recession. Eight service companies listed in the first section of the Tokyo Stock Exchange (TSE) averaged over 20 percent annual sales growth in the last three years (Table 11.14). Hikari Tsushin, a tele-communications agent, was the fastest growing company listed on the

TABLE 11.14
Service Sector Growth Companies

	Average growth 1996–1998 %	1998 Growth rate Sales	1998 Sales ¥
Hikari Tsushin	87.7	30.8	159,619
Fuji Soft ABC	43.4	22.6	44,005
Shoko Fund	42.4	34.5	83,186
Konami	32.8	40.0	100,779
Bell System 24	29.4	25.0	33,871
Daimei	25.8	53.8	143,191
Hokuyo Bank	22.3	71.4	107,363
Mini Stop	21.4	21.0	37,573
Enix	6.7	105.6	24,395
Itochu Techno Science	NA	21.3	149,798

Source: Corporate data of individual companies.

TSE from 1996 to 1998. Game software is also a growth industry. The hit game DragonQuest made Enix the fastest growing company in 1998. In addition, the IPO of Itochu Techno Science, the IT subsidiary of a long-established general trading company, surpassed the current total value of its parent. The stock prices of Softbank and its subsidiaries, which distribute and sell PC software and peripheral hardware equipment and provide network consulting, technical support, and systems integration, have been skyrocketing. In the field of e-commerce, Rakuten, a pioneering virtual shopping mall founded by a former Industrial Bank of Japan employee, is growing rapidly.

The main areas of growth in Japan's service industries involve advanced technology and entrepreneurial development of new businesses. For example, i-mode, NTT DoCoMo's wireless Web service launched in 1998, already has 10 million customers in Japan and the number is growing by 50,000 per day.[4] New business start-ups have initiated pervasive changes in some markets. For example, the market for international travel changed dramatically with the 1992 entry of H.I.S. Co., which specialises in discount air tickets and budget-oriented package tours. Domestic airfares have been falling since 1998 when newcomers such as Skymark Airlines and Hokkaido International Airlines (Air Do) began flying certain routes in Japan. Skymark's $119 one-way fare between Tokyo and Fukuoka was about half that of the existing "big three" Japanese airlines (Japan Airlines, All Nippon Airlines and Japan Air Systems).[5]

CONCLUSION: STILL MORE CHANGE NEEDED

Despite deregulation and corporate restructuring during the 1990s, the service sector cannot yet take over the driver's seat as Japan tries to become competitive in the global economy. In particular, only a few of Japan's service companies that operate in open, markets are profitable (Figure 11.3). A solid business model is required to make profits in an open market. For example, Seven-Eleven Japan has demonstrated high business performance due to its outsourcing strategy for logistics and information technology. As a premise to make Japanese companies competitive in open markets, all parts of the service sector need to become much more open.

Although the transportation and telecommunications industries and the utilities are relatively profitable in Japan, their high performance depends on restrictions to entry and other regulatory controls. Companies in these

FIGURE 11.3
Current Situation of Japan's Service Industries

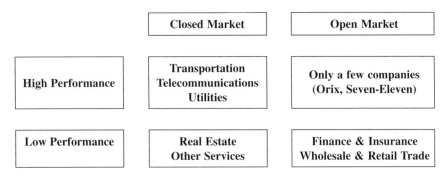

	Closed Market	Open Market
High Performance	Transportation Telecommunications Utilities	Only a few companies (Orix, Seven-Eleven)
Low Performance	Real Estate Other Services	Finance & Insurance Wholesale & Retail Trade

Note: Market openness is based on the amount of inward foreign direct investment. High performance industries are those with a 1998 profit rate higher than the 2.4 percent for manufacturing.
Source: Nomura Research Institute.

industries could not remain profitable if their markets were opened to foreign competitors. The distinction between companies that can create added value and those that cannot is widening the income differences among sectors.

High labour, land, transportation, and utility costs caused by government regulation continue to reduce competitiveness and restrain the service industries, but deregulation alone will not solve Japan's current economic problems. The creation of dynamic new businesses requires promoters, financial supporters, and technology. Information technology is a key to creating successful new service sector businesses. Human resource management is also critical. The seniority-based incentive system and the resulting immobility of workers mean that decision-makers in many Japanese companies tend to be old and inflexible to change.

From a Manufacturing to a Consumer Economy

To allow the service sector to create new jobs and revitalise the economy, the Japanese government should shift the focus of its policies from the supply side (production) to the demand side (consumption). The government should encourage foreign direct investment to stimulate change in other Japanese industries as it did in the retail trade and insurance industries.

Weak protected domestic service industries drag down the whole economy, so Japan's markets must open wider to foreign companies to promote competition and restructuring in the service sector. In addition, the government should encourage the creation of new service industries through deregulation and contracting-out of government services.

Support for Restructuring

To encourage corporate restructuring in 1997 the government relaxed regulations against shareholding companies and share-exchange mergers and it changed the rules that govern M&As among listed companies. Also, the September 1998 introduction of asset-backed securities through special purpose companies diversified the financial instruments available to companies. To promote new business, the government must continue to revise the bankruptcy law and the rules for depreciation of information equipment and to work toward introducing a portable pension system and a system of tax preferences for venture businesses.

Reforming the employment system will also promote restructuring. The failures of the Long Term Credit Bank of Japan and Yamaichi Securities and the rescue of Nissan Motors by Renault showed that even large companies cannot succeed under the traditional employment system. Workers should be freer to move from company to company in order to learn and to spread state-of-the-art skills throughout the service sector. Deregulation of temporary workers and introduction of a portable pension would create a labour market infrastructure that allowed for greater mobility and higher employee motivation.

Notes

[1] Recent introduction of Asymmetric Digital Subscriber Line (ADSL) is expected to reduce the cost of Internet provider service to around ¥6,000 per month for unlimited use. ASDL makes high-speed digital data transfer possible through ordinal metallic cable by use of high frequency.

[2] Sakura Bank and Sumitomo Bank. Merger Agreement between Sakura Bank and Sumitomo Bank. April 21, 2000.

[3] *Nihon Keizai Shimbun,* 25 December 1999.

[4] "Today Tokyo, Tomorrow the World!" For*tune*, 18 September 2000.

[5] <http://www.embjapan.org/JapanNow/>, February 1999.

References

Bank of Japan. 1999. *Comparative Economic and Financial Statistics Japan and Other Countries.* Tokyo: Bank of Japan.

Business Week. "A New Japan?" 25 October 1999.

Doremus, Paul N., Louis W. Pauly, Simon Reich. 1999. *The Myth of the Global Corporation.* Princeton: Princeton University Press.

Economist. 1999. "A Survey of Business in Japan: Restoration in Progress." 27 November.

Henry, D., P. Buckley, G. Gurumukh, S. Cooke, J. Dumagan, d. Pastore, and S. LaPorte. 1999. *The Emerging Digital Economy II.* Office of Policy Development, Economics and Statistics Administration, U. S. Department of Commerce. <http://www.ecommerce.gov/ede/ede2.pdf>.

International Institute for Management Development (IMD). 1999. *The World Competitiveness Report 1999.* Lausanne: IMD.

Masuyama Seiichi. 1999. "Economic Globalization and the Japanese Corporate System." *Chiteki Shisan Sozo.* Tokyo: Nomura Research Institute, December.

Ministry of International Trade and Industry. 1998. *White Paper on International Trade* (Tsusho Hakusho). Tokyo: Ministry of Finance Publishing Bureau.

Ministry of Post and Telecommunications. 1998. *White Paper on Telecommunication* (Tsushin Hakusho). Tokyo: Ministry of Finance Publishing Bureau.

Nihon Keizai Shimbun. Various issues.

Organisation for Economic Co-operation and Development (OECD). 1999. *Strategic Business Services.* Paris: OECD.

THE EDITORS

SEIICHI MASUYAMA is Chief Researcher at the Center for Policy Research of the Nomura Research Institute in Tokyo.

DONNA C. VANDENBRINK is economist at the Center for Knowledge Exchange and Creation at Nomura Research Institute and formerly at the Federal Reserve Bank of Chicago.

CHIA SIOW YUE is Director of the Institute of Southeast Asian Studies in Singapore and was previously Associate Professor of Economics at the National University of Singapore.